ACCESS

TO

JUSTICE

Final Report

By The Right Honourable the Lord Woolf,
Master of the Rolls

JULY 1996

Final Report

to the Lord Chancellor

on the civil justice system

in England and Wales

London: HMSO

ISBN 0 11 380099 1

Printed in the United Kingdom for HMSO
Dd 302932 7/96 C80

Introduction

In June 1995 I presented my interim report on Access to Justice to the Lord Chancellor. Responses to the overall conclusions of the report have been overwhelmingly favourable; criticism was almost universally confined to the detail of particular recommendations. The reaction of both branches of the profession, the judiciary and consumer bodies has been strongly supportive.

This final report is accompanied by a draft of the general rules which will form the core of the new, combined code of rules for civil procedure which was part of the task set for me by the Lord Chancellor. The report and the draft rules take into account the many submissions which I have received since the publication of the interim report. I have paid particular attention to any expressions of concern or criticism which have been made about my earlier recommendations. The report also benefits from the extensive further consultation which has taken place over the last year and the responses to the issues papers which the Inquiry published in January of this year dealing with the fast track, housing, multi-party actions, medical negligence, expert evidence and costs.

I have attempted throughout the Inquiry to give the widest possible notice of my views as they developed. I and members of the Inquiry Team have worked closely with the Legal Aid Reform Team in the Lord Chancellor's Department, and have attended numerous conferences and less formal meetings all over the country where my proposals have been discussed. The organisations I have met range from the governing bodies of sections of the legal, medical and other professions to a tenants' association in a local authority tower block in London. I also visited lawyers' offices specialising in areas of litigation of especial relevance to my Inquiry and a number of academic institutions.

Both the Law Society and the Bar set up committees which have shadowed the work of the Inquiry. In addition to holding joint sessions with the Inquiry they have made formal and informal submissions of great value.

In the second stage of the Inquiry my work on specialist jurisdictions and special areas of litigation has been carried out with the assistance of small working groups whose members had relevant specialist expertise and practical experience. A separate working group was concerned with the drafting of the new rules of court, and another with the development of detailed procedures for the new fast track. I am immensely grateful to the members of the working groups for their wise advice. They are all extremely busy people and it is an indication of the importance they attached to the work of the Inquiry that they were prepared to devote so much time to assist me. Their names are set out in Annex 1. I thank each one of them for the great help they have given me.

The Inquiry has again benefited from research carried out specifically to inform its work on costs. Professor Hazel Genn of University College London and Professor Richard Davies of the Centre for Applied Statistics at Lancaster University have followed up Professor Genn's preliminary analysis of costs in High Court litigation with a more detailed study based on a sample of cases submitted to the Supreme Court Taxing Office during 1990-1995. Adrian Zuckerman, a Fellow of University College, Oxford, has, with the help of one of my assessors, Senior Master Turner, conducted a survey of German practitioners to elicit their views on the fixed costs system in Germany. I am grateful to all of them, and to Chief Taxing Master Hurst for facilitating the work in the Supreme Court Taxing Office.

Before the publication of the interim report I had visited France, the USA and Canada. During the second stage of the Inquiry I have made a further visit to the USA, Canada, Australia and Hong Kong. I am very grateful to all those who were involved in organising my intensive programme.

I have also recently had the opportunity of discussing my approach with specialists in civil procedure from many countries around the world at a conference in Florence organised by the University of New York.

Once again, I would like to thank the five assessors who have continued to assist me: Senior Master Turner, District Judge Greenslade, Rupert Jackson QC, John Bolton and Phillip Sycamore; also Professor Ross Cranston, my academic consultant, and Dr Richard Susskind, my consultant on information technology. I am particularly grateful to James Rennie, the draftsman of the new rules. I offer my congratulations to Master Turner on his recent appointment as Senior Master, and to District Judge Greenslade on becoming President of the Association of District Judges. In addition, I am deeply indebted to the joint secretaries to the Inquiry, Amanda Finlay and Michael Kron, and their team, for their invaluable support and commitment to the Inquiry.

The names of the Inquiry Team and working groups are set out in Annex 1 to this report, Annex 2 provides a list of those who have contributed to the second stage of the Inquiry, whether by written submissions or by organising meetings and visits. The list is intended to be complete, and I apologise for any omissions. I am extremely grateful to everyone who has contributed. The result, in my view, is a programme for change which could radically improve access to civil justice. If it does not, then I accept responsibility. If it does achieve the objective, then this is due to the immense amount of help which I have received from the assessors, the team and the working groups. Without their help I could not have produced this report and the new rules. They are the product of a collective effort.

The Right Honourable the Lord Woolf, Master of the Rolls.

CONTENTS

A N N E X E S

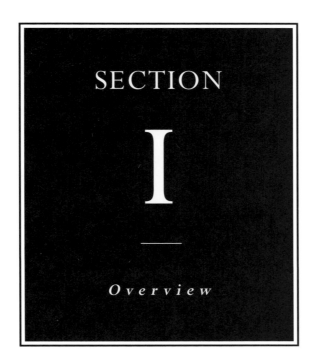

SECTION

I

Overview

The Principles

1. In my interim report I identified a number of principles which the civil justice system should meet in order to ensure access to justice. The system should:

(a)   be *just* in the results it delivers;

(b)   be *fair* in the way it treats litigants;

(c)   offer appropriate procedures at a reasonable *cost*;

(d)   deal with cases with reasonable *speed*;

(e)   be *understandable* to those who use it;

(f)   be *responsive* to the needs of those who use it;

(g)   provide as much *certainty* as the nature of particular cases allows; and

(h)   be *effective*: adequately resourced and organised.

The problems

2. The defects I identified in our present system were that it is too expensive in that the costs often exceed the value of the claim; too slow in bringing cases to a conclusion and too unequal: there is a lack of equality between the powerful, wealthy litigant and the under-resourced litigant. It is too uncertain: the difficulty of forecasting what litigation will cost and how long it will last induces the fear of the unknown; and it is incomprehensible to many litigants. Above all it is too fragmented in the way it is organised since there is no-one with clear overall responsibility for the administration of civil justice; and too adversarial as cases are run by the parties, not by the courts and the rules of court, all too often, are ignored by the parties and not enforced by the court.

The basic reforms

3. The interim report set out a blueprint for reform based on a system where the courts with the assistance of litigants would be responsible for the management of cases. I recommended that the courts should have the final responsibility for determining what procedures were suitable for each case; setting realistic timetables; and ensuring that the procedures and timetables were complied with. Defended cases would be allocated to one of three tracks:

(a)   an expanded small claims jurisdiction with a financial limit of £3,000;

(b) a new fast track for straightforward cases up to £10,000, with strictly limited procedures, fixed timetables (20-30 weeks to trial) and fixed costs; and

(c) a new multi-track for cases above £10,000, providing individual hands-on management by judicial teams for the heaviest cases, and standard or tailor-made directions where these are appropriate.

The second stage of the Inquiry

4. My general analysis of the problems in the present system, and the broad agenda for reform which I proposed in the interim report, have provided the foundation for the more detailed work I have carried out in the second stage of the Inquiry. This has concentrated on particular areas of litigation where, in my view, the civil justice system is failing most conspicuously to meet needs of litigants. These areas are medical negligence, housing and multi-party litigation. I have also developed more detailed proposals on procedure and costs for the new fast track. Another focus of special attention was the Crown Office List, which has a particularly important function in enabling individual citizens to challenge decisions of public bodies including central and local government.

5. In all these areas a particular concern has been to improve access to justice for individuals and small businesses. I am also concerned about the level of public expenditure on litigation, particularly in medical negligence and housing. In both of these areas substantial amounts of public money are absorbed in legal costs which could be better spent, in the one case on improving medical care and in the other on improving standards of social housing. An efficient and cost-effective justice system is also of vital importance to the commercial, financial and industrial life of this country and I was anxious to improve this, especially because of the evidence I received that there was a substantial risk of the existing system changing our competitive position in relation to other jurisdictions. Finally I was anxious to ensure that the judiciary and the resources of the Court Service were deployed to the best effect.

6. All the work I have carried out in the second stage of the Inquiry has confirmed the conclusions I reached in the interim report about the defects in the present system. This report therefore builds on the contents and recommendations of the interim report by:

(a) providing greater detail as to the principal recommendations in the interim report;

(b)   identifying the problems in those areas which have received special attention during the second stage of the Inquiry and the solutions I am recommending to meet those problems;

(c)   describing the new rules; and

(d)   making clear any change in my approach since the interim report.

Rules of court

7.   An important part of my task in the Inquiry was to produce a single, simpler procedural code to apply to civil litigation in the High Court and county courts. This report is accompanied by a draft of the general rules which will form the core of the new code. In the second part of the Inquiry I have looked in detail at the specialist jurisdictions of the High Court with a view to accommodating them so far as possible within the general procedural framework embodied in the core rules. As a result of the work done by the Inquiry, it is apparent that a great many of the existing specialist rules are no longer required. Work is continuing on the more limited body of special rules which are still considered essential. Here I await with interest the views of those engaged in the specialist jurisdictions who could not express a formal opinion as to what extra rules are still needed until they had seen the general rules which have been prepared by the Inquiry.

The new landscape

8.   If my recommendations are implemented the landscape of civil litigation will be fundamentally different from what it is now. It will be underpinned by Rule 1 of the new procedural code, which imposes an obligation on the courts and the parties to further the overriding objective of the rules so as to deal with cases justly. The rule provides a definition of 'dealing with a case justly', embodying the principles of equality, economy, proportionality and expedition which are fundamental to an effective contemporary system of justice. These requirements of procedural justice, operating in the traditional adversarial context, will give effect to a system which is substantively just in the results it delivers as well as in the way in which it does so.

9.   The new landscape will have the following features.

Litigation will be avoided wherever possible.

(a)   People will be encouraged to start court proceedings to resolve disputes only as a last resort, and after using other more appropriate means when these are available.

(b)   Information on sources of alternative dispute resolution (ADR) will be provided at all civil courts.

(c)   Legal aid funding will be available for pre-litigation resolution and ADR.

(d)   Protocols in relation to medical negligence, housing and personal injury, and additional powers for the court in relation to pre-litigation disclosure, will enable parties to obtain information earlier and promote settlement.

(e)   Before commencing litigation both parties will be able to make offers to settle the whole or part of a dispute supported by a special regime as to costs and higher rates of interest if not accepted.

Litigation will be less adversarial and more co-operative.

(a)   There will be an expectation of openness and co-operation between parties from the outset, supported by pre-litigation protocols on disclosure and experts. The courts will be able to give effect to their disapproval of a lack of co-operation prior to litigation.

(b)   The court will encourage the use of ADR at case management conferences and pre-trial reviews, and will take into account whether the parties have unreasonably refused to try ADR or behaved unreasonably in the course of ADR.

(c)   The duty of experts to the court will be emphasised. Single experts, instructed by the parties, will be used when practicable. Opposing experts will be encouraged to meet or communicate as early as possible to narrow the issues between them. The court will have a power to appoint an expert.

Litigation will be less complex.

(a)   There will be a single set of rules applying to the High Court and the county courts. The rules will be simpler, and special rules for specific types of litigation will be reduced to a minimum.

(b)   All proceedings will be commenced in the same way by a claim.

(c)   The claim and defence will not be technical documents. The claim will set out the facts alleged by the claimant, the remedy the claimant seeks, the grounds on which the remedy is sought and any relevant points of law. The defence will set out the defendant's detailed response to the claim and make clear the real issues between the parties. Both 'statements of case' will have to include certificates by the parties verifying their contents so tactical allegations will no longer be possible.

(d)   During the course of proceedings the court on its own initiative, or on the application of either party, will be able to dispose of individual issues or the litigation as a whole where there is no real prospect of success.

(e)   Claimants will be able to start proceedings in any court. It will be the court's responsibility to direct parties or to transfer the case, if necessary, to the appropriate part of the system.

(f)   Discovery will be controlled; in a minority of cases the present scale of discovery will be possible but in the majority of cases there will be a new standard test for more restricted disclosure.

(g)   There will be special procedures, involving active judicial case management, to deal with multi-party actions expeditiously and fairly.

(h)   Instead of an irrational kaleidoscope of different ways of appealing or applying to the High Court against the decisions of other bodies, there will be a unified code.

The timescale of litigation will be shorter and more certain.

(a)   All cases will progress to trial in accordance with a timetable set and monitored by the court.

(b)   For fast track cases there will be fixed timetables of no more than 30 weeks.

(c)   The court will apply strict sanctions to parties who do not comply with the procedures or timetables.

(d)   Appeals from case management decisions will be kept to the minimum, and will be dealt with expeditiously.

(e)   The court will determine the length of the trial and what is to happen at the trial.

The cost of litigation will be more affordable, more predictable, and more proportionate to the value and complexity of individual cases.

(a)   There will be fixed costs for cases on the fast track.

(b)   Estimates of costs for multi-track cases will be published by the court or agreed by the parties and approved by the court.

(c)   There will be a special 'streamlined' track for lower value or less complex multi-track cases, where the procedure will be as simple as possible with appropriate budgets for costs.

(d)   For classes of litigation where the procedure is uncomplicated and predictable the court will issue guideline costs with the assistance of users.

(e)   There will be a new test for the taxation of costs to further the overriding objective. It will be that there should be allowed "such sum as is reasonable taking account of the interests of both parties to the taxation."

Parties of limited financial means will be able to conduct litigation on a more equal footing.

(a)   Litigants who are not legally represented will be able to get more help from advice services and from the courts.

(b)   Procedural judges will take account of the parties' financial circumstances in allocating cases to the fast track or to the small claims jurisdiction.

(c)   Limited procedures and tight timetables on the fast track, and judicial case management on the multi-track, will make it more difficult for wealthier parties to gain a tactical advantage over their opponents by additional expenditure.

(d)   When deciding upon the procedure which is to be adopted the court will, if the parties' means are unequal, be entitled to make an order for a more elaborate procedure, conditional upon the other side agreeing to meet, in any event, the difference in the cost of the two possible procedures.

(e)   The new approach will be supported by more effective sanctions, including orders for costs in a fixed sum which are to be paid forthwith.

There will be clear lines of judicial and administrative responsibility for the civil justice system.

(a)   The Head of Civil Justice will have overall responsibility for the civil justice system in England and Wales.

(b)   The Presiding Judges on each Circuit will exercise their responsibility for civil work in conjunction with the two Chancery judges who will also oversee the business and mercantile lists.

(c) A nominated Circuit judge will be responsible for the effective organisation of each civil trial centre and its satellite courts.

(d) The new administrative structure will establish a partnership between the judiciary and the Court Service.

The structure of the courts and the deployment of judges will be designed to meet the needs of litigants.

(a) Heavier and more complex civil cases will be concentrated at trial centres which have the resources needed, including specialist judges, to ensure that the work is dealt with effectively.

(b) Smaller local courts will continue to play a vital role in providing easy access to the civil justice system. Housing claims, small claims, debt cases and cases allocated to the fast track will be dealt with there, as well as case management of the less complex multi-track cases.

(c) Better ways of providing access to justice in rural areas will be maintained and developed.

(d) There will be a more straightforward system of appeals. Appeals with no real prospect of success will be eliminated at an early stage.

(e) The courts will have access to the technology needed to monitor the progress of litigation.

(f) Litigants will be able to communicate with the courts electronically and through video and telephone conferencing facilities.

(g) Trials will take place on the date assigned.

Judges will be deployed effectively so that they can manage litigation in accordance with the new rules and protocols.

(a) Judges will be given the training they need to manage cases.

(b) Judges will be encouraged to specialise in such areas as housing and medical negligence, and will be given the appropriate training to ensure that they understand the legal and technical issues fully.

(c) Cases will be dealt with by the part of the system which is most appropriate. The distinctions between the county courts and High Court and between the divisions of the High Court will be of reduced significance.

(d)   Judges will have the administrative and technological support which is required for the effective management of cases.

The civil justice system will be responsive to the needs of litigants.

(a)   Courts will provide advice and assistance to litigants through court-based or duty advice and assistance schemes, especially in courts with substantial levels of debt and housing work.

(b)   Courts will provide more information to litigants through leaflets, videos, telephone helplines and information technology.

(c)   Court staff will provide information and help to litigants on how to progress their case.

(d)   There will be ongoing monitoring and research on litigants' needs.

The funding of civil litigation

10. My Inquiry is concerned with the procedure of the civil courts. I have not dealt directly with the funding of litigation, but there are other developments in this area which will affect the new landscape I have just described. The most significant recent development in the funding of civil litigation is the current review of legal aid, on which there has been close co-operation between my Inquiry Team and the Legal Aid Reform Team.

11. It is essential that the reforms of legal aid should take into account and support the recommendations I am making. The reforms of civil procedure which I am proposing will be more effective if:

(a)   legal aid funding is available for pre-litigation resolution and ADR (including the costs of an expert conducting expert adjudication of small claims and cases on the fast track);

(b)   public funding is available for in-court advice services, especially on housing issues;

(c)   legal aid is available for solicitors and barristers providing 'unbundled' legal services to parties conducting their own cases on the fast track;

(d)   the Legal Aid Board's decisions take into account the court's allocation of a case to the appropriate track, and any directions of the court as to the future management of the case; in all cases but especially in multi-party actions;

(e)   the legal aid reforms recognise the importance of ensuring the survival of efficient small firms of solicitors, particularly in remote areas.

12. In addition there is the availability of conditional fee agreements and the growth in legal expenses insurance. Both of these can help to make litigation more affordable, but they cannot in themselves deal with the underlying problems of excessive and unpredictable costs. Both conditional fees and insurance are, at present, available only in limited classes of cases. They will only become more generally available if costs are firmly controlled in the ways that I am proposing.

Implementation of my reforms

13. The Lord Chancellor welcomed my interim report and has made plain his commitment to reform. Having accepted the thrust of my recommendations, he has established an implementation team and embarked on a programme of phased implementation.

14. In January 1996 the Lord Chancellor appointed the Vice-Chancellor, Sir Richard Scott, to take on the duties envisaged for a Head of Civil Justice. This appointment is in itself a very important step. Sir Richard will be able to take charge of implementing many of the other recommendations. He will be able to provide the hands-on leadership for civil litigation which it has lacked in the past. He will be able to have an input into the selection of judges to be responsible for the handling of civil work at trial centres. He will be in a position to oversee the implementation of the other recommendations.

15. The Court Service, in consultation with the judiciary, has started to put into place the supporting structure which will be needed to introduce the new system of case management by the courts. This includes identifying the appropriate number and location of trial centres on each Circuit, and setting up a new arrangement for a partnership between the judiciary and administrative staff. The Judicial Studies Board is preparing for an intensive programme of training for judges involved in case management, based on a survey which the Board wishes to conduct to identify the special interests and needs of judges.

16. Some of my other recommendations which did not need to await this final report have already been implemented. The small claims jurisdiction has been increased to £3,000, except for personal injury claims, as from 8 January 1996. At the same time the test applied by district judges in considering transfer out of the small claims jurisdiction was modified, so that cases qualify for transfer if they are considered 'complex' rather than 'exceptionally complex'. The Judicial Studies Board is making arrangements to provide additional training for district judges in connection with their small claims work and has developed a protocol or best practice guide to promote the consistency of approach which I recommended. The option of paper adjudication, which I recommended, as of benefit in particular to small businesses and the self employed, is being considered by the Lord Chancellor's Department.

17. The effects of the increased jurisdiction are being monitored and research is being considered. I hope that the results of any monitoring or research will be published so that the effects of the increase in jurisdiction can be considered by all those involved, before any further increase is contemplated.

18. I outlined my proposals for an enhanced role for ADR in the interim report and the past year has seen further developments, including a pilot mediation scheme at Central London County Court and plans for pilot mediation and arbitration schemes at the Patents County Court. I also understand that the Lord Chancellor is considering providing assistance with the ADR pilot scheme being conducted by Bristol Law Society and researching the effects of this. I welcome the recent publication by the Lord Chancellor's Department of a plain English guide on ADR entitled *Resolving Disputes Without Going To Court*, designed to make members of the public more aware of methods of resolving disputes which do not involve litigation. The new procedures I propose will emphasise the importance of ADR through the court's ability to take into account whether parties have unreasonably rejected the possibility of ADR or have behaved unreasonably in the course of ADR.

19. The interim report emphasised the importance of providing effective information, advice and assistance to all litigants and recommended that all the Civil Justice Review's recommendations in this respect should be implemented. Provision of such assistance until now has been very much a matter of local initiative and it says much for such local action that about one third of all county courts now host advice schemes. The creation of the Court Service as an agency, with its emphasis on customer service, and in particular the new management structure, now provides an opportunity to take a more strategic approach. The provision of information and advice directs people to appropriate means of resolving disputes, enables them to understand how to progress their cases and contributes to the effective disposal of court business. Just as case management involves spending time to save time, so the provision of appropriate help to litigants will result in a better use of court and legal aid resources. It will also ensure that access to justice is a reality rather than a slogan.

Conclusion

20. In the course of the Inquiry there has been unprecedented consultation with all involved in the civil justice system. Over the last year, judges, practitioners and consumers have worked together to hammer out new ways of tackling problems and to contribute to what is proposed in this final report. I see a continuing need for such involvement in the process of implementation. Much has been done. But much more remains to be done. The continuing involvement of all those who use the civil justice system will be given coherence and leadership by the Civil Justice Council which I recommended in the interim report. Local user committees, a specialist IT sub-committee and working groups developing further detail for the new fast track would all come under its aegis. The Council would continue and develop the process of co-operation and creativity that the Inquiry has benefited from.

21. The civil justice system in this country urgently needs reform. The time is right for change. The public and businesses want change, and the majority of the legal profession agree. The judiciary has strongly supported my Inquiry. I have been given a unique opportunity to help achieve the change which is needed.

22. My recommendations, together with the new code of rules, form a comprehensive and coherent package for the reform of civil justice. Each contributes to and underpins the others. Their overall effectiveness could be seriously undermined by piecemeal implementation. Their implementation as a whole will ensure that all the supporting elements of the civil justice system are directed towards the fundamental reform that is required.

23. Nevertheless, there should be a degree of flexibility in the approach to implementation. All the recommendations I have made, both in the interim report and in this report, are designed to meet the objectives for the civil justice system which I set out at the beginning of this overview. My detailed recommendations are based on a thorough review of the present system, including the wide consultation I have mentioned, but the objectives are of primary importance. The individual proposals should not be too rigidly applied if it is found that there are better ways of achieving the objectives. My overriding concern is to ensure that we have a civil justice system which will meet the needs of the public in the twenty-first century.

SECTION

II

Case Management

Chapter 1 Introduction

1.   In chapters 6 and 8 of my interim report I described the introduction of judicial case management as crucial to the changes which are necessary in our civil justice system. Ultimate responsibility for the control of litigation must move from the litigants and their legal advisers to the court. The reaction to this key message in my interim report has been extremely supportive.

2.   There are already examples of case management being developed at particular courts. In the High Court there is the management of substantial litigation, such as that involving Lloyd's, by the Commercial Court. The same is true of the Official Referees' Court. There are the procedures being adopted at county courts such as Central London, Truro and Wandsworth. The results are very encouraging. Similar developments have been taking place in Scotland, the United States, Canada, Australia and New Zealand. Experience in developing case management in other jurisdictions has indicated that not all cases require the same hands-on management but that a differential approach is needed. Research on existing systems has also shown the efficacy of timetabling. These developments show the way forward.

3.   There are those who have misgivings about the need for my proposals and their ability to effect beneficial change. Concern has been expressed that my proposals for case management will undermine the adversarial nature of our civil justice system. The concerns are not justified. The responsibility of the parties and the legal profession for handling cases will remain. The legal profession will, however, be performing its traditional adversarial role in a managed environment governed by the courts and by the rules which will focus effort on the key issues rather than allowing every issue to be pursued regardless of expense and time, as at present.

4.   It has also been suggested that judges are not well equipped to be managers. I do not see the active management of litigation as being outside a judge's function. It is an essential means of furthering what must be the objective of any procedural system, which is to deal with cases justly. Case management includes identifying the issues in the case; summarily disposing of some issues and deciding in which order other issues are to be resolved; fixing timetables for the parties to take particular steps in the case; and limiting disclosure and expert evidence. These are all judicial functions. They are extensions backwards in time of the role of the trial judge. It should be remembered that not all judges will be acting as procedural judges. I envisage that the function of procedural judges will usually be taken by Masters and district judges, although in more complex cases Circuit judges and High Court judges will perform the task. I see case management as an enhancement of the present role of Masters and district judges, but with clearly defined objectives. Obviously there will be a need for training for both judiciary and court staff in order to improve the necessary skills. The Judicial Studies Board recognises that a substantial training effort is needed and has already begun to consider what is required. I am conscious that some procedural judges may feel that their decisions, for example on limiting evidence or the order in which issues are to be dealt with, may be overturned by the trial judge or on appeal. In the future, I hope that the team system will make for a greater partnership between all the judges in every court and ensure consistency of approach to the handling of cases and the development of case management.

5.   Another concern which has been expressed is that early consideration of cases, reading the papers in the case as well as conducting the conferences and pre-trial reviews, will add significantly to the burdens of already hard-pressed Masters and district judges. It has also been suggested that case management will mean an increase in the number of interlocutory hearings, when the objectives of reducing costs and delay would be better achieved by reducing the number of such hearings. Moreover, given that the majority of cases do not reach trial, it has been argued that time spent on management early in a case will be wasted time.

6.   The concerns about workload and new ways of working are understandable. I accept that any new regime will initially impose additional burdens on those who have to operate it. But the concerns do not take sufficient account of the expectations of active case management by the court. The aim of case management conferences in multi-track cases is that fewer cases should need to come to a final trial, by encouraging the parties to settle their dispute or to resolve it outside the court system altogether, and that for those cases which do require resolution by the court the issues should be identified at an early stage so that as many of them as possible can be agreed or decided before the trial. The pre-trial review should then take further steps to ensure that the trial will be shorter and less expensive. Case management hearings will replace rather than add to the present interlocutory hearings. They should be seen as using time in order to save more time.

7.   This last point is an aspect of the wider concern that what I am proposing will require far more staff and other resources. Both the Bar

Council and the Law Society and many others have drawn attention to this. It is said that if the management of a case is now to be handled by the court instead of by the parties' lawyers, additional judicial and administrative capacity will be needed. There are several ways in which these concerns can be addressed.

(a)   Case management will be proportionate. There will be hands-on judicial intervention only in cases which will require and repay it. Basic management, with a fixed timetable and standard procedure, will be used wherever possible, on the multi-track as well as the fast track.

(b)   Case management conferences will involve a more focused and directed use of time which would otherwise be spent on interlocutory hearings. The number of interlocutory applications will in any event be reduced: the move from formal pleadings to fact-based statements of case, for example, will make applications about further and better particulars less necessary.

(c)   Priorities for resources must be established and resources redeployed where necessary. Generally, this will mean making realistic provision for reading time for judges and more clerical assistance to enable judges to spend more time on judicial functions. It may involve the use of law clerks in heavy cases, which I discuss in chapter 8. Under the new system some tasks, such as taxation of what will become fast track cases, will no longer be needed. Increased use of information technology will provide substantial support for case management by offering easier access to information on the progress of cases and by providing tools to support the management of individual cases. Its use will also mean that court staff can be freed from other tasks to provide support to judges on case management. (I refer here to the important proposals on IT in chapter 21.)

(d)   Two other significant aims of my recommendations need to be borne in mind: that of encouraging the resolution of disputes before they come to litigation, for example by greater use of pre-litigation disclosure and of ADR, and that of encouraging settlement, for example by introducing plaintiffs' offers to settle, and by disposing of issues so as to narrow the dispute. All these are intended to divert cases from the court system or to ensure that those cases which do go through the court system are disposed of as rapidly as possible. I share the view, expressed in the Commercial Court Practice Statement of 10 December 1993, that although the primary role of the court is as a forum for deciding cases it is right that the court should encourage the parties to consider the use of ADR as a means to resolve their disputes. I believe that the same is true of helping the parties to settle a case.

8.   While I have always accepted that some additional resources will be necessary, especially for training and technology, I do believe that when all these considerations are borne in mind the additional resources required should be well within the bounds of what is possible.

9.   It has been suggested that it is simplistic to attribute the problems of the system to one single cause, the uncontrolled nature of the litigation process, and that there is no research to back up this assertion. My approach has been to examine the many symptoms of that single underlying cause, and my proposals are designed to tackle each of those symptoms as well as to provide an overall and coherent framework which addresses the underlying cause itself. The final survey of Supreme Court Taxing Office taxed bills by Professor Genn, summarised in Annex 3, provides detailed information on the wide range of factors which contribute to the problem and the need to provide the system with procedural levers to tackle each of them.

10. It is argued by a minority that cost and delay in civil litigation are not excessive and no remedial action is required. The SCTO survey in fact reveals, in relation to taxed cases, a reduction in overall delay and a holding steady of cost in all case types except medical negligence where cost has been increasing by seven per cent a year. The perception of clients remains, however, that cost is excessive and in many cases disproportionate and that the overall time taken is still too long and when the facts are examined it is clear this perception is far from being without foundation.

11. The survey findings on proportionate cost bear this out. They indicate that average costs among the lowest value claims consistently represent more than 100 per cent of claim value and in cases between £12,500 and £25,000 average costs range from 40 per cent to 95 per cent of claim value. To put it another way, the present system provides higher benefits to lawyers than to their clients. It is only when the claim value is over £50,000 that the average combined costs of the parties are likely to represent less than the claim. These difficulties will be alleviated by my proposals for case management.

12. It has been argued that costs are only disproportionate if they are in excess of what the parties are prepared to pay and that this is not the case in relation to personal injury and other cases where the costs are predominantly met by insurers. I do not accept this argument for reasons which I explained in the interim report. I deal again in detail in chapter 2 of this report with why I do not accept this argument.

13. My proposals tackle not only the cost but also the time taken by cases to reach a conclusion. Although the SCTO survey showed that most cases had an overall duration of 20 to 35 months, personal injury and medical negligence cases lasted a median period of 54 and 61 months. Also of concern is the indication that this period is longer in personal injury cases if the case is simple rather than complex and if it is legally aided. My recommendations in relation to pre-issue disclosure and pre-litigation protocols are designed to achieve an improvement here. There are particular problems in relation to medical negligence cases; that is why I have devoted special attention to this area.

14. The survey found that the cases which lasted longest were the 54 per cent which settled, taking between 42 and 48 months, while those ending after judgment, a quarter of the sample, took on average 25 months. The categories of cases with the highest proportion of settlements are those with the longest duration which are medical negligence, personal injury and professional negligence. My recommendations in relation to timetabling of all cases, to plaintiffs' offers and the requirement on the court to consider and assist with settlement, are designed to improve matters here.

15. In conclusion, I remain convinced that there is a grave need to move to a managed system of dispute resolution and that my proposals accurately address that need.

16. Essential elements of my proposals for case management include:

(a)   allocating each case to the track and court at which it can be dealt with most appropriately;

(b)   encouraging and assisting the parties to settle cases or, at least, to agree on particular issues;

(c)   encouraging the use of ADR;

(d)   identifying at an early stage the key issues which need full trial;

(e) summarily disposing of weak cases and hopeless issues;

(f) achieving transparency and control of costs;

(g) increasing the client's knowledge of what the progress and costs of the case will involve;

(h) fixing and enforcing strict timetables for procedural steps leading to trial and for the trial itself.

17. The fast track will provide these on a standardised basis for straightforward cases under £10,000. My general approach, the detailed procedure and the costs regime are set out in chapters 2, 3 and 4. Chapter 5 sets out my detailed proposals for cases on the multi-track and chapter 6 in this section deals with sanctions.

Chapter 2   Fast Track: General

1.   In my interim report I recommended the establishment of a new fast track for straightforward cases not exceeding £10,000 in value. I recommended a strictly limited procedure designed to take cases to trial within a short but reasonable timescale with fixed costs that would be known in advance so that litigants could estimate their maximum liability for costs even if unsuccessful. I envisaged that the greater certainty of the procedure and the costs would encourage the development of legal expenses insurance because it would provide certainty to solicitors and to insurance companies and would enable the Legal Aid Board and other bulk purchasers of legal services to make better use of their resources.

2.   The fast track was welcomed by the Lord Chancellor. He has asked me to develop detailed procedures and a costs structure for the fast track. This I hope has been achieved thanks to the extremely valuable help of the Fast Track Working Group.

3.   Other jurisdictions, in particular the United States, Canada and Australia, have introduced limited procedures and tracking for straightforward cases. I have examined some of these in operation and been sent valuable material on others. The Inquiry's academic consultant has conducted a survey. Experience elsewhere has been generally positive although some systems are still at an early stage. My approach has many common features with those but is more radical in that it involves a fixed costs regime.

The Fast Track Working Group

4.   The working group included practitioners nominated both by the professional bodies and the Advice Services Alliance (which covers a wide range of advice centres and law centres). The practitioners on the working group (listed in Annex 1) are representative of those who litigate in the civil courts and have experience of a wide range of cases, including personal injury, building and construction, disputes over goods and services, housing disrepair and other housing cases.

Consultation

5.   An issues paper circulated in January 1996 consulted on proposals for the fast track procedures. I and members of the Inquiry Team have discussed the proposals with interested organisations and many individuals. The Inquiry Team has had detailed discussions with representatives of small businesses and the issues paper has been circulated, thanks to the Department of Trade and Industry Small Business Unit, to many of the leading business representatives via bodies such as the Institute of Directors and the Alliance of Independent Retailers and Businesses.

Response to consultation **6.**   The Consumers' Association recommended that the fast track procedure should apply to cases up to £15,000. They said:

> "This would enable more, relatively straightforward disputes relating to, for instance, building works (home extensions and improvements), to be covered by the procedure. We are aware of many consumer complaints that fall into this category but where the risk of liability for disproportionately high legal costs makes litigation an impractical option for all but the wealthy and/or brave."

The National Consumer Council (NCC) commented:

> "Broadly the NCC feels that a fast track could provide lower cost access to justice for fairly straightforward cases of moderate value. In order to ensure that this more rough and ready justice is in fact just, the new proposals need to conform to the basic principles. These are fairness and accessibility, responsiveness to objectives, equality and balance; supported by active case management, adequate resourcing, information and consultation and a non-adversarial approach."

7.   The Law Society and the Bar have been extremely constructive in their contributions. They have submitted a number of very helpful papers to the Inquiry. Their response and that from the profession and consumers, both individuals and businesses, has been overwhelmingly positive. In addition, the Department of Trade and Industry, which has circulated my interim report through its consultative bodies and information channels, has reported overwhelming enthusiasm among business on the proposals for the fast track and on case management generally.

8.   The Law Centres Federation, while it did not accept that any link existed between the complexity of a case and its value, did accept that there was a relationship between the costs of the case and the benefit to the client. It commented:

> "It is clear that a privately paying client would not consider it reasonable that the total cost of the claim should be more than the value of the claim itself in most cases. Given the 'person of moderate means' test applied by the Legal Aid Board then the position is likely to be very much the same for legally aided clients."

9.   The Law Society in its response to my interim report supported my outline proposals for the fast track in principle but said:

"The Society has continued to support the principle of the fast track provided the procedures are not so curtailed as to discourage settlements and lead to more trials and/or lead to rough justice. The Society also supports proportionality between what is at issue between the parties and the procedures and costs."

10. The Society also suggests that "a number of factors, not only monetary value, need to be taken into account when deciding the appropriate track for an action."

11. There are nonetheless a minority who consider that the whole concept of the fast track is wrong in principle and a greater number who, while supporting the proposals in principle, are concerned about the detail. The issues of principle which were raised relate first to the scope of the fast track and the criteria by which cases are included or excluded and secondly to the concept of proportionality.

Scope

12. The fast track is intended to cover the majority of defended actions within the monetary band £3,000 – £10,000. All personal injury cases up to £10,000 will be included except where the claimant is a litigant in person and opts for a claim below £3,000 to be dealt with under the small claims procedure. The fast track will also deal with non-monetary claims such as injunctions, declarations and orders for specific performance which are not suitable for the small claims procedure and do not require to be dealt with on the multi-track. Since the fast track is for defended actions, debt actions, fixed date possession and return of goods actions will not be affected by these proposals unless a substantive defence is filed.

13. The new procedures should enable defended cases up to £10,000 to be progressed fairly within the fast track. Some respondents to the issues paper, notably the Bar, have suggested that all cases should be allocated to the fast track by a given case type, rather than as a result of a presumption based on monetary value. As against this, many respondents have pointed out that all types of cases have the potential to be simple or complex. It is preferable to establish criteria which can be applied to all types of cases and which will enable parties to identify, and the court to decide, whether or not a case is suitable for handling within the 'no frills' procedure of the fast track.

14. I recognise that not all cases under £10,000 will be suitable for the fast track. The criteria for removal from the fast track must be such as can be clearly identified by litigants, advisers and the courts. It is in the interests of all that there should be certainty; I do not wish to devise criteria which will lead to endless applications to transfer.

15. I have carefully considered the responses to the consultation and the conclusions of the working group. I recommend that a case should not be included in the fast track if:

(a)   it raises issues of public importance; or

(b)   it is a test case; or

(c)   oral evidence from experts is necessary; or

(d)   it will require lengthy legal argument or significant oral evidence which cannot be accommodated within the fast track hearing time; or

(e)   it will involve substantial documentary evidence.

16. There are three categories of cases which will normally be excluded because of the criteria outlined above: medical negligence cases, jury trials and cases of deceit. In those cases, the presumption should be that the case will be dealt with on the multi-track. In other types of cases, such as personal injury and other classes of professional negligence, there will be no presumption. Some individual cases will meet the criteria for transfer into the multi-track but others will not. The decision will have to be made by the district judge in the individual case, based on the information in the claim and defence and taking account of the criteria outlined above and the wishes of the parties. It has been argued that all professional negligence cases should be excluded from the fast track. Negligence claims will include claims against builders and garages, as well as claims against the 'learned' professions. There is no reason in principle to treat them differently and no clear dividing line; some of the former may be complex while some of the latter may be straightforward. Both consumers and small businesses value the improved access that the fast track will provide. I do not wish to restrict that access by the exclusion of a particular category of proceedings where their wish for access is well recorded.

Party choice of procedure

17. It has been suggested, by the Bar amongst others, that the decision whether to opt for the limited procedures of the fast track should be a matter for the parties themselves. I am aware that the introduction of a fast track in New South Wales was achieved on this basis. Parties and their representatives had a choice between a fast track and the standard or slow track, and legal representatives were required to inform their clients if they were pursuing the case in the slow track and of their reasons. This is one answer. However, potential litigants, both individuals and small businesses, have indicated to me that they support the concept of the fast track and I think there should be a *prima facie* assumption that the fast track will be used for all cases under £10,000, unless they meet one or more of the criteria for transfer out. To preserve access to justice for all users of the system it is necessary to ensure that individual users do not use more of the system's resources than their case requires. This means that the court must consider the effect of their choice on other users of the system.

18. There are two other compelling reasons for designing the fast track in such a way that the majority of cases under £10,000 will be dealt with under its procedures. The first is the certainty that is provided both to the litigant and to the litigant's legal advisers. This will enable advice to be given to potential litigants on the cost benefit of pursuing any case under the procedures. The second is that without the *prima facie* assumption that most cases would be dealt with under the fast track, there would be numerous disputes as to what the appropriate track would be and this would itself generate expense and involve a considerable drain on judicial resources. The certainty provided by the fast track will be particularly helpful in the merits test for legal aid which looks at the likely cost benefit of the case.

Proportionality

19. My proposals for proportionality for the system of civil justice overall are underpinned by Rule 1 of the new rules which requires the court to deal with cases in ways proportionate to the amount involved, the importance or complexity of the issues, and the parties' financial position. Proportionality underlies the whole concept of the fast track.

20. The argument against proportionality was put by the Association of Personal Injury Lawyers (APIL) in the first part of my Inquiry. The Association has made a number of points to me, and out of respect for its arguments I consider these in detail in what follows. In the first part of the Inquiry, APIL argued that since the costs of personal injury cases were almost invariably recovered from insurers there was no need to introduce the concept of proportionality in these cases and that to do so would have a disastrous impact on lawyers' ability to achieve proper compensation for their clients. APIL has further argued that it would be impracticable to expect its members to work within a range of costs that would be proportionate to the compensation that is awarded. They consider that if they are required substantially to reduce the cost of litigating their cases, and hence their fees, it will result in experienced personal injury solicitors giving up the work.

21. I considered these arguments in stage one of my Inquiry and in my interim report I commented as follows:

> "I have carefully considered these arguments but I reiterate that the cost of litigating moderate claims, as illustrated in APIL's survey, is unacceptable. The public will not be persuaded that a serious effort to bring down those costs is being made unless the amounts allowed are expressly limited at substantially lower figures. In response to the profession's argument that the present levels of costs are unavoidable under existing procedures, I am offering what I believe is a radically simplified procedure which will enable case expenditure to be reduced. Professional practices are not immutable; I would expect efficient and effective firms to adjust their methods and approach (perhaps using IT) so as to work within new cost budgets. This should be regarded not as a threat, but as a challenge and an opportunity because the resulting improvement in access to justice should mean more business for practitioners.

> "If the profession is not willing or able to meet this challenge, then it should not imagine that the status quo can be retained. More fundamental measures, possibly involving the removal of at least moderate-sized injury claims from the litigation system, would have to be envisaged." (Interim report, chapter 7, paragraphs 24 – 25)

22. APIL has maintained its stance, basing it on two rather different considerations. First it argues that it is impossible to investigate and to prove personal injury claims in a way that is proportionate to the compensation eventually awarded because insurers are prepared to throw unlimited sums of money into the defence of quite small claims. Secondly, it argues that disproportionate cost is immaterial since the majority of personal injury claims succeed and the costs of litigating the action are in any event reimbursed to the claimant by the defendant. I accept that the first argument will have weight in a minority of cases; an example is where there are pioneering types of action such as vibration white finger. Actions involving new areas of industrial disease or other cases which are effectively test cases should not come within the fast track. However, in the majority of cases, the insurers will have little scope to deploy excessive resources even if they want to do so, which I doubt will happen, because of the limited procedure. In those cases where a defendant unexpectedly pursues a small action at great expense to the claimant, the judge will provide the protection needed by exercising his discretion to disapply the limit on recoverable costs.

23. The second point goes to the root of the Inquiry and is not to be accepted. A system which usually pays those who litigate cases as much as, and sometimes more than, the victims receive in compensation simply fails to command public confidence. One of the objectives of the Inquiry is to restructure the work that solicitors have to do so that there will be a greater degree of proportionality between the amount of a claim and the cost of pursuing it. As the London Solicitors' Litigation Association pointed out, the only way to limit the costs of a case is to limit the amount of work that the solicitor has to do on the case. That is what the fast track will achieve.

24. Even where individual litigants receive back the full cost of achieving their compensation, that cost must be borne in the first place by the insurers, in the second place by the insured and in the third place by society generally. I accept that the cost of litigating and awarding compensation has a regulatory role in influencing awards of compensation and the costs associated with them may well play a part in deterring employers from perpetuating unsafe practices. But that is also likely to be achieved by proportionate costs, and in any event is more a matter for the insurance industry to achieve through appropriate loading of premiums than through accepting excessive litigation costs. In addition, when insurers consider settling cases they tend to look at the total cost of the claim (the damages payable plus costs). Excessive cost tends to reduce the sum available for damages. Finally, the pattern of high spending on personal injury contaminates other areas of litigation where the costs are less likely to be borne by insurers.

25. More recently, in the final stages of the Inquiry, APIL has argued that the growing use of conditional fee agreements, since their introduction in August 1995, has provided access to justice in personal injury cases for those who previously did not litigate through fear of costs, and that there is no need for personal injury cases to be subject to the fast track since the desired increase in access to justice has been achieved. APIL contends that conditional fee agreements provide claimants with complete certainty as to costs, through the provision of insurance after the event since, if the client loses, the insurance pays all the defendant's costs and the claimant's solicitor must carry his own costs. If the claimant wins, as APIL suggests will happen in 95 per cent of personal injury cases, he/she will recover in the region of 85 per cent of his/her costs from the defendant. Successful claimants pay their own solicitor a success fee, which APIL suggests would normally be between 20 – 30 per cent of solicitor and own client costs. The Law Society recommends that, in any event, it should be no more than 25 per cent of the damages recovered.

26. APIL's concern is that fixed recoverable costs will diminish the amount of costs recovered by claimants on their behalf from defendants because the cost of litigating an individual case may be in excess of the fixed recoverable costs if those are not fixed at a realistic level. If that were to happen, clients would have to meet the extra out of their damages, in addition to the success fee, or solicitors would be pressured to do the work for less. APIL has said that in those circumstances, either clients would cease to use conditional fee agreements or experienced personal injury lawyers would no longer be able to undertake the work. Either outcome would reduce access to justice.

27. The whole concept of the fast track is intended to increase access to justice by removing the uncertainty over excessive cost which deters people from litigating. Conditional fee agreements combined with after the event insurance contribute to the same objective. The two must work together to improve access rather than reduce it. It will be clear, however, from the preceding discussion, that conditional fees do not answer the case for a more economical level of costs. Indeed, they could, taken by themselves, shore up an uneconomic level of costs. An acceptable level of costs can best be achieved by ensuring that the costs regime provides a realistic and fair reward for litigating such cases and that solicitors generally accept this regime of fixed limited costs for solicitor and own client costs. The working group has recommended a structure designed to achieve that, which I outline in chapter 4.

28. The Fast Track Working Group and the work on pre-action protocols have demonstrated the considerable progress that can be made by working groups of judges and practitioners representing both claimants and defendants in devising procedures appropriate to cases under £10,000. I recommend that such groups should carry forward the work on the costs regime on a similar basis.

29. There is a final point to which I attach great importance. It is vital that solicitors should feel able to welcome the fast track system as a new facility which they can commend to their clients as providing access to justice with certainty and economy. Constant pressure to take cases out of the fast track will undermine certainty and increase costs.

Equality of resources

30. Many of those responding to the fast track issues paper were concerned that it might reduce equality between the litigants. That is the opposite of what should be the position. Equality is furthered by setting out the requirements in terms of activity and timetable for both parties at the very start of the case. There will be very limited scope for any party to undertake extra work and no reward for doing so. The timetable will be sufficient for parties to undertake the work that is needed but not so generous as to encourage elaboration. While the fixed costs will be set at a level sufficient to reward the winning party for this work, the resultant procedure will mean that there is little potential for a powerful opponent to drive up costs in a way which is intimidating to the weaker litigant, as can happen in the current system. Sanctions will be more effective, whether they are cost related or inhibit a party's ability to present material in the case. It is particularly important on the fast track for the court to provide protection, on both a preventative and a curative basis, against oppressive or unreasonable behaviour. My proposals for dealing with such behaviour are set out in detail in chapter 6.

Court control

31. My proposal for a court-managed system which sets a timetable for steps to be taken to progress a case to trial in the fast track is a significant change from the current party-driven litigation. It builds on the experience of timetabling at Liverpool and Central London County Courts. On consultation, the overwhelming response to timetabling was positive. The limited period given to parties by fixed dates for trial was seen as beneficial in concentrating attention, ensuring effective preparation and, most significantly, in reducing cost. Litigants in person, in particular, find detailed timetables helpful but complain that at present they are routinely ignored by practitioners, with impunity. That will no longer be possible under my proposals.

32. It is clear that at present party-driven litigation is still taking too long to reach a conclusion. It is unreasonable in my view to expect clients to wait on average two to three years for the resolution of a dispute. It is important for cases to proceed as quickly as is consistent with the interests of justice. The longer the period from the time when the cause of action arose until trial the more difficult it is for clients and witnesses to remember the events clearly. It is also likely that the eventual award will be of less significance to the successful party so long after the event, notwithstanding the possibility of awarding interest on the claim. For this reason it is important that lower value cases, which will be dealt with on the fast track, are resolved as soon as possible. The way to achieve that is for the court to determine an appropriate timetable to bring cases to final disposition.

The judiciary and court resources

33. Particularly in the early stages the fast track will impose a considerable burden on the judiciary, especially the district judges. They will have to consider cases at the outset to determine the allocation to the proper track and will have to deal with applications to remove cases from the track, to vary the timetables, to require opponents to produce documents or experts' reports or to restrain the oppressive activity of opponents. It will be essential for there to be consistency in decision making throughout the country, at each local centre and at every level of the judiciary. This will require judicial training and guidance to ensure that there is consistency of approach both at first instance and appeal. District judges and Circuit judges need to feel that they are operating within a system which will be supported by High Court judges and the Court of Appeal. It is particularly crucial that time is allocated to allow judges to give proper consideration to the papers when the defence is filed, to determine the appropriate track and give the necessary directions for the future conduct of the case. It is also important, for the purposes of trial management, that judges receive the necessary training and that time is allocated to pre-read the papers. Judges will require administrative support from the Court Service to ensure that the new demands of the fast track can be met. Listing systems must enable judges to deal with applications for relief from sanctions within days rather than weeks.

34. If difficulties arise over meeting timetables, these need to be resolved quickly. Whilst the majority of these applications may be dealt with on paper, some may require a hearing. It will also be important that appointments to deal with failure to return the listing questionnaire are given promptly. Appeals, particularly interlocutory appeals, will also need to be disposed of expeditiously and effectively. I deal with appeals generally in chapter 14.

35. I recognise that this presents a considerable challenge, particularly to the Court Service, but I am firmly of the view that listing arrangements need to be more responsive to the needs of litigants. The practical ways in which this will be achieved will need to be worked out locally but experience in many areas, particularly with the Central London Common Listing System, has demonstrated that, with a degree of creativity and ingenuity, cases can usually be heard on the day for which they are listed. The same ingenuity and creativity will now be required throughout the whole system.

36. Cases allocated to the fast track will generally be tried by district judges unless it is more practicable or appropriate for the case to be heard by a Circuit judge. I recommended in my interim report that fast track cases should be heard at local county courts convenient to the parties. I still believe that this should be an option but recognise there will be circumstances in which it is more advantageous for the case to be heard at a civil trial centre. For example, it may enable parties to have an earlier hearing date or it may be more convenient bearing in mind public transport facilities. It is, however, important that there should be a central listing system within each local group of courts to ensure the most effective use of court and judicial resources and provide the listing flexibility needed to deal with cases expeditiously.

37. I outline in more detail in chapter 21 the role which information technology might play in implementing my proposals generally and judicial case management in particular. It is important that systems are introduced to support my proposals for the fast track. In particular, both the judiciary and the courts must be in a position to monitor the progress of individual cases to trial as efficiently as possible. Systems must also be introduced to support the administrative process, particularly that relating to listing. Systems of monitoring which depend solely on papers are clearly inefficient and time consuming. I am aware that the Court Service already has a programme for developing information technology systems in the county courts, known as LOCCS (Local County Court System). The first module of LOCCS, called 'Caseman', will provide courts with a database for court details and will, in the first instance, enable courts to process cases more efficiently and effectively without complete reliance on paper-based systems. It is expected that both 'Caseman' and further modules under the LOCCS programme can be developed to support my proposals for the fast track and case management generally. I understand that 'Caseman' will be available to the largest courts by March 1997 and to all courts by the end of 1998.

Implementation

38. A significant number of the responses to the fast track issues paper have urged that there should be piloting of the new fast track procedures and, in particular, of the costs regime, before the fast track is introduced overall. The fast track depends, as do all the changes which I am recommending, on a change of culture throughout the system which will be supported by the new rules which I am drafting. It will affect judges and court staff as well as the profession. The new system will depend very much on good and clear forms, notes for guidance and practice guides, changes in the listing practices, and appropriate information technology in both courts and solicitors' offices to ensure that the requirements of the timetable are properly diarised.

39. The need for a change in culture will only be achieved by implementing my proposals for the fast track as a whole. It would be difficult to secure such a change if, as has been argued, the procedures were implemented without the costs regime. There would be a real danger that it might replicate, within the fast track, the disproportionate costs that already exist within the current methods of litigation. However, there are some aspects of the procedure where I believe it would be beneficial to consider piloting. Listing practices will need to be reviewed to meet the needs of the fast track and to meet the considerable criticism voiced in relation to current practices. I am aware that the Court Service already has this in hand. New listing systems will take time to develop and it may be helpful for there to be a degree of experimentation to determine the best approach for different areas and different sized courts.

40. Implementation is of course a matter for the Lord Chancellor to consider. It will be for him to decide on the scale and the timetable of preparation if he accepts my proposals for the fast track. For my own part, I would merely suggest the need for a sensible timetable for implementation so that there can be adequate time to convert and train all of those involved; the judiciary, court staff and lawyers, and for practitioners and the Court Service to devise and put in place the structural arrangements, both in terms of staff and information technology, that will enable the new fast track to work effectively.

Chapter 3   Fast Track: Detailed Procedures

1. In this chapter I set out the detailed procedure for the fast track. I start from the point at which the defence is filed. My proposals for starting a claim and for filing a defence and/or counterclaim will apply to all cases and are set out in chapter 12. My proposals for pre-action conduct, including establishing protocols, which will facilitate the speedy progressing of cases on the fast track are set out in chapter 10. Chapter 11 deals generally with claimants' and defendants' offers to settle and will apply to cases on the fast track.

Allocation to the fast track

2. The common procedure, which I recommended in my interim report, will require all cases to be scrutinised by the Master or district judge after a defence is filed. This will enable the claim to be allocated to the appropriate track; that is, small claims, the fast track or the multi-track. In practice, most cases which are candidates for the fast track will be managed by district judges in county courts. In making the decision as to which is the appropriate track, the judge will have to consider the criteria which will prevent a case being included in the fast track, which I set out in paragraph 15 of the previous chapter.

3. Responses to the issues paper suggested that parties should be able to indicate the appropriate track at the outset. I therefore adopt the working group's recommendation that the parties may file an allocation questionnaire with the claim or defence which will provide further information. Among the information which it would provide would be the parties' choice of track together with their reasons for preferring that track, the estimated value of the claim, the number of non-expert witnesses, whether expert reports have been obtained, what further reports are needed, and the type of claim. It should also include any suggested variation in the standard timetable, together with reasons for this and an alternative timetable. It will enable parties to indicate any special considerations and the preferred venue. The precise form of the questionnaire and the information which will be included in the new claim form will need to be developed as part of the implementation process.

4. On the basis of this information the district judge will allocate a 'trial week', set a timetable for the work to be done to ensure that the claim is ready for trial by the date given and give directions generally in relation to disclosure, witness statements, expert evidence and any other particular directions considered necessary in an individual case. This exercise will be conducted on the papers. It will not require a hearing.

5. Both the claim and the defence must set out the facts of the case in a way which allows the judge to identify clearly the issues to be resolved. If either the claim or defence is deficient, the judge will be able to order further details or consider summary disposal. It is the combined aim of the fast track and the new system of statements of case that there should be less need for applications for further and better particulars and interrogatories. When an application is necessary, the decision as to who should pay the costs will depend on whose fault it was that an application was required.

6. The Institute of Legal Executives and the Association of Personal Injury Lawyers (APIL) suggested that every case on the fast track should have a case management conference early in the procedure to determine the way in which it should be run. This would place too heavy a drain on court resources, add substantially to the cost of cases and, in the majority of cases, would be unlikely to provide any corresponding benefit. Questionnaires will elicit the information the judge will require to give his directions. When further guidance is required from the procedural judge, this will normally be able to be done on paper. An interlocutory hearing will be a last resort to resolve matters of particular difficulty.

7. However, litigants in person do face greater difficulties in knowing how to prove their case and assessing whether expert evidence is required. I recommend, therefore, that judges should have the power to direct a preliminary hearing for the purpose of assisting litigants in person to prepare their case. The other party may well wish to attend but will not normally be required to do so.

Venue

8. The existing rules relating to the automatic transfer of cases will no longer apply. Instead, venue will be decided by the judge. Relevant considerations will include the location of the parties, where the cause of action arose and practical factors, such as access by public transport and facilities such as wheelchair ramps and facilities for those with hearing difficulties. The National Consumer Council and the Advice Services Alliance have both stressed to me the importance of such matters for the public. When the transfer of a case is ordered, management directions will be given by the receiving court.

Transfer in or out of fast track

9. It will be within the discretion of the judge to allocate to the fast track defended actions which fall within the small claims jurisdiction or in which more than £10,000 is claimed. The decision will rest with the court and will take into account the wishes of the parties, their means and court resources. Normally applications to transfer cases will be dealt with on paper.

10. A case may become more complex after it has been allocated to the fast track. When this happens the case will be able to be referred to the judge for allocation to another track. An exceptionally strong reason will be needed to transfer a case contrary to the wishes of a weaker party. Legally aided parties may need to satisfy the Legal Aid Board that it is reasonable for the action to proceed on the multi-track. However, I would expect, if a decision has already been made by the court, the Legal Aid Board would rarely, if ever, take a different view from that of the court.

11. A number of respondents were concerned in case spurious counterclaims would be made for the purposes of removing cases from the fast track. Although I do not consider the risk of this abuse is great, the existence of a counterclaim will not, of itself, dictate the track to which a case will be allocated even where the value of the counterclaim exceeds the normal financial band for the track. Instead the judge will exercise his discretion on all the information which is available. The onus will be on the party suggesting that the case should be transferred to justify this. In some cases it may be necessary to handle claim and counterclaim separately. This should reduce the scope for tactical counterclaims.

12. Concern has been expressed about the effect of a succession of applications to amend. The proposed fact-based statements of case should reduce the need for amendments. However, a claim may be amended once, after service of the claim, without leave of the court. Similarly, a defence or counterclaim may be amended once without leave. Any further amendment will require leave of the court. This may mean further directions and an adjustment to the timetable will be needed. Unless there are special circumstances explaining why the amendment is not the fault of the party seeking leave to amend, that party will have to pay the costs assessed by the judge to arise from the amendment forthwith to the other party.

Timetable

13. The timetable I recommended in the interim report was 20 to 30 weeks, with a 'warned week' or fixed date for trial allocated at the time of the initial directions and a definite trial date notified nearer to trial. The working group has recommended a standard timetable outlining the steps which must be completed in preparing the case for trial and the timescale in which this should be done. I accept this recommendation. Experience with pre-trial reviews indicates that in a very high proportion of cases set down for trial, many of the steps which should have been completed prior to setting down have not been taken. In view of this the working group thought that it would be preferable to specify a timescale for each of the key preparatory elements rather than merely specifying an overall date by which they should all have been completed.

14. Taking into account the views of the working group, I propose the following standard timetable which will start from the date of service of the order for directions and will include specific dates on which stages are to be completed. For example, assuming the date of service of the directions order to be 10 June 1996.

(a)   Disclosure must take place by 8 July 1996 (28 days from the date of service of the order for directions).

(b)   Exchange of witness statements must take place by 29 July 1996 (21 days thereafter).

(c)   Exchange of expert reports must take place by 19 August 1996 (a further 21 days thereafter).

(d)   The court will dispatch the listing questionnaire by 19 August 1996 (70 days from the start of the timetable).

(e)   Parties need to return the listing questionnaire by 2 September 1996 (84 days from the start date).

(f)   The trial will take place during the week commencing 18 November 1996 and the court will notify the parties of the fixed date at least eight weeks before the hearing.

Annex 4 is an example of the timetable set out in a Gantt chart.

15. I regard adherence to the overall timetable, with strict observance of the set trial date, as an essential component of the fast track. For this reason, the directions order will be framed as a series of requirements which must be completed by specified dates and will include an automatic sanction for non-compliance unless an extension has been granted prospectively. Parties will be in breach of the order unless they comply with the directions by the date specified. A copy of the directions order will be sent to clients as well as their legal advisers so that they too can monitor the progress of their case.

16. I propose that the automatic sanction in relation to service of expert reports or witness statements should be that the defaulting party is unable to rely on that evidence unless relief has been sought in advance of the date for compliance and allowed. Thus, an example of an automatic sanction contained in the directions order would be that the defendant must serve all witness statements on the claimant by 10 June 1996 and will not be entitled to rely on the evidence of any witness whose statement is not so disclosed.

17. In the case of disclosure, it would not be sufficient merely to debar such evidence as it is usually the party seeking discovery who would be at a disadvantage. For this reason, I recommend that the appropriate automatic sanction would be to debar the party from relying on the document but further to enable the other party to apply *ex parte*, certifying non-compliance with the direction, for an order debarring the party at fault from pursuing their claim or defence if discovery is not complied with within seven days of service of the order. I set out in more detail in chapter 6 my proposals for appropriate sanctions and the circumstances in which parties may obtain relief from sanctions.

18. Parties will always be working to a timetable. Any party wishing to vary a date or the timetable must apply in advance to do so. Applications to vary the trial date or defer the listing questionnaire will always be on notice and will be granted only in the most exceptional circumstances. In addition, even where the court is prepared exceptionally to grant an adjournment, it will not make orders to adjourn generally but will always adjourn to a new fixed date. Applications giving reasons, will be made to the court with a copy to the other party. The court will consider such applications and grant them without a hearing, although the district judge may contact the other party to discover their views. If necessary, he may fix an appointment.

19. I accept that judges may occasionally need to vary the timetable. For example, there could be significant problems with evidence, there may be a change of solicitor or the proceedings may have been issued at the very end of the limitation period. If the prognosis is uncertain but there is no major dispute over liability, an extension may be appropriate but the preferable course will usually be a split trial. It is particularly important from the client's point of view that the issue of liability in these cases is determined at the earliest opportunity. The prospect of an early trial of liability frequently leads to an admission. Once liability is determined, it is unusual to have a trial on quantum because settlements usually follow. This will also foster interim payments being made in cases where the long-term prognosis remains uncertain. These circumstances should be identified by the information provided in the allocation questionnaire. The judge will then provide a timetable which, while realistic, will avoid unnecessary delay.

20. Although the issue of third party proceedings may not, of itself, necessitate a change in the timetable or the costs arrangements, a defence to third party proceedings will require further scrutiny by the judge. At that stage, it will be open to the judge to determine whether the case remains in the fast track, whether there needs to be an adjustment to the timetable, whether the third party proceedings should be dealt with separately or whether the whole case should be transferred to the multi-track. The judge will take into account the effect that such proceedings will have on the parties, particularly the cost consequences, when making his decision.

21. There will also be cases where the overall timetable can be significantly shortened. The facility to apply, in clear cases, for summary judgment either on the application of one of the parties, or of the court's own motion will also be available. Summary judgment is dealt with in chapter 12.

22. The timetabling system for the fast track will be supported by the use of information technology which will enable the court and the judiciary to monitor effectively the progress of cases. The system is being developed by the Court Service as part of the LOCCS (Local County Court Office Systems) programme. One of the modules of this programme, 'Caseman', will provide courts with facilities which can be further developed to provide the sort of case management system which will be needed.

Disclosure

23. There will only be standard disclosure on the fast track, that is:

(a)   *the parties' own documents:* those on which a party relies in support of his/her contentions within the proceedings; and

(b)   *adverse documents:* those of which a party is aware and which to a material extent adversely affect his/her own case or support another party's case.

My detailed proposals for disclosure are dealt with in chapter 12.

24. To alleviate the difficulty in obtaining documents in personal injury cases, a list of documents which should be automatically disclosed forms part of the pre-action protocol which is described in more detail in chapter 10.

Expert evidence

25. It is very important to limit the use of experts on the fast track to achieve my goal of proportionate cost. My detailed proposals on the handling of expert evidence are set out in chapter 13. Under those proposals, the court will have complete control over the use of experts in litigation. The way in which the use of experts on the fast track will be controlled is as follows.

(a)   There will be no oral evidence from experts: the evidence will be in writing.

(b)   Protocols will encourage the use of a single expert agreed between the parties.

(c)   Parties will be able to put written questions to experts.

(d)   The court will have the power to order that a single expert be appointed or that parties put forward names of experts for selection by the court.

(e)   Where a single expert is not agreed or directed by the court, and where a party requires experts from more than one discipline, then they may be instructed, although a party will not be allowed more than two experts in a fast track case without leave of the court.

(f)   Leave of the court will be required to instruct any expert, other than a medical expert, in road traffic accident cases.

Witnesses of fact

26. In the interim report I recommended that in fast track cases the evidence of witnesses should be handled by way of witness summaries. The working group's preference, however, is for brief witness statements, as most witness statements in fast track cases are, in any event, relatively concise and largely factual. If this is the case a summary will not be necessary. However, in any event, witnesses will be allowed to amplify their statements in their oral evidence provided that the additional evidence does not go outside the broad scope of the statement.

Listing questionnaire

27. There is a need to confirm that the parties have complied with the directions in the directions order before the case is allocated a final fixed trial date and time. The court needs information on what has happened and also the parties' estimates of how long the hearing will take. To obtain this information the court will send a listing questionnaire 10 weeks after service of the directions order. Parties will be required to return it within 14 days. If a party does not return the listing questionnaire when required to do so, the court will fix a hearing to resolve any difficulties and to ensure that the case is back on schedule for the trial. Legal representatives will be required to attend court with their clients and this may lead to a 'wasted costs' order. This should take place no less than nine weeks before the intended trial date.

Listing arrangements

28. Once the listing questionnaire has been returned from both parties, the court will give a fixed date for trial at a set time. I attach great importance to trial dates being honoured and I know that the Court Service is already working towards developing an effective listing system to meet the needs of the fast track.

29. Under my proposals for the fast track, the court will give parties a 'warned' week in which their case will be listed at the directions stage. The actual trial date will be within this 'window'. Although many respondents have requested fixed dates from the start, it would be extremely difficult to give a specific date for trial in all cases at the directions stage, given the high proportion of cases which settle between then and the trial date. In some courts the settlement rate is in excess of 80 per cent. Unless the court was able to fill vacated dates at short notice, which seems unlikely, this could result in courts not being utilised four out of five days each week. This in turn would lead to longer waiting times for all cases. Although I favour fixed trial dates I have therefore concluded that it would not be realistic to fix them in all cases at the directions stage.

30. Responses to consultation indicated four areas of concern to judges and practitioners: first, whether the Court Service would be able to provide a judge and a court on the date fixed for the trial; secondly, whether limited hearing times would be eaten into by other urgent matters, as happens at present, so that cases come on very late in the day and have to be adjourned or are not reached at all; thirdly, the impact of the current approach to listing which 'overbooks' because of the high rate of settlement; and fourthly, the practice in some courts of block listing which inevitably results in delay.

31. Fixed trial dates, limited hearing times and trials completed within one day are key components of the fast track and essential if there is to be a significant reduction in cost and delay. Meeting these new requirements will involve changes in working practices for all concerned. Practitioners must provide accurate information in the listing questionnaire to enable hearing times to be calculated on a realistic basis. They must inform the court of any settlement. District judges must make realistic assessments of hearing times based on the information provided. Courts must reconsider their listing arrangements and make provision for hearing urgent matters in ways which do not interfere with fast track hearings. They must provide specific staggered times for hearings rather than block lists.

The trial

32. The key characteristics of fast track trials are that there should be no oral expert evidence; the trial length should be strictly limited and the judge will have responsibility for ensuring that effective and appropriate use is made of the allotted time.

33. The trial length of three hours that was suggested in the issues paper has attracted a great deal of comment. Some respondents have failed to take account of the fact there will be no oral evidence from experts, which will considerably reduce the amount of time required. Many respondents felt that, while three hours was too short, a period of five hours should be sufficient for the majority of fast track cases. I do not regard the three-hour time limit as sacrosanct. When the district judge considers the case at the outset, the decision on whether it is appropriate for the fast track will depend in part on whether it can be dealt with within the normal fast track hearing time of three hours or half a day. If it is suitable in all other ways but might take up to a day then it could remain within the fast track. The important point is that if a case is allocated to the fast track at the directions stage then it must be heard within a day. Only in exceptional circumstances should the case be taken out of the fast track once allocated.

34. The amount of time allocated to a particular case will be derived from the information contained in the listing questionnaire. In order to make the most effective use of the time available, advocates will have to concentrate on the key issues and evidence. Judges will have to exercise control throughout the hearing, as many do at present. To do this effectively, they will need time to pre-read papers. There will also be a greater need to exercise discipline on late applications for additional witnesses and other matters where this is likely to affect the length of the trial. The importance of not overrunning the allocated trial time cannot be overemphasised. It will call for a skilful, professional partnership between judiciary, legal profession and Court Service alike.

35. For the judiciary and the legal profession, the challenge must be to achieve greater accuracy in estimating the time required and to ensure that cases which could settle do so before they are entered in the list. All the players have a responsibility to each other and to others whose cases must, if these skills are not developed, either wait longer for their trial or be exposed to the risks of overlisting. For the Court Service the challenge must be to improve the arrangements for moving cases and to increase the reliability of listing fixtures. If the Court Service fails to meet this responsibility through no fault but its own, and fixed dates are not honoured, then I accept the working group's recommendation that the Court Service should be liable for the costs of the hearing, except where the failure to honour the date is as a result of a specific judicial direction.

Appeals

36. My detailed proposals for both interlocutory and final appeals are set out in chapter 14. It is particularly important on the fast track that interlocutory appeals are dealt with expeditiously to ensure that the timetable for getting cases to trial is not delayed to an extent which affects the trial date.

Recommendations

My recommendations are as follows.

(1)   When appropriate cases shall be allocated to the fast track by a district judge after service of the defence. A case should not be included in the fast track if:

    (a)   it raises issues of public importance; or

    (b)   it is a test case; or

    (c)   oral evidence from experts is necessary; or

    (d)   it will require lengthy legal argument or significant oral evidence which cannot be accommodated within the fast track hearing time; or

    (e)   it will involve substantial documentary evidence.

(2)   Additional information to assist allocation to the appropriate track may be provided by questionnaires filed by the parties.

(3)   When allocating a case to the fast track the judge should decide on venue, allocate a 'trial week' and set a timetable for the steps to be taken which will ensure that the case can be tried by the date given; and give directions for preparing the case.

(4)   Judges should have the power to direct a preliminary hearing where a litigant is in person so as to assist the litigant in the preparation of the case.

(5)   There should be a discretion to allocate to the fast track other defended actions which fall outside the recommended monetary band but which are otherwise appropriate for disposal on the fast track.

(6)   Directions orders will be framed as a series of requirements which must be completed by specified dates.

(7)   Applications to vary the timetable must be made within the relevant time limit. If that time has passed, a sanction will apply automatically, unless relief is applied for.

(8)   There should be no oral evidence from expert witnesses but parties will be able to put written questions to experts.

(9)   Where possible a single expert should be instructed. Any relevant protocols should be observed.

(10) The court will have a residual power to appoint a single expert.

(11) Where a party legitimately requires experts from more than one discipline then they may be instructed, although no more than two experts can be instructed without leave of the court.

(12) Leave of the court will be required to instruct any expert, other than a medical expert, in road traffic accident cases.

(13) The court will give a fixed date for trial at a set time and for a limited hearing time.

(14) Normally cases should be completed in three hours but if otherwise suitable may go up to a day.

(15) Cases are to be heard on the date fixed. If the Court Service fails to honour a fixed date, through no fault but its own, it should be liable for the wasted costs except where the failure is the result of a specific judicial direction.

Chapter 4   Fast Track: Costs

Introduction

1.   In this chapter I set out my approach to establishing a regime of fixed recoverable costs for fast track cases. It is based on the work of the Fast Track Working Group. It seeks to provide an appropriate balance between certainty, proportionality and reasonable remuneration, taking account of:

(a)   the variety of cases which will be handled on the fast track;

(b)   the variations in amount and type of work in each case category;

(c)   the different characteristics of solicitors' practices;

(d)   the differing stages at which cases finish;

(e)   the additional work that may be required in some, but not all, cases.

2.   The provisional results of the working group's consideration were set out in a consultation paper issued in April 1996. Consumer representatives, businesses, judges and practitioners have commented on the paper. Consumers and businesses generally support a fixed costs regime. Small businesses are particularly keen on the certainty that fixed costs will provide, because they will be able to quantify at the outset the likely costs of bringing or defending an action. The proposed regime will also help businesses and individual litigants to negotiate their own solicitors' costs on a more effective and better informed basis. The National Consumer Council has also welcomed the proposals but has warned that, unless the levels of the fixed costs are fair and realistic, the introduction of the fast track will diminish rather than increase access to justice. The judiciary, too, are broadly content with the proposed regime, and have made a number of helpful comments on the detail of the proposals.

3.   The response from practitioners has been divided. Those who tend to represent claimants are concerned that the fixed costs might not properly reward the work required, so that claimants will be at a disadvantage against defendant insurers who can afford to spend more on the defence than they can expect to recover. There is concern that experienced practitioners might stop taking on cases. Defendant solicitors are broadly in favour of fixed costs, but again stress that the costs must be set at the right level.

4.   The Law Society has also drawn attention to the risks which could flow from costs being set too low: lawyers might be persuaded to cut corners to keep within the costs parameters, or actual costs might have to be met from the award won by a litigant which might dissuade people from taking legal action in the first place. But the Law Society has also acknowledged that if the costs projections are pitched fairly, the greater certainty and transparency of fixed costs will encourage more members of the public to seek redress from the courts, bringing lawyers more business.

5. The consultation has led to the proposals being refined. The structure which is now proposed will serve as a basis for further detailed work on the precise amounts which should be payable. The working group has undertaken some initial costings to assist in drawing up a blueprint for a costs regime, based on profiles of the activity which will be required in a number of different case types under the fast track procedure. The activity profiles were drawn up by practitioner and district judge members of the working group, and are based on a fair average of the time that a reasonably competent solicitor would take to do the work. While further work to set the levels of costs will be required by those responsible for implementing my proposals, I believe that the working group's activity profiles provide a good indication of the amount of work which will be required.

6. There has been an almost universal request from practitioners and the National Consumer Council for the new procedures to be piloted to provide information about the realistic costs which should apply. Timetables and the restricted procedure are being, and can continue to be, tested. There are, however, problems in running pilots on costs. How can you have a regime offering benefits to only selected litigants who happen to be in a particular area? Practitioners may choose or avoid the courts in which pilot studies are being conducted. Knowledge of the pilot might itself impact on the level of costs. I consider it would be preferable to set up a series of detailed hypothetical studies of the procedure using actual cases in a number of different areas. This would provide experience for members of the profession and the judiciary, as well as representatives of the Court Service, of working real cases through the proposed procedure to assess the amount of work that will be required. This type of exercise could produce slightly artificial results due to the effect on the participants of being involved in a new project. It would, however, allow the new approach to be tested out repeatedly on a theoretical basis over a much shorter period of time than would otherwise be possible. In addition, there will be a need to monitor the operation of the costs regime to ensure that what is proposed meets the objectives which I have set for it.

Solicitor and own client costs

7. The fast track costs regime will provide a standard system of fixed *inter partes* costs. It will result in the individual litigant knowing at the outset of the proceedings the maximum extent of his liability for his opponent's costs if he loses, and the amount that he will recover from his opponent if he wins.

8. However, the litigant also needs information on what he will pay his own solicitor. To provide this certainty it is imperative that solicitors explain their basis of charging to their clients. They must go beyond quoting an hourly rate to enable clients to appreciate their real maximum exposure. The fact that the fast track provides a greater degree of certainty as to the procedure involved should enable them to do this. It is also my hope that the fixed costs regime will enable clients to negotiate their own solicitors' costs on a more informed basis, and to make a better assessment of whether they wish to pay more than the fixed costs and, if so, what they will receive for the extra expense. I therefore recommend that, unless there is a written agreement between the client and his own solicitor which sets out clearly the agreed terms of business, the costs payable by a client to his own solicitor should be limited to the level of the fixed costs plus disbursements. The agreement will need to set out the likely level of fixed recoverable costs, the basis of charging specifying the hourly rate actually charged, and the likely level of disbursements and expert fees. It should include the best possible information, including all the relevant figures, on the amount which the client will be liable to pay. This information should be updated in the event of a change of circumstances.

Certainty

9. It is suggested that it is both impossible and unfair to estimate in advance the costs of any case. Certainty as to cost needs to be linked to certainty as to procedure. Unnecessary delays and complexities in procedure add to the work required on a case and push up the costs. I accept that at present there are difficulties for practitioners in this respect. But the fast track is designed to overcome these difficulties.

Equality

10. One criticism that has been made of my proposals for fixed recoverable costs is that they will allow the more affluent party to spend more on vigorously pursuing his own case whilst limiting the amount that he will have to pay his opponent if he loses. This is not the case. The limited procedure and strict timetable in the fast track will reduce both the scope for a party to delay or push up the amount of work required by an opponent and the extent to which a party will be able to spend money extravagantly on his own case.

11. The fast track will also be supported by the firm but fair use of sanctions which are described in detail in chapter 6.

Reasonableness

12. The working group, in drawing up proposals for the costs regime, has had in mind the need to ensure that cases on the fast track can be litigated by small firms undertaking a reasonable but not enormous volume of work at this level, either across the whole range of work or within one particular area of litigation. My proposal is for standard fixed recoverable costs. These will not directly reflect the cost of work undertaken in each individual case. The costs regime will, however, provide an amount which overall will represent reasonable remuneration. Today most practitioners who undertake litigation take on more than a handful of cases. Those who do not litigate except on isolated occasions have available to them the services of members of the Bar who deal with litigation regularly. Solicitors either with or without the assistance of the Bar should therefore be able to conduct litigation profitably on the fast track.

13. The working group has not undertaken detailed work on the costings for the new regime. Its effort has been directed at establishing the initial structure. Further detailed work will be required to establish the final figures. In paragraph 6 above, I have recommended that this might be assisted by a series of detailed case studies in different areas of the country. This will provide further information on the realistic cost of progressing cases on the fast track. In the light of information available to me at present, from the initial work on activity profiles, examination of current county court bills by District Judge Greenslade and Professor Hazel Genn, and information on the current cost of legally aided cases, I consider that it should be possible to litigate even the upper band of fast track cases at a total legal cost of up to £2,500, excluding VAT and disbursements. This is based on a preliminary assessment, undertaken chiefly to inform the structure rather than the actual level of costs. Those responsible for implementation will establish the specific figures. It will then be for solicitors together to work within this figure.

Proportionality

14. There are a number of possible options for achieving a proportionate costs regime. The issues paper on the fast track canvassed views on whether the best approach would be to devise a single level of costs for all cases up to £10,000, several bands within the £10,000 limit or a sliding scale of percentages related to case value. While the responses indicated some support for a sliding scale of percentages, since this would provide absolute proportionality in every case, this approach would make it impossible for solicitors to put a figure on the likely costs until the end of the case. There was particular concern that it would be very difficult to achieve both proportionality and a realistic figure at the lower end of the scale – that is, personal injury cases under £3,000 – since there is a basic minimum amount of work which has to be done in all cases. The weight of responses favoured broad bands related to case value.

15. I propose that there should be two value bands: up to £5,000 and up to £10,000. The lower band will include claims up to £5,000 not dealt with within the present small claims limit of £3,000. As now, costs will depend on the award for successful claimants and the amount of the claim for successful defendants. This approach will encourage claimants to make a realistic assessment of their claim. It will also allow solicitors greater certainty at the start of the case because they will be able to assess at the outset the fixed costs for which clients will be liable if they lose (based on the value of the claim) and either the likely amount they will recover or, in cases likely to be near the boundaries of a band, a lower and upper figure.

16. The value of the award will be taken as being the value before deductions for contributory negligence and any damages recouped by the Compensation Recovery Unit in respect of social security benefits paid as a result of the injury, so that the level of recoverable costs is related to the issue at stake and more fairly reflects the amount of work required.

Amount of work required

17. A number of respondents to the fast track issues paper observed that the amount of work required on a case is not necessarily related to the value of the claim. The activity profiles prepared by the working group indicated that most potential fast track cases fell into two broad groups; straightforward cases which tended to require seven to ten hours work, and those involving additional work which tended to require between 13 and 18 hours work. For example, cases involving expert evidence tended to require more work than those which did not. I accept that the cases which will fall within the fast track are not sufficiently homogeneous for me to be sure that a single amount within each value band would provide fair remuneration for both groups. A single fee covering all would not provide adequate reward for cases requiring additional work but would over-reward the straightforward. I therefore propose that there should be two levels of costs within each value band.

18. While it would be attractive, in terms of certainty, to assess whether a case required more or less work according to the type of case, particular case types may vary in the amount of work required. I therefore recommend that individual cases should be considered against specified criteria. This approach should enable litigants and their solicitors to assess with a reasonable degree of certainty into which fee band their case will fall. The district judge will determine the costs band into which the case will fall at the paper review stage once the defence is filed by assessing whether the individual case meets these criteria.

19. A number of criteria which might be good indicators of whether a case will require additional work have been suggested. Some criteria, such as disclosure exceeding that laid down as standard or a multiplicity of experts, are more relevant to the decision on whether the case should be in the fast track or the multi-track. Others, such as a split trial or a limitation issue, would be better taken account of by an additional fee since they relate to procedural activities which occur in only a minority of cases. In the case of children, the vast majority of such cases will be personal injury cases and will meet the first of the identified criteria.

20. I have therefore identified the following criteria as being valid indicators of additional work required on a case:

(a)   the need for expert evidence;

(b)   parties who are patients (as defined by the Mental Health Act 1983) and therefore require a next friend;

(c)   parties who are unable to give adequate instructions in English; and

(d)   multiple defendants with different interests where the case is otherwise suitable for the fast track.

21. The Law Society has recommended that the same level of costs should be payable for cases valued up to £5,000 requiring additional work and straightforward cases valued between £5,000 and £10,000. I consider that this approach adds to the simplicity of the costs regime, and I therefore accept this recommendation. Thus there will be three bands of costs:

Band A   £5,000 ceiling and straightforward

Band B   £5,000 ceiling and additional work factors
         £10,000 ceiling and straightforward

Band C   £10,000 ceiling and additional work factors.

22. Litigants will be able to file an allocation questionnaire with their claim or defence identifying any factors meeting the criteria for the additional work band and making representations about any desired changes to the standard timetable. Where other factors emerge later in the case, either party may apply in writing to the court for directions at any stage. Such directions could include a direction that additional work criteria are present.

Non-monetary claims

23. I have set out my recommended approach to achieving proportionality in cases which have a monetary value. Non-monetary claims are less straightforward in this respect. It has been suggested that such claims could be assigned a notional monetary value by the district judge at the paper review stage. It is, however, less easy to identify factors which would ensure a consistent and predictable allocation of non-monetary cases to the three costs bands and this approach would reduce certainty as to costs for the client. I therefore propose that non-monetary claims should be assigned to the middle costs band (B) or transferred to the multi-track. This approach will also be taken in cases where an injunction is the only relief sought. My proposals for dealing with the costs of interim injunctions and injunctions as part of another claim are set out in paragraphs 52 to 54. Experience of handling non-monetary claims over the initial period should be helpful in indicating criteria for allocation to different notional value bands in the future.

Stages

24. Cases finish or settle at different stages. To ensure that remuneration broadly corresponds to the activity required at different stages within the new fast track procedure, the fixed costs will be divided into tranches relating to the stage the case has reached, although the costs will only become payable at the conclusion of the case. This approach will allow clients to assess their exposure to costs at each stage of the case, and give effect in part to my general recommendation that clients should know how much their case is costing as it progresses. It will ensure that the costs regime provides certainty as to costs for litigants whose cases settle as well as for those who go to trial. It will be important for clients with solicitor and own clients costs agreements to be kept informed about the costs of their cases.

25. The points for stage-related payments should be set at key stages in the fixed procedural timetable where there is external evidence that the stage has been reached. The first key stage is the point at which the case is allocated to the fast track. The second is the filing of the listing questionnaire. Few cases will conclude at the exact point of these key procedural stages. The percentages of costs relating to each stage should therefore reflect the range of work which might be carried out between these stage points. Some cases may settle very shortly after allocation to the fast track, while others may settle after witness statements are served. The percentages should therefore be pitched at a level which will fairly represent work done towards resolution of the case, and encourage settlement early in the stage.

26. The percentage of costs payable for the first stage, up to and including allocation to the fast track will be higher for claimants than for defendants, recognising the amount of work which will be required to prepare the case. I propose that it should be 40 per cent of the fixed recoverable costs for claimants, and 25 per cent for defendants.

27. In the second stage, up to and including the filing of the listing questionnaire, both claimant and defendant will have to do broadly equivalent amounts of work. The percentage of costs should therefore be the same for both parties: 70 per cent.

28. After filing the listing questionnaire, both parties will have to prepare effectively for the trial. There will be a further 20 per cent for this stage. The final 10 per cent of the fixed recoverable costs will be payable only in cases which go to trial or settle in the 48 hours before trial, when all the final preparation will have been completed.

29. Some respondents to my consultation paper on fast track costs have argued that the defendant should not be entitled to very much in the way of costs if the case ends at the first stage. However, there is a need to recognise that defendants will need to file a fuller defence than is currently the practice and I consider that 25 per cent of the fixed costs fairly represents the amount of work that will have been done by that stage.

30. It has also been suggested to me that total costs for defendants in personal injury cases should be less because defendants do much less work than claimants, and that much of the early work may be done by the insurer rather than his solicitor. However, the pre-action protocols for fast track cases will require defendants to do more early preparation in order to meet the requirements of the directions and timetable. In my view it is unrealistic and impracticable to seek to distinguish cases where work is done by defendant insurers or defendant solicitors. The costs regime is intended to apply to all defendants.

31. Claims for fixed amounts for goods or services which become defended will be allocated to the fast track. Generally speaking, very limited work will have been done in such cases prior to the issue of proceedings. The application of the stage costs that I am proposing could lead to unfairness if such a claim was settled very shortly after a defence was filed. I therefore recommend that further work be carried out to establish a fair percentage of the fixed costs to be recoverable for the first stage of such claims.

Offers to settle

32. My proposals for offers to settle are set out in chapter 11. Where an offer to settle by either party is made and accepted, the successful party will be entitled to recover costs up to the date of acceptance. The level of the costs recoverable will be determined by the stage the case has reached. However, the relevant point will be the due date for a particular procedural stage rather than the actual date, if that is earlier, to prevent parties getting ahead of the timetable in order to recover higher costs. Thus it will be for the party making an offer to calculate the effect of the timetable on his liability for costs and time the offer accordingly. For example, if the defendant makes an offer less than 21 days before the listing questionnaire is due and this is accepted after the date for filing the listing questionnaire, the claimant will receive 90 per cent of the fixed recoverable costs. Similarly, where the claimant discontinues, the defendant will be entitled to recover his costs on the same principle.

33. Where the claimant does not accept the defendant's offer to settle but fails to beat the offer at trial, currently the claimant is entitled to recover his costs up to the date of the offer but is liable to pay the defendant's additional costs from that point. On the fast track the same broad principle will apply. For example, where the defendant offers to settle before the listing questionnaires are filed and the case proceeds to trial, the claimant will recover 70 per cent of his costs and will be liable to pay the defendant 30 per cent of his costs plus the advocacy fee.

Costs matrix

34. My proposal is therefore for a range of costs levels combining recognition of factors which are likely to lead to additional work with a broad banding approach to case value, and payment corresponding to the activity required at each stage of the case.

35. In its response to my issues papers, the Law Society suggested that a costs matrix would present simply and clearly the relationship between the amount of work required on a case, the stage reached and case value. I am extremely grateful to the Law Society for this suggestion, which I consider will assist the client's understanding of the costs for which he may be liable. I propose the following outline costs matrix:

BAND	CLAIMANT	Up to and including allocation to fast track (40%)	Up to and including filing the listing questionnaire (70%)	Up to 48 hours before the trial (90%)	Trial (100%)	Advocacy fee
	DEFENDANT	Up to and including allocation to fast track (25%)				
A	£5,000 ceiling and straightforward					
B	£5,000 ceiling and additional work factors £10,000 ceiling and straightforward					
C	£10,000 ceiling and additional work factors					

36. The costs matrix will operate by cases being allocated to a costs band according to the case value and the presence of specific additional work criteria. The district judge will determine whether additional work criteria are present when the defence is filed. Since the criteria for additional work are simple, solicitors should be able to advise their clients on the likely allocation beforehand. Disbursements will be payable in addition to the fixed costs.

Advocacy fees

37. The working group recommended that there should be an advocacy fee covering the immediate preparation for trial (including a conference) and advocacy, payable only in cases which go to trial.

38. The advocacy fee will be based on the same bands as those proposed for solicitors' fixed costs. The Bar has suggested, and I strongly agree, that this should be regardless of the length of the hearing. It will be payable whether the advocate is a solicitor or barrister. A conference, final preparation for trial by the advocate and preparation of a skeleton argument will be included in the advocacy fee, but preparation of bundles and notifying witnesses will fall into the trial stage of the fixed costs. Payment for more than one counsel will not be allowed.

39. At present Law Society rules of conduct provide that where counsel has been instructed, the instructing solicitor is under a duty to attend or arrange for the attendance of a responsible representative throughout the proceedings, except in specified circumstances. The costs of such attendance will be included in the trial stage of the solicitor's fixed costs. The amount included will take into account that a junior member of the solicitor's staff would normally be able to carry out this function. Rules of conduct of this kind impose additional costs on the fast track. I recommend that they should be changed.

Cancelled hearings

40. At present, a considerable proportion of cases settle shortly before trial and very often at the last minute. The working group considered whether cancellation fees should be payable to advocates if trials did not take place. This would be a move away from the current practice that once the brief is delivered counsel is entitled to payment in full even if the case immediately settles (although in practice a reduced fee may be negotiated). I think that the correct approach is to pay for work actually undertaken, such as conferences. The new arrangements should, however, recognise that shorter hearing times will require considerably more preparation by advocates. In straightforward cases this is likely to be undertaken, as at present, just before the hearing, and conferences if required will take place on the day of the trial. In other cases, the advocate will usually arrange a conference with the client and prepare for trial a good way in advance.

41. I propose, therefore, that where a case settles after the brief has been delivered and a conference has been held, advocates will be entitled to receive 40 per cent of the advocacy fee to cover the work done on the conference. However, where the advocate is a solicitor who is a member of the firm which has had conduct of the case, I do not consider that it should be necessary for a conference to be held. I do not, therefore, propose to make any provision for payment for a conference in these circumstances.

42. If the case settles less than 48 hours before the hearing, the solicitor advocate from the conducting firm will be entitled to 40 per cent of the advocacy fee, to cover the preparation that will have been done by this stage. For other advocates, there will be an entitlement to the full fee.

Waiting time

43. I have already set out the importance for the operation of the fast track of using the most effective listing arrangements to minimise the interruption of trial time for urgent business. This approach should reduce the amount of waiting time on the day of hearing. The advocacy fee is intended to be appropriate for all hearings up to one day. I therefore do not consider that it is necessary to make additional payment for waiting time.

Travel time and costs

44. A small amount of travel time and costs to cover time spent travelling to and from court for the trial will be included in the advocacy fee. This is intended to cover the time spent travelling by advocates 'local' to the court, and swings and roundabouts will operate within this amount. Costs associated with longer journeys may be allowed, and further work is needed to establish the amount.

Additional costs

45. The costs matrix covers the core costs of the solicitor in the majority of cases. However, there are some costs which are not suitable for inclusion in the costs matrix, either because they relate to particular procedural stages which will only feature in a small number of cases (such as injunctions) or because they may vary greatly between cases (such as disbursements and experts' fees). While these additional costs will reduce certainty as to the total cost for the client, at this stage in the introduction of the fast track it would not be appropriate to recommend their inclusion in the overall fixed costs. The solicitor will, however, be required to give the client an estimate of experts' fees and of the standard disbursements associated with the particular type of case at the outset of the case. Where there is a written agreement setting out agreed terms of business between the client and his solicitor, it should include an estimate of disbursements. Where the estimate is likely to be exceeded, the client should be informed.

Disbursements

46. Disbursements, including court fees, will be recoverable in addition to the fixed costs. It has been suggested that this might encourage solicitors to use solicitor agents or non-solicitors for work for which payment is included in the fixed costs and then claim the cost as a disbursement, thereby obtaining double-payment. Examples that have been given are where accountants are instructed to carry out simple mathematical calculations within a solicitor's competence, or where enquiry agents are used to interview witnesses. Disbursements will be subject to scrutiny by the court to ensure that any such claims are disallowed.

47. In order to assist in determining the disbursements to be allowed, each party should, at the end of the case, submit a form to the court setting out all disbursements incurred and attaching relevant vouchers. This may then be challenged.

Experts

48. Since the use of experts will be considered in determining whether a higher level of costs is appropriate, it will be particularly important for the rules to allow judges to control effectively the use of experts. It will be important to differentiate clearly between experts and the use of agents for work for which payment is covered by the standard costs. Many respondents have been reluctant to place any limit on experts' fees although there is at the same time concern about the high fees charged. On the fast track this is a particular worry. I recommend that further work should be carried out to establish standard fees for experts' reports. The level of a maximum or standard fee will need to take into account the ability of an opponent to ask questions of an expert.

49. The overall number of experts will be reduced by pre-action protocols and other steps encouraging parties to agree a single expert's report. There will be an overriding discretion to disallow the costs of experts' reports where they are unreasonably incurred. This will apply where it was not appropriate to obtain a report on the particular issue, or where separate reports are commissioned but the district judge considers it unreasonable not to have instructed a single expert.

Split trials

50. There may be occasions, even on the fast track, where an early trial on liability alone may be required but quantum cannot be decided at that stage because of uncertainty over the prognosis. In many cases a trial on liability alone will lead to settlement. If it does not and there is a later trial on quantum alone, there will still be a need for a further advocacy fee and a degree of preparation by the solicitor. In those circumstances, the solicitor's total fixed costs will be increased by 20 per cent.

Interlocutory applications

51. It is of particular importance in reducing the cost of lower value cases that there should, in the main, be no interlocutory hearings. Pre-action protocols, informative claims and detailed defences all have a part to play in making this possible. There may, however, be occasional cases where an interlocutory hearing is necessary, such as where there is an application for extension of the timetable or for relief from a sanction. Because the circumstances will vary, I recommend that the district judge should make a costs order in each individual case and that, if the hearing was occasioned by the default of a party, that party should normally pay the costs forthwith. Such costs orders will be separate from the fixed fee. In such cases, if for example a solicitor has not adhered to the timetable and as a result has to appear before the court, the client should be informed about the costs order against him so that he can apply for a wasted costs order against his solicitor if the solicitor was at fault.

Injunction hearings

52. In paragraph 23, I recommended that non-monetary claims should be assigned to costs band (B). Where an injunction only is sought, those provisions will apply. Where an injunction is linked to a claim for damages, the costs will be determined by the amount of damages recovered (or claimed in the case of a successful defendant).

53. Other claims may involve an application for an interim injunction, usually immediately after the issue of proceedings. I propose that there should be an additional 'bolt-on' fee to cover the immediate preparation for and the hearing of the application. The costs recoverable for the claim as a whole, depending on the stage which the claim reached, would then be determined at the conclusion of the case.

54. However, situations will arise in which the interim injunction effectively resolves the case. Where this occurs before the case is allocated to the fast track, I recommend that a separate fixed fee should apply. Those responsible for implementation will decide what this should be.

Children and patient settlements

55. Where a claim is issued to approve a settlement, the fast track costs regime will not apply since there will be no defence. Where a case is already in the fast track and a settlement is reached which requires the court's approval, I recommend that, in addition to the costs applicable to the stage at which settlement was reached, an additional fixed fee should be allowed to cover the preparation for and advocacy at the hearing to approve the settlement.

Counterclaims

56. In cases involving counterclaims, case value will be determined for the purpose of costs by looking at the value of the claim and counterclaim separately, rather than allowing the parties to ask for the value to be determined on the balance.

Indemnity principle

57. The indemnity principle provides that a party may recover from his opponent only as much as he owes his lawyer. The indemnity principle will need to be modified so that the costs recoverable are the fixed costs, subject to any court order on, for example, interlocutory costs. Thus, the fixed costs will be recoverable even if the solicitor and own client costs would be lower.

Mechanism for ordering the costs to be paid

58. There will no longer be a need for costs payable *inter partes* to be taxed. Where a case proceeds to trial, the court will certify the total costs, including disbursements at the end of the trial. The order for costs will then be included in the judgment.

Conditional fees

59. The extent to which conditional fee agreements are available will not be affected by the existence of the fast track costs regime. Indeed, their adoption could well be assisted by the ability to base the percentage increase on the fixed costs, thus giving more certainty to the client. A conditional fee agreement for a fast track case will need to set out the relationship between the fixed costs, the likely amount of solicitor and own client costs and the proportion of those costs represented by the success fee if the client wins.

Geographical variation

60. Consideration may have to be given to whether the levels of fixed costs should vary according to the geographical location of the court or solicitor's office.

Litigants in person

61. In chapter 7 I have recommended that there should be a review of the provisions relating to the costs of litigants in person. This review will need to take into account the effect of the fixed costs regime and, in particular, the need to ensure that the total of the litigant in person's costs, plus the cost of any legal advice, does not exceed the total fixed recoverable costs which would have applied had the litigant been represented.

Evaluation and review

62. There will need to be a general and continuous evaluation and review of the operation of the new rules and the costs regime. The levels of the fixed costs should be reviewed each year, and the general operation of the fixed costs regime should be reviewed every three years by a committee representing judges, a representative selection of litigants, consumers and their representative bodies and practitioners. This committee should report to the Lord Chancellor through the Civil Justice Council.

63. To inform the evaluation and review of the costs regime, it will be necessary to collect data on the level of costs recovered in fast track cases, particularly in the first year of operation. Information on costs recovered in cases which settle before trial, on levels of experts and fees and on the type and amount of disbursements incurred will be particularly useful to inform further development of the regime.

Recommendations

My recommendations are as follows.

(1)   There should be a regime of fixed recoverable costs for fast track cases.

(2)   The guideline maximum legal costs on the fast track should be £2,500, excluding VAT and disbursements.

(3)   The costs payable by a client to his own solicitor should be limited to the level of the fixed costs plus disbursements unless there is a written agreement between the client and his solicitor which sets out clearly the different terms.

(4)   The costs regime should reflect case value in two bands; up to £5,000 and up to £10,000. There should be two levels of costs within each value band, one for straightforward cases and the other for cases requiring additional work.

(5)   The fixed costs should be divided into tranches relating to the stage the case reaches.

(6)   There should be a fixed advocacy fee for each band payable in cases which go to trial whether the advocate is a solicitor or a barrister. A cancellation fee should be payable to the advocate to cover work undertaken on cases which settle shortly before trial.

(7)   The Law Society's rule of conduct requiring a solicitor to attend trial with counsel except in specified circumstances should be revoked.

(8)   The costs of interlocutory hearings, applications for interim injunctions and hearings for the court to approve a settlement should be additional to the fixed costs.

(9)   The indemnity principle should be modified so that the costs recoverable are the fixed costs.

(10) There should be further detailed work to establish the levels of the fixed costs, standard fees for experts' reports and an appropriate fee for defended debt cases.

(11) The levels of the fixed costs should be reviewed each year, and the general operation of the fixed costs regime should be reviewed every three years by a committee reporting to the Lord Chancellor through the Civil Justice Council.

Chapter 5   The Multi-Track

Case management

1. There are various options for case management open to the court ranging from light control to full judicial hands-on case management. In reaching its decision on management, the court can take account of the parties' proposals for management and, if it approves, adopt them. It can do any one or more of the following:

(a)   fix a case management conference;

(b)   issue directions in writing for the preparation of the case;

(c)   fix a date for the trial;

(d)   specify a period within which it is intended that the trial shall take place;

(e)   fix a pre-trial review.

In this chapter I set out in detail the way in which the court will reach a decision on those options and the considerations it will take into account.

A different approach

2. The multi-track will include a wide range of cases, from straightforward cases just above the fast track limit to the most complex and weighty matters involving claims for millions of pounds and multi-party actions with many claimants. Case management will reflect this. The central principle is that the court will manage every case, but the type of management will vary according to the needs of the case.

3. In broad terms, this means that simpler cases will need less of a hands-on approach by the courts and more complex cases will require greater judicial involvement. But whatever the type of management, the parties must co-operate with it. So, in straightforward cases, if standard directions are all that are required, the parties must carry out these directions and not complicate or delay matters; in the heaviest cases, when the court will be seeking to ascertain and refine the issues at an early stage, a case management conference must not be treated as a formality, with the client knowing nothing of what is being done and his solicitors being represented at too low a level.

4. The nature of management required will be decided by the procedural judge as part of the initial scrutiny. I described this scrutiny in the interim report:

> "It will determine whether the case can be dealt with by standard directions and timetable, or whether more active case management

is required and the appropriate judge for both management and eventual trial. A particularly important part of the process will be to identify those cases which are sufficiently complex to justify individual management from the outset by a more senior judge and those which will need to be tried by a High Court judge." (Interim report, chapter 8, paragraph 3).

Initial scrutiny

5.   Case management on the multi-track will start with the court scrutinising the case once the defence is received to determine the choice of track, where the case should be dealt with and the appropriate degree of management. In straightforward cases, where the procedural judge can see to the end of the case because the main issues are clear and there is no apparent complexity of evidence or multiplicity of issues and little scope for ADR, the procedural judge, having considered any request from the parties for a case management conference, will be entitled to give written directions as to witness statements, expert evidence and disclosure of documents, and fix a 'window' for the trial and direct when the listing questionnaire should be served. It will then be unnecessary for there to be a case management conference, although in some cases a telephone conference may be helpful. As one of the aims of case management is to dispose summarily of weak cases and hopeless issues, in the clearest cases the procedural judge may be able to direct an immediate trial or fix a summary disposal hearing.

6.   In less simple cases, he may need to decide first whether there should be an early case management conference or a pre-trial review or both. The judge will have to weigh their advantages as against the expense. Are the directions that could be given going to save time and costs in the long run? Is a conference likely to lead to a settlement? On the other hand are the circumstances such that it is better to leave matters to a pre-trial review when the evidence will have been disclosed and the trial is imminent? In a case of substance, both a case management conference and a pre-trial review will be justified.

7.   However, the procedural judge must bear in mind the costs of case management conferences, in terms both of the parties' costs and of court resources, and they should not be ordered unless they would clearly be of value. The need to control the costs of a case is particularly important in smaller value multi-track cases. In such cases the procedural judge should be more willing to consider paper directions, not dissimilar to the standard directions in fast track cases, but with a slightly more relaxed timetable. I envisage that there will be many straightforward multi-track cases of, say, between £10,000 and £25,000, which will not need a case management conference. In paragraphs 29 – 31 below I suggest the development of a 'streamlined procedure' which would enable many smaller and more straightforward cases on the multi-track to be dealt with swiftly and economically.

8.   There will be actions, including certain actions now begun by originating summons or motion, in which there will be no need for substantial case management, because it will be possible for the court to determine the case at the first hearing. For such cases, it will be possible for the claimant to indicate that all that is required is a hearing at the outset and, where appropriate, it can then be disposed of at the first hearing. When the claim is issued the court will fix the day for the first hearing and insert it on the claim, or indicate an approximate date, or say that a date will be fixed later. If it is not possible to determine the case at the first hearing, that hearing will in effect be a case management conference at which the court will give directions for the progression of the case. Where the facts are not in dispute it should be possible for there to be standard directions and a standard timetable.

Questionnaires

9.   Although my proposals for case management place greater responsibility for the progress of a case in the hands of the court, it is essential, as the Council of Circuit Judges has pointed out, for the court to have sufficient material on which to base the important early decisions about the handling of cases. This includes the views of the parties on how the case should be managed. The statements of case are not intended to provide all such material. It should therefore be possible for the parties to provide information on matters relevant to the progress of the case and for the court to call for such information by means of a questionnaire. This will avoid the court holding a case management conference simply for the purpose of obtaining information. It will also enable the parties to play a part in the initial decision as to how the case will best be managed. Questionnaires will bind neither the parties nor the court, but I have no doubt that they will often be helpful.

10.   It would be undesirable to lay down fixed rules as to when the parties should file their questionnaires setting out their proposals for the management of the case. In the interests of expedition they should be able to do so at the same time as they file their statements of case. The claimant may however feel that he cannot do so until he knows that the claim is being contested and he has seen the defendant's case. Following helpful suggestions by the Commercial Court Group and others, the questionnaire could indicate:

(a)   whether specific disclosure will be sought;

(b)   what are the principal issues and whether they are ones of construction, fact, expert evidence or law;

(c)   whether any directions concerning factual or expert evidence would be helpful at an early stage;

(d)   whether ADR has been or is about to be attempted;

(e)   whether there is any way in which the court can assist the parties to resolve their dispute without the need for a trial, or a full trial;

(f)   how much time they need for any specific disclosure, witness statements or experts' reports;

(g)   when the case will be ready for trial;

(h)   the present estimate of the length of the trial;

(i)   the costs to date and an estimate of the total costs;

(j)   whether there should be a case management conference and, if so, when it is considered it should take place.

At a later stage in the case the court will require equivalent information in a listing questionnaire.

Case management conference

11. At a case management conference the procedural judge should aim to achieve the following:

(a)   identify the key issues;

(b)   earmark issues for summary disposal;

(c)   explore the scope for ADR or settlement;

(d)   give directions as to witness statements, experts' reports and the disclosure of documents, including setting a limit where appropriate;

(e)   set a timetable for the case;

(f)   consider the trial date or trial window, the date when the listing questionnaire should be sent out, whether there should be a pre-trial review and the estimated length of the trial;

(g) find out what costs have been incurred to date and control likely future costs.

12. A further element of case management, which I discuss more fully in paragraphs 32–34 is that it should be open to the parties and the court to agree that a case can be determined without an oral hearing.

Timing of case management conferences

13. The timing of the first case management conference can be flexible, subject to the principle that its object is to set the agenda for the case before too many costs have been incurred and too much time has elapsed. In more complex cases, it will often be desirable for it to take place before standard disclosure since there is a greater danger of unnecessary time and costs being expended on this, in the absence of judicial control. The Commercial Court and Chancery groups thought that the procedural judge might consider that a case management conference would be more effective after standard disclosure has taken place, because by then the issues will have become clearer. In such cases the conference should be as soon after standard disclosure as practicable. Occasionally it may even be desirable to have a case management conference before the defence has been served, for example in very complex areas such as some Official Referees' cases. In multi-party actions, where it has been necessary for much work to be carried out before the claim can be served, there may well be a case management conference as soon as a multi-party situation is certified, as discussed in chapter 17.

Lists of issues

14. The identification and rolling disposal of the issues is a key element in the reforms. It will therefore be necessary for the parties to file statements of issues, if possible agreed beforehand, for case management. Again the approach must be that it is worth spending time in order to save more time. I do not agree with those who have expressed doubt about the value of having lists of issues on the grounds that in a simple case they will be unnecessary and, in a complex case, will take too long to prepare. If it takes a long time to prepare a statement of issues in a complex case it is an indication that the issues do need to be ascertained more clearly. If it is a simple case the statement will not involve more than minimal effort.

Parties attending case management conferences

15. The conference is a significant opportunity to take important decisions about a case, including the possibility of settlement or referring the dispute to ADR, and to consider the costs so far and the estimate of the future costs. The client must be enabled to know what has happened and be involved in the decisions about the future of the action. The litigation is his responsibility. He has both an interest in being involved and a duty to be involved. The presence of the parties will ensure that the lawyers take the event seriously and prepare for it properly. It was for these reasons that I proposed in chapter 8, paragraph 8, of the interim report that the lay client, or someone fully authorised to act on his behalf, should be required to attend the case management conference and pre-trial review in a multi-track case. The specialist working groups agree that it is something which should be strongly encouraged by the court, although they have expressed reservations about making this a requirement in every case.

16. There may be both practical difficulties and questions of expense in the case of a foreign party (individual or corporate) attending a case management conference. Nor may it always be possible for a representative of a large company or of a government department, for example, to be able to give undertakings at a conference which bind the party. Nevertheless, I am aware of at least one major insurance company which has been able to authorise its representative to enter into settlements at pre-trial reviews. At first sight there is a difference between an international company which is well used to litigation and an individual who is bringing a personal injury claim never having come into contact with the courts before. In the latter case, there is a clear need for the litigant to know what is going on in his case, how much it is all costing and how the court intends to handle the case. However, in the case of large corporations as well, it may be undesirable to leave everything in their lawyers' hands. They must also bear in mind the needs of other cases in the system. Experience in the Queen's Bench Division has shown that requests to adjourn hearing dates which are made in the absence of the parties themselves are seldom renewed when the judge requires the parties to attend such applications. When the parties know what is being done on their behalf and in their name they do not always endorse it.

17. To ensure the effectiveness and emphasise the importance of case management conferences and pre-trial reviews, I believe that it is essential for the lay client to attend, or for someone to attend on his behalf, unless this is very difficult to arrange. Exhortation is not enough. The onus must be on the parties, before the conference, to give very good reasons to the court why they are not attending.

Alternative dispute resolution

18. In the interim report I welcomed the growth of alternative dispute resolution and expressed the view that the court should play an important role in encouraging its use in appropriate cases. I continue to be of that view. I also remain of the view, though with less certainty than before, that it would not be right for the court to compel parties to use ADR and to take away or postpone their right to seek a remedy from the courts, although this approach is being successfully adopted in a number of other jurisdictions. Nevertheless, where a party has unreasonably refused a proposal by the court that ADR should be attempted, or has acted uncooperatively in the course of ADR, the court should be able to take that into account in deciding what order to make as to costs.

The timetable

19. The court will have control over the timescale of cases from the point at which they are allocated to a track. Cases will always be proceeding on a timetable, whether a standard timetable or a tailor-made timetable drawn up by the procedural judge. The timetable will specify actual dates for each stage and for particular steps such as the exchange of witness statements and experts' reports. There will be no adjournments generally; the court should always fix a date for the next step in the case.

20. The critical date is the trial date. At the meetings which I have held with judges they have made clear their view that fixing the trial date or a trial window is the most effective mode of controlling a case. Research from other jurisdictions where case management is being introduced, such as Ontario, also shows that the earlier in a case the trial date is fixed, the more effectively the case can be managed.

21. I originally suggested that it should not be possible for the parties to agree between themselves that a time limit set by the court should be extended. The specialist groups have all expressed doubts about this proposal. Sometimes there may be good reasons why a party cannot adhere to a time limit. The Intellectual Property Group points out, for example, that in its field there may well be concurrent litigation in other parts of the world and that the timetable of a case in this country may be affected by the progress of a case in another country. But if the court here is made aware of this, it will in many cases be able to set a timetable to take account of the other litigation or adjourn the case to a fixed date at which the situation can be reviewed.

22. There are certain key management stages, or 'milestones', in a case which should be established at the outset and which it should not be possible to move except with the permission of the court. These stages would be the case management conference, the pre-trial review and the trial date. But apart from these key stages the parties would be able to agree changes to the timetable subject to the overriding power of the court to intervene if appropriate. Any such agreement to vary a timetable, and the reasons for it, must be sent to the court (and to the client). Any extension must be for a specific period and the parties should file a new timetable.

23. Where one party seeks an extension of time to which the other does not agree, he may apply prospectively for an extension of time. If that time has passed he would have to apply to the court for relief from the sanction which would be imposed in the event of his non-compliance with the time limit. He would have to satisfy the court that he had complied with other directions and that there was a good reason why he was unable to comply with the direction in question. Save in exceptional circumstances he would also have to pay the other side's costs of the application immediately.

Listing questionnaire

24. Just as the court requires information at the start of the case for initial case management, so too there is a need for further information before trial to confirm that directions have been complied with and to inform the decision on hearing time. A listing questionnaire should be sent out by the court in advance of a pre-trial review if one has been fixed. In other cases the listing questionnaire will indicate whether such a review is required. In straightforward cases the court will need no more than the information in the listing questionnaire, or can request additional information in writing or by telephone. In other cases where more detailed examination is required, a pre-trial review will be necessary.

25. The questionnaire should therefore be sent out in sufficient time to allow a pre-trial review to be held, if necessary, in good time before the trial date or window.

Pre-trial review

26. The purpose of a pre-trial review is to prepare a statement of issues to be tried and to set a programme and budget for the trial. It enables the court to check that directions given at case management conferences have been complied with and can also help in promoting settlement. I would expect the pre-trial review to take place about eight to 10 weeks before the hearing. Experience from Wandsworth County Court, which has a system of pre-trial reviews, and in other courts, shows that very often the parties are not ready for the review at that date, let alone nearly ready for the trial. However, such reviews at present are similar to the proposed case management conferences rather than the new pre-trial reviews which I am recommending. It is important to remember that in the new system the court will already have been managing the case, so that the parties will know what steps they should have taken by the time of the review.

27. Since January 1995, pre-trial reviews have been held in all Queen's Bench Division cases estimated to last for more than 10 days. The impression is that they have accelerated settlements of some cases and have made for better prepared trials in others. The difficulty has been in trying to arrange for the review to be held by the eventual trial judge. I hope that more widespread case management will assist in overcoming this difficulty by creating more certainty as to which cases will proceed to trial and as to the length of trial. As my reforms take effect I hope this will enable my target of pre-trial reviews by the trial judge to be met more frequently.

The trial

28. An important task at the pre-trial review is to determine the timetable of the trial. A number of people have written to me since the interim report with encouraging examples of better managed trials. Periods for examination and cross-examination of witnesses are fixed in advance. Disruption to the parties' and witnesses' business is reduced and counsel prepare their questions and argument on a concentrated and specific basis. Listing by the court will then be able to be more accurate and precise. A number of solicitors have written to me saying that until they experienced a timetable for a long trial they did not believe timetables could work; they are now convinced of their practicability and benefits. Counsel have said the same. High Court judges and Official Referees, too, have given me examples of trials which have operated successfully with timetables. There is no doubt, however, that fixed timetables for trials impose greater burdens on both judges and practitioners in preparing for and handling trials. I would therefore repeat the recommendation in the interim report that in multi-track trials the court should not normally sit on Fridays. The efficient use of this day will, I believe, lead overall to shorter trials.

Streamlined procedure

29. The needs which underlie the fast track procedure – to know in advance what procedure, timetable and costs will be involved in litigation, and to dispose of a case expeditiously at an affordable cost – apply to all cases. The court will already be able to go a long way to meeting these needs in multi-track cases by the exercise of its powers to manage a case, for example by limiting disclosure and expert evidence, setting a short timetable for the steps that are to be taken before the trial, and limiting the length of the trial. There are a number of areas in which I believe that it is especially important that the court should seek to streamline the procedure. The first is that of small medical negligence claims which fell within the financial limits of the fast track but could not meet the timetable, largely because of the scope of the expert evidence involved. I deal with this in chapter 15. Secondly, Crown Office cases where the applicant is an individual and the respondent a public body (chapter 18). Thirdly, intellectual property cases where there is substantial disparity between the financial status of the parties and the smaller party would find it difficult to bring or defend a claim without the protection of a limited procedure and costs. An example of such a case might be one in which a defendant has stopped infringing the claimant's patent but the claimant nevertheless pursues his claim. Both the Intellectual Property Working Group and the judge of the Patents County Court have been considering my proposals for a streamlined procedure, with benchmark costs. I look forward to their bearing fruit.

30. Furthermore, there is a large class of cases where the value and complexity do not justify hands-on judicial case management. I recommend that, as part of implementation, work should be done to establish a general streamlined procedure which would be applicable to such cases. An important feature of the streamlined procedure would be a system of controlled costs, which, while less restrictive than the fast track, would provide many of the same benefits to parties.

31. I set out in the costs chapter my approach to providing benchmark costs for such cases. These will be predicated on the development of a standard streamlined procedure. I suggest that the court with user groups should be able to provide benchmark costs. First, however, it will be necessary to devise standard streamlined procedures with the assistance of judges and practitioners.

Determinations without an oral hearing

32. I also recommend that it should be possible for suitable cases to be determined on the statements of case, without the need for an oral hearing, where this would save time and costs. Appropriate cases would be judicial review or other Crown Office cases, Chancery Division cases such as construction summonses, where the facts are not in dispute and there are no more than one or two easily identifiable points of law.

33. The Chancery Group have considered the possibility of paper determinations in this type of case. They suggest that the parties would have to certify that the case was suitable for a paper determination and the court would have to agree. There would be an agreed statement of facts and written arguments on each side. The court would need to be satisfied that all relevant legal issues had been adequately dealt with in the written submissions. If necessary, the judge would be able to call the person named in the written argument to make oral submissions. The group recognised that paper judgments could take longer than oral judgments to prepare, and suggested that the judge should be able to give a short basic judgment which would be expanded only at the request of the parties. The details of the procedure could be fleshed out in a practice direction. The group thought that paper determinations could be beneficial if used properly but could create considerable problems if abused. I agree with their views and suggest that this is a candidate for monitored pilots. The Crown Office Group has made a similar recommendation which I adopt.

34. Further work will have to be done to introduce paper determinations in appropriate multi-track cases.

Consistency

35. It is essential that there should be effective and consistent case management for the court system as a whole. Unpredictability causes difficulties, especially for those who are not regular litigants. Parties ought not to find themselves disadvantaged because they are unfamiliar with a particular court or judge. At present there is an unsatisfactory proliferation of local practices in county courts, which makes it harder to conduct litigation. The new rules will provide that only the Lord Chancellor and the Head of Civil Justice will be able to issue practice directions.

36. I also recommend an end to the practice in some courts of each judge working from his own standard directions. It is not acceptable for judges' approaches to be so different as to lead to significant differences in costs between similar cases. This is likely to result in forum shopping, which must be discouraged. The approach of different judges will, of course, never be identical and the need to handle each case as that case requires means that case management will always vary. However, so far as possible, the initial approach of the judiciary to case management should be the same. At the same time, I do not encourage rigidity in the handling of multi-track cases, but there should be the appropriate degree of consistency. There is still room for innovative approaches to case management, but these must be under the control of the Head of Civil Justice.

Recommendations

My recommendations are as follows.

(1)   On the multi-track the nature of management required will be decided by the procedural judge as part of the initial scrutiny once

the defence is received. The court can:

(a) fix a case management conference;

(b) issue directions in writing for the preparation of the case;

(c) fix a date for the trial;

(d) specify a period within which it is intended that the trial shall take place;

(e) fix a pre-trial review.

(2) Information to assist the judge may be provided by the parties in a questionnaire and called for by the court.

(3) The objective of the case management conference is to set the agenda for the case before significant costs have been incurred and too much time has elapsed. At a case management conference the procedural judge will narrow the issues, decide on the appropriate future work and case management required, set a trial date and a timetable for the case, and consider ADR and the question of costs.

(4) Parties should file statements of issues, if possible agreed beforehand, for the conference.

(5) Where a party has refused unreasonably a proposal by the court that ADR should be attempted, or has acted unco-operatively in the course of ADR, the court should be able to take that into account in deciding what order to make as to costs.

(6) The dates of the case management conference, the pre-trial review and the trial date cannot be changed except with the permission of the court. Parties would be able to agree other changes to the timetable subject to the overriding power of the court to intervene if appropriate, and any such agreement should be notified to the court, with the proposed new timetable.

(7) Applications to vary the timetable must be made within the relevant time limit. If that time has passed, a sanction will apply automatically, unless relief is applied for.

(8) A listing questionnaire should be sent out by the court at a time specified in the initial directions to establish whether directions have been complied with and to inform the decision on hearing time.

(9) At a pre-trial review about eight to 10 weeks before the hearing the judge will settle the statement of issues to be tried and set a programme for the trial.

(10) A general streamlined procedure should be developed with the assistance of judges and practitioners for more straightforward cases on the multi-track. This should involve limited disclosure and expert evidence, a short timetable and limited trial time and a system of controlled costs, which, while less restrictive than the fast track, would provide many of the same benefits to parties.

(11) Particular streamlined procedures should be developed for small medical negligence claims, Crown Office cases and intellectual property cases where there is substantial disparity between the financial status of the parties.

(12) It should be possible for suitable cases to be determined on the statements of case, without the need for an oral hearing, where this would save time and costs.

(13) The new rules will provide that only the Lord Chancellor and the Head of Civil Justice will be able to issue practice directions to ensure that case management systems are uniform and consistent.

Chapter 6   Sanctions

1. When considering the problems facing civil justice today I argued in chapter 3 of my interim report that the existing rules of court were being flouted on a vast scale. Timetables are not adhered to and other orders are not complied with if it does not suit the parties to do so. Orders for costs which do not apply immediately have proved to be an ineffective sanction and do nothing to deter parties from ignoring the court's directions.

2. There was overwhelming support from all sides for effective, appropriate and fair sanctions among those who have commented on my interim report and the issues paper on the fast track. Members of the judiciary saw sanctions as a key element, while recognising that their application must not be allowed to generate additional litigation. Consumers' groups pointed to the need for sanctions which were sufficiently powerful to prevent games playing and oppressive behaviour. As I have commented elsewhere, one of the greatest grievances of litigants in person is the apparent impunity with which practitioners breach procedural orders.

3. I would stress four important principles.

(a)   The primary object of sanctions is prevention, not punishment.

(b)   It should be for the rules themselves, in the first instance, to provide an effective debarring order where there has been a breach, for example that a party may not use evidence which he has not disclosed.

(c)   All directions orders should in any event include an automatic sanction for non-compliance unless an extension of time has been obtained prospectively.

(d)   The onus should be on the defaulter to apply for relief, not on the other party to seek a penalty.

4. If the new regime, and especially case management by the court, is to work, it is essential for there to be an effective system of sanctions for non-compliance with rules, directions and orders. But there is a further need for sanctions. A party may not be guilty of any breach of a particular rule or order but may nevertheless frustrate the overriding objective of the rules by pursuing his litigation in an oppressive manner. The overriding objective is to enable the court to deal with cases justly and there is an express duty on the parties to help the court to further it. An example of unreasonable behaviour in a fast track case might be sending an inordinately long list of questions to the other party's expert. Where this happens the innocent party should seek the protection of the court without delay and the court must warn the offending party that he is acting unreasonably and that if he continues to do so a sanction will be imposed. A costs sanction alone may not be sufficient. The court must consider taking strong measures, such as excusing the innocent party from answering the questions, in the example I have given, or refusing to receive a report from the expert of the party who is acting unreasonably. If the behaviour was repeated the court should consider debarring the party from continuing his claim or defence. The control of oppressive behaviour which does not infringe a specific rule or direction is an essential condition for maintaining the credibility of the fast track.

5.   The Advice Services Alliance has stressed the need for litigants to be provided with adequate information at the outset, in order to ensure that timetables are complied with. There should be clear instructions as to what is required of parties under the timetable and the possible consequences of inaction, what action they should take if they are unable to comply with directions and how and where to obtain advice.

6.   In fast track cases it will be possible for the court to order the party at fault to pay the other party's costs in excess of the fast track fixed costs whatever the outcome of the case. I have also received suggestions that the court should be able to award an additional sum, by way of a fine to the court, a penalty in interest or significantly higher compensation or costs, where one party has behaved in a notably oppressive or excessive manner. The greatest enthusiasm has been for additional sums on top of the existing award. Although I am attracted by the simplicity of this idea, I do not propose to pursue it as part of my recommendations in this report. Monitoring of the proposed approach will clarify whether additional sanctions are needed.

7.   I recognise the difficulties involved in the application of sanctions. Recent attempts at strengthening the court's powers to deal with delays and defaults of the parties have not met with complete success. The provisions in Order 17, rule 11(9) of the County Court Rules for the automatic striking out of cases if no request is made for a hearing date within a fixed time have been the subject of a number of appeals to the Court of Appeal. This was partly because of a lack of clarity as to how the rule should operate. But the vast majority of cases were struck out under the rule because of a failure by practitioners to appreciate its effect or to comply with its requirements. The experience with the rule shows up the advantage of effective case management throughout a case; even the most severe sanction does not change practitioners' behaviour when it is delivered without an adequate warning, while effective management should avoid a situation to which Order 17, rule 11(9) applies arising.

8. Wasted costs orders, which were introduced by the Courts and Legal Services Act 1990, are in danger of creating "a new and costly form of satellite litigation", as the Court of Appeal put it in *Ridehalgh v Horsefield* [1994] Ch 205. The procedure is too cumbersome and can add to cost and delay instead of reducing them. I do not propose that wasted costs orders should be abolished; the principle that legal advisers should be responsible for costs incurred as a result of their improper, unreasonable or negligent acts or omissions is one which I would endorse. But I do not believe that such orders should always be the first response to the problem. They are best reserved for clear cases.

9. Sanctions are dealt with in part 5 of the new rules. The court may:

(a) strike out a statement of case or part of one if there has been a failure to comply with any rule, practice direction or direction given by the court;

(b) direct that a party may not call evidence on a particular issue, or call a particular witness or use a particular document;

(c) make a wasted costs order;

(d) order indemnity costs;

(e) fix or assess costs and order them to be paid immediately;

(f) order costs to be taxed and paid immediately;

(g) impose a higher rate of interest on costs than would otherwise apply;

(h) order interim costs of a fixed amount to be paid within a specified time.

10. Sanctions must be relevant and proportionate. They should be tailored to fit the seriousness of the breach to the other party. They should also where possible relate to the particular breach. Thus the court will be able to order that a party is not to be entitled to rely on documents or an expert's report, or to call a witness, where the document, report or witness statement has not been timeously disclosed. In the case of a failure to disclose a document it will usually be the innocent party who wishes to rely on the document, in which case an order debarring the party at fault from relying on it will be ineffective. In such circumstances it should be possible for the innocent party to apply *ex parte* for an order debarring the other party from continuing with his case if the document is not disclosed within seven days of service of the order.

11. Striking out an entire claim or defence must remain as a weapon in the court's armoury, but I accept that it is a draconian sanction and that it should not be imposed too readily. Cases should be kept running if possible, so that they can be resolved either by a substantive determination by the court or by a settlement agreed by the parties. Nonetheless, where parties do fail without reasonable excuse to comply with the court's directions, particularly where they do so more than once, the court must be willing to exercise appropriate discipline over them.

12. There is no doubt in my mind that orders for costs have an important part to play. As I have said, such orders are ineffective if they do not bite until the end of case, when they can be lost among all the other orders for costs. The courts must make more use of their power to tax or assess costs of an application and order them to be paid immediately. I also welcome the proposal made to me by the Intellectual Property Working Group that having made an order for costs against a party the court should be able to order that party to make an interim payment of the costs. I also refer to orders for costs as sanctions in chapter 7.

13. Orders for costs, although important, cannot provide a complete solution. Parties may accept an order for costs against them as a price worth paying for the delay and inconvenience which their action causes the other party. It is essential that case management itself, and other sanctions, should play their part in suppressing misbehaviour rather than leaving it to a costs order, even one for immediate payment, to compensate the innocent party afterwards.

14. There must of course be some limited right to apply for relief from a sanction. In my view the onus should be on the party in default to seek relief, not on the other party to apply to enforce the sanction. The application should be made before the date of expiry of the specific requirement. It is important that the conditions for relief should be set out clearly in the rules. I recommend, broadly following the test in *Rastin v British Steel* [1994] 1 WLR 732, that relief should not be granted unless the court is satisfied that the breach was not intentional, that there has been substantial compliance with other directions and that there is a good explanation. The court will need to consider whether the failure was due to the default of the client, whether the default had been or could be remedied within a reasonable period, whether the trial date, or next milestone date, could still be met if relief were granted, and whether granting relief would cause more prejudice to the respondent than refusal would to the applicant. The normal order in these cases will be for the costs of the application, as assessed by the court, to be paid immediately by the party at fault. In many cases the applicant's solicitor would have to pay the respondent's costs and would not be entitled to recover them from his client. Where relief is not applied for until after the relevant time has expired it will only be allowed in exceptional circumstances and the applicant would normally bear the costs. In considering whether there is prejudice the courts must be prepared to acknowledge that delay in itself is prejudicial to a party who is seeking a decision. The client should personally be sent any costs order made against him and be made aware of his right to apply for a wasted costs order against his solicitor. He should also be sent a copy of any order breach of which will lead to striking out, so he knows the directions of the court and the effect of non-compliance.

15. To a large extent the effectiveness of sanctions will revolve around judicial attitudes. There is no doubt that some judges at first instance, especially Masters and district judges, will need to develop a more robust approach to the task of managing cases and ensuring that their orders are not flouted. They must, in particular, be resistant to applications to extend a set timetable, save in exceptional circumstances. But these judges must also be supported both by the trial judge and by courts hearing appeals. Many people who commented also stressed the need for consistency between the trial judge and the judge who had imposed sanctions for earlier procedural breaches. If the fast track, in particular, is to work it will be necessary for the rules to make it clear that it will not normally be acceptable to overturn earlier procedural decisions unless there has been a material and unforeseeable change of circumstances and it would not be possible to deal with the case fairly without doing so. So far as appeals are concerned, procedural decisions must not be overturned lightly but only when judges have misdirected themselves as to the facts or the law or made errors of principle. This is not simply a matter of limiting appeals. It goes to a change of culture, in which judges can make orders confident that parties will not feel that they can ignore orders or that they can escape unscathed by appealing. As Steyn LJ said in *AB v John Wyeth & Brother Ltd* (1993)

4 Med LR 1, 6, "the judge invariably has a much better perspective ... of the needs of efficient case management than the Court of Appeal can ever achieve". He was speaking particularly of group actions, but I believe that the point is true of all cases.

16. In such a new climate, sanctions will be able to play their proper role, which is prevention rather than punishment. What is needed is for the threat of a prompt, relevant punishment to prevent the offence. Where a sanction does have to be applied, it must be fair, relevant and simple to administer and must not create additional costs or delay for the party not at fault. Sanctions are an integral part of case management. They are properly to be applied as an aid to positive case management, the purpose of which is not to destroy cases but to resolve them.

Recommendations

My main recommendations on sanctions are as follows.

(1)   As part of a case-managed system, sanctions should be designed to prevent, rather than punish, non-compliance with rules and timetables.

(2)   The rules themselves should specify what will happen where there has been a breach. All directions orders should include an automatic sanction for non-compliance.

(3)   The court should intervene and impose sanctions on parties who conduct litigation in an unreasonable or oppressive manner even if they have not breached specific rules, orders or directions.

(4)   The courts should make more use of their power to tax or assess the costs of an application and order them to be paid immediately.

(5)   The onus should be on the party in default to seek relief from a sanction, not on the other party to apply to enforce the sanction.

(6)   The power to make wasted costs orders should continue, but they should be reserved for clear cases and not allowed to develop into satellite litigation.

(7)   The client should personally be sent any costs order made against him and be made aware of his right to apply for a wasted costs order against his solicitor. He should also be sent a copy of any order, breach of which will lead to striking out, so that he knows the directions of the court and the effect of non-compliance.

Chapter 7   Costs

**The importance
of costs**

1. I began the chapter on costs in the interim report by saying:

"The problem of costs is the most serious problem besetting our litigation system."

2. The year which has elapsed since the interim report has not caused me to alter that assessment. Costs are a significant problem because:

(a)   litigation is so expensive that the majority of the public cannot afford it unless they receive financial assistance;

(b)   the costs incurred in the course of litigation are out of proportion to the issues involved; and

(c)   the costs are uncertain in amount so that the parties have difficulty in predicting what their ultimate liability might be if the action is lost.

3. The adverse consequences which flow from the problems in relation to costs contaminate the whole civil justice system. Fear of costs deters some litigants from litigating when they would otherwise be entitled to do so and compels other litigants to settle their claims when they have no wish to do so. It enables the more powerful litigant to take unfair advantage of the weaker litigant. The scale of costs per case has an adverse effect on the scope of the legal aid system. It also adversely affects the reputation of our civil justice system abroad and may be making this country less attractive for overseas investment and as a forum for the settlement of commercial disputes. As I pointed out in the interim report, it is incorrect to assume that high costs are not a problem merely because they are met out of a relatively deep pocket or are passed on in insignificant amounts to individual consumers. They still constitute an unnecessary cost to the economy as a whole and are not acceptable however they are distributed.

4. Costs are also of great importance to my Inquiry because the ability of the court to make orders as to costs is the most significant and regularly used sanction available. The court's power to make appropriate orders as to costs can deter litigants from behaving improperly or unreasonably and encourages them to behave responsibly. Cost orders can also have a salutary effect on members of the legal profession.

5. Costs are central to the changes I wish to bring about. Virtually all my recommendations are designed at least in part to tackle the problems of costs. They are intended to:

(a)   reduce the scale of costs by controlling what is required of the parties in the conduct of proceedings;

(b)   make the amount of costs more predictable;

(c)   make costs more proportionate to the nature of the dispute;

(d)   make the courts' powers to make orders as to costs a more effective incentive for responsible behaviour and a more compelling deterrent against unreasonable behaviour;

(e)   provide litigants with more information as to costs so that they can exercise greater control of the expenses which are incurred by their lawyers on their behalf.

6.   These objectives are to be achieved in part by the expansion of the small claims jurisdiction to £3,000 and the establishment of a new fast track for straightforward cases up to £10,000, both with restricted costs. The remaining problem is the multi-track.

7.   On the multi-track I recommended that at case management conferences and pre-trial reviews, the information available for the hearing should include an estimate of the amount of costs already incurred and the costs which would be incurred if the case proceeded to trial. I also recommended that it should be a professional obligation for lawyers to explain their charges to clients, including the potential overall cost of a case, and to give reasonable notice where an estimate is likely to be exceeded; and that legal professional bodies should encourage their members to undertake litigation, where this is practical, on fixed fees either for stages of the proceedings or for the proceedings as a whole.

8.   English courts are wedded to the dual concept that costs should be treated as a whole and that costs should follow the event. In the interim report I recommended that courts should pay greater regard than they do at present to the manner in which the successful party has conducted the proceedings and the outcome of individual issues. I suggested that the court should use its powers over costs to encourage co-operative conduct on the part of litigants and to discourage unreasonable conduct. This can apply to pre-proceedings conduct as well as conduct after proceedings have been commenced. The court should also be more willing to identify areas where it considers that costs have been unnecessarily incurred. I suggested that running up excessive costs would continue unless the court was prepared to take action (Interim report, chapter 25, paragraph 23).

9. I also recommended that RSC Order 62, rule 3(3), which provides the general rule that costs follow the event, should be relaxed so that the court could use to the full its very wide statutory discretion over costs to support the conduct of litigation in a proportionate manner and to discourage excess. This new approach will be given effect by the overriding objective which is set out in Rule 1 of the new rules which at 1.3(g) requires the court to further the overriding objective by actively managing cases appropriately, in particular:

> "(g) by considering whether the likely benefits of taking a particular step will justify the cost of taking it".

10. This will give the court an effective weapon for the first time. Generally, the response to the interim report and to the issues papers indicated that practitioners would welcome such an approach from the bench.

Research

11. There is little research information on the costs of the existing system. There is, however, almost total agreement among all those engaged in the civil justice system that costs are excessive. It would therefore have been inappropriate for me to defer my Inquiry until empirical research had been carried out. This would have prolonged the Inquiry unreasonably.

12. However, I was concerned that the Inquiry should commission some research which could be carried out within the two years laid down by the Lord Chancellor for the preparation of this report and the new procedural rules. I therefore asked the Supreme Court Taxing Office (SCTO) to collect information from bills submitted. A preliminary analysis of the first 673 cases was included as Annex 3 to the interim report. A complete analysis of 2184 cases is set out in a report, *Survey of Litigation Costs*. A summary of that report appears in Annex 3.

13. The survey confirmed that it is among the lowest value claims (£12,500 or less) that costs are most disproportionate. In 40 per cent of these cases the costs of one party alone are close to, or exceed, the total value of the claim. This emphasises the importance of the fast track in bringing costs under control. I have referred in more detail to some of the findings of the research in the introduction to this section on case management.

14. Annex 5 to the interim report contained a schedule of fixed costs which applied to litigation in Germany in 1994. The object of including the schedule was to illustrate a radically different approach to costs. The costs set out in the schedule are substantially lower than the uncertain sums which parties in this jurisdiction are likely to have to pay for the equivalent representation. Following the publication of the interim report, Adrian Zuckerman, Fellow of University College, Oxford, was requested to conduct a survey of German practitioners about the German litigation cost system. That survey will be made available at the same time as this report. The survey provides an outline of German civil procedure, noting in particular that although the judge is in charge of proceedings, the system is not an inquisitorial system. Nor is the task of the German lawyer easier than that of his English counterpart, although its emphasis differs. The chief focus of the survey was to establish German practitioners' views of the system of fixed costs, in relation to concerns expressed here that such a system would result in lawyers charging above the official scales and that, were they not able to do so, clients might not be able to secure legal representation in low value litigation. A further worry was that, where lawyers did take on low value claims, they would tend to provide superficial services to compensate for the low return. The survey shows that while lawyers' fees in Germany are substantially lower than in England, there appears to be no difficulty in securing legal representation. This is the position even for low value claims where the figures are particularly modest by comparison with those that would be charged in England.

15. I do not refer to the survey with a view to recommending the adoption of the German approach to costs. I do so because the German survey indicates that, unlike in England, in Germany it has been possible to make litigation substantially more affordable, provide lawyers with what they regard as an acceptable level of income and, so far as can be judged, provide an acceptable standard of justice. This surely presents a challenge to all those responsible for our civil justice system to do better than at present to make justice affordable.

Controlling costs

16. In order to explore the issue of costs further, the Inquiry published an issues paper by Adrian Zuckerman, which discussed a number of mechanisms for controlling costs in advance, such as budget-setting, fixed fees related to value, fixed fees related to procedural activity or a mixture of the two.

17. The paper occasioned a general outcry from the legal profession. Prospective budget-setting was seen as unworkable, unfair and likely to be abused by the creation of inflated budgets. The ability of judges to be involved in the hard detail of matters such as cost was generally doubted. The imposition of fixed fees, even relating only to *inter partes* costs, was seen as unrealistic and as interference with parties' rights to decide how to instruct their own lawyers. There was widespread concern that these suggestions heralded an attempt to control solicitor and own client costs. The restrictions were generally seen as "artificial and unworkable". But the debate which they occasioned has been both instructive and encouraging.

18. In my interim report I quoted the London Solicitors' Litigation Association who said:

> ". . . it is impossible to limit costs without limiting procedural activity."

That is what the fast track and judicial control on the multi-track are designed to achieve. The Association, in response to Adrian Zuckerman's paper, suggested that:

> ". . . costs reductions in litigation can only follow a vigorous attack on the roots of the problem: unnecessary delays, complexity in procedure and the service provided by the courts themselves."

19. The Association welcomed procedural reforms which would achieve these costs reductions but did not believe that in themselves they would provide a complete answer to the vexed question of ever-increasing litigation costs. To achieve this, the Association said:

> ". . . it will be necessary to impose costs restraints".

The impact of procedural reform

20. My recommendations, together with the new rules, are intended to ensure that litigation is conducted less expensively than at present and to achieve greater certainty as to costs. The emphasis will be on using case management to:

(a)   reduce the steps which parties have to take to enable the court to dispose of the case justly;

(b)   ensure that the way in which the case is handled is proportionate to the nature of the issues involved;

(c)   narrow the areas of dispute as early as practicable either by achieving the agreement or summary determination of issues when this is possible;

(d)   restrict discovery and evidence to that which is appropriate;

(e)   set timetables for progressing the proceedings and the hearing so the parties and their lawyers can perform their roles efficiently.

21. The court will also have an increased focus on costs relating to pre-action behaviour as a result of recommendations made elsewhere in this report. In three areas, the court will assess compliance and overall behaviour in making orders for costs:

(a)   compliance with the new pre-action protocols (chapter 10). A party who has not complied with a protocol will find that he is at a disadvantage in seeking or opposing an order for costs;

(b)   the introduction of pre-action offers to settle by prospective claimants and defendants (chapter 11);

(c)   wider powers of pre-action disclosure to enable such offers to be made (chapter 12); if necessary, the court will be able to order disclosure.

22. In addition, I recommend that the court should have power to deal with the question of costs even where all the other issues in dispute have been resolved without the need for litigation. If all that is left in issue is costs, it will be open to a party to make a claim to have the outstanding issue determined by the court. This will facilitate pre-litigation settlement of disputes.

Focusing attention on costs as a sanction

23. Many respondents called for costs sanctions to deal with the tendency of parties at present to make numerous interlocutory applications. These are generally of a tactical nature which may be of dubious benefit even to the party making the application or which may not be warranted by the costs involved. It was agreed that the answer here is for costs orders to be made at the end of interlocutory hearings, to be payable forthwith by the party who has occasioned the hearing. At present such applications are made with impunity because the liability on the loser to pay is usually postponed until the end of the case when it is lost in the overall settlement of costs.

24. Orders for costs should reflect not only whether the general outcome of the proceedings is favourable to the party seeking an order in his favour but also how the proceedings have been conducted on his behalf. I have already referred to the need to assess compliance with protocols. Judges must therefore be prepared to make more detailed orders than they are accustomed to do now. The general order in favour of one party or another will less frequently be appropriate. Different orders will need to be made on different issues, eg, where there has been a departure from a protocol or an offer to settle that issue has been unreasonably refused.

25. In addition, failure to comply with directions and orders should produce orders for indemnity costs, payable forthwith.

26. Unless the court is prepared to take the time necessary to elevate decisions as to costs above the conventional approach adopted at present, the parties will not take as seriously as they should the obligations which a managed system will place on them. Orders for costs must in future reflect the obligations the new rules place on the parties. In addition the court should have powers to require solicitors to inform their clients of orders which have been made and why they were made.

Control by the client

27. The Chief Taxing Master has suggested to me:

> "that the most effective and simple method of keeping costs under control is to keep the client informed at all times as to what is proposed in his name."

28. I agree this is extremely important. I have recommended in the interim report that it should be a mandatory requirement for a solicitor to tell prospective clients how fees are to be calculated and what the overall costs might be; and to give reasonable notice when that estimate is likely to be exceeded and the reasons. If, in the past, the uncertainty of what might occur in proceedings provided justification for not making this a mandatory requirement, that justification would no longer exist under the more predictable system which I am proposing.

29. For the same reason I am recommending that clients should be present at case management conferences and pre-trial reviews, where the judge will be informed about the level of costs incurred to date and the likely amount of future costs that would be incurred by the programme of work that he is setting at the conference. The presence of the client should be a powerful incentive to adopt a realistic approach.

30. Clients have other methods of control which they can exercise. It has been suggested that all clients or funders should impose eight requirements on their solicitors:

(a)   prevent major litigation strategies without instructions;

(b)   eliminate unnecessary research and detail;

(c)   control the hiring and use of barristers and experts;

(d)   forbid interlocutory/discovery activities without prior approval;

(e)   prevent convening of meetings when telephone calls will suffice;

(f)   control the level of manning;

(g)   agree the level and method of charging;

(h)   emphasise that the case belongs to the client.

31. If clients were to impose these requirements this would go a long way towards achieving my objectives. Increasing client consciousness of costs would also increase their awareness of the need to act responsibly as litigants.

Estimates of costs and control by the court

32. It is important that the court is aware of the parties' estimate of the expenditure which has been and will be incurred when considering the future conduct of a case. The parties' estimates will be dependent upon how they are proposing that the case should be conducted. If one method of dealing with the case would be beyond the resources of one of the parties, then dealing with the case justly may involve not adopting that procedure. This could be particularly important where, for example, one party wishes a case to remain on the fast track but the other is arguing for the case to be transferred to the multi-track.

33. Estimates need not go into detail and would therefore not disclose confidential information which might be of tactical value to an opponent. They would fall short of the radical proposals set out by Adrian Zuckerman in the issues paper. The estimates would be indications to help the procedural judge decide the best course of action rather than budgets which limited what parties could recover. My other recommendations need to be 'bedded down' before proceeding further in this direction on costs.

34. In an exceptionally complex case the procedural judge may need further assistance. In such a case, I recommend that taxing masters should be able to give guidance, as they do now on applications for security for costs. The guidance would be in a broad terms and would not be equivalent to a prospective taxation.

Benchmark costs

35. There are, however, some multi-track proceedings in which further steps could be taken to assist the parties and the courts. These are proceedings which have a limited and fairly constant procedure. Here the court, with the assistance of user groups and the information available to the SCTO, should over time be able to produce figures indicating a standard or guideline cost or a range of costs for a class of proceedings. An obvious candidate for this approach would be cases which do not substantially turn on issues of fact, for example, those dealt with in the Chancery Division using the originating summons procedure.

36. Judicial review is also a possible example. The steps taken in the majority of cases are standard. Variations are limited to the number of affidavits on either side and the difficulty of the point involved.

37. While the arrangement a party chose to come to with his own lawyers would not be of direct concern to the court, a party to a 'normal' application for judicial review would have to justify seeking to recover from the other side more than the published benchmark cost. Where a lawyer proposed to charge his client more than the guideline figure, the Law Society could require a written agreement to be entered into which would set out the client's acceptance of the increase. The figures for benchmark costs would have to be kept up to date with the assistance of those who were responsible for the original figures. I therefore recommend, as a first step, that work should be put in hand to identify provisional categories of case suitable for standard treatment and costs data collected to test the range of costs incurred and the factors associated with any significant variations.

Reconciling the needs of parties with differing resources

38. There will be some cases which require the full procedure of the multi-track because of the wider importance of the case but which one of the parties is unable to afford. Medical negligence and patents are areas where this is quite likely. Is the stronger party to be deprived of the full assistance of the legal process which he reasonably desires because of the lack of means of the other party? To meet this situation I recommend that the court, in deciding upon the procedure which is to be adopted, should be entitled to make its order conditional upon the other side agreeing, whatever the outcome, to meet the difference in the costs of the two procedures to the weaker party if the more elaborate and expensive procedure is adopted. This would ensure that a stronger party is not deprived of the benefits of the full procedure and at the same time enables the weaker party to continue to contest the proceedings.

39. There are precedents for a similar approach being adopted. For example, under the Banking Ombudsman scheme, if the bank decides not to accept the Ombudsman's decision because there is an issue of principle involved, it is entitled to take the matter to court, but only on the basis that it meets the whole of the other side's costs. It can be a condition of leave to appeal being given, particularly to the House of Lords, that the appellant will meet the respondent's costs in any event and the order for costs made in the court below is not disturbed.

40. The court should be able to award interim costs in appropriate cases, in the same way as interim damages would be payable. That is to say, interim costs would be payable forthwith, although ultimate liability would remain subject to the court's determination, where the opponent has substantially greater resources and where there is a reasonable likelihood that the weaker party will be entitled to costs at the end of the case.

Taxation of costs

41. The function of taxation is not to undertake an independent assessment of the charges claimed as a whole but to resolve disputes over items between the paying and receiving party. The process therefore depends upon the paying party identifying those items on the bill which are capable of being challenged effectively. The taxing officer or Master does not give his opinion of the reasonableness of the bill as a whole. Thus there is no objective assessment of what would have been be a reasonable sum for conducting a particular case; instead, it is a retrospective check on the reasonableness of the costs in fact incurred by a party over the course of the litigation. As long as a party, judged by the conventions of current practice, was acting reasonably in the way in which he conducted the case and the charges for the actual work done were reasonable in the circumstances, the taxing process does not intervene. The taxing system is therefore not a method of controlling costs absolutely but a safeguard against claims for costs which can be shown to be out of line with the norm. Taxation provides no encouragement to litigants to conduct litigation in the most economical manner.

42. Although it is not, practically speaking, possible to change the retrospective nature of taxation, I would however make one recommendation designed to improve the process. The new overriding objective in Part 1 of the new rules should be a constructive influence on the process because of the duty which it imposes on litigants. Taxation would however be more in accord with the general message of this report that litigants should act reasonably if the test on taxation was changed clearly to reflect this. The test I would recommend is based on the wording of the Solicitors' (Non-Contentious Business) Remuneration Order 1994; it is that the amount allowed should be what is "reasonable to both parties to the taxation". This would be the new standard approach. The indemnity basis would remain as it is.

Litigants in person and costs

43. In the interim report I indicated the number of litigants in person is increasing. I stated that they should cease to be seen as problems for the system but, instead, the court should adopt a pro-active role in providing information and advice for them. I did not, however, in making my recommendations, address their position in relation to costs.

44. The amount of costs recoverable by a litigant in person is what would be allowed if the work had been done and disbursements had been made by a solicitor on his/her behalf together with any payments made by him/her for legal advice. This is, however, subject to two qualifications:

(a) where the litigant in person has not suffered any pecuniary loss in preparing his/her case or attending court he/she is only allowed £8.25 per hour for time reasonably spent on the case;

(b) he/she is limited to two-thirds of what would be allowed on taxation if he/she had been represented.

45. These provisions bear heavily on litigants in person. They are complex to operate. They do not accord with my general approach that litigants who are compelled to come to the court for a remedy should receive recognition for what this requires them to undergo. A distinction based on whether pecuniary loss can be shown is sometimes arbitrary in application. My proposals for fixed recoverable costs on the fast track and in relation to the position of companies both raise further considerations. I therefore recommend that the operation of the rule should be re-examined, with a view, if possible, to dispensing with the need to show pecuniary loss, perhaps in conjunction with a reduction in the overall proportion of what is allowable. Such a consideration should take account of the desirability of promoting arrangements whereby litigants could undertake much of the preparation of their case but with access to legal advice and representation as necessary. This is often known as "unbundling". Such an approach is of greater significance in view of the Bar's recent decision to allow referrals from Citizens Advice Bureaux, which already provide significant assistance to litigants in person.

Costs and insurance

46. In the future, insurance could have a larger part to play in funding litigation. This could apply both to parties' own costs and to liability for the other side's costs. A rapid increase in the availability of insurance is important to greater access to the courts. It is also important to the legal profession. However the ability to assess the risks involved is important if insurers are to increase their involvement. Certainty as to costs and moderation in their amount is critical to insurers offering affordable terms.

Costs and training

47. Although most respondents thought that judges would be able to achieve the aims of case management, there was considerable concern that judges did not have the appropriate background to make informed decisions about costs. This is, however, a shortcoming which can be dealt with by training and experience.

48. I recognise that my reforms involve learning new skills. These will have to be learned not only by judges but by members of the profession generally. The profession as well as the judiciary must pay more attention to and be better informed about costs than they are at present. My objective is to require greater attention to be focused on costs throughout the process of resolving disputes by everyone involved: judges, litigants and lawyers.

Recommendations

My recommendations are as follows.

(1)   Orders for costs need to reflect more precisely the obligations the new rules place on parties.

(2)   The court should have power to deal with the question of costs even where all other issues have been resolved without litigation.

(3)   Where one of the parties is unable to afford a particular procedure, the court, if it decides that that procedure is to be followed, should be entitled to make its order conditional upon the other side meeting the difference in the costs of the weaker party, whatever the outcome.

(4)   The court should be able to order payment of interim costs in cases where the opponent has substantially greater resources and where there is a reasonable likelihood that the weaker party will be entitled to costs at the end of the case.

(5)   Benchmark costs should be established by the court with the assistance of user groups, for multi-track proceedings with a limited and fairly constant procedure.

(6)   The new standard basis of taxation should be based on the wording of the Solicitors' (Non-Contentious Business) Remuneration Order 1994, ie, that the amount allowed should be what is "reasonable to both parties to the taxation". The indemnity basis should remain as it is.

(7)   There should be a review of the rules on the costs recoverable by a litigant in person with a view to simplifying them.

Chapter 8   The Supporting Structure

1.   I said in the interim report that effective case management would need to be supported by an appropriate court structure and suitable arrangements for judicial administration and the deployment of the judiciary. Among my specific proposals on these topics were recommendations that:

(a)   there should be a Head of Civil Justice with overall responsibility for the civil justice system in England and Wales;

(b)   one of the Presiding Judges on each Circuit should be nominated as having primary responsibility for civil work;

(c)   the two Chancery judges responsible for overseeing Chancery work on Circuit should be involved in the supervision of commercial work, and should be invited to attend the regular meetings of Presiding Judges;

(d)   outside London there should be three or four designated civil trial centres on each Circuit;

(e)   there should be a Senior Civil Judge appointed for each trial centre and its satellite courts;

(f)   the Court Service should appoint officials corresponding to the judges responsible for judicial administration to act in partnership with them;

(g)   case management on the multi-track should be handled by teams of judges, each including a Master or district judge as the manager of the team and, except in unusually complex cases, as the procedural judge;

(h)   High Court and Circuit judges should concentrate on fewer areas of work without becoming single subject specialists; and

(i)   there should be training and monitoring of judges, under judicial supervision, in relation to case management.

2.   Some of these recommendations have already been implemented, and others are in the process of being implemented. In January 1996 the Lord Chancellor appointed the Vice-Chancellor, Sir Richard Scott, to take on the duties envisaged for a Head of Civil Justice. This has enabled me to keep in close touch with Sir Richard during the later stages of the Inquiry. He will now be able to take charge of implementing many of the recommendations, and to provide the hands-on leadership for civil litigation which it has lacked in the past.

3. I also regard it as important that the new rule-making authority which will be needed to enact the new combined rules should contain in its membership people who can advance consumer, advisory and other lay viewpoints, as a counterbalance to the professional legal interests.

4. One major step which I recommended in the interim report has not yet been taken. That is the establishment of a Civil Justice Council to include representatives of the court service and the Judicial Studies Board, and of a wide range of court user organisations to contribute to the development of the reforms I am proposing. I see a clear need for such a body to ensure the continuing involvement of all those who use the Civil Justice system. I repeat my recommendation.

5. It is essential that the appropriate infrastructure for successful case management is put into place as soon as possible, without waiting for legislation or the new rules. It has, however, become clear that there is considerable scope for flexibility in the implementation of my proposals in this area. The aim is to establish a consistent system of case management in courts throughout the country, but the arrangements required to underpin this will vary in different geographical areas, and sometimes in different courts within each area. It is important, therefore, that the detailed recommendations in the interim report are not interpreted too rigidly. Where there are better or more appropriate ways of achieving my objectives, then these should be adopted.

Organisation and supervision of civil work on Circuit

6. As I recommended in the interim report, the two Chancery judges responsible for overseeing Chancery work on Circuit are now included in the regular meetings of Presiding Judges. I also recommended that a Presiding Judge on each Circuit should be nominated as having primary responsibility for civil work. I still regard this as desirable but I understand that the Presiding Judges see practical difficulties because of the way in which they divide their administrative work and because only one Presiding Judge is usually on a Circuit at any one time. Here, I am content that it should be agreed between the Presiding Judges appointed to a Circuit at a particular time whether one or both should be responsible for civil work on their circuit. The Presiding Judges should, however, keep in mind that the objective of my recommendation is to raise the profile of civil justice so that it does not always take second place to criminal and family work.

7. As regards my recommendation on civil trial centres, I am pleased to hear that the Court Service is conducting a review of existing accommodation to identify which of the courts on each Circuit might be suitable. I understand that progress is constrained by the nature of the available court buildings and the need for longer term planning of any substantial changes to the estate. The important point is to establish the principle that substantial civil work on Circuit should be concentrated at selected centres of expertise, and to identify the appropriate courts as soon as possible. How this is done, and how many such centres are needed for each Circuit, is a matter for the Court Service. I do, however, emphasise that the use of existing buildings with a main court and a cluster of satellite courts is a way of achieving my objectives.

8.   In the interim report I referred to the Circuit judge who should be responsible for each civil trial centre and its satellite courts as a "Senior Civil Judge". I envisaged that this judge would perform a similar role at each trial centre to that which the Presiding Judges should perform for civil work on the whole of the Circuit, and suggested that his additional management responsibilities should be reflected in his salary.

9.   I have now had the opportunity to discuss these proposals with the Council of Circuit Judges. They agree that there is a need for a senior judge to perform the role I have in mind, but they are concerned to avoid the creation of two tiers of Circuit judges, which they believe would have a damaging effect on the status, morale and cohesion of the Circuit bench as a whole. I understand that salary leads are at present confined to a small number of senior Circuit judges with exceptional administrative responsibilities such as the Recorders of Manchester and Liverpool and the senior judge at Central London County Court. Judges with administrative responsibilities will exercise these in relation to civil trial centres of varying size and workload. There is also the responsibility which derives from undertaking the heaviest and more complex judicial work, notably in those cases heard by Circuit judges designated to hear High Court work. Judicial salaries are, in any event, currently under review by the Senior Salaries Review Body. It is proper that decisions on salaries should be taken in that overall context.

10. There is a need, however, to designate and distinguish by an appropriate title the judge who is to be responsible for each trial centre. It is also important that such judges should be designated as soon as the centres are identified. This will be a task for the Head of Civil Justice, in consultation with the Presiding Judges and the Lord Chancellor's Department.

11. I am particularly pleased that the Court Service and the judiciary agree that the way forward is, as I suggested in the interim report, "a partnership between the judiciary and the administrators where the partners have distinct roles but work together to further an agreed policy". Following an extensive review of its management arrangements, the Court Service is currently putting into place a new management structure. As part of that process the Court Service has, in response to my proposals, started to develop partnership arrangements between administrators and judges at all levels. This will, of course, be an evolutionary process, and that emphasises the importance of early preparation before the new system of case management comes fully into effect.

The organisation of case management

12. In the interim report I indicated that the deployment of the judiciary for case management should seek to achieve:

(a)   continuity of management;

(b)   management and trial by judges of the right level; and

(c)   the flexible and efficient deployment of judges.

13. It is not easy to achieve all these aims in combination. The American 'single docket' system, where each case is handled by the same judge from start to finish, achieves maximum continuity but minimises flexibility in deployment. In an attempt to balance these conflicting aims, I recommended case management by teams of judges. I envisaged that each team would include as its manager a Master or district judge who would, in the majority of cases, act as procedural judge. I did not, however, intend that all district judges should carry out the full range of procedural judges' duties, and I emphasise again that the procedural judge is not a new type of judge. It is a function, not a title.

14. I remain firmly convinced that the team approach is the way forward, but that approach itself must be applied flexibly. In some of the heavier cases the approach I would encourage is for a district judge or Master, acting as procedural judge, to work in a team with the intended trial judge from an early stage in the litigation. In others it may be appropriate for a Circuit judge to carry out the function of procedural judge. High Court judges, too, have a role in case management; as I recommended in the interim report, the best arrangement for cases which are to be tried by a High Court judge is that, if practical, the judge himself should conduct the pre-trial review. For fast track cases, and smaller cases on the multi-track, the approach I envisage is that teams of Circuit and district judges would be led by the senior judge at each trial centre, with a degree of supervision by the Presiding Judge. The aim would be to ensure that they act along common policy lines, hence making appeals less common and easier to predict.

15. I also envisaged in the interim report that there may need to be different arrangements in particular courts or in specialist jurisdictions. In the Chancery Division and in general Queen's Bench Division work the Masters will continue to carry out their existing role as procedural judges. In the Commercial Court and the Official Referees' Courts all interlocutory work is taken by the judges, and the Queen's Bench Division Masters play no part in cases in these specialist courts. In the Patents Court the judges handle more of such work than in general Chancery cases, and in judicial review cases any interlocutory application may be made to a judge and not only to the Master.

16. All four working groups in these areas consider that the present arrangements should continue (with some modifications in the case of the Crown Office Group). The Official Referees', the Commercial Court and the Crown Office Groups believe that it would be neither appropriate nor necessary to have a second tier of procedural judges involved in the case management of their business. Their report recommends the rules should ensure that cases may continue to be dealt with by the same Official Referee throughout on a 'cradle to grave' basis. I should again draw attention to the fact that in my interim report I expressed the view that there should be flexibility in the use of judges across the Divisions, and that judges might be attached to a number of lists in different Divisions).

17. The Commercial Court Group say that the reason for the Court's popularity with the commercial community in the City and abroad is that all interlocutory matters are dealt with by the Commercial judges. However, they welcome the suggestion that there should be a move towards establishing two judge teams. This would be for cases which would respond to continuity of management. Having two judges would mean one of the judges should always be available. The team would avoid a number of judges having to deal with applications relating to the same case. This can involve undesirable duplication of work both by lawyers and by the judges.

18. In the Queen's Bench Division of the High Court in London it has not proved possible, except in a small minority of particularly important cases, to identify the trial judge early enough to ensure that he also conducts the pre-trial review. This is because of the Circuit commitments of the Queen's Bench judges. I have discussed the problem with the judges currently responsible for judicial deployment in the Queen's Bench Division, and they have been testing the extent to which it is possible to put the team concept into practice.

19. In future, the added certainty provided by case management should make it easier to plan the deployment of Queen's Bench judges further ahead. Developing technology may reduce the problem of the judge's absence from the court where the case is being handled. In the meantime, although it remains desirable for the trial judge to be identified at an early stage and to conduct the pre-trial review, I have to accept that this will only be possible in a limited number of the more complex cases. As part of the team approach, the judge who conducts the pre-trial review should regard it as part of his responsibility, where he is not going to conduct the trial, to inform the trial judge fully of what occurred during the pre-trial review. The trial judge, in turn, needs to honour any preliminary decisions made by the procedural judge.

20. These questions of judicial deployment will be largely for the Head of Civil Justice. It will be for him to set out the division of responsibilities between High Court judges and Masters on the one hand and Circuit judges and district judges on the other, and to consider who should act as procedural judges in particular types of case. The new rules will provide the flexibility needed to allocate work in the most appropriate way. The needs of the High Court as a whole and the overall use of judicial resources will have to be taken into account.

Specialist lists

21. In the interim report I recommended that there should be a General, Personal Injury and Damages list in the Queen's Bench Division, a General Business List in the Chancery Division and a number of specialist lists, including: Commercial, Admiralty, Patents, Official Referees, judicial review, company and insolvency, intellectual property, revenue, trusts, probate and real property. I indicated that I would change the titles of some of the specialist lists, and possibly combine the Patents Court with the intellectual property list, and that I would reach a final decision on this after considering the specialist jurisdictions during the second stage of the Inquiry. I have now discussed this with the Head of Civil Justice, and agreed that it should be for him to make the decision in consultation with the judges concerned. In chapter 15 of this report, I am proposing that a new medical negligence list should be added to the specialist lists.

22. I believe that a system of specialist lists is an important means of ensuring that cases receive the appropriate management, both in the interlocutory stages and at trial. This means that they will be managed and tried by judges who have some knowledge of the relevant subject matter and experience of handling similar cases. In a culture where the legal profession is becoming increasingly specialised, I do not consider it sensible to expect either procedural judges or trial judges to deal with all types of cases. Case management will require both procedural judges and trial judges to take on a more interventionist role than they are used to, and to have more understanding of the substance of the cases before them.

23. It is not my intention, however, that more judges should become exclusive specialists in one area of civil business, or that the list system should interfere with the flexible and effective deployment of the judiciary. What I proposed in the interim report was that a High Court judge could be nominated for a period, according to his or her expertise, to one or more of the general and specialist lists, irrespective of the Division to which the lists belong. If that system is adopted, as I still think it should be, it will be possible for every High Court judge to be allocated to at least one of the specialist lists, and for the general list work to be shared among a number of judges who will be doing a mixture of general and specialist work. As part of the team approach, Masters and district judges should similarly have responsibility for particular areas of litigation. This could be especially valuable in specialist fields such as medical negligence.

24. I would recommend that this approach is taken forward by nominating judges for appropriate areas of specialisation. Especially for Circuit judges, the type of cases which they are required to handle can be of considerable significance. I also therefore recommend and adopt the suggestion of the Judicial Studies Board (JSB) that a record of judges' interests as to the type of cases which they would prefer to try should be established and taken into account in determining to what specialised areas different judges should be allocated. Obviously the wishes of the individual judge can only be a factor in furthering this approach.

Judicial training

25. The proposed reforms will, in some areas, substantially change judges' duties. If judges are to be able competently to handle the new system in a consistent way throughout the country, a structured training effort is what is required. This will be important for public confidence in the reforms. Judges must be seen to be in full command of the new procedures. It is for the JSB to provide the appropriate training. It is already providing training for the increased small claims jurisdiction. When decisions have been reached as to the implementation of the other proposed reforms a training programme for them will need to be fully defined. In the meantime, I understand the JSB is considering how training should be set up for the other changes. Because of the importance of training to my proposals, both my team and myself have kept in close contact with the JSB and its officers. In particular, the Chairman, Lord Justice Henry and the Director of Studies, His Honour Judge Sumner, accompanied me on my visit to Australia. I am indebted to them and their staff for their advice.

26. In the interim report I recommended an increase in the small claims jurisdiction from £1,000 to £3,000. This was implemented on 8 January 1996, though the jurisdiction for personal injury cases remained at £1,000. In my report I identified the need for a more consistent approach by district judges in handling small claims. This was as a result of representations I received and also the research which was carried out by Professor Baldwin. I recommended (Recommendation 44): "All district judges and deputy district judges should be trained in handling small claims, to ensure a more consistent approach."

27. This is now being tackled by the JSB. All deputy district judges have to attend a one week residential induction course at which the handling of arbitration is a key feature, and all the points made by Professor Baldwin are covered. This training is designed to ensure a consistent approach while allowing judges to retain their inherent discretion. In addition to this, deputy district judges 'sit in' with experienced district judges to see arbitrations being conducted and gain practical experience. District judges will have to attend residential refresher course lasting four days every three years. Again, part of the time on these courses is devoted to arbitrations. Both sets of courses are kept under continual review.

28. In addition to training in how to conduct arbitration, the JSB has commendably set up a working party late in 1995 under His Honour Judge Sumner in order to produce a protocol, or guide to good practice, for the conduct of small claims arbitrations. This working party included a QC and three experienced district judges. Its draft proposal is nearly complete and will be presented for approval to the Main Board in July 1996. When it is approved the JSB will circulate it to all district and deputy district judges.

29. My proposals for the fast track and multi-track also involve a new approach. They create a number of new duties which judges will have to carry out in order to manage cases properly. Judges will have to resist pressure both on the fast track and on the multi-track for disclosure and expert evidence when it is not appropriate. They will have to enforce the timetable on practitioners who may wish, for whatever reason, to delay. They will also be expected to draw the existence of any available alternative dispute resolution mechanisms to parties' attention where this is appropriate or desirable.

30. The responsibility for many of these steps will rest with procedural judges. The JSB is considering an intensive residential course for judges at all levels who will have to carry out these duties. This residential course might be between two and three days long and should include practical examples of cases for procedural judges to work out.

31. The disposal of fast track cases will require new skills. In the case of complex multi-track cases the trial judge will be expected to conduct a pre-trial review. The preliminary JSB view is that between one and two days training is likely to be needed to give trial judges a better understanding of the full implications of the reforms. They should have an opportunity to conduct a pre-trial review. It would also be beneficial if the judges could have some practical exercises in the issues which may arise during the hearing of a case under the new procedures.

32. Judges will also need training in new IT systems. It may well be that it would be advantageous for the JSB and the Court Service to organise joint training on purely IT matters.

33. In addition to face to face training, the JSB is planning on including in its benchbook advice to judges on how to use the new system. This might appropriately include flow charts, setting out the various decision-making points in the new procedures, as well as advice on how discretion within the new rules might be used.

34. Both the training and the revisions to benchbooks would need to be in place prior to implementation of reforms.

35. One consistent theme in this final report is the proposed requirement for judges dealing with certain categories of case – notably medical negligence and housing – to have the necessary specialist experience and expertise. If judges are to develop expertise in areas such as these, it would be desirable to provide specialist training. This need not, however, be exclusively judicial training. Shared training with the profession, under the general aegis of the JSB, may be appropriate.

36. The ability of the JSB to carry out the necessary training will depend on its resources. In order to determine the resources it will need, the JSB will need to know the number and categories of judges who are likely to be involved. The Court Service should help the Head of Civil Justice to identify the numbers who should be involved with rolling programmes of training.

Assistance for judges

37. I emphasised in the interim report the need for support for the judiciary. This needs to be provided in various ways. First, it is essential that procedural judges have adequate clerical and secretarial support to enable them to carry out their new duties in relation to case management effectively.

38. Secondly, I suggested in chapter 11 of the interim report that it might be helpful to High Court judges if they could have the assistance of recently qualified barristers and solicitors as law clerks in complex litigation. They would be able to assist in legal research and the preparation of summaries of documents. There have been a small number of cases in which this has been done, and it has been a success. The Commercial Court Group says that, whatever changes are necessary as a result of the new system of case management, it will be desirable for the Commercial judges to have assistance of this kind. The Crown Office Group also supports the use of law clerks, and considers that their introduction would be more useful than having nominated judges delegating work to Queen's Bench Division Masters. I am pleased to note that there is now a budget at the Royal Courts of Justice, albeit a very small one, for this purpose. I hope that the budget will be increased so that more use can be made of law clerks in the future, and that it will be recognised that there are real benefits to be obtained. This is the clear message that I have received from the United States, Canada, Australia and New Zealand.

39. In the course of the meetings that I had with the working group on multi-party actions, it became apparent that a potential source of assistance to the courts would be senior solicitors with experience in the efficient management of these highly complex cases. I therefore recommend that the Lord Chancellor's Department should maintain a list of practitioners (either those still in practice or recently retired from practice) who would be prepared to act in this role. They would be appointed as a deputy Master in relation to a specific case. The advice which I received from the working group was that candidates should be readily forthcoming. The appropriate candidates would be easy to identify. Because of their experience, they would carry considerable conviction with litigants in this very difficult area, whether they were making the decisions themselves or assisting the judge in marshalling material in order to make his decisions.

40. I outlined in the interim report the valuable role which such senior solicitors could play in providing assistance as procedural judges in all areas of complex litigation. Responses to the report have reinforced my conclusion that a valuable resource remains untapped because the current methods of recruitment, involving part-time sitting over a period of years, are well suited to barristers' patterns of working but are less easily accommodated in the careers of solicitors with litigation practices. The continued supply of high quality candidates for appointment as procedural judges is of importance to the future of the system. A more flexible approach to the requirement of part-time sitting, perhaps by allowing this to be continuous rather than spread over time, would allow for the necessary appraisal before a full-time appointment was made and would also encourage applications from those whose talents the system requires.

41. I also see a need for encouraging court staff to develop relevant expertise. Managing clerks in the past and legal executives today have always played a prominent role in managing the progress of litigation in the solicitors' offices. The Institute of Legal Executives has an effective system of training and qualification for legal executives. In a managed system, members of the Institute of Legal Executives could play a role which cannot be played by staff who have no legal qualification. I would recommend the Court Service to encourage appropriate existing and future members of the staff to become members of the Institute. I recommend the same for the clerks to High Court judges.

Recommendations

My recommendations are as follows.

(1)   A Civil Justice Council should be established to contribute to the development of the proposed reforms.

(2)   The new rule-making authority which will be needed to enact the new combined rules should contain in its membership people who can advance consumer, advisory and other lay viewpoints, as a counterbalance to the professional legal interests.

(3)   A Circuit judge responsible for each civil trial centre and its satellite courts should be designated by the Head of Civil Justice as soon as the centres are identified.

(4)   Judges should be nominated for appropriate areas of specialisation. A record of judges' preferences should be established and taken into account in determining the allocation of judges to specialised areas.

(5)   Judges who specialise in areas such as medical negligence and housing should be given appropriate training. The possibility of providing joint training with the legal profession, under the general aegis of the Judicial Studies Board, should be explored.

(6)   Procedural judges should be given proper clerical and secretarial support to enable them to carry out their new duties in relation to case management effectively.

(7)   The Court Service should encourage members of staff, including clerks to High Court judges, to become members of the Institute of Legal Executives.

(8)   High Court and Court of Appeal judges should have law clerks, initially on a selective basis.

SECTION

III

*Procedure and
Evidence*

Chapter 9   Introduction

1.   This part of the report deals with matters of practice and procedure. A general theme of the interim report and of this report has been the need to bring the uncontrolled features of the adversarial system under proper discipline. Another has been to promote more, better and earlier settlements. At the same time, it has been my aim to refocus the rules of the system, which have tended to become over-technical and detached from their proper purposes. I explained in the interim report that the proliferation of rules has itself become an obstacle to access to justice. In the new rules, I have sought to advance a simpler, more economical approach to procedure. Eradication of unnecessary distinctions in terminology and substantive treatment have been part of this approach. These themes are reflected in the procedural topics mentioned in this chapter and dealt with in this part of the report.

2.   In this part, I draw attention to some of the more noteworthy procedural changes which I am putting forward. One of the most significant, the introduction of pre-action protocols (chapter 10), lies outside the scope of the formal rules of procedure, which in the main apply only to proceedings in court. The protocols would extend back to the pre-action stage something of the discipline I am seeking for formally litigated proceedings. They will render less distinct the difference between pre-action activity directed to case disposal and that which takes place after proceedings have begun. They are not intended, however, to provide a comprehensive legislative code. They will be worked out largely by agreement between groups representing relevant litigant interests and they will deal only with the main pre-action requirements and with matters which have caused particular difficulty.

3.   Offers to settle, which are dealt with at chapter 11, are an important means of promoting settlement. I am recommending that claimants as well as defendants should be able to make offers with teeth, ie, with adverse financial consequences for a party who unreasonably fails to accept such an offer. It should be possible to make an effective offer in this sense before as well as after proceedings have begun. Just as the court will be able to take into account the extent to which parties have complied with pre-action protocols, so they will be able to take account of whether or not reasonable, pre-action offers to settle were made.

4.   A conspicuous area of divergent practice and nomenclature is the initiation of proceedings. Both the High Court and county courts have several different ways of starting proceedings. I am proposing that all claims and appeals should be started on a single claim form with appropriate variations. This will apply not only to fact-based disputes currently brought by writ or summons but also to claims involving construction of documents brought by originating summons and to claims for remedies in public law.

5.   Chapter 12 also deals with the contents of statements of case (as I recommend that pleadings should in future be called). In cases where the facts are potentially in dispute, the emphasis in future will be on the clear statement of factual allegations by the claimant and on equally clear answers by the defendant. The aim is to put an end to the evasive and obscure pleading which often discredits our civil procedures at present. Scrutiny of statements of case by the court for case management purposes will stimulate those drafting statements of case to achieve a better standard. The new rules will require a litigant or his legal adviser to certify belief in the truth of allegations contained in statements of case. This is already a requirement for evidence contained in witness statements. This approach, which is another means of emphasising the obligation of parties to act reasonably in litigation, will reduce the distinction between statements of case, witness statements and affidavits.

6.   Service of court process is in a sense a mechanical process but is nevertheless an important part of civil procedure. It secures a basic element of procedural justice, namely, that a party is informed of a case against him and put in a position to reply. Confidence that service has been properly carried out also enables the court to grant appropriate remedies even in the absence of a response by a defendant. I believe, nevertheless, that this too is an area where technical distinctions can be reduced, allowing a less prescriptive approach concerning methods of service. I am therefore recommending a more flexible system for service of documents.

7.   In contested cases, disclosure of documents (as I now recommend discovery should be called) is an area of procedural activity which I am seeking to curb. In the interim report, I explained the need to find a half-way-house between a system with little or no disclosure and the present, unlimited obligation of disclosure. I recommended that disclosure should be limited in the first instance to relevant documents of whose existence a party is aware. This test obviously causes difficulties in a corporate context in which 'awareness' depends on the recollection of more than one individual. In chapter 7, I explain further how the test might apply in that situation. I acknowledge that practical application of the test will still not be free of difficulty, though the existing test of relevance is itself not without difficulty in practice and it will remain possible to supplement the disclosure of documents which the awareness test produces by application for specific disclosure. I emphasise that here, as in the new procedure as a whole, what we must seek to achieve is a more proportionate but workable system, not one which is theoretically impeccable but unaffordable.

8. Finally, this part deals with expert evidence. In the interim report, I explained that this too was an area where certain excesses needed to be restrained: in particular the cost, especially in smaller cases, and the temptation for parties and their legal advisers to deploy expert witnesses as a party weapon rather than as a source of objective assistance to the court. My recommendation that there should be greater use of single experts has caused much controversy. In chapter 13 I examine the matter further, but still conclude that there is considerable scope, even within a procedure which will remain essentially adversarial in character, for greater use of a single expert. The development of protocols provides a potential voluntary route to achieving this in many instances. Here, as in some other respects, many of those who have acknowledged the need for change in principle hesitate before the practical implications of that recognition. I fully understand their unease. But this is the kind of choice which has to be made if practical improvements of any significance are to be achieved.

Chapter 10   Pre-action Protocols

1.   This chapter sets out my proposals for the development of pre-action protocols. These are intended to build on and increase the benefits of early but well-informed settlements which genuinely satisfy both parties to a dispute. The purposes of such protocols are:

(a)   to focus the attention of litigants on the desirability of resolving disputes without litigation;

(b)   to enable them to obtain the information they reasonably need in order to enter into an appropriate settlement; or

(c)   to make an appropriate offer (of a kind which can have costs consequences if litigation ensues); and

(d)   if a pre-action settlement is not achievable, to lay the ground for expeditious conduct of proceedings.

2.   It is a characteristic of our civil justice system that the vast majority of cases are settled without trial, by negotiation between the parties or their legal advisers. There are many more potential claimants who settle their disputes without starting legal proceedings at all. It is my intention to build on this. My approach to civil justice is that disputes should, wherever possible, be resolved without litigation. Where litigation is unavoidable, it should be conducted with a view to encouraging settlement at the earliest appropriate stage.

3.   However, settlement is not an end in itself. Settlement must be appropriate to the needs of both parties, and be achieved without excessive cost or delay. At present too many cases settle at the door of the court. This is the least appropriate stage to settle because maximum cost and delay have been incurred. Other cases settle for no better reason than that the claimant is tired of waiting, or does not have the energy or resources to pursue the claim any further. This may arise because of the deliberate tactics adopted by the parties.

4.   Delay before the start of proceedings is just as undesirable (and can be just as expensive) as delay in the course of litigation. There would be no point in offering a fast track timetable of 20 or 30 weeks to a claimant who had spent two or three years in fruitless negotiations before bringing the case to court at all. What is needed is a system which enables the parties to a dispute to embark on meaningful negotiation as soon as the possibility of litigation is identified, and ensures that as early as possible they have the relevant information to define their claims and make realistic offers to settle.

5.   In my view, this can only be achieved if the court itself takes more account of pre-litigation activity than has traditionally been the case. Once a protocol has been adopted, the parties' compliance (or failure to comply) with it will be taken into account when the court is dealing with the future conduct of the case. In particular, if one party has unreasonably refused to accept a pre-action offer to settle, that will have consequences in costs once litigation has started.

6.   Pre-action protocols will be an important part of the new system. They are not intended to provide a comprehensive code for all pre-litigation behaviour, but will deal with specific problems in specific areas. They will set out codes of sensible practice which parties are expected to follow when they are faced with the prospect of litigation in an area to which a protocol applies. Protocols will make it easier for parties to obtain the information they need, by the use of standard forms and questionnaires wherever possible. This will be assisted by wider powers for the courts to order pre-action disclosure. (See chapter 12 of this report.) Protocols will also be an important means of promoting economy in the use of expert evidence, in particular by encouraging the parties to use a single expert wherever possible. Unless this happens before the commencement of proceedings, it will frequently be too late because the parties will already have established an entrenched relationship with their own expert. In addition, protocols will encourage the use of any appropriate alternative mechanisms for the resolution of disputes. If litigation proves necessary, observance of the protocols should put the parties in a good position to meet the timetable imposed by the court. This will be particularly important on the fast track, with its tight standard timetable.

7.   Work is already well advanced on the development of protocols for some areas of litigation which particularly concern the Inquiry. The Law Society has played a particularly important role in work on pre-litigation procedures, both by helping the Inquiry directly and through independent initiatives such as its protocol for the disclosure of medical records. Elsewhere in this report I mention the progress made on a disrepair protocol by the Housing Law Practitioners' Association and the associations representing local authority landlords (the Association of District Councils, the Association of London Government and the Association of Metropolitan Authorities). Chapter 15 refers to the new 'umbrella' group for medical negligence litigation, which will also be taking forward work on a protocol. I also understand that a group of construction industry professionals is working to produce guidelines which would encourage the resolution of disputes through arbitration rather than litigation.

8.   Another group, involving members of the Association of Personal Injury Lawyers (APIL) and the Association of British Insurers (ABI), is working on a pre-action protocol for personal injury cases. This started in the context of the Inquiry's work on the fast track, but the approach is relevant to all personal injury work. The main points on which agreement has been reached so far are as follows.

(a)   The content and broad format of a notification of claim have been agreed. The letter will be sent to the defendant (and, where known, the defendant's insurer) as soon as the claimant is aware of sufficient facts to show that there is a possible claim. It will contain enough information to enable the defendant to investigate and broadly value the claim.

(b)   Where the claimant does not know the identity of the defendant's insurer, the defendant would be requested to forward a copy of the letter to his insurers and notify the claimant of their identity and his policy number within 28 days of receiving the notification.

(c)   Within three months of receiving notification of a claim, the defendant must reply saying whether or not liability is accepted. If it is not, the defendant must give factual reasons for disputing liability and send copies of relevant documents.

(d)   A list of the documents which should be automatically disclosed by the prospective parties in common types of personal injury cases has been drawn up. It is intended that, as recommended by the group, the exchange of these documents will be prescribed by practice direction. In most cases, this will obviate the need for any further disclosure after proceedings have begun. The group has also identified the documents that should be provided on request in particular circumstances.

9.   The group has also been able to agree a protocol for instructing experts which provides that the claimant's solicitor may, in the first instance, put forward more than one expert's name. The defendant may indicate that one or more of these is unacceptable. The group considered that this would have advantages for both claimants and defendants. Provided at least two names are acceptable to both parties, the claimant may reject a report by the expert of his first choice without letting the defendant know that he has done so. The advantage for defendants is that they can identify at an early stage if the claimant is intending to use an expert whom they regard as partisan and whose report they are unlikely to accept.

10. If the other party does not object to the claimant's expert he will not be able to rely on any other expert in that speciality unless the claimant agrees or the court so directs, or unless the report commissioned by the claimant has been amended and the claimant is not prepared to disclose the original report.

11. Instructions to experts will follow a standard format and they should refer to any protocol that may be agreed between the Law Society and the British Medical Association (BMA) or other medical organisation as to the format of the report. Either party may deliver written questions on the report relevant to the issues to the solicitor instructing the expert. Answers to the questions will be sent separately to each solicitor.

12. The group has also suggested that there should be a central register of insurance policies to enable a claimant to identify the potential defendant's insurer. This is a particular difficulty in employer's liability cases where the company or firm has gone out of business. I endorse this proposal.

13. Protocols will be most effective if they are agreed, broadly speaking, on behalf of those likely to be frequent users of the procedures, whether as litigants or as professional advisers. All the groups whose work I have mentioned have made commendable progress, but there are some detailed points on which the claimants' and defendants' representatives have not yet reached agreement. I hope that discussions will continue after this report is published, and will lead to agreed protocols.

14. It is important that protocols are devised within a general structure of court approval. The Civil Justice Council will have a significant role to play here in advising and assisting the Head of Civil Justice. When a protocol is established for an area of litigation, I recommend that it is incorporated in the relevant practice guide. Unreasonable failure by either party to comply with the relevant protocol will be taken into account by the court, for example in the allocation of costs or in considering any application for an extension of the timetable.

15. I am aware that there is some scepticism as to whether insurance companies will comply with the protocols. My discussions with insurers, and their co-operation (led by the ABI) in the development of protocols, do not support this. I have no reason to think that the industry leaders will not honour the protocols. It will, in any event, be in their interest to do so if they wish to avoid the sanctions that will be imposed, if necessary, by the courts.

16. There are also practitioners who fear that the use of pre-issue protocols will lead to the unnecessary front-loading of costs. While the protocols will certainly bring work forward by comparison with usual present practice, this is to be welcomed. The work has to be done to enable cases to be resolved, and bringing the work forward will enable some cases to settle earlier. Where this is not possible the work will not have been wasted. The insurers have pointed out that cases cannot settle until sufficient information is available for a realistic commercial assessment of the value of the claim. This has been accepted by the Association of Personal Injury Lawyers.

17. If the procedure laid down in protocols proves to be over-elaborate in more straightforward cases, it will be a simple matter to allow for this. The courts should initially be flexible in their enforcement of compliance with the protocols. The operation of the protocols will have to be monitored and their detailed provisions modified so far as is necessary in the light of practical experience.

Recommendations

My recommendations on protocols are as follows.

(1)   Pre-action protocols should set out codes of sensible practice which parties are expected to follow when faced with the prospect of litigation. They should not cover all areas of litigation, but should deal with specific problems in specific areas, including personal injury, medical negligence and housing.

(2)   When a protocol is established for a particular area of litigation, it should be incorporated into the relevant practice guide.

(3)   Unreasonable failure by either party to comply with the relevant protocol should be taken into account by the court, for example in the allocation of costs or in considering any application for an extension of the timetable.

(4)   The operation of the protocols should be monitored and their detailed provisions modified so far as is necessary in the light of practical experience.

Chapter 11   Offers to Settle

1. In chapter 24 of the interim report, I explained that a greater role for offers to settle was an important part of my general approach of promoting early settlement of cases. My main recommendations on offers can be summarised as follows.

(1)   The system of payments into court should be replaced by a system of offers.

(2)   Any party, the claimant as well as the defendant, should be able to make an offer to settle.

(3)   Offers could be in respect of the whole case or of individual issues (including liability) or claims.

(4)   Offers could be made before the start of proceedings.

(5)   There should be financial incentives to encourage claimants, in particular, to make offers.

(6)   Where an offer has been made, the court should exercise a wider discretion in respect of costs and interest than it habitually does at present.

2. My proposals for offers remain essentially the same as those set out in the interim report. This chapter therefore deals mainly with matters where I have modified or extended my original ideas. I would stress, however, that the importance which I attach to offers to settle has, if anything, increased since I wrote the interim report. I believe they are capable of making an important contribution to the change of culture which is fundamental to the reform of civil justice.

Basic system

3. In the interim report, I did not attach importance to the retention of payments into court as a means of achieving the kind of benefits which I believe will flow from my proposed system of offers. However, the Law Society and others who made representations in response to the interim report, while generally supporting my proposals on offers, argued that a payment into court was a useful way of assuring claimants of the substance of an offer. The fact that the money was actually available made it more likely that the offer would be accepted. Up to a point, I accept this reasoning and therefore do not now recommend the abolition of payments into court.

4. Allowing for the fact that my proposals would enable claimants as well as defendants to make offers, it is of course important that rules of court relating to offers and to payments into court respectively should diverge as little as possible. I therefore recommend, in respect of defendants' offers, that the making of the offer itself should be the critical step, while the backing of a payment in will be secondary and optional. This means that *Cutts v Head* [1984] Ch 290, which prevents the making of a Calderbank offer where a payment into court can be made, will no longer apply under the new rules. When considering the exercise of its discretion as to costs at the end of a case, the court will therefore have to give primary consideration to the terms of the defendant's offer regardless of whether there was also a payment into court. In practice, it should only be in an unusual case that the absence of a payment in should be taken to undermine the reasonableness of an offer.

Withdrawal of offers

5. A matter not mentioned in the interim report was the withdrawal of offers. I recommended there that, as with payments into court now, an offer should normally remain open for acceptance for 21 days or more. In theory, a party could make an offer stipulated to be open for a shorter period, but I would recommend that rules of court should direct the courts to disregard any such offer in exercising the costs discretion. There needs to be a minimum period for the 'offeree' to consider the offer and, if necessary, to ask for more information about it. Subject to the 21 day provision, it should be open to the offeror at any time to withdraw or vary an offer subsequently, by notice in writing to all the other parties. This differs from the existing position for payments into court, where the circumstances in which a payment in can be withdrawn are extremely narrow. Obviously the court would not take account of a withdrawn offer when considering costs except when considering the reasonableness of the parties' conduct generally.

Incentives to make offers

6. I consider that the defendant's potential entitlement to all his costs from the date of his offer is a sufficient incentive to defendants to make offers. Imposing any more rigorous sanction on a claimant for not accepting an offer would constitute undue pressure to settle. I therefore do not recommend any change here.

7. However, the claimant clearly needs a significant incentive to balance up the risk to which the defendant can subject him by making an offer. In the interim report, I suggested that this should take the form of additional interest above that which would ordinarily be payable on damages. Since writing the interim report, I have come to the conclusion that significantly higher incentives than I had originally suggested are needed. I therefore recommend that the figures should be 25 per cent above the rate which would otherwise be payable on awards up to £10,000, 15 per cent from £10,000 to £50,000 and then an additional 5 per cent. Thus if, for example, the conventional rate was 5 per cent, then the rate on an award up to £10,000 would be 30 per cent, and so on. The rate would be tapering, ie, 25 per cent on the first £10,000, 15 per cent on the next £40,000 and 5 per cent on the rest. This is necessary because otherwise a claimant who is awarded £49,950 would be better off than a claimant who was awarded £50,000. The extra rate of interest is higher on lower value claims because otherwise the incentive to make an offer in such cases would be insufficient.

8.   The normal date from which interest would be payable would be the date 21 days after the offer was made. The court could, however, order that interest should run from a different date. This might be appropriate where, for example, the defendant could not reasonably have been expected to accept the offer until certain information had become available to him.

9.   These incentives for claimants and defendants are in addition to the court's power to award indemnity costs and interest on costs where the court considers a party has acted unreasonably.

Recovery of the whole sum claimed

10.   If a claimant has specified the exact amount which he is claiming and recovers that amount at trial, he will be in the same position as a claimant whose offer to settle was the same as the court's award. Like such a claimant, he too should be entitled to additional interest.

Recommendations

I make the following, further recommendations in respect of offers.

(1)   A defendant's ability to make a payment into court should be retained, but the making of an offer, in accordance with rules of court, should be the primary requirement, with payments in being a secondary and optional means of backing an offer. The absence of a payment in should not normally influence the court's view of whether an offer was reasonable.

(2)   A party may withdraw an offer, but an offer which is open for less than 21 days should be disregarded by the court for costs purposes.

(3)   The rates of additional interest which I now recommend should be payable to a claimant who makes an offer which is not accepted and which the claimant matches or exceeds at trial are:

awards up to £10,000   25%

more than £10,000 and up to £50,000   15%

above £50,000   5%

(4)   Extra interest will normally run from the date of the offer, but the court may order a different start date where appropriate.

(5)   A party who recovers at trial the amount which he claimed should be treated as if he had made an offer for that amount, and be entitled to extra interest.

Chapter 12   Practice and Procedure

Starting a claim

1. In my interim report I argued that the complexity of the present rules of court could be seen as an obstacle to access to justice. A prime example of that complexity is the fact that there are four different ways of starting proceedings in the High Court, and another four in the county courts: the writ, originating summons, originating motion and petition in the High Court; and the summons, originating application, petition and notice of appeal in the county courts. Within those categories there can be further variations: there are three types of forms of originating summons, and a number of different forms of summons. In many cases there is a choice of methods, each having different consequences.

2. More specific examples have been provided by the specialist working groups which have been assisting me. The Chancery Working Group has pointed to the unnecessary distinction in RSC Order 102 whereby some applications under the Companies Act have to be by petition, some by originating motion and some by originating summons. The Intellectual Property Working Group has noted that there are similarly confusing requirements in RSC Order 104. Needless complexity is introduced into the system at the outset.

3. I therefore propose that all proceedings should be begun by means of a claim. There should be a single claim form with could be used for every case. I regard this as an important step towards achieving simplicity in civil litigation. I suggest that the necessary degree of uniformity can be achieved by having the same first page for every claim, containing exactly the same information (the names of the parties and of the issuing court, and the case number) with the following pages varying according to the type of claim.

4. Because judgment for failure to defend can be obtained in some cases but not in others, the second page can contain the different notices to the defendant which will be necessary to set out the consequences of doing nothing. These will follow the lines of the existing wording, for example: "If you do nothing, judgment may be entered against you without further notice" in the county court form N1, or: "Failure to attend may result in judgment being entered against you" in the county court forms N3 and N4.

5. The form will then go on to the claimant's statement of case. It will be possible to tailor it so that, for example, standard claims can be used in personal injury and other fast track cases, and for appeals and Crown Office cases.

6. I am proposing for both fast track and multi-track cases that the claimant and defendant should be able to complete a directions questionnaire which would indicate, among other things, the court where they consider the case should be heard and their reasons why the case should be dealt with on a particular track. The importance of the case to the parties will be relevant, as well as the nature of the claim. Because of the number of undefended claims it is undesirable to require the claimant to file a questionnaire with this claim, but he can do so if he knows that the case would be defended. The procedural judge may call for one where the statement of case does not provide him with enough information to give directions about the handling of the case. The final decision as to allocation and the other matters like venue will, of course, rest with the court.

7. In cases which are at present begun by originating summons, originating motion and originating application, the claim will combine the information now contained in the originating document and the principal affidavit in support. This will be possible because of the requirement for the claimant or his legal representative to certify that he believes the contents of the claim to be true. In the same way a defence will contain the defendant's contentions and will replace the principal affidavit in reply. In some cases, for example an appeal from a tribunal or an arbitrator, the defence need only say that the defendant supports the order for the reasons given by the tribunal or arbitrator.

8. It will continue to be possible for the claimant to ask the court to fix a hearing date when the claim is issued, for example in mortgage possession cases. In cases at present begun by originating summons, motion and application where judgment for failure to defend is not available, the procedural judge will look at the papers when the acknowledgement of service is received, or the time for filing it has expired. If there is no acknowledgement of service or the defendant indicates that he does not intend to put in a defence, the judge will fix a date for the hearing. If there is to be a defence he will consider the matter again when the defence has been received and either fix a date for the hearing or give directions as to how the case is to proceed. Where it appears that the facts are in dispute and that witness statements and disclosure of documents are required, he may allocate the case to a more managed track.

9. The new rules will provide that proceedings may be started in any court which has jurisdiction to hear and determine them, subject to two exceptions. First, a claim may not be started at the Royal Courts of Justice unless it is appropriate to be tried in London and unless the claimant certifies that his claim, where it can be valued, is worth over £50,000, or that it is a multi-track case which ought to be dealt with by a High Court judge. Secondly, where the claimant seeks possession of land the case must be started in the county court in whose area the land is situated or in the Royal Courts of Justice if there is a London certificate.

10. It will, of course, be most convenient for the parties and the courts if a claim is lodged in the court where it ought to be determined and this should be strongly encouraged. Nevertheless, the courts must be willing to assist litigants in person who may be unsure where their case ought to be brought. In the future, I hope that developments in the use of information technology by the courts will make it easier for them to act as a post box for the appropriate court. In the meantime staff should either seek to persuade the litigant to issue his claim in the more suitable court or to accept it for issue and then let it be transferred judicially. The commencement of proceedings in the wrong court will not mean that the proceedings are a nullity.

Statements of case
Claimant's case

11. The basic requirements of a claim are that it should:

(a)   set out a short description of the claim and a succinct statement of the facts relied on;

(b)   certify that the claimant believes the contents to be true;

(c)   indicate the remedy claimed;

(d)   specify any document on which the case depends;

(e)   certify the claimant's belief, where he is claiming money, that he reasonably expects to recover:

   (i)   up to £3,000;

   (ii) between £3,000 and £10,000;

   (iii) over £10,000.

12. There will continue to be specific requirements for particular types of case. In the case of personal injury claims, for example, the claimant will have to provide a statement of any special damages which are claimed and, in the case of appeals, the decision under appeal must be attached.

13. The claimant must also specify the date of service of the claim and the date by which the defendant must file a notice of intention to defend (14 days) and a defence (28 days unless the parties agree on a longer period, which can be up to three months). Only one agreement to extend will be allowed; any further extension can only be made by court order. I accept that in some technical areas of litigation, for example claims involving medical negligence or patents, extensions beyond 28 days may not be uncommon, but I have no doubt that these should be the exception and not the rule.

14. The notice of intention to defend, which is similar to the present High Court procedure, will apply to all claims other than appeals. This step is needed for a number of reasons. First, it is important that creditors are not prejudiced by the longer period which the new rules allow for filing a defence. Secondly, it will enable a defence to be dispensed with where it is necessary, for example where the matter is not contentious but the defendant is a necessary party. Thirdly, it will enable defendants to challenge the jurisdiction of an English court to hear the case, without needing to file a full defence. In any claim the defendant may choose to file a defence within 14 days instead of returning the notice of intention to defend within that time.

15. I should make it clear that my proposals are not intended to affect undefended debt claims, which form the vast majority of all claims. The procedures between issue and judgment, in particular, for the defendant to admit the claim and seek time to pay, which will be based on the existing county court procedures, will continue.

Defence

16. The defence must:

(a)   indicate

(i)   which parts of the claim the defendant admits,

(ii) which parts he denies,

(iii) which parts he doubts to be true (and why),

(iv) which parts he neither admits nor denies, because he does not know whether they are true, but which he wishes the claimant to prove;

(b)   give the defendant's version of the facts in so far as they differ from those stated in the claim;

(c)   say why the defendant disputes the claimant's entitlement to any, or to a particular, remedy or the value of the claim or assessment of damages; and

(d)   specify any document vital to the defence.

Reply

17. I suggested in chapter 20 of my interim report that there should be no further formal pleadings beyond a reply, and that that itself would be rare and should not be permitted unless the court gave leave. The Commercial Court and Chancery Working Groups say that replies are often necessary in order to set out the claimant's challenges to the defence and that the need to obtain a court order where none is now necessary will add to delay and expense. I accept their recommendation that it should still be possible for the claimant to put in a reply without having to seek the leave of the court, provided it is served before any case management conference. However, in fast track cases any reply is not to be taken into account with regard to costs, nor should it defer the timetable. And there should be no further statements of case at all.

18. I also recommend the use of a reply in debt cases. If the defendant states in his defence that he has paid the whole of the money claimed, the claimant must file a reply. If he fails to do so within three months of the filing of the defence, the claim will be deemed to be struck out (although the claimant may apply for the position to be restored under the general rules about relief from sanctions).

Amendments to statements of case

19. It will be possible for the claimant to amend his statement of case after service once, without leave, and for the defendant to amend his defence once without leave.

Service of documents

20. The machinery for the service of documents relating to court proceedings is of fundamental importance in ensuring that justice is achieved, since it is the means by which parties are notified of claims against them and put in a position to respond. Furthermore, if the court is to take steps in proceedings on the assumption that a party has been properly served, it too must have confidence in the reliability of the methods used. In order to achieve these purposes, it follows that the system for service must be reasonably reliable in bringing knowledge of court process to the attention of those whom it may affect. For this reason, rules of court have tended to restrict permissible methods of service. This is true of both the Rules of the Supreme Court (RSC) and County Court Rules (CCR). Indeed, the RSC are drafted in a way which still reflects the former emphasis on the primacy of personal service, ie, physical service directly on the party concerned. (The RSC were changed only in 1979 to allow postal service.) In the county courts, service by first class post is also permitted and is overwhelmingly the normal method in use. This is the method used by the Summons Production Centre, which issues around 1,163,000 summonses each year, approximately 47 per cent of the county court total.

21. Other methods permitted by the rules include leaving the process at a party's address, and service on a solicitor if he has authority to accept service on behalf of his client. The rules provide that the court can also direct service by a method not expressly sanctioned by the rules ('substituted service'). If necessary, it can order service to be dispensed with entirely.

22. There are differences between the practice in the High Court and in county courts. In the former, once the court has formally issued the process by sealing it, it is the initiating party's responsibility to serve it. The court itself does not serve any process. In the county courts, the norm is for the court itself to serve the process by first class post. Indeed, in many cases, the county court itself prepares the formal process from particulars provided by the claimant, though there is now provision for claimants themselves to prepare process ready for issue. In personal injury cases only, the claimant may serve the claim himself.

23. The basic methods allowed for the service of originating process and other documents are the same, but there are some variations. When originating process is served by first class post, it is deemed to have been served seven days after posting. For other documents, the 'ordinary course of post' rule of the Interpretation Act 1978 is applied; this is treated in practice as meaning two days after posting by first class post and four days for second class post. Originating process may not be served by FAX or through a document exchange.

Proposals for change

24. The recommendations which follow relate only to service of domestic court process in this country. The final version of the rules will deal with service of foreign process in this country and with service abroad of domestic process but those matters are not considered in this report.

25. In principle, there should be no restriction on the methods by which documents can be served. Before any procedural step which depends on proper service of a document can take place, the court would have to be satisfied that the method used either had put the recipient in a position to ascertain its contents or was reasonably likely to enable him to do so within any relevant time period. (I refer to putting the recipient in a position to ascertain a document's contents to deal with situations where the recipient deliberately avoids informing himself.)

26. Subject to this, there would be two 'standard' methods of service: first class post and service on a solicitor who intimates that he has instructions to accept service. Use of either of these methods would involve a lighter burden of proof of service, for example, when it comes to entering judgment for failure to defend ('default judgment'), the commonest situation where proof of service is relevant. Service by first class post would have to be to the appropriate address specified by the rules, for example, the residential address of an individual or, in the case of a business, an office or place of business connected with the dispute. I treat first class post as a standard method because it is estimated to be the most commonly used method of service; it is cheap and generally effective. Accordingly, therefore, the burden of proving service should be a light one. As now, it will consist effectively of no more than an assertion that first class post had been used, that the document has not been returned through the post and that it is reasonably likely that the recipient would be in a position to ascertain the document's contents.

27. Service on a solicitor who intimates that he can accept service speaks for itself in terms of reliability and proof.

28. By contrast, the use of all other methods of service would require the serving party to state what method he had used, the date of service and why it was expected to be effective. So parties would be free to choose other methods, but there would be an advantage in using the primary methods.

29. I also recommend that a party should be free in all cases to choose to serve process himself. The amount of costs allowed for service should be very low to reflect the fact that, if the court were serving the document, it would use first class post and that it is reasonable in most cases to expect the party himself to use that method.

30. Where a party does not wish to serve the document, the only method which the court would use is first class post. This means that, in the county courts, the option of bailiff service, which is already restricted to situations where other methods of service have failed, would no longer be available.

Summary judgment

31. In the interim report I explained that the important purposes of case management are stopping weak cases from dragging on and reducing complexity and cost by eliminating issues as the case proceeds. One means of achieving these purposes is for the court to exercise its power of summary disposal on a wider basis than it does at present.

32. In the interim report I recommended a single procedure for summary disposal, applying a single test for its exercise. The single procedure would replace existing, separate procedures which currently allow:

(a)   summary judgment on the application of the plaintiff;

(b)   summary determination of a point of law;

(c)   striking out pleadings which disclose no cause of action on the defendant's application.

33. The new procedure in effect merges several different procedures into one. It thus conforms with my overall approach of integrating and harmonising rules and procedures wherever possible.

34. The procedure would be available on the application of any party or of the court's own volition. The test for making an order would be that the court considered that a party had no realistic prospect of succeeding at trial on the whole case or on a particular issue. A party seeking to resist such an order would have to show more than a merely arguable case; it would have to be one which he had a real prospect of winning. Exceptionally the court could allow a case or an issue to continue although it did not satisfy this test, if it considered that there was a public interest in the matter being tried.

35. The procedure would be available from the beginning of the case: for example, a claimant could issue an application at the same time as he served his statement of case while a defendant could apply even before he had filed a defence in a suitable case. Although parties would be expected to make an appropriate application as early as they reasonably could, the procedure would be available throughout the proceedings, up to and including the trial. Whenever it had occasion to consider the case, the court would have to ask itself the question: "Can the case or part of it be disposed of without the full apparatus of trial?"

36. The procedure will be flexible: the court could require oral evidence as well as written statements if it considered that it could dispose of the case more economically than at a full trial.

Disclosure of documents

37. In chapter 21 of the interim report, I discussed the need to curtail the process for discovery of documents (which I now recommend should be called 'disclosure'). I said that the process had become disproportionate, especially in larger cases where large numbers of documents may have to be searched for and disclosed, though only a small number turn out to be significant. Nevertheless, I considered that disclosure contributes to the just resolution of disputes and should therefore be retained, but in a more limited form.

38. My recommended solution involved the identification of four categories of documents which at present have to be disclosed. These are:

(1)   the parties' own documents, which they rely upon in support of their contentions in the proceedings;

(2)   adverse documents of which a party is aware and which to a material extent adversely affect his own case or support another party's case;

(3)   documents which do not fall within categories (1) or (2) but are part of the 'story' or background, including documents which, though relevant, may not be necessary for the fair disposal of the case;

(4)   train of inquiry documents: these are documents which may lead to a train of inquiry enabling a party to advance his own case or damage that of his opponent.

39. In fast track cases, the basic duty of disclosure, ie, that which would arise by virtue of standard case management directions given by the court, will be limited to categories (1) and (2) ('standard disclosure'). Indeed that will normally be the limit on fast track disclosure in any event, though I do not rule out the possibility of the court allowing what I called 'extra disclosure' (categories (3) and (4)) in an exceptional case. On the multi-track, the initial obligation will also be to make standard disclosure only.

40. Extra disclosure will be by court order only. I should make it clear that it will also be possible to apply for disclosure of documents in categories (1) or (2) which should have been included in standard disclosure. When ordering extra disclosure, the court would have to be satisfied not only that it was necessary to do justice but that the cost of such disclosure would not be disproportionate to the benefit and that a party's ability to continue the litigation would not be impaired by an order for specific disclosure against him.

41. It is no use, however, limiting the categories of document which a party has to disclose if he still has to search through all his documents to identify those in categories (1) and (2). I therefore recommended that initial disclosure should apply only to relevant documents of which a party is aware at the time when the obligation to disclose arises. I recognise that this is the most difficult aspect of my proposals in practice. The test of awareness is particularly problematic where the disclosing party is not an individual; in a company, firm or other organisation, it is likely that a number of people will have known about relevant documents. My proposal here is that there should be an obligation for the organisation to nominate a supervising officer whose task would be to identify individuals within the organisation who were likely to recollect relevant documents. On the basis of their combined recollections, documents would be extracted and disclosed (subject to any claim of privilege). When it made its list of documents in accordance with rules of court, the company, etc, would also include a statement of the identity and status of the supervising officer and those whose recollections he had canvassed. This would assist the other party to make an appropriate application for specific discovery if he thought that inquiries should reasonably have been made of some additional person or department in the organisation.

42. I am not recommending that the supervising officer should have to pursue his inquiry with former employees of the organisation who have had knowledge of relevant documents. In practice it would be impractical to enforce co-operation with such an inquiry. This is to be distinguished from the requirement, to which I recommend no substantive change, that a party must list documents which have been but are not currently in its possession. In some circumstances this may require a party to seek to obtain documents from an external source, such as a subsidiary company.

43. I received a number of responses to my original proposals. I can summarise these by saying that, while they all endorsed what I was trying to achieve in principle, all found objections to my proposals in practice. Among the arguments, it was suggested that my formulation would be easy to evade; that it would positively encourage parties to turn a blind eye to documents which might damage their case or at least would encourage a slapdash approach to disclosure; and that the line drawn by the test of awareness is artificial and unsatisfactory, depending as it does on the chance recollections of available individuals.

44. I have no doubt that these views are sincerely held. However, following this advice would mean making no recommendation to improve a state of affairs generally acknowledged to be unsatisfactory for domestic litigants and for the international competitiveness of the English legal system.

45. Discovery depends at present on the honesty and diligence of the parties. Withholding documents cannot necessarily be detected so the temptation to do this already exists; the facts of decided cases and comments which I have received confirm that it is not unknown in practice. It has to be recognised that the alternatives to my proposal would be to dispense with disclosure entirely (like the continental systems) or to limit initial disclosure to documents on which a party intended to rely. Both of these go too far; the latter would be inefficient because it would simply increase the volume of routine applications for disclosure. My proposal has the effect of preventing a party, if he acts reasonably honestly, from putting forward a case which he knows to be inconsistent with his own documents. It thus offers not a perfect, but a realistic, balance between keeping disclosure in check while enabling it still to contribute to the achievement of justice.

46. Despite its imperfections, I therefore have no doubt that a solution on the lines I have indicated is necessary and will bring about some improvement. If the principle of disclosure is to be retained at all, it is important not to make the non-existent ideal the enemy of the better-than-nothing solution. It should of course be kept in mind that standard disclosure can be supplemented by applications for specific disclosure; if it is apparent in a particular case that documents disclosed on such an application should plainly have been produced by way of standard disclosure, the court can impose appropriate sanctions.

Pre-action disclosure

47. An important part of my thinking is the need for parties to adopt a sensible and co-operative approach from the earliest stages at which a potential claim begins to materialise. As I have explained in chapter 10, key elements of this approach include early notification of claims coupled with sensible exchange of information. Chapter 10 describes the work which the Inquiry has initiated on pre-action protocols with a view to ensuring good practice before proceedings are ever initiated.

48. In support of this strategy, I recommend that parties should be able to make pre-action applications for disclosure against potential defendants in all cases. At present, the court's power to make such orders is confined to potential claims in respect of personal injury or death.

49. There may be some apprehension about the unforeseen consequences of such an extension. In relation to claims for injury or death, it was fairly clear against which categories of potential defendants such applications were likely to be made. When the jurisdiction to make pre-action orders was first introduced, applications for medical records tended to be hard-fought and often acrimonious. I understand that it is now rarely necessary even to make such applications, since documents are usually provided directly in response to a reasonable request. I have no doubt that the recent protocol prepared by the Civil Litigation Committee of the Law Society for use in this context will have helped further to simplify the process. This involves the use of standard forms of request and response, and has been approved by the NHS Management Executive.

50. Opening up the range of cases in which pre-action applications may be made obviously widens the range of potential defendants who might be subject to such applications. But it must be remembered, first, that any such application would have to be in respect of specific documents, which will have to be shown to be in the possession of the respondent; secondly, that there is a likelihood that the respondent would indeed be a defendant if proceedings were initiated; and, thirdly, that the documents sought are relevant to a potential claim. These requirements simply extend the provision currently made by statute and rules of court for injury cases. In my recommendations about disclosure generally, I have not explicitly proposed exclusion of category (3) and (4) documents from the scope of relevance, but I have made it clear that the court would apply a rigorous cost-benefit analysis when considering an application for such documents. It perhaps hardly needs saying that the court should apply the cost-benefit test to pre-action applications; I believe that its effect would be that the court would invariably not allow disclosure of category (3) or (4) documents at a stage when issues had not been fully elaborated between the parties. On this basis, I believe that the proposed extension of the jurisdiction is justified.

51. In relation to claims in respect of personal injury or death, I recommend a further, specific extension of the court's jurisdiction. At present in such cases, the court may order disclosure of documents:

(a) before proceedings, against a potential defendant; and

(b) once proceedings have begun, against any non-party.

52. There are often circumstances in which a prospective claimant needs documents - usually medical records - from health providers other than the prospective defendant. Not infrequently, such documents are provided on a voluntary basis. However, where access is refused, there are difficulties. The claimant may have to issue proceedings prematurely in order to be able to seek disclosure from the third party. This is a waste of resources, in particular, of public health service resources. It not infrequently results, for example, in an expert's report having to be modified in the light of documents which only become available much later. I therefore recommend, for claims in respect of personal injury or death only, a limited extension of the court's power, so that it may order a third party to disclose documents before proceedings have begun, whether or not it is intended to join them as a defendant. The criteria for making such an order would otherwise be the same as for an application against a potential defendant. Without experience of how the power would work in relation to the limited category of personal injury and death claims, I would not put it forward on a wider basis.

Witness statements

53. In fact-based disputes, it is now a standard requirement, laid down in rules of court, that a party who intends to adduce factual evidence at trial must provide the other parties with a written statement in advance of the evidence which the witness is expected to give. It has also now become standard practice, especially since the practice direction issued jointly by the Lord Chief Justice and the Vice-Chancellor in January 1995, for such witness statements to stand as the evidence in chief of the relevant witness. In chapter 22 of the interim report, I described the problems which have begun to beset what should have been a very useful procedural development. Indeed, despite the problems which have emerged, nobody has suggested to me that the principle of openness on which the use of witness statements is founded is wrong and that their use should be discontinued. 'Cards on the table' is universally accepted as the proper approach to conducting litigation.

54. Nevertheless, the problem which I noted in the interim report is a serious one. Witness statements have ceased to be the authentic account of the lay witness; instead they have become an elaborate, costly branch of legal drafting. Although the general view of judges appears to be that the use of witness statements shortens trial time, the great majority of cases do not go to trial: the costs of preparation are incurred in all cases but the savings of trial time in only a few.

55. Part of the problem lies in the fear that a witness will not be permitted to depart from or amplify his statement at the trial itself. Whether or not this fear is well-founded, it has led to the elaborate over-drafting which I described in the interim report, with a view to ensuring that the witness statement is complete in every detail.

56. To tackle this, I recommended in the interim report that judges should be flexible in allowing a witness to amplify what he has said in a witness summary or a witness statement. Many judges are no doubt flexible in allowing witnesses to depart from the letter of their statements where it is reasonable to do so. A number of judges have commented that it is in any event helpful to them to hear the witness give evidence in his or her own words before coming under the pressure of cross-examination. It also helps to put the witness at ease. I would not quarrel with this, so long as the overall need for economy is kept in mind, especially on the fast track.

57. The new rules will provide that the court can allow evidence which has not been foreshadowed by a witness statement to be given at trial where admitting the evidence will not cause any other party injustice. It should be noted that, in the light of the overriding objective at the start of the new rules, additional expense to a party caused by a late, unjustified change of tack by his opponent can be regarded as a potential aspect of injustice. Departing from present assumptions, however, this type of prejudice should not be regarded as remediable simply by an order for costs. There may accordingly be cases where the court has to refuse to allow the additional evidence to be given.

58. If the courts are flexible about allowing a reasonable degree of amplification of witness statements at trial, then they can expect the lawyers to be less concerned to draft absolutely comprehensive statements. This is not to be taken as encouragement deliberately to omit relevant material, but simply to rein back the excessive effort now devoted to gilding the lily. In the interim report, I recommended that courts should disallow costs where they thought the drafting of witness statements had been disproportionate. Trial judges, and to some extent procedural judges, will need to make a real effort, especially in the early phase of the new system, to scrutinise witness statements rigorously. This is the only way in which they will be able to pinpoint repetitious or inappropriate material, such as purported legal argument or analysis of documents. This is a fault which must in the main be attributed to the legal profession and not to its clients; wasted costs orders may therefore be appropriate in some instances of grossly overdone drafting. Only if the legal profession is convinced by demonstration that it has an active judicial critic over its shoulder will it be persuaded to change its drafting habits.

59. In connection with this change of approach, I make the following recommendations about the content and form of witness statements:

(a)   witness statements should, so far as possible, be in the witness's own words;

(b)   they should not discuss legal propositions;

(c)   they should not comment on documents;

(d)   they should conclude with a statement, signed by the witness, that the evidence is a true statement and that it is in his own words.

60. When the Civil Evidence Act 1995 is brought into force, hearsay evidence will become admissible, with only a minimum of formality required to identify it. The lawyers' present task of editing a witness statement so as to remove hearsay will become unnecessary, thus saving cost. Since a witness statement will in future be able to refer to matters beyond the direct knowledge or observation of the witness, the statement should indicate, where appropriate, the sources of knowledge, belief or information on which the witness himself is relying. In this respect the difference between witness statements and affidavits will diminish.

Representation of companies

61. At present a company has no right to represent itself in proceedings in the High Court or in the county courts. It may do so only at the court's discretion. County courts commonly, though not invariably, exercise the discretion in favour of companies; the High Court will almost never do so. I make recommendations below to extend a company's ability to represent itself.

62. I have received numerous representations about the inconvenience and additional expense which the present restrictions impose. They are particularly irksome in relation to routine procedural steps, such as an application to register a county court judgment for enforcement in the High Court. Steps such as these require no special skills. This has not gone without comment by the courts. The Court of Appeal, in *Jonathan Alexander Ltd v Proctor,* [1996] 2 All ER 334, held that a company representing itself should be entitled to the same costs as a litigant in person.

63. The rationale of the limitations on company representation is unclear. It is true that a company, being a legal and not a physical entity, cannot physically 'appear' in court. It follows, as the Court of Appeal confirmed in *Alexander v Proctor*, that a company cannot be a litigant in person. On the other hand, an officer or employee of a company, not being the litigant in person either, is prevented (except at the discretion of the court) from acting as a representative because he does not qualify under Part II of the Courts and Legal Services Act 1990.

64. A justification which is put forward for the present restriction is that it is simply the consequence of a company's limited liability. Directors cannot have it both ways by saying that the company has a separate legal personality but that they can act for it in person. To my mind that is not a sufficient answer. Incorporation is intended to provide public as well as private benefits. If it contains features which are burdensome to companies but which are not obviously justifiable in the public interest, then those features should be re-examined.

65. What are the arguments against allowing companies to represent themselves? First, it would mean in effect that the courts would have to deal with more litigants in person. However, unlike the position in some continental countries, it has never been the policy here to oblige litigants to employ professional lawyers to represent them in the courts. I cannot, therefore, see a basis in principle for distinguishing the treatment of companies in this respect. Despite the undoubted difficulties which the policy of openness can create for the courts, I believe that it is desirable to maintain this tradition. In the interim report, I made recommendations for improved advice facilities for litigants in person, and these would also help the courts. Small companies may also need assistance, though not exactly the same kind as individuals. If companies are to have a wider facility to represent themselves, bodies representing their interests may wish to consider how guidance and advice might be provided. In line with my general approach, any such guidance should include guidance on the availability of ADR.

66. A second objection is that company employees are not subject to the same duty to the court or to the same professional discipline as solicitors. But they are in no different position from litigants in person. Under my proposals, the court will certainly have sanctions (if it does not already have them) to prevent abuse and maintain case progress. In addition, I see no difficulty in a company being held liable for the defaults of its duly authorised representative. There has been a suggestion that, in certain circumstances, the representative as well as the company could be joined as a party in order to make him more directly amenable to sanctions. I believe that such a step would normally not be necessary.

67. Thirdly, it is argued that a representative may not be genuinely representing the interests of the company but may be exploiting it. As a general rule, I would require a representative to show due authorisation to act from the company. I recognise that this does not deal with the situation where the representative effectively controls the company and is acting contrary to its interests. If that fact became apparent, then I believe that the court would have power under its inherent jurisdiction to refuse to allow the misbehaving representative to continue in that capacity. The company would then either have to obtain professional representation or discontinue the proceedings.

68. Finally, it may be argued that allowing company employees rights to litigate and to act as advocates cuts across the regime for approving litigators and advocates established under the Courts and Legal Services Act 1990. Such a change would either enable in-house lawyers to do what they are not at present able to do under that regime or make them worse off than their non-lawyer colleagues. My answer in principle would be that, if it is right that companies should be allowed to represent themselves, then the identity of the representative is immaterial, subject to the conditions which I have already indicated. So long as the position of in-house lawyers remains as it is under the 1990 Act, those representing companies would be treated as lay representatives; they would not have the status of lawyers though, as I have explained, their acts would bind the company; they would be subject where appropriate to the court's sanctions and the company itself would be liable to be penalised for their misbehaviour.

69. It is not the case that all companies are uniformly better able to afford representation than individual litigants. We have a huge number of very small companies in this country, for whom the potential costs of litigation (especially under the present arrangements) are daunting and burdensome. It is for this reason that those representing the interests of small businesses in particular have welcomed my proposals for the fast track. Legal aid is generally not available to companies. Under the existing legislation, they are unlikely to be able to take advantage of conditional fee arrangements unless they are insolvent. By no means all steps in proceedings require professional legal skills. In certain areas of work, such as debt recovery and small claims, company employees regularly involved may become as competent as any solicitor. Furthermore, a company is more likely than an individual to be capable of judging when professional help is needed, assuming it is affordable.

70. Companies are at present frequently represented by their employees in county court proceedings, subject to the court's discretion. It has not been suggested that this has harmed the administration of justice. The objections to a right of self-representation need to be weighed against that fact. This would not be a leap in the dark. At the same time, I recognise that it would be desirable on the whole not to move too far away from the regime established under Part II of the Courts and Legal Services Act for extending rights of advocacy and representation.

71. I therefore recommend that rules of court should no longer require a company to act by a solicitor and that, subject to the court's discretion, a duly authorised employee of a company should normally be permitted to take any steps on behalf of the company which a litigant in person could take on his own behalf in High Court and county court proceedings. Exercise of the facility would be subject to the court being satisfied that the representative was duly authorised to act and to the right of the court to stop any advocate who misbehaves from addressing it. In effect I am recommending that the discretion to allow companies to represent themselves should be exercised on county court lines as opposed to High Court lines. To ensure that the discretion is exercised in a consistent and reasonable way, I also recommend that the Head of Civil Justice should set out in a practice direction the considerations which would be relevant to the court's decision. It should normally be possible for a company which is acting reasonably to be confident in advance that it will be able to act on its own behalf.

72. The question was raised in *Alexander v Proctor* whether companies should be entitled to the same costs as litigants in person. My recommendation about this is a provisional one, since I believe that the matter needs further consideration. A company has potentially more scope for incurring time-based costs on a scale which most individual litigants would be unlikely to approach. The fact that unreasonable costs could be reduced on taxation is not a complete answer. It would not be desirable to encourage companies to set up informal litigation operations in larger cases where they would be better advised to seek professional help. However, on the fast track, I am recommending that the costs recoverable by litigants in person, like those of solicitors, should be capped (see chapter 4). In cases on the multi-track, I am recommending (chapter 7, paragraphs 35–37) that the courts should develop an approach to limiting costs, at least in the more standard cases. These limitations would also apply to a company representing itself. I therefore consider that it is reasonable in principle to allow companies the same costs in those cases as litigants in person. This will be subject to the general review of litigant in person costs which I am recommending.

Recommendations

My recommendations are as follows.

(1)   It will usually be possible to start proceedings in any High Court district registry or county court. Claims for possession of land will be an exception, being brought in the court where the relevant land is situated. It will normally not be possible to bring claims worth £50,000 or less in the Royal Courts of Justice in London. The commencement of proceedings in the wrong court will not nullify them.

(2)   All claims should be started on a single claim form with appropriate variations.

(3)   The defendant will be required to complete a notice of intention to defend, within 14 days of service of the claim, and the period for filing a defence will be 28 days, unless the parties agree to extend it.

(4) In debt cases the claimant must file a reply if the defendant's defence is that he has paid the whole of the money claimed. In other cases it will be possible for the claimant to file a reply without the leave of the court, before any initial case management conference.

(5) One amendment of the claim, after service, and one amendment of the defence will be allowed without leave.

(6) In principle there should be no restriction on the methods by which court process can be served. Instead the court will have to be satisfied that the method used had either put the recipient in a position to ascertain the document's contents or was reasonably likely to enable him to do so.

(7) Service by first class post and service on a solicitor will be the 'standard' method of service, with a simpler burden of proving service than other methods. A party who uses another method will have to describe the method, the date of service and why the method was expected to be effective.

(8) A party should be free in all cases to serve process himself.

(9) The test for summary judgment would be that there was no realistic prospect of success at trial. Exceptionally, notwithstanding that the test was satisfied, the court could allow a case or issue to continue if it considered there was a public interest in the matter being tried.

(10) Summary judgment would be available at all stages of a case up to judgment.

(11) The test for documents to be initially disclosed is whether a party is aware of those documents at the time when the obligation to disclose arises. In the case of a company, 'awareness' will be that of individual employees with relevant knowledge. A company will be required to appoint a supervising officer to identify such individuals.

(12) A potential claimant in proceedings for injury or death should be able to make a pre-action application for disclosure against a person who is not expected to be a defendant.

(13) Pre-action applications for disclosure will have to be in respect of specified documents which will be relevant to a potential claim; the court must be satisfied that the benefit of allowing such disclosure will outweigh any cost and inconvenience to the disclosing party.

(14) Witness statements should:

    (a) so far as possible, be in the witness's own words;

    (b) not discuss legal propositions;

    (c) not comment on documents;

    (d) conclude with a signed statement by the witness that the evidence is a true statement and that it is in his own words.

(15) When the Civil Evidence Act 1995 is in force, allowing a witness statement to refer to matters beyond the direct knowledge or observation of the witness, the statement should indicate where appropriate the sources of knowledge, belief or information on which the witness relies.

(16) Especially on the fast track, witness statements should be concise.

(17) Rules of court should no longer require a company to act by a solicitor.

(18) The court should normally exercise its discretion in favour of allowing an employee of a company to take any steps on behalf of the company which a litigant in person could take in High Court or county court proceedings.

(19) The employee would have to show, if required, that he was duly authorised to act by the company.

(20) A practice direction should indicate the considerations relevant to the exercise of the court's discretion.

Chapter 13   Expert Evidence

Introduction

1.   It was a basic contention of my interim report that two of the major generators of unnecessary cost in civil litigation were uncontrolled discovery and expert evidence. No-one has seriously challenged that contention.

2.   A large litigation support industry, generating a multi-million pound fee income, has grown up among professions such as accountants, architects and others, and new professions have developed such as accident reconstruction and care experts. This goes against all principles of proportionality and access to justice. In my view, its most damaging effect is that it has created an ethos of what is acceptable which has in turn filtered down to smaller cases. Many potential litigants do not even start litigation because of the advice they are given about cost, and in my view this is as great a social ill as the actual cost of pursuing litigation.

3.   It was to meet these concerns that, in chapter 23 of the interim report, I recommended that the calling of expert evidence should be under the complete control of the court. Within that framework, I argued for a wider use of 'single' or 'neutral' experts who would be jointly selected and instructed by the parties, or, if the parties could not agree on a single expert, appointed by the court. I also put forward a number of other recommendations designed to achieve a more economical use of expert evidence in cases where opposing experts were involved, by narrowing the issues between them as early as possible.

4.   In the second stage of the Inquiry I issued an issues paper on expert evidence, in which I reviewed the approach adopted in the interim report and its underlying objectives, and sought views as to the best way in which arrangements for experts could be improved to meet my overall aims. In particular, I invited responses from those with experience of the use of expert evidence in areas of litigation which were not considered in any detail in the interim report, such as intellectual property, housing, and construction cases, as well as of expert evidence in personal injury which was my main focus of attention in the interim report.

5.   There is widespread agreement with the criticisms I made in the interim report of the way in which expert evidence is used at present, especially the point that experts sometimes take on the role of partisan advocates instead of neutral fact finders or opinion givers. My detailed proposals on experts, however, have provoked more opposition than any of my other recommendations. Most respondents favour retaining the full-scale adversarial use of expert evidence, and resist proposals for wider use of single experts (whether court-appointed or jointly appointed by the parties) and for disclosure of communications between experts and their instructing lawyers.

Expert evidence within an adversarial framework

6. In the interim report I made it clear, in general terms, that I wanted to retain what was best in the English adversarial system. Any substantial curtailment of the parties' rights to adduce the expert evidence of their choice would certainly be a significant move away from the adversarial tradition. For that reason alone, many contributors to the Inquiry regard it as unacceptable. My concern, however, is with access to justice, and hence with reductions in cost, delay and complexity. The argument for the universal application of the full, 'red-blooded' adversarial approach is appropriate only if questions of cost and time are put aside. The present system works well for lawyers and judges, but ordinary people are being kept out of litigation. Where commercial litigants are concerned, the English courts are becoming uncompetitive because of unacceptable cost and delay.

7. The purpose of the adversarial system is to achieve just results. All too often it is used by one party or the other to achieve something which is inconsistent with justice by taking advantage of the other side's lack of resources or ignorance of relevant facts or opinions. Expert evidence is one of the principal weapons used by litigators who adopt this approach. The present system allows them to withhold from their opponents material which may be damaging to their own case or advantageous to their opponents'. This practice of non-disclosure cannot be justified, because it inevitably leads to unnecessary cost and delay, and in some cases to an unfair result.

8. The traditional English way of deciding contentious expert issues is for a judge to decide between two contrary views. This is not necessarily the best way of achieving a just result. The judge may not be sure that either side is right, especially if the issues are very technical or fall within an area in which he himself has no expertise. Nevertheless, he hopes to arrive at the right answer. Whether consciously or not, his decision may be influenced by factors such as the apparently greater authority of one side's expert, or the experts' relative fluency and persuasiveness in putting across their arguments.

9. In continental jurisdictions where neutral, court-appointed experts are the norm, there is an underlying assumption that parties' experts will tell the court only what the parties want the court to know. For the judge in an inquisitorial system, the main problem is that it may be difficult for him to know whether or not to accept a single expert's view. There is no suggestion, however, that he is inevitably less likely to reach the right answer than his English counterpart.

10. Less adversarial forms of dispute resolution are not, in any event, completely alien to our tradition. The various Ombudsman schemes have for a number of years provided a valuable service based on an impartial investigation by a neutral third party. Within the court system itself there are precedents for limiting the scope of expert evidence, in particular in the Family Division, where no expert evidence may be adduced without leave of the court and there is considerable emphasis on use of single experts.

Court control of expert evidence: a flexible approach

11. The basic premise of my new approach is that the expert's function is to assist the court. There should be no expert evidence at all unless it will help the court, and no more than one expert in any one speciality unless this is necessary for some real purpose.

12. I do not recommend a uniform solution, such as a court-appointed expert, for all cases. My overall objective is to try, from the start, to foster an approach to expert evidence which emphasises the expert's duty to help the court impartially on matters within his expertise, and encourage a more focused use of expert evidence by a variety of means. We should avoid mounting a contest between opposing experts where justice (in the widest sense) can be achieved between the parties without it. The key to achieving this is flexibility: above the fast track, there is no single answer that would apply to all cases.

13. Under the system of case management which I proposed in the interim report, the court will have complete control over the use of evidence, including expert evidence. The new rules will say that no expert evidence may be adduced without the leave of the court, which may be given as part of its own directions or specifically on application. There will be a range of options which the court will have a discretion to apply according to the type of case, or to the circumstances of an individual case. The options for limiting the scope of expert evidence will be:

(a)   directing that no expert evidence is to be adduced at all, or no expert evidence of a particular type or relating to a particular issue;

(b)   limiting the number of expert witnesses per party, either generally or in a given speciality;

(c)   directing that evidence is to be given by one or more experts chosen by agreement between the parties or appointed by the court (this will extend the court's existing power under RSC Order 40, which permits the appointment of a court expert only on application by one of the parties);

(d)   requiring expert evidence to be given in written form without the expert's attendance at court.

14. In cases where opposing experts are involved, the court already has power to direct the parties' experts to meet, before or after the experts have disclosed their reports, so as to identify and reduce areas of difference. Under the new rules the experts will be required (not simply authorised, as at present) to produce a report identifying matters agreed and outstanding areas of difference after such a meeting.

15. In fast track cases the exercise of the court's discretion will be more restricted. For the vast majority of cases falling within the financial limits of the track (that is, cases up to £10,000) the principle of proportionality of cost dictates that the scope of expert evidence must be limited. The rules on expert evidence on the fast track will therefore limit the parties generally to one expert per side in any single speciality (with an overall limit of two per side) with no oral evidence. Single experts will be used wherever possible. These proposals are explained in greater detail in chapter 3.

Single experts

16. Since the publication of the interim report, resistance to my proposals on single experts has remained particularly strong, and it is clear that the idea is anathema to many members of the legal profession in this country who are reluctant to give up their adversarial weapons.

17. It needs to be understood that a neutral expert, under the system I am proposing, would still function within a broadly adversarial framework. Wherever possible, the expert would be chosen by agreement between the parties, not imposed by the court. Whether appointed by the parties or by the court, he or she would act on instructions from the parties.

The appointment of a neutral expert would not necessarily deprive the parties of the right to cross-examine, or even to call their own experts in addition to the neutral expert if that were justified by the scale of the case. Anyone who gives expert evidence must know that he or she is at risk of being subjected to adversarial procedures, including vigorous cross-examination. This is an essential safeguard to ensure the quality and reliability of evidence.

18. The consultation process I have carried out has, at least, revealed a measure of agreement that single experts would be acceptable in certain types of cases or in certain limited circumstances, particularly on issues of quantum. Acceptance of a single expert on liability issues is generally limited to cases where the amount in issue is very small, or where there is little scope for disagreement. This is a helpful start, but without further measures it is unlikely to have any significant impact on cost.

19. I do not think it would be appropriate to specify particular areas of litigation where a single expert should or should not be used. There are in all areas some large, complex and strongly contested cases where the full adversarial system, including oral cross-examination of opposing experts on particular issues, is the best way of producing a just result. That will apply particularly to issues on which there are several tenable schools of thought, or where the boundaries of knowledge are being extended. It does not, however, apply to all cases. As a general principle, I believe that single experts should be used wherever the case (or the issue) is concerned with a substantially established area of knowledge and where it is not necessary for the court directly to sample a range of opinions. The expert's duty to the court will require him to set out in his report his view of the range of possible opinions. Too often under the present regime the experts are in fact agreed upon the range of opinion, but their reports only set out the extreme positions.

20. Given the strength of opposition to my proposals, it would not be realistic to expect a significant shift towards single experts in the short term. What is needed to initiate such a shift is a clear statement of principle in the rules, coupled with procedures to ensure that parties and procedural judges always consider whether a single expert could be appointed in a particular case (or to deal with a particular issue); and, if this is not considered appropriate, that they indicate why not.

21. A single expert is much more likely to be impartial than a party's expert can be. Appointing a single expert is likely to save time and money, and to increase the prospects of settlement. It may also be an effective way of levelling the playing field between parties of unequal resources. These are significant advantages, and there would need to be compelling reasons for not taking them up. It is certainly not sufficient to say that a party is entitled to adduce separate expert evidence provided he is willing to pay for it.

22. It has been suggested to me that by the stage at which case management starts, it will be too late for the court to control the scope of expert evidence because parties will already have appointed their own experts. There are of course circumstances in which a party will need to consult an expert before proceedings have started, sometimes even before legal action is in contemplation. It does not, however, follow that each party is entitled to rely on its own expert evidence for the purposes of litigation. Once litigation appears likely, the use of experts will be subject to different considerations: impartiality is of paramount importance, and because of the costs shifting rule, parties need to be protected against the extravagant use of experts by their opponents.

23. The use of experts before litigation has started cannot be directly controlled by the courts, but pre-action protocols of the kind that I am recommending in chapter 10 can help to encourage the parties to agree on a single expert. Failure to comply with the protocol should normally have consequences in costs. There will of course be cases where either party would be justified in not adhering to the protocol requirements, especially in relation to experts on liability rather than quantum, but the onus will be on the party to justify his decision.

24. I have said that in some cases there are good reasons for each side to appoint its own expert or experts. That need not, however, preclude a co-operative approach between the opposing experts, which should ideally start as soon as they are instructed. It should wherever possible include a joint investigation and a single report, indicating areas of disagreement where these cannot be resolved.

Impartiality

25. There is wide agreement that the expert's role should be that of an independent adviser to the court, and that lack of objectivity can be a serious problem. This may sometimes arise because of improper pressure on experts from solicitors, as was found in a survey of clinical and educational psychologists, the results of which were reported in the May 1996 issue of *The Psychologist.*

26. The present system has the effect of exaggerating the adversarial role of experts, and this helps neither the court nor the parties. As the Court of Appeal has recently remarked:

> "For whatever reason, and whether consciously or unconsciously, the fact is that expert witnesses instructed on behalf of parties to litigation often tend . . . to espouse the cause of those instructing them to a greater or lesser extent, on occasion becoming more partisan than the parties." *(Abbey National Mortgages plc v Key Surveyors Nationwide Ltd and others* [1996] EGCS 23)

27. The clear implication of this is that a new approach is required which emphasises experts' impartiality. In cases where the option of a single expert is not pursued, it is particularly important that each opposing expert's overriding duty to the court is clearly understood. This is partly a matter of good practice on the part of instructing solicitors, who may themselves need guidance as to the appropriate form of instructions to experts. In my view, clarification in the rules of court is also needed.

28. Contributions to the Inquiry from experts themselves suggest that there is a degree of uncertainty among them as to their duties, and a perceived conflict between their professional responsibilities and the demands of the client who is paying their fee. Experts would welcome some formal recognition of their role as advisers to the court rather than advocates of the parties.

29. The rules will provide that when an expert is preparing evidence for potential use in court proceedings, or is giving evidence in court, his responsibility is to help the court impartially on the matters within his expertise. This responsibility will override any duty to the client. The rule will reaffirm the duty which the courts have laid down as a matter of law in a number of cases, notably *Whitehouse v Jordan,* [1981] 1 WLR 246, when Lord Wilberforce said:

"It is necessary that expert evidence presented to the court should be and should be seen to be the independent product of the expert uninfluenced as to form or content by the exigencies of litigation." (Cited by Cresswell J in *The 'Ikarian Reefer'* [1993] 2 Lloyds Reports 68).

30. There was wide support for the proposal in my interim report that an expert's report intended for use as evidence in court proceedings should be addressed to the court. I now propose that there should be a requirement to this effect in the rules of court to apply whenever litigation is contemplated. This is a formal but important requirement. It does not imply that the expert is to be instructed by the court, but is intended to concentrate the expert's mind as he writes the report on his paramount duty to the court.

31. One of the recommendations in my interim report was that, once an expert had been instructed to prepare a report for the use of a court, any communication between the expert and the client or his advisers should no longer be the subject of legal privilege. My intention was to prevent the suppression of relevant opinions or factual material which did not support the case put forward by the party instructing the expert. There is, I believe, no disagreement with that intention, but it has been put to me very strongly that waiver of legal privilege is not the way to achieve it. The point has been made that experts must be free to submit drafts to clients and their legal advisers, so that factual misconceptions can be corrected. A further objection is that a great deal of time could be wasted if all these documents were disclosable, because the opposing party would have to comb through the various versions of a report to identify any changes, the reasons for which would not always be clear in any event. Another possibility is that lawyers and experts might begin to subvert the system by avoiding written communication in favour of off the record conversations.

32. I accept, in the light of these arguments, that it would not be realistic to make draft experts' reports disclosable. I do not, however, consider that privilege should apply to the instructions given to experts. The Chancery Working Group has pointed out that major problems can arise when opposing experts are working from different instructions, which leads to reports that are hard to compare and use. Joint or agreed instructions would meet this specific point, but even a single expert's report may be unclear or open to misinterpretation unless the instructions on which it is based are known.

33. Under the new system, transparency of instructions to experts will be particularly important. The effectiveness of pre-action protocols will depend on it. On the fast track, in cases where there are diverging opinions in two reports, it will be absolutely essential for the parties and the judge to know the basis on which the experts have been instructed. I therefore recommend that expert evidence should not be admissible unless all written instructions (including letters subsequent upon the original instructions) and a note of any oral instructions are included as an annex to the expert's report.

34. A further recommendation in the interim report was that any expert's report prepared for the purpose of giving evidence to a court should end with a declaration that it includes everything which the expert regards as being relevant to the opinion which he has expressed in his report and that he has drawn to the attention of the court any matter which would affect the validity of that opinion. That recommendation was widely supported on consultation, and I have come to the conclusion that a declaration along the lines I have proposed, coupled with the requirement for instructions to be disclosed, should be sufficient to meet my concerns about the disclosure of all relevant material.

35. The Working Group on Intellectual Property has proposed a form of declaration which would include statements that the expert:

(a)   understands that his primary duty is to the court, both in preparing his report and in giving evidence;

(b)   has endeavoured in his report to be accurate and complete, and to mention all matters which he regards as being material to the opinions he has expressed;

(c)   has drawn the court's attention to any matter of which he is aware which might adversely affect the validity of his opinions;

(d)   has indicated the source of his factual information if he has based an opinion on facts of which he has no personal knowledge;

(e)   has not included anything in the report which has been suggested to him by anyone (including particularly his instructing lawyers) without forming his own independent view on the matter;

(f)   will notify his instructing lawyers immediately in writing if for any reason he considers that his existing report requires any correction or qualification; and, if the correction or qualification is significant, will prepare a supplementary report as soon as possible; and

(g)   understands that

    (i)   his report will form the evidence he will give under oath, subject to any corrections he may make before swearing as to its correctness;

    (ii)   he may be cross-examined on his report by a cross-examiner assisted by an expert; and

    (iii)   if the court concludes that he has not fairly tried to meet the standards set out in the declaration, he is likely to be the subject of public adverse criticism by the judge.

36. I should like to see added to this a statement that where there is a range of reasonable opinion, the expert has indicated the extent of that range in his report.

37. Some elements in the working group's suggested declaration may be controversial; in particular, it might be argued that a reference to the possibility of adverse criticism could deter competent experts from giving evidence. I believe, however, that the outline broadly sets out the points which should be included in an expert's declaration. It could usefully form the basis of discussion between the Law Society, the Academy of Experts and any other interested bodies, with a view to drawing up a standard declaration for use in experts' reports.

Access to evidence: inequality of resources

38. One of the fundamental principles of my approach to civil litigation is that there should, so far as possible, be a level playing field between litigants of unequal financial or other resources. A particular problem arises when one party, often the defendant or potential defendant, has an easily available source of expertise to which the other party does not have access. This happens, for example, in medical negligence, where a health authority or hospital trust can use its own doctors; or in actions against large companies with in-house technical experts. The potential claimant, on the other hand, may not even know whether he or she has a case worth pursuing without paying for an independent expert to carry out an investigation.

39. I suggested in the issues paper that one way of redressing this imbalance would be to introduce a new procedure enabling claimants to apply to the court (either before or after proceedings have started) for an order requiring the defendant to provide an in-house expert's report on a particular situation. It seemed to me that such a procedure would be particularly helpful to claimants who did not qualify for legal aid, although it could also save money for the legal aid fund. The provision of an in-house report would not prevent the opposing party from instructing his or her own expert at a later stage if it emerged that there was a case worth pursuing.

40. This proposal was generally opposed by respondents to the consultation paper. Prospective defendants considered it unfair, and claimants' representatives questioned whether an in-house report could be accepted as impartial and independent, because of the fear that an in-house expert would come under pressure to report in favour of the defendant. In the light of this reaction, I have considered whether there may be a more acceptable way of achieving my objective than a specific power to direct a prospective defendant to carry out investigations or tests.

41. I have concluded that the court should have a wide power, which could be exercised before the start of proceedings, to order that an examination or tests should be carried out in relation to any matter in issue, and a report submitted to the court. Any such order would indicate by whom the examination or tests were to be carried out, and at whose cost. This will cover a wider range of situations than I originally had in mind, and can be applied flexibly by the courts to meet particular circumstances.

Narrowing the issues: experts' meetings

42. Among the criticisms I made in my interim report was that the present system does not encourage narrowing of issues between opposing experts, or the elimination of peripheral issues. There has been widespread support for my suggestion that experts' meetings were a useful approach to narrowing the issues. In areas of litigation (such as Official Referees' business) where experts' meetings are already the usual practice, there is general agreement that they are helpful. In areas where they are not at present widely used, including medical negligence, the majority of respondents accept that they could be helpful. (This is not, however, the view of the Intellectual Property Working Group, which believes that sequential disclosure of reports may be a better way of narrowing the issues in some cases, or that each expert might usefully be asked to take the opposite side's report and underline the passages with which he or she disagrees.)

43. Two principal reservations have been expressed, even by those who support experts' meetings in principle. The first (mentioned in my interim report) is that meetings can be futile because the experts are instructed not to agree anything; or, alternatively, are told that any points of agreement must be referred back to their instructing lawyers for ratification. This subverts the judge's intention in directing the experts to meet, because the decision as to what to agree becomes a matter for the lawyers rather than the experts. I recommended in the interim report that it should be unprofessional conduct for an expert to be given or to accept instructions not to agree, and this has been widely supported.

44. On the basis of the consultation I have carried out, it is far from clear whether these are widespread problems, although there is certainly evidence that they do happen on occasions. The solution lies in a clear requirement that the experts must produce for the court, at the end of their meeting, a written list of agreed matters of professional opinion and issues still in dispute. It must be made clear that the discussion is to cover only matters within the experts' professional competence, and that it is for the parties and their legal advisers to consider the effect of any agreement or disagreement on the future conduct of the case.

45. At least in the heaviest cases where expert issues are likely to be most complex, the agenda for the experts' meeting should be set by the court. Narrowing the issues to be put before the court, including issues of expert opinion, is one of the fundamental purposes of the system of case management I have proposed. The procedural judge conducting a case management conference should not only direct an experts' meeting but define (with the help of the parties and their legal advisers) the subject matter to be covered.

46. The second reservation about the need for experts' meetings relates to cost. It is said that meetings are expensive to set up, especially if they are attended by the parties' legal advisers. My answer to this point is that, provided a clear agenda is set and the meeting is properly conducted, the investment, in the vast majority of cases, will be well worthwhile. Where the meeting does not lead directly to settlement, it will reduce the scope of further work on the case and either facilitate settlement at a later stage or ensure that the trial focuses on the essential issues. In any event, the net result should be a saving of costs.

47. It is also worth pointing out that, at least in the more straightforward cases, it may be possible to hold a 'meeting' by using telephone conferencing and video conferencing technologies, at less expense than bringing the experts physically together. The important point is that they communicate with each other.

48. It is important, too, that experts communicate at the earliest possible stage in the case, to establish that they are answering the same questions or addressing the same issues. A useful starting point for discussions between experts would be to prepare an agreed chronology and statement of facts, with a summary of important or disputed points. This should be done as soon as possible after submission of the defence, with a view to identifying non-contentious points from the outset so as to define the scope of the experts' reports. In some cases, the first meeting may be only after the exchange of experts' reports. At that stage, in any event, the reports themselves will provide a clear and agreed basis for the discussion.

49. In areas of litigation where the use of experts' meetings is well established, it seems to be accepted that there is no difficulty in allowing them to be conducted in private, with no-one present apart from the experts themselves. In other areas, it has been suggested that experts' meetings should take place only in the presence of the parties' lawyers, or of a neutral third party such as an independent lawyer or the procedural judge. In medical negligence, for example, it is thought that such an arrangement would be needed to overcome the traditional attitude of suspicion between the parties. In particular, it is said that private meetings between experts would not be acceptable to patients, because of the common perception that doctors 'hang together'.

50. In the majority of cases I see no reason why the experts should not meet alone, but I accept that there are circumstances in which this will not be appropriate. When the court directs a meeting, I suggest that the onus should be on the parties to apply for any special arrangements. In considering any such application, the court should bear in mind the expense of attendance by the parties' lawyers. When the lawyers do attend, it must also be made clear that they are present simply as observers to ensure fair play, and not to participate in the discussion or inhibit legitimate agreement between the experts.

51. Given the potential advantages, and the flexibility of the possible arrangements, it is difficult to see why there should not be at least one experts' meeting in all cases where opposing experts are involved. Certainly, I would not expect to see any substantial case come to trial under the new system without at least one such meeting having taken place.

Improving the quality of experts' reports

52. Since the publication of the interim report an appreciable level of concern has been expressed about the quality and reliability of experts' reports. This can relate to the problem of partisan reports which I have already discussed, or to the inclusion of irrelevant material, a tendency to stray beyond the expert's field of professional competence, or failure to address the real issues.

53. There are a number of ways of tackling these problems, of which training for experts is one. Some people would like to see a compulsory system of training and accreditation of experts in particular fields, along the lines of what is already provided by bodies such as the Academy of Experts. This would mean that only fully qualified and accredited experts would be permitted to appear before the courts or prepare reports for forensic use. (Special arrangements would have to be made to meet the situation in some areas of litigation such as intellectual property, where experts commonly act on a 'one-off' basis. For example, experts could be permitted to act in up to, say, three cases before accreditation was required.) Such a system would include the exercise of sanctions against experts who failed to meet the required standard.

54. I certainly support the provision of training for experts, both through attendance at courses and through the dissemination of published material such as the model form of expert's report which has been produced by the Academy of Experts. Professional people who take on responsibilities as expert witnesses need a basic understanding of the legal system and their role within it. They also need to be able to present their evidence effectively, both in written reports and orally under cross-examination. Training in presentational skills, however, should never lose sight of the fundamental point that the expert's duty is to assist the court. Otherwise it is not in the interests of justice because it may result in the truth being concealed.

55. I do not recommend an exclusive system of accreditation. Such a system could exclude potentially competent experts who choose for good reasons not to take it up. It might, in fact, narrow rather than widen the pool of available experts. It could foster an uncompetitive monopoly, and might encourage the development of 'professional experts' who were out of touch with current practice in their field of experience.

56. Another way of improving the quality of experts' reports is by ensuring that experts are given adequate instructions. From the comments

I have received on this point it appears that solicitors' instructions vary from detailed to perfunctory. "Please provide your usual report" is an example that has been mentioned to me, and it may well be that this is adequate for an experienced expert who is frequently instructed by the same solicitor. Many experts have, however, indicated that they would welcome more detailed and explicit instructions, and I have no doubt that solicitors would benefit from guidance in this area.

57. The Law Society has already published pro forma instructions in its *Directory of Experts*, and, jointly with the British Orthopaedic Association, a model letter of instruction to medical experts. A number of other initiatives which have begun in the course of the Inquiry will help to take this work forward under the new system. These include a working group set up by the ABI to develop a protocol for the instruction of experts, and an APIL/ABI working party on pre-action protocols for the fast track which has produced a model letter of instruction.

Expert assessors

58. In the interim report I recommended that the courts should make wider use of their powers to appoint expert assessors to assist the judge in complex litigation and, in appropriate cases, to preside over meetings between the parties' experts and help them to reach agreement.

59. There has been some resistance to these proposals, largely on the grounds that an assessor would usurp the role of the judge. I do not agree that this would necessarily be the case: where there are complex technical issues the assessor's function would be to 'educate' the judge to enable him to reach a properly informed decision. In the most complex cases this function could be performed by two assessors, one instructed by each party.

60. Clearly the use of an independent assessor in addition to the parties' experts and the judge will not be cost-effective except in the heaviest cases. In smaller cases, such as boundary disputes or complaints about domestic appliances, there may also be technical issues which are not agreed between the parties. In these circumstances I see no objection to appointing an independent expert as adjudicator. This may well be the most economical way of disposing of the case, and the result is no less likely to be satisfactory to the parties than a decision by a judge who has little or no expertise in the subject matter of the dispute. The county courts already have a power (albeit rarely used) to appoint outside arbitrators for small claims.

Recommendations

My main recommendations are as follows.

(1)   As a general principle, single experts should be used wherever the case (or the issue) is concerned with a substantially established area of knowledge and where it is not necessary for the court directly to sample a range of opinions.

(2)   Parties and procedural judges should always consider whether a single expert could be appointed in a particular case (or to deal with a particular issue); and, if this is not considered appropriate, indicate why not.

(3)   Where opposing experts are appointed they should adopt a co-operative approach. Wherever possible this should include a joint investigation and a single report, indicating areas of disagreement which cannot be resolved.

(4)   Expert evidence should not be admissible unless all written instructions (including letters subsequent upon the original instructions) and a note of any oral instructions are included as an annex to the expert's report.

(5)   The court should have a wide power, which could be exercised before the start of proceedings, to order that an examination or tests should be carried out in relation to any matter in issue, and a report submitted to the court.

(6)   Experts' meetings should normally be held in private. When the court directs a meeting, the parties should be able to apply for any special arrangements such as attendance by the parties' legal advisers.

(7)   Training courses and published material should provide expert witnesses with a basic understanding of the legal system and their role within it, focusing on the expert's duty to the court, and enable them to present written and oral evidence effectively. Training should not be compulsory.

Chapter 14   Appeals

Introduction

1.   An effective system for appeals is an essential part of a well-functioning system of civil justice. There can be no doubt about the importance of the availability of appeals to ensure that redress can be obtained for mistakes by a lower court, although it should be noted that international human rights instruments such as the European Convention on Human Rights and the International Covenant on Civil and Political Rights only guarantee the right to an appeal in criminal, and not in civil, proceedings. Save in exceptional cases, an individual who has grounds for dissatisfaction with the outcome of a case should in my view have at least the right to have his case looked at by a higher court, if only to consider whether to allow an appeal to proceed any further.

2.   Appeals serve two purposes: the private purpose, which is to do justice in particular cases by correcting wrong decisions, and the public purpose, which is to ensure public confidence in the administration of justice by making such corrections and to clarify and develop the law and to set precedents.

3.   These purposes must, nevertheless, be achieved without introducing unnecessary costs, delay and complexity. The principles set out in the first chapter of my interim report and in the overview of this report which must be met in order to ensure access to justice apply to appeals just as they do to hearings at first instance. So too do the methods of dealing with a case justly which will be set out in the new rules, among them expedition, proportionality, saving expense and assisting settlement.

4.   The problems of delay and cost are particularly relevant. There has always been the possibility of using appeals as a delaying tactic on occasions, but there is a real risk that numerous appeals could undermine the new system of case management by the court, especially in cases on the fast track, in which the fixed timetable will have a key role. The greater the number of important management decisions which the court takes, the more likely it is that parties will wish to appeal. This may happen particularly in regard to the summary disposal of cases or issues. A balance has to be struck between the need to ensure that the fast track, in particular, is effective, and the need to ensure that parties are not unfairly prevented from bringing appeals.

5.   On the positive side judges exercising appellate functions will have a significant part to play in giving effect to the new system of case management, first, by laying down principles to be followed in exercising the new powers of case management. It should be borne in mind, however, that management decisions are pre-eminently matters of discretion with which an appeal court would seldom interfere. Secondly, where there is an interlocutory appeal, there is an opportunity for the appeal court itself to be more active in considering how the case is to continue, for example by clarifying the issues. In fact, under RSC Order 59, rule 10(3) the Court of Appeal already has the power not only to make any order which ought to have been made, in place of the order appealed from, but "to make such further or other order as the case may require."

6. On 26 March 1996 the Lord Chancellor announced a review of civil appellate procedure, to begin work two months after publication of this report. It would not be right for this report to pre-empt the decisions which are properly for the review. Nevertheless, my report would clearly be incomplete if it did not make recommendations for those appeals which lie to courts below the Court of Appeal or propose changes to the appeals system which are consequent upon other changes which I am recommending. I also offer some suggestions on other issues affecting appeals which are relevant to my Inquiry.

Appeals as to management and determinative decisions

7. Active case management will require procedural judges to take more positive steps than they do at present to control the progress of cases, notably by fixing timetables and by defining the issues at an early stage and disposing summarily of other issues. Some of these decisions, such as fixing a date for a pre-trial review or refusing a request for an adjournment, can be described as management or procedural decisions, as distinct from determinative or substantive decisions, such as striking out a claim as statute-barred or for delay or granting an interlocutory injunction. In order not to delay the progress of cases, there is something to be said for barring appeals from purely management decisions. However, if such a distinction were to be drawn by means of a definition, it would be likely to lead to arguments as to which category a decision came within, and the objective would often be nullified. Similarly, although a more pragmatic approach might be adopted by taking a list of orders or powers and placing them in one category or the other, any decision, whether management or dispositive, can have a crucial effect on a case (eg, fixing a date for a hearing which it is said that an essential witness cannot attend) and it does not therefore seem reasonable to bar appeals from management decisions altogether. Furthermore, even if there were to be no appeal from such decisions, judicial review would continue to lie in respect of county court decisions, and this would probably cause more delay than an appeal.

8. I therefore remain of the view which I expressed in my interim report, chapter 8, paragraph 20 of which said that for practical reasons there should be no difference in practice between a management decision and a determinative decision. This would apply to both the fast track and the multi-track.

Leave to appeal

9. If management decisions and determinative decisions are not to be distinguished, then the current distinction between final and interlocutory orders will apply. At present leave to appeal is not required in the case of an interlocutory appeal from a Master or district judge to a High Court or Circuit judge, but it is required in the case of an interlocutory appeal to the Court of Appeal from a first instance decision of, or a further appeal from, a Circuit judge or High Court judge (see RSC Order 59, rule 1A). Leave is not required from most final orders. Some means of weeding out unmeritorious appeals is clearly needed (as Lord Donaldson has said, "it is no kindness to allow an appeal to go forward which will quite clearly fail"), although even taking one step in seeking to appeal may be enough to disrupt the progress of a case. I recommend that leave to appeal be required for all interlocutory appeals. It has been suggested that such appeals should be defined more clearly and simply than is done by the present list of orders. It is questionable whether a better approach is possible, but I recommend that the matter be considered further.

10. The leave stage might be renamed as a preliminary consideration, as the Law Commission has recommended for applications for judicial review, to indicate that the appellant has a right to such a consideration and that the court has wider powers than simply deciding whether to grant leave to appeal or not. It may, for example, ask the respondent to make representations.

11. It should be possible to seek leave from the lower or the higher court, but the leave process should not be made complex. If leave from the lower court is sought it should be done at the hearing, immediately after the decision, not by a subsequent application, thus avoiding delay. If the higher court refuses leave there should be no further application for leave to another court. If the higher court would be minded to refuse leave to appeal because of a previous decision but nevertheless thought that the appeal might be arguable in a superior court, it could give leave to appeal and then dismiss the appeal, thus opening up the possibility for a further appeal.

12. Another way of limiting appeals from procedural judges' interlocutory decisions, as well as requiring leave to appeal, would be to provide that leave should only be given if a point of principle is involved on appeals which seek to challenge the way in which the court's discretion has been exercised, or where there has already been an appeal. As against this, such an approach would greatly reduce existing rights of appeal.

13. As I say, I am proposing that leave to appeal should be required for all interlocutory appeals, in both fast track and multi-track cases. I have received differing views as to the introduction of a leave requirement in multi-track cases. On the one hand, it has been said that the present system in the High Court, where leave is not required from Masters' interlocutory decisions, works well and should not be changed. It has been suggested that introducing an application for leave would generate more work and expense than it would save. On the other hand, it has been urged upon me that it would be inconsistent with my aim of removing complexity and avoiding unnecessary differences of procedure if the same provisions as to leave did not apply in both fast track and multi-track cases. Provided that applications for leave do not impose an unjustified burden on the court and the parties, I believe that there should be consistency between the two tracks.

To which court should appeals lie?

14. The simplest and most consistent approach to determining to which court or courts appeals should lie is to say either that all appeals from particular types of order should be to the same court or that all appeals from one level of the judiciary should lie to a single higher level of judiciary. However, the first option, for which the Court of Appeal would be the only suitable court, because the same types of order are made by all levels of judiciary sitting at first instance, is impracticable because it would lead to an unmanageable workload for the Court of Appeal. The weakness of the second option is that the more appellate courts there are, the more likely it is that there will be divergences of approach in appellate decisions, where coherence is essential. As at present, therefore, some degree of inconsistency in the structure of appeals is probably inevitable.

Interlocutory appeals

15. My interim report recommended in chapter 8, paragraph 23 that procedural appeals should lie, with leave, from a district judge or a Master to a High Court judge. For reasons of speed, geographical convenience, and the best use of judicial resources, however, I now consider that it would be preferable for such interlocutory appeals from district judges to be to Circuit judges. Because decisions on appeal will have an important role in ensuring that the new system develops coherently, it is important that the Circuit judges who hear appeals should be full-time judges who spend a substantial amount of their time handling civil work. It will be for the Presiding Judges and the judge responsible for each civil trial centre to decide which Circuit judges should hear interlocutory appeals from district judges. The different arrangements for the deployment of Circuit judges in different courts point to flexibility in the choice of judges, although ideally there should be a sufficient number to avoid delay in the hearing of the appeals, but few enough to achieve consistency. In selecting the Circuit judges the need to promote the team concept should be taken into account.

16. It should also be made possible for the Circuit judge, on giving leave to appeal, to refer the case to a Presiding Judge if its complexity made this appropriate or, after consulting the Presiding Judge, to refer it to the Court of Appeal.

17. I suggest that a further appeal should lie, from the Circuit judge to the Court of Appeal, in similar circumstances to those in which appeals lie to the Court of Appeal under the Arbitration Acts: leave to appeal would have to be obtained either from the Circuit judge or from the Court of Appeal, and it would be necessary for the Circuit judge to certify that there was an important point of principle or practice or one which for some other special reason should be considered by the Court of Appeal. I believe that this will provide the necessary restriction on further interlocutory appeals.

18. Appeals from interlocutory decisions in multi-track cases by Masters and district judges should continue to lie to a High Court judge, but with leave. It would be preferable if they, too, were to be to nominated judges or judges in the same team as the Master, in order to ensure greater consistency of decisions. The High Court judge would be able to refer a complex or important appeal to the Court of Appeal.

19. Appeals from interlocutory decisions by Circuit judges should continue to lie to the Court of Appeal, with leave. However, I am concerned about the need to hear such appeals speedily. The current state of the workload of the Court of Appeal makes this difficult. I therefore recommend, first, that the Court of Appeal should have the power to delegate the exercise of its jurisdiction in such cases to any Supreme Court judge or, as in criminal appeals, to request a Circuit judge to sit as a member of the Court and, secondly, that these appeals should be determined on the papers, unless the court directed an oral hearing. Ideally, the appeal should be heard locally.

20. Appeals from interlocutory orders by High Court judges (who would make such orders either because of the nature of the order, eg, an interlocutory injunction, or because they performed the role of procedural judges, as in the Commercial Court) would lie, as they do now, to the Court of Appeal, with leave.

Final appeals

21. It was the clear view of those who responded to the fast track issues paper that appeals from final orders in fast track cases should be to the same court, whether the trial was before a district judge or a Circuit judge. I sympathise with those who have suggested that such appeals should be to the High Court rather than the Court of Appeal, in the interests of speed and so as to avoid adding to the already excessive workload of the Court of Appeal. However, the majority of consultees favoured an appeal to the Court of Appeal and I am reluctant to recommend that appellate jurisdiction should be conferred on the High Court. As with interlocutory appeals from Circuit judges, I recommend that the Court of Appeal should be able to delegate its jurisdiction to hear final fast track appeals to any judge of the Supreme Court and to request a Circuit judge to sit as a member of the Court, and to determine an appeal without an oral hearing.

22. At present the County Court Appeals Order 1991 requires leave to appeal from a number of final orders, including contract and tort cases where the value of the appeal does not exceed £5,000. I recommend that leave to appeal should be required from all final orders on the fast track.

23. In the case of final appeals on the multi-track I recommend that they should lie, as most final appeals from High Court orders do now, to the Court of Appeal.

Preliminary consideration by the Court of Appeal

24. I recommend that there should be a procedure involving the preliminary consideration of all appeals to the Court of Appeal, with the power to dispose of appeals with no merit summarily. The preliminary consideration could be by a single judge.

Time limit for appealing

25. Expedition in bringing and handling interlocutory appeals, particularly on the fast track, will be essential. As I have said, an application for leave which is made to the judge taking the decision should be made there and then. If he refuses leave an application may be made *ex parte*, in writing, to the appellate court. Allowing too long a period for such an application will make it more likely that parties will seek fresh evidence, which should only be allowed exceptionally: cases should be fully prepared for the first hearing. But too short a period within which to seek leave – say, 24 or 48 hours – might encourage parties to appeal almost automatically, without proper reflection. A period of three days would be preferable.

26. I also recommend that this period of three days should apply for all interlocutory appeals from procedural judges, whether on the fast track or the multi-track and whether in London or outside London. At present CCR Order 13, rule 1(10) provides that an appeal lies on an interlocutory order from a district judge to the judge, on notice given within five days after the order. RSC Order 58, rules 1 and 3 provide that a notice of appeal from a Master is to be issued within five days after the order and served within five days after issue, or seven and three days in the case of an appeal from a district judge.

27. Where the court appealed from gives leave to appeal, the appeal should be listed for hearing within 10 days. I very much hope that in the first year of the new system it will be possible to give priority to hearing appeals quickly, so that they do not hinder the progress of cases and case management.

Simplified procedure

28. As well as requiring that interlocutory appeals should be brought expeditiously, consideration should be given to ensuring that the procedure for determining them is as simple and efficient as possible. There was considerable support among those who responded to the fast track issues paper for greater use of paper determinations and of skeleton arguments and written submissions. I welcome this, although I accept that, while their use might save the parties costs, the savings of time for the court are unlikely to be substantial, partly because time would have to be found for a written judgment which might not be needed at an oral hearing. I recommend that the appellate judge to whom an application for leave is made should decide on the papers whether:

(a)   to refuse leave to appeal, stating his reasons; or

(b)   to seek the views of the respondent, in writing; or

(c)   to direct that there be an oral hearing of the appeal; or

(d)   to direct that the parties lodge written submissions within 10 days for a determination of the appeal on the papers.

In making his decision there are a number of factors which he should bear in mind. There is the need for expedition and minimising cost and the need to ensure that both parties feel that the procedure is fair. The respondent would not be involved unless the court thought fit, although the applicant would be obliged to serve him with the application. He could apply to set aside an order directing a hearing or written determination, like any *ex parte* order, but it would usually be preferable to wait until the substantive hearing or determination. In the interests of time and expense the application should be entirely in writing: the applicant would not be able to make oral representations.

29. There should also be scope to minimise the respondent's involvement in final appeals, which lie as of right and where the respondent cannot therefore be protected by a requirement for leave to appeal. As I have said, it should be possible for the appellate court to dismiss a hopeless appeal at a preliminary consideration stage. It should also be possible for the court, if it was minded at that stage to dismiss the appeal, to be able to ask only the appellant to make representations as to why it should not do so.

Effect on the fast track's limited costs regime and fixed timetable

30. The possibility of an interlocutory appeal in a fast track case also raises the question of how this is to affect the limited costs regime which is an integral part of my proposals for the fast track. It would not be right, in my view, to include in the fixed limited costs a sum to cover appeals. However, the Court of Appeal, in consultation with the Supreme Court Taxing Office, should publish standard costs for such an appeal, which would apply unless the court otherwise ordered. So far as the fixed timetable is concerned, I hope that it will be possible for appeals to be heard without interfering with it, but I believe that the court from which the appeal is brought should be able to set a new timetable to take account of the appeal.

Small claims

31. An award in small claims proceedings may only be set aside for misconduct or error of law by the arbitrator; notice must be given 14 days after entry of the award as a judgment (CCR Order 19, rule 8). The application to set the award aside lies to a Circuit judge. Rule 8 also enables a party to apply to the arbitrator for a fresh hearing if the award was made in his absence. My interim report made no recommendations in this area. I propose that, in order to cut down the large number of misconceived 'appeals', applications to set aside should be subject to a paper preliminary consideration stage. Where the arbitrator was the district judge or an outside arbitrator, these would be dealt with by a Circuit judge; in the rare case that the arbitrator was a Circuit judge the preliminary consideration would be by the Court of Appeal.

The nature of the hearing

32. There are three broad categories of review or appeal.

(a) A complete rehearing, in the sense that the whole matter is heard *de novo* (although the appellant, not the original applicant, opens it). The appellate court is not bound by the exercise of the lower court's discretion. Where the appeal is from a trial, the oral evidence would be heard again (as happens in criminal appeals to the Crown Court). Arguably, this is not an appeal at all but a second hearing.

(b) A rehearing, in the sense used in RSC Order 59, rule 3(1), in that although the issues in the appeal are narrowed by the requirement for grounds of appeal to be given, the whole of the evidence and the course of the trial may be reviewed on the documents, and the appellate court may substitute its own decision for that of the court or judge below. But oral evidence is not heard and fresh evidence only allowed in limited circumstances.

(c) A review of the decision, which, if held to be defective, is then remitted to the court below for the matter to be heard again. This is more akin to judicial review or to the civil law *cassation*.

33. In a small number of cases a second hearing is appropriate. Examples are the fresh hearing on account of the absence of one of the parties from the first hearing, in the small claims jurisdiction, and a hearing on an application to set aside a judgment in default of defence. But these are not really appeals. Where there is a true appeal, I believe that the second type, an appeal, on precisely stated grounds, meets the needs of justice and is preferable to the first, rehearing *de novo*, type. There may, of course, be some litigants who are determined to have their day in court, whatever the time and cost involved, but most litigants would probably favour the second. An appeal should focus on specific alleged errors, and is not an opportunity to litigate the whole matter over again, except in those circumstances where the appellate court feels that a new trial by the lower court is desirable.

34. The second type of appeal is also more expeditious than the third type, in that a further hearing by the original court is rarely required. Unlike judicial review, where the court is concerned with the decision-making process, a court hearing an appeal is concerned with the decision, and ought to reach its own conclusion on what the decision should be. This will also, of course, help in the setting of precedent. That said, the third type is at least a reminder of the need for the parties to limit the matters in issue on the appeal, and to indicate the matters of fact and law on which they are agreed.

35. In the interests of simplicity and uniformity I therefore recommend that all true appeals (as opposed to second hearings) should be of the second type. This would mean that interlocutory appeals from a Master or district judge to a High Court judge, or from a district judge to a Circuit judge would no longer be complete rehearings of the first type but would follow the Court of Appeal model. The discretion to accept further evidence should nevertheless be retained.

Principles on which appeal court acts

36. At present the Court of Appeal will seldom interfere with findings of basic or primary fact or with the exercise of discretion. The judge at first instance will have seen and heard the witnesses and will have been in a better position to judge the truth of the evidence, even though it will be open to the appellate court to draw different inferences from the facts found by the trial judge. So far as the exercise of discretion is concerned, the appellant must show either that the judge has failed to apply well-settled principles by making an error of law, or on Wednesbury grounds of unreasonableness.

37. I am not suggesting that these principles should be changed. However, it might be helpful if they were set out in a guide, to make it clear to would-be appellants that there is a high threshold which has to be crossed before an appeal can succeed. This could be particularly valuable for litigants in person, who may be less willing than others to accept an adverse decision and may have over-optimistic expectations of their chances of success on an appeal.

Open court or chambers

38. I recommend that all appeals should be heard in open court. This general principle applies all the more strongly to appeals, since, as has been noted, an appeal system has not only the private purpose of doing justice between the parties in a particular case but also the public purpose of ensuring public confidence in the administration of justice by correcting errors. This would mean a change in the present arrangements for appeals from Masters to High Court judges, although in the case of appeals in the Chancery Division it would be a resumption of the practice which was followed until 1982. Such a change would accord with the change in the nature of the proceeding, from a second hearing to a true appeal.

Encouraging settlements

39. I welcome the announcement by the Court of Appeal that it hopes to be able to identify cases which might be susceptible to settlement by mediation ([1995] 1 WLR at 1188). This is in line with my interim report, in chapter 18 of which I commented that litigation is not the only means of resolving civil disputes, or necessarily the best and proposed that the courts should encourage parties to use satisfactory alternative methods of dispute resolution. Mediation is clearly most appropriate in the case of final appeals to the Court of Appeal. There may, nevertheless, be some occasions on which it might also be encouraged in the case of interlocutory appeals, for example where an interlocutory injunction has been granted or in multi-party proceedings. I recognise, however, that there is a danger that this could lead to unacceptable delays in the final determination of disputes.

Simplification and harmonisation

40. There is scope for greater simplification and harmonisation. Even without the new proposals for case management and different tracks for cases, the existing rules on appeals are complex and need reviewing. There are separate provisions in RSC Order 58, for example, for appeals in interpleader proceedings. These should be dealt with by the final/interlocutory distinction rather than in a special rule. There is also a separate rule for appeals from Official Referees' decisions on questions of fact, for which leave to appeal is required. This has been an area of some difficulty in the past, which I hope that the review of the Court of Appeal will consider.

Reference of cases to an appellate court

41. In criminal cases there is a power in the Attorney General to refer decisions to the Court of Appeal so as to ensure proper development of the law. I believe that there is a similar need in civil cases where the finding of a lower court is clearly unsatisfactory but where no appeal has been brought or is possible. The court to which an application would be made would be the House of Lords where a decision of the Court of Appeal was in question and the Court of Appeal where it concerned conflicting High Court decisions. I recognise that the position is more straightforward in criminal cases, where there are more limited rights of appeal and where the Crown Prosecution Service is in a position to draw issues of concern to the attention of the Attorney General. In civil cases it might be appropriate for the Law Commission to play an advisory role in this, since it is part of the Commission's statutory function to keep the law under review with a view to its systematic development. I realise, however, that it is often difficult for bodies to take on additional work. It will be necessary to ensure that there is proper representation of both sides, perhaps by the Treasury Solicitor or the Official Solicitor. Another matter of concern is that of responsibility for the costs of such applications to the appellate court. I believe that it would be in the interests both of legal advisers advising their clients and of the courts themselves if this opportunity of clarifying the law were to be available. It would also open the way to necessary changes to the law being made without having to wait for primary legislation. I recommend that further consideration be given to the proposal, including the possibility of costs being payable out of public funds where there are no parties who could be expected to pay the costs.

Submissions by third parties

42. There should also be the possibility of enabling third parties, and enabling the court to ask third parties, to make submissions to the Court of Appeal or House of Lords where it would be helpful to have wider views than those of the two parties to the appeal. I have in mind, in procedural appeals, bodies such as the Council of Circuit Judges and the Association of District Judges, whose knowledge of practice and procedure would be useful to the Court of Appeal.

Statutory appeals and applications

43. There is a vast array of statutory provisions which give a right of appeal to, or review by, the High Court. There are different provisions in Acts and rules as to leave, time limits, evidence, service and the constitution of the court and, as both the Law Commission and the Crown Office Working Group have said, there is a real need for rationalisation. This will be done in the new rules.

44. The following paragraphs deal with appeals and applications which are administered by the Crown Office. I see no reason why the approach I indicate cannot, subject to any statutory requirements, be applied to other appeals, so that eventually there will be a single procedure for all appeals to the courts. I hope that the working groups will give assistance on this, covering, for example, appeals which are heard in the Chancery Division and appeals from arbitrators.

45. In my view the normal rule for statutory appeals should be that if there have been two stages already (eg, to an industrial tribunal and then to the Employment Appeal Tribunal) the appeal should be to the Court of Appeal, and if not more than one stage, then to the High Court.

46. I believe that it is preferable to have the same basic procedure for all applications and appeals, using a claim and defence. Where any special requirements are justified these will be included in additional rules and there will also be a general rule to make it clear that the rules are subject to the relevant empowering legislation.

47. The claim will indicate whether it is an appeal or a statutory application and the decision or case stated will be attached to it. It will set out the relevant statutory provisions, the relief required and the grounds relied on, and a summary of the claimant's contentions if they are not already clear from the grounds. The claimant will be able to join an application for judicial review if there is good reason for doing so. In such a case the procedure for judicial review would then be followed. The defence will set out a summary of the defendant's contentions. The defendant may choose to say no more than that the decision below is relied on. The claim and defence will have to be verified. This will help to limit vexatious proceedings and will make an affidavit unnecessary.

48. Unless the primary legislation provides otherwise, the time for initiating the claim will be 28 days from notification of the decision.

49. There will be a preliminary consideration of the claim without the attendance of the parties (before the claim, where leave is needed, and after the filing of the defence otherwise). The judge will be able to dispose of the proceedings summarily either by refusing to allow the claim to proceed or dismissing it or granting the relief claimed. A party against whom a summary order was made would normally be given an opportunity to be heard. The general approach, however, will be to give such directions as will result in the case being heard on a date identified as precisely as possible.

50. The proceedings, if in the High Court, should be heard initially by a single judge, who should have extensive powers to remit the case to the body from which it emanated and to make any decision which could have been made by that body. There should be an appeal, with leave, to the Court of Appeal.

Recommendations

My main recommendations are as follows.

(1)   Leave to appeal should be required for all interlocutory appeals.

(2)   Appeals from interlocutory decisions should lie, in fast track cases:

    (a) from a district judge to a nominated Circuit judge;

    (b) from a Circuit judge to the Court of Appeal;

and, in multi-track cases:

    (c) from a Master or a district judge to a High Court judge;

    (d) from a Circuit judge or a High Court judge to the Court of Appeal.

In case (a) the Circuit judge should be able to refer the appeal to a Presiding Judge or, with his agreement, to the Court of Appeal. In cases (a) and (c) there should be a further appeal to the Court of Appeal with leave if there was certified to be an important point of principle or practice or one which for some other special reason should be considered by the Court of Appeal.

(3) It should be possible to make an application for leave to appeal from an interlocutory order to the judge taking the decision, there and then, or *ex parte* in writing to the appellate court within three days. The appellate judge should decide on the papers whether to refuse leave, or to direct that there be an oral hearing of the appeal or a determination on the basis of written submissions. Where the judge appealed from gives leave to appeal the appeal should be listed for hearing within 10 days. There should be no further renewal of the application for leave.

(4) Appeals from final decisions should be to the Court of Appeal. Leave to appeal would be required from final decisions in fast track cases.

(5) The Court of Appeal should be able to delegate its jurisdiction to hear interlocutory and final fast track appeals to any judge of the Supreme Court or to request a Circuit judge to sit as a member of the Court. It should also be able to determine such appeals without a hearing.

(6) There should be a procedure involving the preliminary consideration of all appeals to the Court of Appeal, usually by a single judge, with the power to dispose of appeals with no merit summarily.

(7) All appeals should be of the limited Court of Appeal rehearing type and not complete rehearings.

(8) All appeals should be heard in open court.

(9) There should be greater uniformity in the procedure for statutory appeals to the courts.

(10) Further consideration should be given to enabling decisions to be referred to the House of Lords or Court of Appeal where no appeal has been brought or is possible, so as to ensure proper development of the law.

(11) It should be possible for third parties, with the leave or at the request of the court, to make submissions to the Court of Appeal or House of Lords.

(12) The rules on appeals should be rationalised. Eventually there should be a single procedure for all appeals to the courts, using a claim and defence and with a preliminary consideration by the court at which it will be possible to dispose of the proceedings summarily. If there have been two stages already the appeal should normally be to the Court of Appeal, and if not more than one stage then to the High Court.

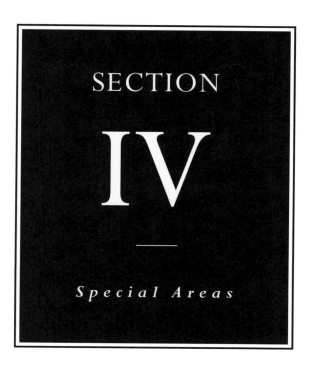

SECTION

IV

Special Areas

Chapter 15   Medical Negligence

Reasons for looking at medical negligence

1. Why have I singled out medical negligence for the most intensive examination during Stage 2 of my Inquiry? (I am using the term 'medical negligence' in this report to refer to any litigation involving allegations of negligence in the delivery of health care, whether by doctors, nurses or other health professionals.) It may appear a surprising choice, because medical negligence cases have no special procedures or rules of court. They are a sub-species of professional negligence actions, and they also belong to what is numerically the largest category of cases proceeding to trial, personal injury. Neither of these is singled out for special attention.

2. The answer is that early in the Inquiry it became increasingly obvious that it was in the area of medical negligence that the civil justice system was failing most conspicuously to meet the needs of litigants in a number of respects.

(a) The disproportion between costs and damages in medical negligence is particularly excessive, especially in lower value cases.

(b) The delay in resolving claims is more often unacceptable.

(c) Unmeritorious cases are often pursued, and clear-cut claims defended, for too long.

(d) The success rate is lower than in other personal injury litigation.

(e) The suspicion between the parties is more intense and the lack of co-operation frequently greater than in many other areas of litigation.

3. The cost of medical negligence litigation is now so high that smaller claims can rarely be litigated because of the disproportionate cost. It is difficult for patients to pursue a claim of any value unless they are eligible for legal aid. In the Supreme Court Taxing Office survey (see Annex 3 to this report), 92 per cent of successful parties in medical negligence cases were legally aided. An analysis by the Law Society of a survey by Action for Victims of Medical Accidents (AVMA) of 376 cases conducted by solicitors' firms on its specialist panel indicates that 90 per cent of cases which reached the stage of litigation were legally aided. If these figures are representative of medical negligence litigation generally, then in the vast majority of cases both sides are funded from the public purse. Here the cause for concern is the amount of money spent by NHS trusts and other defendants on legal costs: money which would be much better devoted to compensating victims or, better still, to improving standards of care so that future mistakes are avoided.

4. The new system of case management by the courts which I proposed in my interim report could do much to reduce cost and delay in medical negligence, and to encourage a more co-operative approach, enabling cases to settle on appropriate terms at an earlier stage. In particular:

(a)   Clearer statements of claim and fully pleaded defences should speed up the progress of cases by helping to establish a factual matrix and define the real issues at an earlier stage.

(b)   Claimants' offers will encourage earlier settlements on realistic terms.

(c)   Extended summary judgment may help to weed out weak claims or defences at an earlier stage.

(d)   Improved training and greater specialisation should help judges to identify weak cases, narrow and determine issues and limit the scope of evidence.

(e)   More use of split trials will limit unnecessary work on quantum of damages in cases where liability is in issue (although this should not inhibit early work on quantum in cases where a valuation of the claim is possible).

(f)   Greater emphasis on early definition of issues between experts should encourage a more co-operative approach and reduce cost and delay.

5. The difficulty of proving both causation and negligence, which arises more acutely in medical negligence than in other personal injury cases, accounts for much of the excessive cost. The root of the problem, however, lies less in the complexity of the law or procedure than in the climate of mutual suspicion and defensiveness which is still all too prevalent in this area of litigation. Patients feel let down when treatment goes wrong, sometimes because of unrealistic expectations as to what could be achieved. Doctors feel they are under attack from aggrieved patients and react defensively. The patients' disappointment is then heightened by what they perceive to be a refusal to acknowledge fault and an attempt to cover up.

6. Case management alone cannot provide the answer to this. A key requirement for achieving the necessary change is designing procedures for handling these cases, both at the pre-litigation stage and by the courts, so that a more co-operative and conciliatory approach to dispute resolution is achieved.

7. A Medical Negligence Working Group was convened for my Inquiry by Sarah Leigh. This has already laid the foundation for the more co-operative approach which is so urgently needed in this area of litigation. It has brought together a considerable number of those involved on all sides of medical negligence litigation to discuss for the first time the problems which exist. I am particularly pleased to report that the group has established a new 'umbrella' organisation which will be open to all those with an interest in medical negligence litigation. One of this organisation's principal tasks will be to discuss and advance the further reforms which are needed after the Inquiry has finished.

The broader context

8. My Inquiry has coincided with a period of significant change in the handling of claims within the NHS. The National Health Service Litigation Authority (NHSLA) came into existence in November 1995. It now administers a voluntary scheme which, in effect, almost acts as a mutual insurer of those NHS trusts which opt for membership. This is known as the Clinical Negligence Scheme for Trusts (CNST). Its membership already comprises about 384 NHS trusts, 89.5 per cent of the trusts in England. The CNST's coverage is limited to claims involving incidents which occurred after 1 April 1995. Because of the timescale involved in resolving this class of claims it will be some time before the full effect of the scheme will become apparent. However, its creation is undoubtedly a positive move which should result in a more satisfactory approach being adopted by defendants.

9. A separate scheme, effective from 1 April 1996 and also administered by the NHSLA, covers all claims against NHS bodies relating to incidents which occurred before 1 April 1995. This is the Existing Liabilities Scheme, under which an NHS body can apply to the NHSLA for reimbursement of any payment out under a claim, provided it has complied with the conditions imposed by the scheme.

10. As an indication of the scale of the task faced by the NHSLA, it is estimated that there are currently about 20,000 claims outstanding against the NHS. About 2,500 of these have a value in excess of £100,000. About 5,000 claims are settled or adjudicated each year, but the number of settlements is matched by the number of new claims entering the system.

11. I am glad to say that the recently appointed Chairman of the NHSLA, Sir Bruce Martin QC, has responded positively to the general thrust of my proposed reforms, and has made it clear that the NHSLA will support any steps taken to improve the legal process.

12. Different arrangements apply to claims against general practitioners and doctors of consultant status working in private hospitals. These are still dealt with by the defence organisations of which the medical practitioners involved are members, and which formerly dealt with all claims against hospital doctors. (One of these organisations, the Medical Protection Society, is about to take on a role within the management of the CNST.) The defence organisations have also made it clear that they support my objectives. Junior doctors and nursing and other staff working in private hospitals are indemnified by their employers who in turn have insurance arrangements.

13. I have no doubt that these changes, combined with reforms of court procedure, will lay the foundation for a much improved system of handling medical negligence claims which will be to the advantage of both patients and doctors.

14. Two further significant changes were introduced in the NHS on 1 April 1996, as part of the Government's response to the Wilson report on complaints handling in the NHS. The first is a new, more open complaints procedure, covering all NHS staff, which includes an independent review stage. The new machinery has been widely welcomed in principle, but the detailed way in which it is intended to operate has attracted some criticism, in particular because cases where the patient has indicated an intention to claim compensation are excluded.

15. The second change is an extension of the Health Service Ombudsman's statutory jurisdiction to include clinical complaints against all NHS staff, normally provided that the complainant has exhausted the internal complaints system. The particular advantages of the Ombudsman scheme are that it is free of charge to claimants and that it provides an inquisitorial approach, with a single, neutral investigation, but the Ombudsman's extended jurisdiction will not cover claims for financial compensation.

A blueprint for reform

16. A system for resolving disputes about medical treatment must be designed to meet the needs of doctors and other health professionals as well as patients. It should not be designed to suit the interests or convenience of lawyers, except in so far as this is necessary to ensure that the work is done properly.

17. Many people involved in medical negligence litigation have justifiably pointed out to me the importance of establishing at the outset what an injured patient wants. Proceedings often start because the claimant cannot get the information he is seeking, or an explanation or apology, from the doctor or hospital. Historically, solicitors have had no alternative but to advise legal action, which is unlikely to be appropriate in all cases unless the client's main or only objective is to obtain financial compensation.

18. Patients' needs and wishes may not be the same in all cases, and are not always compatible with those of health professionals. An obvious point is that both sides want to win, and for some individuals this may override considerations of speed, economy, or even fairness. Some patients want financial compensation, but they may also want to prevent a repetition of the mistreatment or misdiagnosis which occurred, or to get an apology or explanation for what went wrong. Sometimes, especially in cases where the physical injury was less serious, these non-monetary factors are the most important. Whatever form of redress they are seeking, most patients probably want:

(a)   impartial information and advice, including an independent medical assessment;

(b)   fair compensation for losses suffered;

(c)   a limited financial commitment;

(d)   a speedy resolution of the dispute;

(e)   a fair and independent adjudication; and

(f)   (sometimes) a day in court.

19. Doctors and other healthcare professionals agree with patients in wanting a speedy resolution of any disputes, but this is not always compatible with their understandable wish for a fair assessment of their conduct, with a right of comment and hearing. Doctors in particular also want:

(a)   a discreet, private adjudication, which some would prefer to be by a medical rather than a legal tribunal;

(b)   an expert of their own or their solicitor's choice; and

(c)   an economical system, which does not encourage NHS trusts to settle cases over their heads, regardless of liability.

20. There is no easy way of satisfying everyone, but I hope to provide a set of practical and sensible recommendations which will have an impact on cost and delay while ensuring that all parties are treated fairly.

A change of culture

21. The extent of patients' mistrust of doctors and other hospital staff is illustrated by the submission I have received from Action for Victims of Medical Accidents (AVMA). They argue that the real reason for defendants' reluctance to investigate complaints where there is a possibility of legal action is a concern that such an investigation might indeed disclose negligence:

> "[The defendants] do not in fact want a relatively simple and cheap way of investigating a complaint which might expose that there has been negligence".

22. If that mistrust is to be removed, the medical profession and the NHS administration must demonstrate their commitment to patients' well-being by adopting a constructive approach to claims handling. It must be clearly accepted that injured patients are entitled to redress, and that professional solidarity or individual self-esteem are not sufficient reasons for resisting or obstructing valid claims.

23. Patients and their representatives, for their part, must recognise that some degree of risk is inherent in all medical treatment, and that even the best practitioners do sometimes make mistakes. They should not pursue unrealistic claims, and should make every effort to resolve disputes without recourse to litigation.

24. It is fundamental to my approach to civil litigation in general that legal proceedings should be treated as a last resort, to be used only when other means of resolving a dispute are inappropriate or have failed. When someone has a potential negligence claim against a doctor or hospital, the first essential step is to find out what the patient wants to achieve. If his or her main need is for substantial financial compensation to cover future loss of earnings or the cost of continuing care, then litigation may be (but is not always) the best way to proceed. If the patient is chiefly concerned to get an explanation or apology for what went wrong, or to ensure that procedures are changed so that future accidents can be avoided, then litigation is less likely to be the best course. Recourse to the NHS complaints procedures and, if necessary, the Health Service Ombudsman, may offer a more appropriate means of redress.

25. The existing litigation system may allow an untenable case to come to court, several years after the event, in which there has at no stage been any personal contact between the healthcare professionals involved and the injured patient or his family. That simply should not happen, and doctors, trusts and lawyers all have a part to play in preventing it. In some cases, an explanation from the doctor of what went wrong, coupled with a personal apology, would resolve the matter without any further action. Many claims managers, who act as the hospital's first point of contact with aggrieved patients, concentrate on trying to achieve this in suitable cases.

26. One innovative suggestion which has been put to me is that there should be a new, non-pecuniary remedy available from the courts. A patient would, in effect, be able to apply to the court for a formal statement from the hospital explaining the incident of alleged negligence.

27. This idea has some attraction, but I do not recommend it because I think it would send out the wrong signals about the role of the courts and might even encourage unnecessary litigation. It is, as I have already stated, a fundamental part of my approach to access to justice that litigation should be treated as a last resort, and it is far better for patients and hospitals to resolve their disputes through other channels wherever possible.

28. The best way of dealing with the problem of delay before claims are started would be a policy of more open communication on the part of hospital staff. Effective communication of course needs to start before things go wrong. All patients who are about to undergo treatment should understand that the outcome of medical treatment can be uncertain, and should be told about the range of possible outcomes in their particular case. Wherever practicable, the advice should be confirmed in writing. Doctors and hospitals should encourage patients to report any unsatisfactory outcome as soon as possible, and to seek an explanation direct from the individual doctor or hospital before going to a solicitor.

29. Every patient who has suffered an adverse outcome is entitled to an explanation, and, where appropriate, an apology. In appropriate cases, there is no reason why an offer of compensation should not be made before any legal claim is notified, provided the patient is encouraged to seek independent advice on the offer. I understand that some hospitals offer to pay for such advice, to ensure that patients are not deterred from seeking it through fear of the cost.

30. I can understand why this approach is unwelcome to many doctors, in particular. There is a natural reluctance to admit that one has been at fault, and sometimes a fear that any form of apology will amount to an admission of legal liability. Such an admission could have implications for the doctor's professional reputation and career prospects. A face to face meeting with an injured patient may be a very daunting prospect for the doctor concerned. From the trust's point of view, an immediate offer of compensation may not appear to be an effective or prudent use of resources.

31. There are, nevertheless, good reasons for adopting such an approach. Most importantly, unless the patient himself opts to go elsewhere, the hospital and the individual doctor have a continuing obligation to care for a patient who has been injured by negligent treatment. In some cases, at least, that obligation includes the provision of financial compensation to pay for rehabilitation. Secondly, from the hospital's point of view it will be easier to trace the relevant records and carry out an investigation if a potential claim is identified as early as possible. Finally, an open approach is also in the interest of the doctor because an explanation or apology will resolve some cases without the need for litigation.

32. In my discussions and correspondence with doctors, I have been encouraged by the extent to which this more open and enlightened approach to patients is now increasingly recognised and accepted as a matter of good practice. This is, however, far from universally the case, although the system of clinical audit encourages doctors to report adverse outcomes. Doctors need support in any subsequent investigation or litigation and disciplinary proceedings against the minority of incompetent doctors should be clearly separate from this procedure.

33. I have no doubt that the more systematic and professional approach to claims management which the NHSLA is encouraging will help to achieve the necessary change of culture. This is, however, not the only way of tackling the problem. The fear of litigation among so many doctors is often based on ignorance of the legal system. I have heard, for example, of doctors who were unclear about the difference between civil and criminal proceedings, and afraid they might be sent to prison if they were 'found guilty' of medical negligence. To ensure that they are properly informed, I believe that all doctors should be given, as part of their basic medical training, an introduction to the legal context of their work, including an indication of what is involved in a claim for negligence.

34. One specific suggestion which has been made to me in the course of the Inquiry is that there should be an obligation on doctors, as part of their ethical code, to inform their patients if they discover an act or omission in their care and treatment which may have caused injury, and that doctors who fail to comply with such a duty should be subject to disciplinary action. It is suggested that nurses, midwives and other healthcare professionals should have corresponding obligations. There is a comparable requirement in the Law Society's code of professional conduct for solicitors to notify their clients when they become aware of a possible negligent act or omission.

35. It is, in fact, arguable that such an obligation already exists under the common law. In 1987 Sir John Donaldson, then Master of the Rolls, said:

> "I personally think that in professional negligence cases, and in particular in medical negligence cases, there is a duty of candour resting on the professional man . . . It is but one aspect of the general duty of care, arising out of the patient/medical practitioner or hospital authority relationship. . . ." *(Naylor v Preston Area Health Authority* [1987] 2 All ER 353 at 360)

There has, however, been no binding decision of the courts as to the existence of such a duty.

36. I recognise that there may be considerable difficulties in defining such an obligation so that it could be meaningfully embodied in a rule of conduct. What is appropriate for lawyers cannot be assumed to be right for doctors, because of the very different ways in which the work of the two professions is organised. Moreover, the doctor/patient relationship is a uniquely personal and sensitive one. Nevertheless, I suggest that the General Medical Council and other regulatory bodies could usefully consider how to clarify and promulgate the responsibilities of healthcare professionals in these circumstances.

Pre-litigation procedure

37. Some of the major sources of cost and delay in medical negligence cases arise at the pre-litigation stage.

(a) Inadequate incident reporting and record keeping in hospitals, and mobility of staff, make it difficult to establish facts, often several years after the event.

(b) Claimants must incur the cost of an expert investigation in order to establish whether they have a viable claim.

(c)   There is often a long delay before a claim is made.

(d)   Defendants do not have sufficient resources to carry out a full investigation of every incident, and do not consider it worthwhile to start an investigation as soon as they receive a request for records, because many cases do not proceed beyond that stage.

(e)   Patients often give the defendant little or no notice of a firm intention to sue. Consequently, many incidents are not investigated by the defendant until after proceedings have started.

(f)   Doctors and hospital staff in general are traditionally reluctant to admit negligence or apologise to or negotiate with claimants, for fear of damage to their professional reputation or career prospects.

38. An effective pre-action procedure for medical negligence cases therefore needs to:

(a)   encourage early communication between claimants and defendants, and ensure that any appropriate apology or explanation is always offered to the claimant;

(b)   set a challenging but realistic target for disclosure of medical records by defendants;

(c)   ensure that the claimant knows what options are available (including ADR) and what each will involve;

(d)   require the parties to consider whether joint instructions to an expert would be possible, at least on some of the issues in the case; and

(e)   provide an early opportunity for defendants to identify cases where a full investigation is required.

39. Under the present arrangements a hospital faced with the possibility of a medical negligence claim has a number of very real practical problems to contend with. The difficulties of finding patients' records and tracing former staff are endemic problems which, in many cases, are unfortunately exacerbated by late notification of the claim to the defendant, and by the hospital's own failure to record adverse incidents. When a medical procedure goes wrong, it is natural that the first reaction of both doctor and patient is to take restorative measures. The patient may not even consider the possibility of a claim until a protracted course of treatment has been completed. Late notification of a claim creates difficulty for the claimant in establishing liability, while the defendant is faced with all the problems of carrying out an investigation possibly several years after the event, when records may have been lost and staff who have moved away are difficult to trace. This is a situation which can only accentuate the lack of trust between the two sides.

40. In the NHS the establishment of the NHSLA is likely to have a significant impact on the standards of record keeping and incident reporting in hospitals. Improved technology and information systems could, in any event, have a significant impact on record storage and retrieval. I am very encouraged by what I have learnt about the current practice of the more progressive NHS trusts, which have already appointed professional claims managers to adopt a more pro-active approach to risk management. I look forward to a more general movement in this direction once the administrative changes come fully into effect. I am pleased to say that my Inquiry has already contributed to this development, by providing a forum for discussion and spreading the message about best practice among doctors and health service administrators.

41. Patients seeking access to their medical records for possible use in litigation had, in the past, been faced with a slow and expensive procedure. This situation has improved following the Access to Health Records Act 1990, which makes it more difficult for a hospital or trust to justify withholding records which a patient is entitled to see under the Act. The NHS Code of Practice on Openness, which has been in force since June 1995, is non-statutory and does not add to the rights of access created by the 1990 Act, but it should contribute to a climate of greater openness in the NHS. Those who are unable to gain access to the information they request from the responsible NHS body may complain to the Health Service Ombudsman.

42. There was a further step forward in August 1995 when the Law Society, with the support of the Department of Health, launched a protocol designed to make the process quicker and cheaper through the use of standard forms of application and response. This is a very encouraging development, although I understand that the protocol is not yet universally followed either by claimants' solicitors or by hospital trusts. It is, in any event, limited in scope. I hope that in due course it will be possible to build on this approach by introducing an extended protocol covering pre-litigation activity more generally.

43. There are occasionally disputes between parties on the breadth of discovery to be provided in a potential clinical negligence claim. Under the existing rules of court a potential claimant can apply to the court before proceedings have commenced for discovery (disclosure) of documents by the potential defendant, but cannot apply for disclosure by a third party until after the issue of proceedings. This may cause difficulty in medical negligence cases, where the patient's previous medical history is often relevant to the claim and access is needed to records held by the patient's general practitioner or by another hospital. Time and money may be wasted if an expert writes his initial report on the basis of an incomplete history, and then changes his view once the rest of the records become available. I therefore recommend that legislation should be amended to enable potential claimants to apply to the court for pre-action disclosure of documents by someone who is not a party to the proposed litigation.

44. The problem of tracing former staff should, in time, become less serious as procedures in general are speeded up. In the meantime, however, more positive ways of tackling this need to be considered. At present I understand that NHS trusts normally keep employment records for around 6 years, and superannuation records are kept permanently. There may be some scope for extending this or making more use of the existing information.

45. I have already mentioned that one of the difficulties faced by NHS trusts is that of deciding whether a potential claim is worth investigating, and at what stage. The point has been made to me (by, among others, the Law Society) that it is anomalous that potentially serious negligence claims are not automatically investigated until proceedings are issued, whereas the new NHS complaints procedure requires an investigation of all complaints.

46. I agree that any attempt to distinguish 'complaints' from 'claims' must in some respects be artificial. To the extent that a valid distinction can be drawn, it would appear more logical to concentrate resources on the investigation of the more serious complaints, which are likely to include those involving allegations of negligence. I do accept, however, that it would be unreasonable to expect hospitals to instigate a full investigation every time a patient asks for disclosure of medical records, given the number of potential claims which do not proceed beyond that stage. A more pro-active system of incident reporting in hospitals should facilitate a more informed and rational approach to the identification of cases in need of investigation. I am glad to hear that this is already beginning to happen, particularly in hospitals where professional claims managers have been appointed. It would also help if claimants gave an indication with their request for records that they are considering making a claim and not simply asking for information.

47. So far I have concentrated on the part to be played by health providers in constructive pre-litigation activity. Claimants (or potential claimants) and their legal advisers must also make a significant contribution. First, if a genuine change in ethos is to be achieved, it is important that solicitors acting for patients do not adopt an unduly adversarial attitude, and that they find out at an early stage what their clients want. It should always be remembered that clients do have their own views, and it is particularly important to establish whether they are mainly seeking financial compensation. Solicitors should not automatically advise litigation, but should explore and provide information about any available alternatives such as mediation or the Ombudsman service. The primary objective of their initial approach to the prospective defendant should be to obtain the relevant information about the patient's treatment (unless the patient has already done this) and then to resolve any dispute by discussion or negotiation. The possibility of mediation or some other form of alternative dispute resolution should be considered at all stages of the case.

48. Once the patient has made a firm decision to litigate, that decision should be notified to the defendant in a letter before action. Wherever possible, the defendant should be given at least three months' notice that a statement of claim is to be served. The letter before action should give the fullest available information about the basis of the intended claim, in the light of the expert evidence obtained by the patient, and, whenever possible, include an offer to settle. At that stage, defendants who have not already done so should initiate a full investigation of the claim, unless they agree to settle on the claimant's terms. If liability is disputed, defendants must provide a reasoned answer. As part of my proposed system of case management by the courts, any unreasonable delay by either side should be taken into account by the court in setting timetables and making directions for the conduct of the case, and in the award of costs.

49. I understand that the new 'umbrella' organisation has undertaken, as one of its initial tasks, to carry forward the development of a pre-litigation protocol for medical negligence cases. I believe that the adoption of such a protocol will reduce the volume of medical negligence litigation by diverting some cases to alternative methods of dispute resolution and promoting settlement in others. For cases where litigation is unavoidable, the benefits of the protocol should become apparent in an early definition of the issues between the parties and a speedier resolution than is normally possible under the existing, less co-operative approach.

Alternative dispute resolution

50. There is in existence an expanding range of alternative dispute resolution mechanisms for medical negligence claims which may be better suited than litigation to the needs of both patients and doctors. This applies especially to smaller claims, and to those where financial compensation is not the patient's main or only requirement. It is, however, important to ensure that informal procedures do not put claimants at a disadvantage because of the inevitable imbalance of knowledge and power between patients and hospitals.

51. The first possibility, at least for hospitals with professional claims managers, is in-house resolution. This need not have any cost to the patient, has the advantages of speed and informality, and is most likely to be effective when the claims manager has full authority to agree financial compensation up to a limit set by senior managers. It also has the flexibility to provide non-monetary redress when that is what the patient wants. In-house resolution does, however, carry the risk – whether real or perceived – of providing a solution which under-compensates the patient or fails to take his or her interests fully into account. I believe that the benefits outweigh the risks provided that claims managers are properly trained and act responsibly. They should recognise their obligation to put the patient's interests first, and should be able to identify cases which are too complex, or where the potential quantum is too high, for informal resolution. Above all, they should always advise patients as to the need for independent advice, and consider advancing the cost of this. Provided these conditions are met, I believe that in-house resolution may be the best means of settling relatively small and simple claims.

52. Mediation offers a further possibility for out of court resolution. In April 1995 the Department of Health set up pilot mediation schemes for medical negligence cases in two regions: Anglia and Oxford, and Northern and Yorkshire. Participation in the schemes is voluntary, and they are concentrating on cases where legal proceedings have already started. There will be an independent evaluation which is due to report in the autumn of 1997. The Department of Health has also considered the possibility of an arbitration scheme for medical negligence cases, but concluded after consultation that claimants would be unlikely to accept the binding nature of an arbitration award.

53. Work carried out by the ADR sub-group of the Medical Negligence Working Group suggests that it may be possible to mediate cases successfully before proceedings are started, provided the claim can be valued. Exchange of experts' reports and witness statements may in some cases be unnecessary; the basic requirements are for both sides to have a condition and prognosis report which they are happy to use, a reliable estimate of value, copies of the medical records and their own expert reports.

54. I regard this as a very promising development, and one which could result in a significant number of medical negligence claims being resolved without litigation. I understand that work on pre-litigation mediation is continuing, and I hope that in due course it will be possible for guidelines to be produced and incorporated in a pre-action protocol. As I have said elsewhere in this report, this approach will be more effective if legal aid is made available for pre-litigation resolution and ADR.

55. I have considered the suggestion that some form of ADR should be a compulsory precursor to litigation, at least in smaller medical negligence cases. Such a requirement would not, in any event, be realistic at present, given the limited availability of ADR, and as a matter of principle I think it is preferable to encourage rather than to compel its use, as I proposed in the interim report. If the development of in-house resolution and mediation continues, these are likely to prove attractive options for smaller cases on economic grounds. Their use can be encouraged by protocols, and failure to follow the protocol should be taken into account by the court in any subsequent proceedings.

Do medical negligence cases need special treatment by the courts?

56. Medical negligence cases in the High Court are at present treated as part of the general business of the Queen's Bench Division. I proposed in my interim report (chapter 12, paragraph 25) that the work of that Division should be divided between a general list (to be known as the General, Personal Injury and Damages List) and a number of special lists. Medical negligence work is significantly different from, and in many cases more complex than, ordinary personal injury cases, and effective case management (including trial management) requires a degree of familiarity with standard medical practices and procedures which is unlikely to be acquired by judges who only occasionally deal with medical negligence cases. I have therefore concluded that the special lists in the Queen's Bench Division should include a separate medical negligence list. I believe that arrangement will foster the appropriate degree of special experience and expertise among the judiciary which is needed for the efficient and effective disposal of these cases.

57. Outside London, I propose that medical negligence cases, at both High Court and county court level, should be handled at specially designated court centres where both the judiciary and staff will have the opportunity to build up experience and expertise in this work. I have received clear indications that litigants and their legal representatives would be prepared to travel a considerable distance to have access to specialist procedural and trial judges. The problems of distance will be overcome in time by the use of video conferencing and other technology, and there is already scope for using telephone conferencing facilities for straightforward procedural matters.

58. Depending on the volume of cases there should be regional lists, or perhaps a national list, to facilitate the flexible allocation of cases for trial and reduce delay. The precise solution to be adopted will depend on the volume of cases going through the courts, which will need to be ascertained as part of the process of implementing my proposals for case management generally.

59. The question of specialisation leads naturally to that of training. Medical negligence is a highly technical area where judges (unless they happen to belong to the minority who have medical as well as legal qualifications) will inevitably know a great deal less about the subject matter of the litigation than other participants, notably the defendant, the expert witnesses, and the lawyers who are becoming increasingly specialist in this area of litigation. If case management is to work effectively, it will be essential for the procedural judge to have some understanding of the substantive issues in the case. I believe that trial judges would also benefit from specialist training, although I have no doubt that it is possible for a trial judge to acquire enough background information on a particular case to make a reasoned decision on the issues. Indeed, it is one of the functions of the parties' representatives, and in particular of the expert witnesses, to ensure that he does so. However, it takes longer to conduct a case if the judge has to be 'educated' in this way. It is also difficult for the judge to have the authority needed to manage a case well if he is less experienced than the lawyers who are appearing before him.

60. There are ways in which it can be made easier for both the procedural judge and the trial judge to assimilate the essential knowledge for a particular case. For example, the parties' advisers can produce summaries of technical documents, core bundles of essential papers, or a glossary or synopsis of the relevant medical issues. Some judges, I know, would gladly accept this level of help, but do not see the need for any wider training in medical issues.

61. Again, while I can understand that position, I do not think it goes far enough. Under the new system of civil litigation which I have outlined in my interim report, both procedural judges and trial judges will play a much more active part than they do at present in the management of cases. They will be expected, for example, to narrow and define issues as the case progresses, and will have extended powers to exclude evidence. They will not be able to carry out this new role effectively if their grasp of the technical background to the case is solely dependent on briefing from the parties and their advisers; they will need to have sufficient confidence to form an independent judgment and overrule the parties when necessary.

62. For these reasons I believe that some form of training in medical issues is essential for judges who seek to become specialists in this area, to reinforce the expertise they will acquire through regular handling of these cases. I therefore recommend that the Judicial Studies Board should investigate, with the help of appropriate medical experts, the scope and content of training in medical issues for procedural and trial judges; and organise the necessary training. I have no doubt that the appropriate expert help can be provided by the various medical royal colleges and by AVMA, all of whom have told me in the course of the Inquiry of their willingness to assist, for example by giving advice or providing specialist lecturers.

Expert evidence

63. Medical negligence differs from other personal injury litigation in the parties' greater reliance on expert medical evidence for issues of causation and liability as well as quantum. Causation is more difficult to establish than in other personal injury cases. This is because the effects of the allegedly negligent treatment must be distinguished from those of the patient's underlying condition which gave rise to the need for treatment. Liability is often very difficult to establish. It must be determined by the principle stated in *Bolam v Friern Hospital Management Committee* [1957] 1 WLR 582:

> "[A doctor] is not guilty of negligence if he has acted in accordance with a practice accepted as proper by a responsible body of medical

men skilled in that particular art . . . Putting it the other way round,
a man is not negligent, if he acts in accordance with such a practice,
merely because there is a body of opinion who would take a contrary
view."

64. This is not significantly different from the test used in any professional
negligence litigation, but it causes greater difficulty for the courts than
would a claim for negligence against, say, a lawyer or an accountant,
because of the technical issues involved. The assessment of damages,
although essentially a similar exercise in all personal injury cases, is often
complicated in medical negligence, because the court must compare the
claimant's actual condition and prognosis with the hypothetical condition
and prognosis if the patient had received competent medical treatment. The
court must only compensate for the injuries caused by negligent treatment,
not for any underlying condition.

65. For the resolution of all three issues – causation, liability and quantum
of damages – the parties and the courts are dependent on medical and
other expert evidence. This is not only expensive, especially if experts from
several specialities are used by each side, but may also be a source of delay
because of the time taken by the experts to produce their reports.
Generally speaking, expert witnesses in the medical field have less time to
spare for legal work than experts in other fields.

66. All practitioners in this field know the peculiar difficulty of finding the
information necessary to determine whether a potential claimant has a
case. This is not simply a matter of establishing the facts, although that in
itself is often difficult enough, but of finding an expert medical opinion to
support the claim.

67. Traditionally, there has been an understandable reluctance on the part
of doctors and other healthcare professionals to criticise their colleagues.
Their reluctance was accentuated by the fact that the defence in the
majority of medical negligence cases was conducted by the medical
protection bodies, of which doctors themselves were members. This
resulted in a shortage of medical experts who were willing to work on
behalf of claimants, which in turn led to heavy demands on those who were
prepared to do the work, and to a tendency for them to spend more time
preparing medico-legal reports than providing treatment. The end result
was that their standing in the profession was lowered, and other doctors
were even more reluctant to be associated with claimants.

68. It would be difficult to exaggerate the effect on potential claimants of the problems they encounter in obtaining information, coupled with the knowledge that defendants have easy access to medical information and opinion. I am glad to say there have been some improvements since my own experience in practice, but many claimants still feel strongly that the system is weighted against them, and in particular that professional solidarity among doctors is a barrier to justice for ordinary people. Whether or not this feeling is always justified, I have no doubt that it is encouraged by the lack of openness between parties which still prevails in this area of litigation.

69. My general approach to expert evidence in the context of a case-managed system was set out in chapter 23 of the interim report. I recommended that the scope of expert evidence in a particular case should be under the control of the court; that a single expert (whether jointly instructed by the parties or appointed by the court) should be used wherever possible; and that, where this was not appropriate, the issues between opposing experts should be narrowed and outstanding areas of disagreement defined as early as possible.

70. In chapter 13 of this report I have given an account of the Inquiry's work on experts since the interim report, and explained how my general approach is to be put into effect through the new code of procedural rules. I revert to the subject in the present chapter in order to consider how the approach will work in the specific context of medical negligence litigation.

71. The vast majority of people consulted by the Medical Negligence Working Group, including many with whom I have discussed the matter personally, see no scope for the joint appointment of liability experts in medical negligence, except perhaps in the smallest and most straightforward cases. The most commonly cited reason for this is the special nature of the Bolam test (see paragraph 63 above), which requires the court to be apprised of the whole range of acceptable medical practice in a given speciality.

72. I accept that in some medical negligence cases the issues of causation and liability will be too complex to be decided on the basis of evidence from one medical expert in the relevant speciality or specialities. I do not, however, agree that it is an inevitable consequence of the Bolam test that each side must instruct its own experts on all issues in every case. In a straightforward case it may be perfectly possible, and appropriate, for a consultant to advise the court not only of his own practice in relation to the alleged negligence, but of the range of practices regarded as acceptable by his colleagues. Conversely, in an exceptionally complex case, or one where the treatment given was at the 'cutting edge' of medical science, it is by no means self-evident that two opposing experts will be able to represent the whole spectrum of professional opinion.

73. It is part of my approach to expert evidence in general, as set out in chapter 13 of this report, that parties must consider whether a particular case or issue could be dealt with by a jointly instructed expert. In medical negligence cases, I suggest this will apply in particular to:

(a)   quantum issues, such as future care costs;

(b)   medical issues which are uncontroversial (such as the precise nature of a tumour, for example);

(c)   condition and prognosis in straightforward claims; and

(d)   liability in claims under £10,000.

74. As I see it, one of the fundamental problems in medical negligence litigation is polarisation of experts: the situation is all too common where neither side knows until a very late stage in the case on what evidence the other is to rely. Joint instruction of an expert by both parties is clearly one way of overcoming the problem; but, as I have already discussed, that will not be appropriate in all cases. In cases where opposing experts are involved, it must be a prime objective to identify areas of agreement and disagreement between the experts as early as possible, and, if the case proceeds to trial, to ensure that the outstanding issues are clearly identified for the court.

75. The principle of mutual and simultaneous disclosure of expert evidence is well established in medical negligence litigation, and is strongly supported by a number of those who have contributed to this part of the Inquiry. Nevertheless, I believe it is worth reconsidering. Sequential rather than simultaneous disclosure of expert evidence could, at least in theory, reduce delay and cut down the amount of work needed on medical negligence claims. Defendants tend to support this, on the basis that the claimant's report would be disclosed first and might persuade some defendants to settle without going to the expense of obtaining their own ·reports. The opposing argument which has been put to me is that simultaneous disclosure is a more effective way of establishing the true facts of the case. On this view, sequential disclosure encourages the defendant's expert to focus on (and possibly attack) the points made by the claimant's expert, instead of carrying out a full and independent investigation. This, it is said, is in neither party's real interest, because a factually inaccurate view of the incident is unsafe and likely to be exposed at trial, sometimes at enormous expense.

76. For ordinary personal injury litigation, pre-action protocols are being developed on the basis that the claimant will instruct an expert who is approved by the defendant, and that the defendant will accept the claimant's report without instructing a separate expert. In principle, I see no reason why a similar approach could not be adopted in medical negligence, at least for the smaller and more straightforward cases. For the time being, I have to recognise that this would not be acceptable to claimants, but I strongly urge that it should be seriously considered by those concerned as part of the more co-operative approach which I am aiming to establish.

77. It emerged from the working group's consultation exercise that meetings between opposing experts were rarely used in medical negligence cases, but that there was a strong view that they might be a helpful way forward. I have dealt with the arguments for and against experts' meetings in chapter 13 of this report, where I concluded that in the majority of cases the benefits should outweigh any disadvantages in terms of cost and inconvenience. I mentioned the particular problem in medical negligence that private meetings between experts would not be acceptable to patients. To meet this, I proposed that experts' meetings should normally be held in private, but that when the court directs a meeting the parties may apply to the court for any special arrangements.

Quantification of medical negligence claims

78. One particular feature of medical negligence litigation (and, indeed, of personal injury claims in general) which has come to my attention in the course of the Inquiry is the enormous amount of time and money which is spent on quantification of the more substantial claims. There are a number of ways of tackling this, all of which will require a greater emphasis on co-operation and joint planning of quantum resolution. Particularly in larger cases, this is a matter that should be dealt with, either by the parties themselves or with the help of the procedural judge, as part of the case management process.

79. First, to avoid waste of resources, it is important to ensure that detailed quantification work is done at the most appropriate stage of the case. Defendants want claimants to value cases at an early stage, because it encourages early settlement or at least enables the defendant to estimate his liability. But in complex cases where prognosis and needs are unclear, this is too expensive and leads to repetition. Early quantification can also be wasteful of resources when there is a real dispute on liability; in such cases, consideration should be given to deferring quantum evidence until the issue of liability has been dealt with.

80. Working out the detailed cost of a care regime for a severely injured patient requires contributions from experts in a number of different fields, including, for example, architects, employment consultants, nurses, physiotherapists, and accountants. Wider use of single experts in each speciality will go some way to reducing the cost of the exercise, but without a more radical approach this is likely to produce only limited savings. Standard tables should be drawn up and, wherever possible, used to reduce the need for separate calculation in individual cases.

Case management in the multi-track

81. Chapter 5 of this report explains how my proposals for case management on the multi-track will be embodied in the new rules. My overall approach is that uniform rules should apply, so far as possible, to all types of cases, with special provisions kept to a minimum. The general rules will be sufficiently flexible to accommodate appropriate variations of practice and procedure for particular categories of cases, such as medical negligence, or for individual cases. For example, the standard time allowed for filing of a defence will be 28 days, which is unlikely to be sufficient in any but the most straightforward medical negligence cases. The rule will permit parties to agree an extension up to three months, and to apply to the court for any further extensions.

82. As experience is gained of the new system, I would expect the rules to be supplemented by judicial practice directions, and published practice guides, which will indicate how the rules are to be applied to different classes of cases. Ideally, the production of the various guides should be supervised by the Civil Justice Council whose establishment I recommended in the interim report. In the particular instance of medical negligence, the work could be started at an early date by the new 'umbrella' organisation, building on the detailed work on case management and procedure which has already been done by the working group.

How to deal with smaller cases

83. I have already pointed out that the problem of disproportionate cost is particularly acute in smaller medical negligence cases. This creates a drain on the legal aid fund, as well as on the resources of the NHS. It also denies access to justice for potential claimants who are not eligible for legal aid, and for whom litigation would be uneconomic.

84. In the interim report I proposed a new 'fast track' procedure, which would enable most straightforward cases up to about £10,000 to be litigated simply, quickly and at a proportionate cost. A more detailed procedure is set out in chapter 35 of this report.

85. I accept that the standard fast track will not be suitable for the vast majority of smaller medical negligence cases. Preliminary investigations can be just as lengthy and expensive whatever the value of the claim, and expert evidence on liability may be just as strongly contested. These are the main factors which would make it impossible to impose the normal fast track timetable and costs limit in small medical negligence cases.

86. I have considered in chapter 2 of this report the arguments put forward by APIL and others that proportionality of costs to compensation would be a denial of access to justice because parties must be allowed to argue their cases fully, regardless of cost. This view has been expressed particularly forcibly by some contributors to the Inquiry in respect of medical negligence. I agree that the special features of medical negligence claims, which I have already identified, make them more expensive to litigate than ordinary personal injury cases of equivalent value, and that this must be reflected in the level of recoverable costs. Even on the standard fast track, as I have explained in chapter 4, I accept that there will need to be different levels of costs for the straightforward and the more complex cases. In other words, strict proportionality, in the sense of a fixed percentage to apply to all cases of the same value, is not a realistic proposition.

87. This does not mean, however, that we should abandon all attempt to achieve a more proportionate use of resources in medical negligence, or in any other areas of litigation. On the contrary, I believe that the disproportionate use of resources in this area is unsustainable. Excessive cost and delay deny access to justice and divert scarce human and financial resources in the NHS away from its primary objective of providing health care.

88. In February 1996 Nottingham Law School organised a one-day conference for the Inquiry on the scope for a fast track for medical negligence cases. It was set up as a hypothetical case study, moderated by Lord Justice Otton and assembled in sections for claimant lawyers, defendant lawyers, managers, doctors and neutrals. There was an interactive voting system which enabled conference delegates to give their views on a range of questions at various stages of the proceedings. One of the most significant findings, in my view, was that the majority of people thought the present cost of litigating small medical negligence claims was too high.

89. With the help of the working group, and of other contributors to the Inquiry, I have explored various options for dealing with smaller medical negligence claims in a more proportionate way. The three main options to emerge from this work, which were examined at Nottingham Law School's conference by reference to two hypothetical case studies, are:

(a)   a 'modified fast track', with

   (i)   a simplified procedure focusing on joint instruction of a single jointly chosen expert;

   (ii) only one lawyer for each side attending the trial;

   (iii) an overall costs cap of £3,500 applying to all cases on the fast track;

(b)   a 'best practice' approach which:

   (i)   is based on existing procedure but assumes a more efficient approach by litigators and the courts;

   (ii) does not attempt an arbitrary pre-set costs limit, but suggests a budget related to defined stages of litigation which would amount to a total of around £4,000 on each side; and

(c)   the 'streamlined track' which I have proposed in chapter 5 of this report for cases at the lower end of the multi-track, and which would include:

   (i)   a tailor-made procedure and pre-set budget for each case;

   (ii) a target maximum timescale of 18 months;

   (iii) a requirement for joint instruction of a single expert after the case management conference, to act as adviser to the court and neutral evaluator of the evidence put forward by the parties' experts.

90. Any of these options would achieve the objective of enabling smaller medical negligence cases to be litigated on a modest budget known in advance. I believe it would be inappropriate at this stage to prescribe a single, mandatory system, and that the Court Service should facilitate pilot studies enabling each of the possible approaches to be tested at selected courts.

91. I have already mentioned that alternatives to litigation may provide the best solution for smaller medical negligence cases. There is a view, held, among others, by the Law Society, that it is better to channel smaller medical negligence claims out of the court system than to make it easier for them to be litigated. The Society has accordingly proposed that claims up to £10,000 should be dealt with under a modified version of the new NHS complaints procedure, as a compulsory precursor to litigation. I have some sympathy with the idea of a combined procedure for complaints and claims, particularly for cases where the monetary value is below £5,000. It would not, however, be realistic to recommend it at present, given that the new NHS procedures are expressly designed to deal with complaints separately from claims for compensation. In any event, I have reservations about making such a system compulsory, especially since the length of the proposed procedure (up to 18 months) would cause serious delay in cases which could not be resolved without subsequent litigation. I hope, however, that the scope for including smaller medical negligence claims will be reconsidered in the context of any future changes to the NHS complaints system.

The future

92. If my recommendations for reform in this area of litigation are successfully implemented, the overall result should be that more patients who have suffered negligent medical treatment obtain the redress they are seeking (whether financial or otherwise) within a shorter timescale and at a significantly reduced cost. That does not necessarily imply a large growth in the volume of litigation, provided that informal negotiation and alternative dispute resolution mechanisms are used in the ways I have suggested. The system should be fairer and more open than it is at present, and I believe that the benefits of this will be felt by doctors, other healthcare professionals and health service administrators as well as by patients.

93. Some contributors to the Inquiry have suggested that more radical change is needed, such as a modification of the test of negligence which is currently applied by the courts or replacement of tort-based litigation with a system of no-fault compensation for some or all medical negligence claims. These matters are not within the remit of my Inquiry; consideration of them is a matter for others if they think it is appropriate.

Recommendations

My recommendations are as follows.

(1)   The training of health professionals should include an introduction to the legal context of medical work, including an indication of what is involved in a claim for negligence.

(2)   The General Medical Council and other regulatory bodies should consider whether a rule of professional conduct is needed to clarify the responsibility of healthcare professionals to their patients when they discover an act or omission in which they may have been negligent in their care and treatment.

(3)   The NHS should consider tackling the problem of tracing former hospital staff, by improving hospital record systems or making more use of existing information.

(4)   A pre-litigation protocol for medical negligence cases should be developed. As part of the protocol, claimants should be required to notify defendants of a firm intention to sue in a letter before action. The letter should include the fullest available information about the basis of the intended claim, and should wherever possible give at least three months' notice that a statement of case is to be served. If liability is disputed, defendants should be required to provide a reasoned answer.

(5)   The use of alternative dispute resolution mechanisms should be encouraged in medical negligence, especially for smaller claims. Solicitors acting for patients should not automatically advise litigation but should inform their clients of all the available options, including the Health Service Ombudsman, and consider the possibility of alternative dispute resolution at all stages of the case.

(6)   The specialist lists in the Queen's Bench Division of the High Court should include a separate medical negligence list.

(7)   Outside London, medical negligence cases at both High Court and county court level should be handled at specially designated court centres.

(8)   There should be regional lists, or a single national list, to facilitate the flexible allocation of cases for trial and reduce delay.

(9) The Judicial Studies Board should investigate, with appropriate medical experts, the scope and content of training in medical issues for procedural and trial judges, and organise the necessary training.

(10) Standard tables should be used wherever possible to reduce the cost of quantifying complex medical negligence (and other personal injury) claims.

(11) There should be a practice guide to indicate how the new rules on case management and procedure will apply in detail to medical negligence litigation. The guide should be developed by the new 'umbrella' organisation for medical negligence or under the aegis of the Civil Justice Council.

(12) The Court Service should facilitate a pilot study of the various options for dealing with medical negligence claims below £10,000, to establish which is the most effective procedure for enabling these cases to be litigated on a modest budget.

Chapter 16   Housing

Introduction

1. I decided to include a special study of housing litigation in my Access to Justice Inquiry because of the fundamental importance of this area of the law to those involved. The two main categories of housing cases I have looked at are: possession (including actions for possession on the grounds of harassment or nuisance) and disrepair. These cases often raise very difficult problems, involving the rights and obligations of individuals and sometimes the constitutional functions of public bodies. I am aware that procedural reform can have only a limited impact on these problems, but it is nevertheless important that the civil justice system is organised to deal with the problems as effectively as possible when they come before the courts.

2. I set out my general approach to housing litigation in the interim report. The main points were that:

(a)   there was a need for proper advice and representation for those who were less able to pursue or defend proceedings on their own in areas such as disrepair;

(b)   reform of the substantive law on housing could do more than anything to reduce cost and delay;

(c)   information technology could help in extending the availability of guidance, for example through the use of legal information systems to support non-specialist advisers;

(d)   given the complexity of the present law, the court should be prepared either to transfer all defended non-possession cases involving an unrepresented litigant to the small claims jurisdiction, or to the new fast track on grounds of complexity or the litigant's inability to manage unaided; and

(e)   it would be helpful to establish a cadre of district judges with specialist expertise in housing law.

3. In the second stage of the Inquiry I have considered the need for specific reforms in greater detail, bearing in mind especially the following factors:

(a)   the cost of housing litigation to individuals as well as to public funds;

(b)   the need to take account of the interests of all those involved, including both public and private sector landlords and tenants and mortgage lenders and borrowers;

(c)   the need to provide access to justice for tenants who are not eligible for legal aid as well as those who are.

4. After the publication of the interim report I had discussions with the Housing Law Practitioners' Association, whose members act for tenants in housing litigation, and with the various associations representing public sector landlords: the Association of District Councils, the Association of London Government, the Association of Metropolitan Authorities and the National Federation of Housing Associations. I set up a working group, comprising representatives of these bodies and two district judges with wide experience of housing litigation. I am very grateful to all of them for the time they have devoted to the Inquiry and for their help in producing recommendations. Their names appear in Annex 1.

5. On 26 February 1996 I held a seminar on housing issues at Manchester Crown Court, at which private as well as public sector landlords and tenants were represented, and the Local Government and Housing Association Tenants' Ombudsmen were among the speakers. The main topics discussed on that occasion were disrepair, possession cases and alternative means of resolving housing disputes outside the courts. These were among the issues canvassed in a consultation paper which I issued in January, and to which I have received around 50 replies. Respondents included the Bar Council, the Law Society, and the Law Centres Federation as well as solicitors' firms and individuals. I have also met a group of local authority tenants to hear at first hand about the problems caused by anti-social behaviour on council estates, and I have myself visited an estate in London to see the problems caused by disrepair. I should like to thank everyone who has participated in this consultation process, either by attending meetings or by sending in written submissions to the Inquiry.

6. Some contributors to the Inquiry have suggested that housing cases would be dealt with more effectively and expeditiously by a separate Housing Court. I do not favour that approach because it would not encourage the flexible use of judicial and other resources within the civil justice system as a whole. I believe that the necessary improvements can be achieved by encouraging a much higher degree of specialisation among judges, and providing more training to ensure that they are aware of the special problems in this area.

7. Although substantive law reform is not within my remit, I remain concerned that reform of court procedures can have only a limited impact in an area where the main source of difficulty is the complexity of the substantive law itself. I referred to this in my interim report, and it is a point which has been made again and again by respondents to my consultation process. Questions such as whether a person is a licensee, a tenant, or a sub-tenant raise issues of law which in some cases have had to be decided by the Court of Appeal or the House of Lords. A tenant whose home is in a state of disrepair may have a claim against his or her landlord in contract or in tort, under the Landlord and Tenant Act 1985, the Defective Premises Act 1972, or the Environmental Protection Act 1990. It is difficult, if not impossible, for tenants to decide these questions without advice. The complexity of housing law makes it a particularly difficult area for advice workers who are not legally qualified. When lawyers do become involved, the complexity of the issues increases the amount of time they have to spend on a case, and, consequently, the level of fees they have to charge.

8.   While I accept that some degree of complexity inevitably arises from the need to balance the rights of tenant and landlord, I recommend that the Department of the Environment should look at this as a matter of urgency. The Law Commission should be invited to carry out a review of housing law with a view to consolidating the various statutory and other provisions in a clear and straightforward form.

Small claims

9.   Following the recommendations in my interim report, the financial limit of the small claims jurisdiction was increased to £3,000 with effect from 8 January 1996. Special provision has been made for limited costs to be recoverable in cases involving applications for injunctions and orders for specific performance, in the light of the Court of Appeal's ruling in *Joyce v Liverpool City Council* [1995] 3 All ER 110 CA that such applications could be dealt with under the small claims jurisdiction. The amount recoverable for an expert's fee has been increased to £200. A further rule change has made it possible for district judges to transfer cases out of the small claims jurisdiction on grounds of 'complexity' rather than 'exceptional complexity'.

10.   All these changes will have an effect on some types of housing cases. Although it is clearly too soon to assess the impact of the new system, I invited comments in my consultation paper on:

(a)   the types of housing cases (if any) in which the reforms to the small claims jurisdiction were likely to be of particular benefit;

(b)   whether any further steps could be taken to help litigants dealing with housing cases as small claims;

(c)   whether any types of housing cases were inherently unsuitable to be dealt with as small claims; and

(d)   how the 'complexity' criterion for transfer out of the small claims jurisdiction should operate in relation to housing cases.

11. I have been made aware that there is a strong body of opinion, mainly among lawyers who regularly represent tenants, that almost all housing cases are inherently too complex to be handled satisfactorily by unrepresented litigants, even under the simplified small claims procedure. The Law Society and the Housing Law Practitioners' Association take this view, suggesting that only the most straightforward disrepair cases, where there is no need for expert evidence and where the tenant is able to represent himself, should be treated as small claims. Other respondents have suggested specific types of cases which should be excluded from small claims: the main categories are claims for non-monetary remedies such as injunctions; disrepair actions; and claims involving violence, intimidation or harassment.

12. There is some measure of agreement, however, that the extended jurisdiction could be of benefit to tenants who are not eligible for legal aid, especially in cases such as disrepair, and to private tenants with minor contractual claims.

13. The Legal Aid Practitioners' Group suggests that the criteria for transfer out of the small claims jurisdiction on grounds of complexity should include multiplicity of experts, heavy documentation, and a dispute with a complex history. I agree with this, and with the response of the Chancery Bar Association that any dispute of law "should potentially be considered complex".

14. I do not consider it appropriate at this stage to recommend any restrictions on the scope of the small claims jurisdiction in relation to housing cases. As the Court of Appeal said in *Joyce v Liverpool City Council*, ". . . for the great mass of small and relatively simple claims the arbitration procedure must be the norm. Section 11 claims cannot form any general exception." The relaxation of the criteria for transferring a case out of the small claims jurisdiction should provide tenants with the protection they need.

15. I have always had in mind the needs of those who are denied access to justice under the present system because they are not eligible for legal aid but cannot afford the cost of private litigation. I do, however, consider it essential that the number and types of housing cases dealt with as small claims, the outcomes of these cases and the operation of the criteria for transfer from small claims to the fast track should be monitored. I am pleased to hear that the Lord Chancellor's Department intends to monitor the effect of the increased small claims limit, and I understand that the Law Society is also considering some research specifically on housing cases which are dealt with as small claims.

Possession cases: general

16. Actions for the possession of land do not fit in to the three-track framework for case management proposed in my interim report. They are already dealt with under a relatively simple procedure, and I do not propose any radical changes to that. There are, however, a number of ways in which the existing procedure could be improved.

17. At present there are several different High Court and county court procedures for possession of land, including summary proceedings for the eviction of squatters under RSC Order 113 and CCR Order 24. The general principle of the new code of procedural rules will be to aim for uniformity and simplicity. Accordingly, in my consultation paper I asked whether the new code should provide a single possession procedure, with all cases starting in the county court of the district in which the property is situated.

18. There is general agreement that all claims for repossession of domestic property, including actions for the eviction of squatters, should start in the local county court. It should be possible for cases to be listed before a High Court judge, if there are exceptional circumstances which make this necessary. I accept that a single, standard procedure for all possession cases will not be feasible, but special provisions should be restricted to cases such as the eviction of squatters.

19. There are, I believe, four principles which are common to all residential possession cases, and on which an appropriate procedure should be based. They are that:

(a)   possession should be granted only to a claimant who can prove his right to possession;

(b) the claimant must prove that any statutory conditions have been met;

(c) there should always be a judicial determination of the proceedings; and

(d) all proceedings should be determined at an oral hearing or on a specified date.

Rent arrears

20. It is generally agreed that the present procedure for possession of tenanted property on grounds of arrears is unsatisfactory. One criticism is that fixed date hearings, which are rarely more than a formality because the majority of defendants do not attend, are wasteful of court time and legal costs. A more fundamental point is that the procedure does not reflect claimants' needs, because in most cases (especially those involving social landlords) the claimants primarily seek repayment of arrears rather than possession of the property. Under the present system, however, landlords' options are limited, and it is often said that the threat of possession is the only effective weapon against tenants' reluctance to pay.

21. Judges, recognising that possession may not really be in the interests of either party, often seek to give the tenant a last chance to pay by granting a suspended possession order. This raises the question whether the virtually automatic making of suspended orders in many courts recognises the statutory requirement for the court, in cases involving secure tenancies, to be satisfied that it is reasonable to make the order. Even when it is reasonable, the use of suspended possession orders in these circumstances can cause serious difficulties. If an order is breached, the unintended effect will usually be the loss of the secured or assured tenancy. This arises from the Court of Appeal's decision in *Thompson v Elmbridge Borough Council* (1987) 19 HLR 526 CA, where the court held that a secure tenancy determines as soon as there is a breach of the terms of a suspended order.

22. Another way of postponing a final possession order is for the court to make an order requiring the repayment of arrears and costs by instalments, in addition to the current rent, while the possession claim itself is adjourned. This 'adjournment on terms' approach avoids the problems associated with suspended possession orders, but still has the disadvantage that a hearing is required before an order for repayment can be made.

23. In the issues paper I suggested a new, two-stage procedure for rent possession actions, building on the 'adjournment on terms' approach. The first stage would be a paper procedure leading to a court order for the repayment of arrears. Failure to comply with its terms would lead to a second stage involving a hearing, which could then result in an order for possession. This would avoid the cost and inconvenience of a court hearing in every case, while at the same time carrying a greater threat of repossession if the attempt to recover arrears failed. It would, I believe, be more effective than the county court rent action, which was abolished in November 1993 because it was little used. The weakness of the rent action as a mechanism for the recovery of arrears was the lack of a direct link with the stronger threat of possession.

24. Most respondents to my consultation paper have welcomed the idea of a two-stage procedure in principle, but some have expressed reservations about the way in which it would work in practice. Landlords are understandably anxious to avoid delay, and are concerned that the proposed two stages might extend to three if breach of a court order for repayment of arrears was not followed by effective action to recover possession. Others, including the Law Society, have pointed out that the rules for the first stage must require the landlord to provide full details of the rent due and paid since arrears began to accrue, together with details of housing benefit claims paid. There must also be an opportunity for the occupier to make an offer to pay the arrears and for the landlord to investigate whether the offer is satisfactory and feasible. Otherwise, assuming that defendants will not always reply on paper, there will be a problem as to what order the court should make.

25. I believe it is possible to devise a two-stage procedure that would overcome these problems. The details will of course need careful consideration, but the outline proposed by the working group, as described below, should be a helpful starting point.

(a) The landlord starts the case by a claim, supported by a declaration of truth. The claim should be accessible to the tenant and should include or have attached the following information:

  (i) a copy of the rent account, showing when it first fell into arrears;

  (ii) a copy of the tenancy agreement;

(iii) the notice of intention to bring the proceedings;

(iv) a statement whether, to the landlord's knowledge, the tenant is in receipt of housing benefit, and if so, how much;

(v) a suggested instalment figure to be paid off the rent arrears; and

(vi) all other information required on the claim form.

(b)   With the documents, the tenant will be sent a form to complete. He/she will be asked if he/she agrees with the level of arrears and the suggested instalment figure for repayment. The form will include a warning that if the tenant does not respond within a specified number of days, then an order will be made on the basis of the landlord's figure. There will be a space for tenants to give details of their financial circumstances, even if the tenant is in agreement with the arrears figure and the suggested instalment figure. The tenant will be encouraged to complete this section, even though the landlord will have given details of the tenant's circumstances on the claim form so far as these are known to him. The form will also encourage the tenant to obtain advice from an advice agency such as a CAB.

(c)   The district judge then checks all the documentation, and makes an order (either for what the landlord has suggested or what he/she thinks fit) without there being a hearing.

(d)   On the tenant's initial reply form there should also be space for the tenant to indicate if there is a defence to the claim for arrears, or a counterclaim, eg, for disrepair, and brief details. If the district judge considers there is a *prima facie* defence or counterclaim, then a preliminary hearing will be fixed.

(e)   The order will be sent to both parties. It will include a warning to the tenant that if he/she breaches the order, then his/her home is at risk and the claim can be restored. Failure to comply with an order will increase the risk of a possession order being made. The order will also tell the tenant that if his/her financial or other circumstances change so that he/she would like the order changed then he/she must tick a box on an enclosed form and send it back to the court. The order could be varied without a hearing, if sufficient information had been provided.

(f)   If the tenant breaches the terms of the order, the landlord applies for a hearing.

(g)   The notice of the hearing to the tenant would make clear that it would be in a private room.

26. The success of the new system will depend, in the first instance, on the effectiveness of the paper procedure for recovery of arrears. The arrears order will need to include a strong warning to the tenant about the increased possibility of possession if the order is breached.

27. Secondly, there needs to be a concerted effort to encourage the attendance of defendants at court. In cases where breach of an order does lead to a hearing for possession, the importance of defendants' attending must be acknowledged by all concerned. Claimants, as well as the courts, must play a part in urging defendants to attend.

28. Whether or not the tenant is present, reasonableness under Section 85 Housing Act 1985, must be fully considered by the judge before a possession order is made. Suspended possession orders would still be used, albeit more rarely. If the proposed procedure has been followed, many of the matters likely to be taken into account in considering reasonableness will already have been identified, and evidence on them may already have been given, at the earlier stages. A suspended possession order would therefore carry a far more serious threat of repossession if breached than at present (and this should be made clear to the tenant). Therefore, applications to set aside warrants would be more difficult and less likely to be successful, unless there had been a change in circumstances since the suspended possession order was made.

29. I do not think it would be appropriate for a two-stage procedure to be compulsory in all cases, although landlords should be encouraged to use it. A landlord would be entitled to ask for a full hearing of his possession claim immediately, but he would have to satisfy the court at the hearing that it was reasonable to have done so, and might be subject to a costs sanction if the court did not agree. The procedure has been developed mainly with social landlords in mind, and it has been suggested that it will be less attractive to private landlords because they are more likely to want immediate possession. There is, however, no reason why private landlords should not use the two-stage process in cases where they are more concerned to recover rent arrears than to repossess the property.

Mortgage arrears

30. It would be difficult to apply the proposed two-stage procedure to mortgage possession proceedings, because of the lender's right to possession where he can prove arrears and the limited discretion of the court to delay possession under the terms of the Administration of Justice Acts. The hearing can, in any event, serve a more useful purpose in mortgage than in rent cases, and I would not wish to recommend any radical changes to the existing procedure. However, the points I have made about access to advice, and the importance of defendants' attendance at court, apply equally in mortgage as in rent cases.

The accelerated possession procedure

31. My issues paper invited comments on the working of the accelerated, papers-only possession procedure which was introduced in November 1993. This applies only to assured shorthold tenancies under the Housing Act 1988, and to certain other types of assured tenancy where there is no security of tenure beyond a fixed date or where the landlord has a mandatory ground for possession under the Act.

32. Some respondents, including the Law Society and a number of practitioners' groups, have indicated that the procedure is not successful because the statutory requirements and the forms are too complicated. Consequently, landlords often do not fill in the forms correctly, and this results in the need for a hearing in any event.

33. The point has also been made that, in fairness to defendants, in cases where there is no hearing there should at least be a nominal date for the court's consideration of the case, so that the parties know when to expect a decision.

34. I understand that the Department of the Environment, in consultation with the Court Service, has commissioned research by the London Research Centre into the effectiveness of the accelerated possession procedure in reducing the time and cost involved in possession proceedings. The researchers are due to report in September 1996. A further stage in the research will then be considered, which would look at the feasibility of widening the scope of the procedure to cover grounds for possession which are currently excluded. I recommend that the need for reform of the procedure should be considered in the light of the responses to my consultation paper, and of the results of the DoE's research.

Chambers or open court?

35. Elsewhere in this report, in the context of case management, I have discussed the possibility of a conflict between the principle of open justice and the need for privacy when matters of a personal or commercially sensitive nature are being discussed. Similar issues arise in relation to possession proceedings, where there is currently a distinction between mortgage cases, which are heard in chambers, and rent cases, which are heard in open court.

36. Those who have responded to my consultation paper are virtually unanimous in the view that the current distinction between rent and mortgage actions is indefensible, and that all hearings involving discussion of a party's financial affairs should be held in private. There are, however, arguments for not excluding the public altogether. A rigidly enforced rule would exclude advice workers and others, including potential litigants, with a legitimate reason for wanting to observe a hearing. There is also the point that private hearings do not encourage consistency of judicial decision making. Finally, there may be a public interest in a judge's comments on, for example, the general practice of a particular mortgage lender or public sector landlord.

37. On balance, I believe the best approach is for all possession proceedings to take place in the informal surroundings of chambers. There should be no overall ban on public attendance, but either party should be able to apply for members of the public to be excluded.

Anti-social behaviour

38. It has been brought to my attention in the course of the Inquiry that serious problems arise in cases where possession is sought on grounds of harassment or nuisance amounting to serious anti-social or criminal behaviour. I have heard, both from local authority officers and direct from tenants, of the serious harassment undergone by residents who complain about the behaviour of an anti-social minority. Harassment can take the form of verbal abuse, threats of violence, drug dealing and even actual physical violence. Tenants who regard themselves as innocent victims are sometimes forced to move, and this exacerbates the problems because an estate can quickly become a ghetto.

39. There are two main criticisms of the way in which actions for possession on the grounds of serious harassment or nuisance are currently dealt with by the court system. The first is that cases take far too long, sometimes even years, to reach a final hearing. The second problem is that witnesses may be reluctant to give evidence of harassment or nuisance through fear of intimidation.

40. I am particularly disturbed by reports that the courts do not recognise the special significance of these cases, and consequently fail to treat them with the appropriate degree of urgency. There is no reason in principle why this could not be dealt with locally by administrative arrangements, but in the light of the apparent inconsistencies it is clear that some more authoritative central guidance is needed. In my view, this problem also underlines the need for a degree of specialisation by judges with training and experience in housing cases. I recommend that specialist housing judges should regard it as part of their duty to visit local council estates and hold structured discussions with tenants' representatives to give them a better understanding of the problems faced by litigants in this area. I am grateful to the local authority associations who have offered their help in arranging such visits and discussions.

41. In the context of the current campaign by the Local Authority Working Group on Anti-Social Behaviour, a number of measures are already being taken to combat anti-social behaviour by tenants. The Housing Bill, which is currently before Parliament, gives social landlords, and private landlords of properties occupied by secure and assured tenants, a new right to start possession proceedings as soon as a notice for possession has been issued, where there is nuisance or annoyance to neighbours. It extends the ground of nuisance or annoyance to include behaviour likely to cause nuisance; this ground applies to behaviour in the locality of the tenant's property, and includes behaviour by visitors to the property. The extended ground will make it possible for landlords to rely on 'professional' witnesses such as council officials or police officers to prove conduct which is 'likely' to cause nuisance. Residents who have been victims of such conduct may not need to be involved to the same extent.

42. Conviction for an arrestable offence in the locality of the tenant's property will now also form grounds for eviction. In addition, the Bill provides a power of arrest for breach of injunctions against anti-social behaviour by tenants of social landlords and others, where violence has occurred or is threatened.

43. In addition to these new measures, the government has recently issued guidance for local authorities on how to get the best out of the court system in cases involving nuisance neighbours. The points covered include:

(a)   applying for injunctions for the protection of people or property before or during possession proceedings;

(b)   requesting an expedited hearing, or a shortened timetable between issue and hearing;

(c)   applying for non-molestation orders for witnesses or non-disclosure of their addresses; and

(d)   providing information on court procedures to witnesses, and arranging for them to use a separate waiting area in court from the defendants.

44. I am hopeful that the new powers in the Housing Bill, coupled with the guidance on court procedures, will provide considerable assistance to public sector landlords in their efforts to combat this problem. In my consultation paper I asked whether there were, in addition, any other procedural steps that could be taken, to address in particular the specific problems of delay and witness intimidation.

45. Respondents who addressed the point did not always think it necessary to introduce a special new procedure for these cases; many thought the essential point was to ensure an appropriate degree of expedition. In particular, it was hoped that the introduction of a two-stage procedure for recovery of arrears would in itself create a new order of priority, enabling cases where possession is genuinely sought to be handled faster.

46. I have concluded that some modifications to the standard possession procedure are appropriate, including an element of case management, for claims by local authorities, housing action trusts, charitable housing trusts or registered social landlords within the meaning of the current Housing Bill, where it is alleged that:

(a)   a tenant, or a person for whom the tenant is responsible under the terms of his tenancy agreement, has assaulted another resident or a member of the landlord's staff; or

(b)   a tenant or a person for whom the tenant is responsible under the terms of his tenancy agreement has threatened to assault such a person; or

(c)   there are reasonable grounds for fearing such an assault; or

(d)   a tenant or a person for whom the tenant is responsible under the terms of his tenancy agreement has caused serious damage or threatened to cause serious damage to another resident's home or property.

47. The claim in such a case should be accompanied by:

(a)   An affidavit of a housing officer or person in a similar capacity, proving the facts within his/her own knowledge and exhibiting statements which have been signed by witnesses in accordance with the rules. If the housing officer has reasonable grounds for fearing a repetition of the violence, threats or damage, or that witnesses may be intimidated, the names, addresses and signatures of the witnesses may be omitted. The housing officer must state the grounds for his/her fear.

(b)   A copy of the tenancy agreement.

(c)   A statement of rent, current arrears and entitlement to housing benefit.

(d)   A copy notice seeking possession.

(e)   (If sought) a claim for an *ex parte* injunction restraining continuance of the nuisance, interference with witnesses or potential witnesses, and any other breach of the tenancy agreement, until 7 days after the pre-trial review.

48. An application for an injunction should be heard forthwith by a judge, who should take into account the effect of failure to grant an injunction on neighbours, potential witnesses and staff of the claimant landlord. The claim for possession, claim for an injunction, and injunction should be served personally by the landlord. The court should fix a pre-trial review not less than 10 days and not more than 15 days from the issue of proceedings.

49. At the pre-trial review, if the defendant does not attend, and the court is satisfied as to the ground for possession and as to reasonableness, possession may be ordered on production of signed statements. Alternatively, the court may give directions for:

(a)   defence;

(b)   disclosure of signed witness statements;

(c)   (in exceptional circumstances) continued anonymity until the trial;

(d)   protection of witnesses, for example by the use of screens or video evidence;

(e)   trial and expedition of the trial; and/or

(f)   continuation of the injunction.

50. The target date for the trial should be within 10-13 weeks of issue of proceedings. I consider this a realistic maximum, given the need for both sides to prepare their case. As one of the tenants at the Manchester meeting pointed out, a 'fast track' system is open to abuse, and rights must not be removed. Provided that is borne in mind, however, there is no reason why the overall timetable could not be even shorter in cases of particular urgency.

51. I see very serious difficulty in guaranteeing the anonymity of witnesses beyond the pre-trial review, as has been suggested by local authorities and tenants' associations. They would like vulnerable witnesses to be interviewed in private by a neutral third party (perhaps a district judge or solicitor acting for the court, or a police officer or housing officer) who could give evidence on behalf of the anonymous witness. New rules on hearsay, under the Civil Evidence Act 1995, will make this approach easier, but it must be doubtful how much weight could be given to such evidence. In particular, it would be essential to ensure that the defendant had a proper opportunity to be heard, and to challenge evidence against him or her. In any event, the 'anonymous' witness would probably still be readily identifiable in the majority of cases.

52. There are a number of practical steps which can be taken to reassure and protect vulnerable witnesses when they attend court, such as the use of screens or video evidence, and the provision of separate waiting areas. In some cases it might also be appropriate for witnesses to be cross-examined by the defendant's legal representative in the absence of the defendant. In addition to this, I believe that prospective witnesses may be more ready to come forward if they have the assurance that an expedited procedure will produce a swift conclusion to the case.

Disrepair

53. Landlords and tenants have a common interest in maintaining housing stock in good condition. Local authority landlords have a duty to maintain their property in good repair and eradicate poor housing, and tenants have a right of access to the courts to enforce their landlords' obligations to carry out repairs. Where there is a written tenancy agreement, this may set out the mutual rights and obligations of landlords and tenants. All those who have contributed to this part of my Inquiry, both landlords and tenants, would agree in principle that court action should be treated as a last resort.

54. Sadly, the reality is that problems and disputes over disrepair do arise all too frequently, and landlords and tenants view the situation from very different perspectives. Tenants who have recourse to litigation, and their representatives, say that this is sometimes the only effective way of getting repairs carried out, and to obtain appropriate compensation. Landlords point to overstretched resources as the underlying reason for any failure to carry out their obligations. They say that tenants who resort to litigation are effectively jumping the queue, which results in an unfair distribution of limited resources among the body of tenants as a whole. They claim that court orders often oblige them to carry out repairs which they do not regard as urgent or necessary, because surveyors who inspect and report on premises on behalf of tenants often find additional items of disrepair which the tenant did not previously know about.

55. The use of legal aid in disrepair actions is another point of contention. Landlords suggest that solicitors drum up business by leafleting estates, and that tenants who are eligible for legal aid gain an unfair advantage over others who cannot afford to litigate privately. From my perspective, the main cause for concern is the expenditure on both sides of public funds which could be put to better use. Local authorities understandably dislike paying legal costs from their housing budgets, which in turn limits the amount available to be spent on repairs. As an example, I am told that one major local authority, deplorably, has to spend 20 per cent of its response repairs and maintenance budget on litigation. The remedy against 'drumming up business' is in part in the landlords' hands. If they had clear and understandable programmes, tenants would not turn so readily to lawyers for help.

56. It would be naive to suggest that reform of court procedures could have more than a very limited impact on problems of this kind on the scale that exists around the country. I do not, in any event, want to encourage unnecessary litigation, in this area or any other. Where court action is unavoidable, however, the procedures should be as simple, quick and inexpensive as possible. The majority of disrepair actions under the new system are likely to be dealt with either as small claims or as fast track cases. (Detailed procedures for the fast track are set out in chapter 3 of this report.) This should reduce cost and delay, and provide wider access to the courts for tenants who do not qualify for legal aid.

57. It is important that tenants who are contemplating litigation are properly informed about alternative means of obtaining redress. One existing alternative for local authority tenants is provided by the 1994 Right to Repair Regulations, which provide strict timetables for the completion of specified repairs upon notice to the landlord by the tenant. It appears, however, that this option is not widely used because of its limited scope and the low level of compensation available. The Local Government Ombudsman, whose work I describe in more detail below, also deals with a significant volume of complaints about disrepair. Information about these options, and any others such as local mediation schemes, should be provided by county courts, solicitors, law centres and any other agencies dealing with enquiries about housing matters.

58. Above all, tenants should not be advised to start legal proceedings, or pursue a complaint about disrepair through any outside agency, until they have reported the disrepair to their landlord through the normal channels and allowed a reasonable time for the landlord to respond.

59. I believe that unnecessary litigation might be avoided, and repairs carried out more speedily, if landlords' and tenants' representatives could agree a pre-action protocol which sets out a clear procedure to be followed by both sides, and which would be enforceable by the courts in the event of breach. Early in the second stage of my Inquiry I had separate meetings with the Housing Law Practitioners' Association and with the public sector landlords' bodies, following which each side drew up its own version of a possible protocol. Subsequently, under the aegis of the working group which I then set up, the two sides have held a number of meetings in an attempt to agree a joint protocol. I have also had useful representations from the Law Society and the Bar Council. I agree with the Bar Council that it is desirable for a protocol to be incorporated into tenancy agreements.

60. While the proposals for a protocol have been developed mainly with social landlords in mind, I believe it is right in principle that they should also apply to landlords and tenants in the private rented sector. Primary legislation would be required to import the terms of a protocol into private tenancy agreements, but in the meantime compliance should be encouraged as a matter of good practice.

61. I am very encouraged by the progress made by the Housing Law Practitioners' Association and the landlords' associations. Subject to two points which I discuss below, they have reached broad agreement that the protocol should provide for:

(a)   landlords to identify and advertise a clear procedure for tenants to follow in reporting disrepair;

(b)   tenants to report disrepair in accordance with the procedure prescribed by the landlord;

(c)   landlords to issue receipts for reports of disrepair, and, within a specified time, either carry out the necessary work or give a reasoned response to the tenant's request. (This could, for example, explain why the landlord disagreed with the tenant's request, or propose a date on which the repairs would be carried out); and

(d)   a list of approved experts to be established by each local authority, in consultation with representative bodies for tenants and lawyers dealing with housing issues in their local area.

62. If the landlord's response was not satisfactory, or if the repair had not been carried out in accordance with proposals, the tenant could ask for an expert to inspect and report on the premises at the landlord's expense. The landlord would select the appropriate expert from the locally agreed list. It is suggested that the landlord would instruct the expert within 14 days, and that the expert would then have 14 days within which to inspect and report.

63. The next stage would be that the landlord would have 21 days to reply to the expert's report, indicating what work was to be carried out and by what date. The reply could also, in appropriate cases, include an offer of compensation to the tenant.

64. If the tenant remained dissatisfied with the landlord's proposals, or with the compensation offered, or if the work was not carried out satisfactorily, the tenant could start court proceedings. The case would be allocated either to the small claims jurisdiction or to the fast track in accordance with its value and complexity.

65. This approach has a number of significant advantages. First, a clear system for reporting disrepair and acknowledging such reports will reduce the scope for disputes as to what was reported when, and encourage landlords to deal with reports of disrepair systematically. Secondly, a straightforward procedure with standard 'tick box' forms will make it possible for tenants to reach at least the stage of applying for an expert inspection without legal assistance. Thirdly, the period of 14 days within which the expert is required to carry out an inspection will give the landlord an opportunity, in appropriate cases, to reconsider its initial decision and agree to carry out the repair.

66. If a protocol along these lines were to be generally adopted and properly followed, the result should be that court proceedings would be issued in only a minority of cases. In cases that did go to court all the necessary documentation, including an expert's report, should be readily available, and that should significantly reduce the length and cost of proceedings.

67. The first point of disagreement between the landlords and the Housing Law Practitioners' Association is on the issue of receipts for reports of disrepair (paragraph 6 above). The Association believes that receipts should be issued for all reports of disrepair, while the landlords would prefer not to issue receipts where they do not consider they are liable for the repair, for example because it is the tenant's responsibility.

68. If the landlords' approach is accepted, the protocol will be effective only in cases where the landlord accepts legal liability for the repair. That in itself would be a significant step forward, but I think it would be preferable for landlords to acknowledge all reports of disrepair, giving written reasons where they do not accept liability for the repair. This could be done by using a pre-printed form with tick boxes, and need not be unduly onerous. The important point, in my view, is that tenants would be given proper information about the status of their claim, and that any future disputes about the reporting of disrepair could be avoided.

69. The second and more fundamental disagreement relates to the instruction of experts. The landlords insist that the expert's report should be restricted to the particular disrepair which is the subject of the tenant's complaint. The only exception they would allow is the inclusion of any additional disrepair which is actually causing a danger to the tenants or a potential injury to their health.

70. In my view it would not be realistic to expect a surveyor's report to ignore additional problems except those he considers dangerous. All disrepair will need to be dealt with in due course, and should be identified as early as possible. It does need to be made clear, however, that the court would not necessarily include any additional repairs in an order for specific performance, unless reasonable time had been allowed for the repairs to be done.

71. First of all, it is up to the tenant to decide whether he or she wants to make a claim in respect of additional repairs identified by the surveyor. In some cases, no doubt, the tenant will choose to concentrate on a major item of disrepair which is causing serious inconvenience. When a claim does include several items of disrepair, it is open to the landlord to identify those which are regarded as urgent and to put forward a timetable for carrying out both urgent and non-urgent repairs. The civil courts have a discretion as to whether or not to make a mandatory order requiring a landlord to carry out repairs. When the landlord can demonstrate that relatively minor repairs are to be carried out as part of a planned programme, the court should take that into account in the exercise of its discretion, for example by adjourning the question of a mandatory order pending implementation of the landlord's repair programme. It would be helpful if this position could be clarified in the rules. (Different considerations would apply in cases brought under the Environmental Protection Act 1990 in the magistrates' courts, which have a more limited discretion than the civil courts.)

72. There will clearly need to be further discussion on the protocol after this report is published. Now that I have indicated my views I very much hope the landlords will accept my approach. I do not suggest, as a matter of general policy, that protocols should be imposed on parties to litigation, but where there is substantial agreement on both sides it may be appropriate for the court to help the parties to come to an appropriate solution on any outstanding points of difficulty by adopting its preferred solution. Once a protocol is established, it should be included in a practice guide on housing cases. If the protocol set out in the practice guide is not complied with by the parties, this should be reflected in the court's approach to costs and discretionary relief.

Judicial review

73. At present the only way of challenging local authorities' decisions in cases involving homelessness is by way of application to the High Court for judicial review. There is also a growing tendency for judicial review to be used in other housing disputes, for example by tenants seeking transfer or owners seeking house renovation grants, or in disputes about housing benefit. It is questionable whether judicial review, which is primarily concerned with issues of wider public interest, is the appropriate procedure for these cases. There are also practical difficulties: the process is a relatively lengthy and expensive one, and is perceived as inaccessible by many of the people involved because applications for judicial review can only be made in London.

74. The Law Commission's report on judicial review (LAW COM. No 226) agreed that there should be a simpler procedure for homelessness appeals, but expressed the view that an internal review procedure could not be regarded as a substitute for a right of appeal to an independent court or tribunal. The Commission therefore recommended that judicial review in homelessness cases should be replaced by a right of appeal either to an independent tribunal or to a county court. (The report pointed out that the county court had the advantage of being locally based and that it already dealt with other housing matters.) In response to this, the government has sought to improve the standard of local authorities' decision making on homelessness, and thus reduce the volume of applications for judicial review in this area, by requiring each authority to establish a formal internal appeal mechanism. The new Housing Bill provides a right to request a review of an authority's decision.

75. My issues paper on housing asked whether it should be possible for housing cases which are dealt with by way of judicial review to be heard outside London, and whether there should be a new right of appeal to an independent tribunal or a county court. Respondents were strongly in favour of a more localised system for homelessness appeals, not only because of the inconvenience for many people of travelling to London, but because the issues would be more appropriately considered by adjudicators with knowledge of local conditions. It was thought that the county courts would provide the most appropriate forum, and that these cases should be heard by specialist Circuit judges who had had the opportunity to build up some expertise on housing matters.

76. There was also a strong, though not unanimous, view that any new county court procedure for homelessness should continue to provide an appeal on points of law only, not on the facts, because it would be inappropriate for the courts to overturn the administrative decisions of local authorities. I agree that this approach is most in keeping with the new arrangements for internal review by local authorities, and I therefore recommend that there should be a new route of appeal to the county courts, on judicial review principles, against local authorities' decisions on homelessness.

Multi-party actions

77. In the context of housing litigation, common issues of law and fact may arise when large numbers of cases are brought by:

(a)   tenants of the same public or social landlord all experiencing the same problem, eg, of disrepair; or

(b)   people affected by a decision of a public body (who under the existing arrangements might apply for judicial review); or

(c)   long leaseholders of the same landlord with a common problem, such as the appointment of receivers.

78. At present, however, the scope for representing collective rather than individual interests in the courts is unclear, because of the courts' restrictive interpretation of the rules on representative procedures. As a result, most lawyers involved in housing tend to deal with individual claims without addressing the wider issues. This means that individual cases cost more than necessary, and costs for the courts and legal aid are increased because effective action can be achieved only through litigation on a case by case basis.

79. I have dealt at some length with multi-party actions in chapter 17 of this report. The procedures I have proposed there should be applicable, in a simplified form, to housing cases, which are likely to be more straightforward and involve smaller numbers of claimants than many other multi-party actions. In the case of housing, there is no reason why multi-party actions should not be managed and tried at county court level.

80. There is a particular need in the housing field for the existing rules on the standing of organisations to bring representative actions to be clarified and made less restrictive. Attempts to address broad policy questions on housing by way of judicial review are sometimes frustrated because there is no applicant to bring the point before the court, or because the potential respondent has settled individual claims on a case by case basis. That situation need not arise if a representative organisation could apply to the court for declaratory relief. The new rules should make provision for this.

Ombudsmen

81. At present both the Commissioner for Local Administration (the Local Government Ombudsman) and the Housing Association Tenants' Ombudsman (HATO) provide an alternative to the courts in many types of housing dispute, including disrepair and homelessness, and some types of multi-party action.

82. The Local Government Ombudsman was established to deal with injustice arising from maladministration. The legislation specifies that the Ombudsman is not to investigate cases where a remedy is available in a court of law, but there is a discretion to accept complaints where it is not reasonable to expect the complainant to resort to a legal remedy. In practice, that discretion is widely exercised. Housing complaints make up 37 per cent of the Local Government Ombudsman's cases, and 10 per cent of the overall caseload is disrepair.

83. The average cost to the public purse of a disrepair case handled by the Local Government Ombudsman, in the financial year 1995-96, was £445, although the cost of a case involving a full investigation could be as much as £3,000. The normal time to achieve a settlement and get repairs done is about 24 weeks, but the overall timescale is nearer 18 months in the minority of cases where a report is issued.

84. The HATO was established in 1993, and is paid for and supported by the Housing Corporation. The Ombudsman currently deals with about 20 complaints a week. The Housing Bill provides for the establishment of statutory Ombudsman schemes which will replace the HATO.

85. The Ombudsman system has a number of advantages in housing cases. It is cheaper than the courts, and there is no charge to the complainant. The process of investigating complaints is informal, flexible and non-confrontational. Unlike the courts, the Ombudsman can recommend changes to a landlord's practice in general. The Local Government Ombudsman has developed a procedure for grouping systemic complaints, such as the handling of housing benefit by a single London borough.

86. The HATO's terms of reference do not permit group actions as such, so that he can only proceed by way of a test case. His determinations are, however, taken as applying to other cases, and the regulatory role of the Housing Corporation is a powerful means of securing compliance with recommendations on systemic failure. The way in which the new statutory schemes will operate is not yet known, but I hope they will have effective powers to deal with complaints involving groups of tenants. Both the Local Government Ombudsman and the HATO can have a powerful influence on future practice through the publication of annual reports and reports of their formal inquiries. The new statutory schemes will have similar powers.

87. The main disadvantages of the Ombudsman system, as compared to the courts, are lack of enforcement powers and lower compensation. Some users of the system also complain that it takes too long, and some have also pointed to a lack of expertise and specialisation among the Local Government Ombudsman's staff in certain parts of the country.

88. I recommended in my interim report that the discretion of the public ombudsmen to investigate issues involving maladministration which could be raised before the courts should be extended. It appears that the Local Government Ombudsman's discretion in relation to housing cases is, in practice, already being exercised in the way I had in mind. It would, nevertheless, be helpful if this could be put on a formal basis, to underline the importance of the Ombudsman's role as an alternative to litigation.

89. I also recommended that the relationship between Ombudsmen and the courts should be broadened, enabling issues to be referred by the Ombudsman to the courts and the courts to the Ombudsman with the consent of those involved. In the housing context, in particular, it has been suggested to me that it would be helpful if the Ombudsman could refer points of law (including questions of statutory interpretation) to the courts, and if compensation recommended by the Ombudsman were enforceable through the courts.

Other forms of ADR

90. There is a limited but important role for other forms of alternative dispute resolution in housing cases. Mediation, in particular, is widely recognised as being the most effective way of resolving many disputes between neighbours, although it is clearly not appropriate in cases of serious nuisance or anti-social behaviour. A minority of local authorities already provide mediation services, and it would be helpful if these could be extended.

Recommendations

My main recommendations are as follows.

(1)　Judges should be encouraged to specialise in housing cases, and more training should be provided to ensure that they are aware of the special problems in this area.

(2)　The Law Commission should be invited to carry out a review of housing law with a view to consolidating the various statutory and other provisions in a clear and straightforward form.

(3) All claims for repossession of domestic property, including actions for the eviction of squatters, should start in the local county court. It should be possible for cases to be listed before a High Court judge only if there are exceptional circumstances which make this necessary.

(4) There should be a new, two-stage possession procedure for arrears of rent cases. The first stage would be a paper procedure leading to a court order for the repayment of arrears. Failure to comply with its terms would lead to a second stage involving a hearing, which could then result in an order for possession.

(5) The need to reform the accelerated possession procedure for assured shorthold tenancies should be considered in the light of the responses to the Inquiry, and of the results of research by the Department of the Environment.

(6) All hearings involving discussion of a party's financial affairs should be held in private. The best approach is for all possession proceedings to take place in the informal surroundings of chambers. There should be no overall ban on public attendance, but either party should be able to apply for members of the public to be excluded.

(7) There should be an expedited possession procedure, including an element of case management and a target date for trial within 10-13 weeks, for claims by local authorities and registered social landlords within the meaning of the current Housing Bill, where it is alleged that there has been violence or harassment.

(8) County courts, solicitors, law centres and any other agencies dealing with enquiries about housing matters should provide information to potential claimants about the 1994 Right to Repair Regulations, the Local Government Ombudsman, and any other options such as local mediation schemes.

(9) There should be a pre-action protocol for housing disrepair cases including:

(a) a clear procedure for tenants to report disrepair;

(b) an obligation on landlords to issue receipts for reports of disrepair; and

(c)   provision for inspection of the property by a single expert chosen from an agreed list.

If the agreed protocol, or the protocol set out in the practice guide, is not complied with by the parties, this should be reflected in the court's approach to costs and discretionary relief.

(10)   There should be a new route of appeal to the county courts, on judicial review principles, against local authorities' decisions on homelessness.

(11)   The existing rules on the standing of organisations to bring representative actions in the housing field should be clarified and made less restrictive.

(12)   The discretion of the public Ombudsmen to investigate issues involving maladministration which could be raised before the courts should be put on a formal basis. The Ombudsman should be able to refer points of law (including questions of statutory interpretation) to the courts, and compensation recommended by the Ombudsman should be enforceable through the courts.

Chapter 17   Multi-Party Actions

Introduction

1.   The second part of my Inquiry was partly intended to deal with types of litigation causing particular problems for the system of civil justice. It was also designed to examine specific developments which would further access to justice. Clearly the arrangements for multi-party actions must be near the top of the list in both respects. As the National Consumer Council said in its submission to the Inquiry:

> "As we become an increasingly mass producing and mass consuming society, one product or service with a flaw has the potential to injure or cause other loss to more and more people. Yet our civil justice system has not adapted to mass legal actions. We still largely treat them as a collection of individual cases, with the findings in one case having only limited relevance in law to all of the others."

2.   Unlike the position in some other common law countries, there are no specific rules of court in England and Wales for multi-party actions. This causes difficulties when actions involving many parties are brought. In addition to the existing procedures being difficult to use, they have proved disproportionately costly. It is now generally recognised, by judges, practitioners and consumer representatives, that there is a need for a new approach both in relation to court procedures and legal aid. The new procedures should achieve the following objectives:

(a)   provide access to justice where large numbers of people have been affected by another's conduct, but individual loss is so small that it makes an individual action economically unviable;

(b)   provide expeditious, effective and proportionate methods of resolving cases, where individual damages are large enough to justify individual action but where the number of claimants and the nature of the issues involved mean that the cases cannot be managed satisfactorily in accordance with normal procedure;

(c)   achieve a balance between the normal rights of claimants and defendants, to pursue and defend cases individually, and the interests of a group of parties to litigate the action as a whole in an effective manner.

3.   In 1992 the Court of Appeal said that there might be a strong case for legislation to provide a jurisdictional structure for the collation and resolution of mass product liability claims *(Nash v Eli Lilly & Co.* [1993] 4 All ER, at p.409). The Legal Aid Board has called for new procedures tailored to multi-party litigation, which will emphasise the central issues rather than investigating every individual claim in detail. Other common law jurisdictions have similarly found the need to enact statutory provision for multi-party actions. Nearer to home, the report of the Scottish Law Commission has been completed and is being published.

4. During the second stage of the Inquiry, a working party of the Civil Litigation Committee of the Law Society has prepared a report. The working party included practitioners who act regularly for claimants and for defendants. On nearly all issues the working party reached a consensus and a number of detailed recommendations for change were formulated. These included a new rule which deals comprehensively with the conduct of group actions from their initiation to judgment or settlement. Their recommendations are especially valuable because they have applied the philosophy of case management, espoused in the interim report, to the problem *(Group Actions Made Easier,* A Report of the Law Society's Civil Litigation Committee, September 1995).

5. The Inquiry published an issues paper raising a number of further questions in January 1996, and held a seminar involving many of those practising in this area of litigation and representatives of claimants and defendants. I have received 55 responses to the issues paper from practitioners, judges and others who were generous in offering lessons from their own experience. I have also benefited from the deliberations of a small working party, and I am indebted to the Inquiry's academic consultant, Professor Ross Cranston, for a detailed commentary on the experience in other jurisdictions. This, most notably in the United States, draws attention to problems which should be taken into account in developing new multi-party rules in England and Wales.

6. In this area of litigation more than any other my examination of the problems does not pretend to present the final answer but merely to try to be the next step forward in a lively debate within which parties and judges are hammering out better ways of managing the unmanageable.

Existing rules

7. Although the existing rules of court provide means of dealing with multi-party actions, they were not drafted with group actions in mind and therefore none has provided a sufficient answer to the problems they create. Representative actions are provided for by RSC Order 15, rule 12 but the experience here and in comparable jurisdictions is that there are definite limits to the weight the rule can bear. Cases can also be joined or consolidated under Order 15, rule 4 and Order 4, rule 9(1). But consolidation deals with situations where actions have already been begun, and it is better that multi-party litigation be dealt with on a collective basis before then, and joinder is not satisfactory where the interests of claimants differ.

The problems with multi-party litigation

8. The problems of cost and delay identified in my interim report are magnified in the context of group actions. Cases take on a life of their own and there is insufficient independent continuing consideration of whether the cost of the litigation is justified by what is at stake. There is a great risk that actions involving large numbers of claimants will become management or organisation driven because of the sheer scale of the numbers involved. Decisions which in a single case might have a small negative impact, when multiplied many hundreds or even thousands of times, can produce waste of effort and resources on a large scale. In addition the complexity and intractability of the intrinsic subject matter can generate major discovery exercises and escalating use of experts to an even greater extent than in ordinary litigation. The large numbers of potential claimants can mean that substantial cost becomes the norm.

9. The positions of claimants and defendants appear inevitably to become polarised over strategy: the claimants' wish to broadly focus on the common or generic issues, the defendants' wish to identify and investigate each individual case. A confrontational climate develops which fuels this divergence of views.

10. The differing interests of group members, even where there are substantial common issues or interests, give rise to difficulties in establishing generic issues applicable to the entire group, maintaining overall progress of the case and achieving settlement for the whole group. Separate claimants with separate representatives may find themselves at odds with each other or unnecessarily duplicating effort and expense. Although most attention is generally given to the problems of high profile 'disaster' cases, similar problems arise in relation to a wide variety of cases. In housing cases, for example, tenants in high rise blocks may have different objectives from those in low rise housing; long lessees from weekly tenants; tenants who wish repairs to be executed from those who seek rehousing.

11. The desire of defendants to know the scale of the action they face leads to the setting of cut-off dates which in turn can cause the swamping of valid claims with weak or hopeless claims. Defendants may suffer from the adverse publicity resulting from the number of potential claimants and may have to bear the expenses of the individual investigation of such cases. There are also problems arising from the need to protect the rights of individuals who are not part of the group and to balance this need against the desire of the defendants for finality. Settlement of some cases or settlement without any court supervision of lead or test cases may undermine the viability of the group as a whole.

12. In larger actions, the costs may be so enormous and so uncertain that only those eligible for legal aid can contemplate involvement. The escalation of costs in such cases can put the initial cost benefit analysis at risk. In more modest actions, the cost is more proportionate but current legal aid and court arrangements do not always contribute to the most cost effective resolution of the issues. The present rules on legal aid funding appear to rule out the funding of representative actions and yet these may provide a more cost effective solution than litigating a group of many individual cases. Lack of clarity about cost sharing arrangements and what costs are recoverable create significant problems on taxation.

13. In the absence of legislative support, courts have had to tackle these problems pragmatically, making decisions on a creative and improvised basis with regard to cut-off dates, on how investigation should be conducted, on whether to process some or all cases in the group and on costs. While many judges have risen to the challenge, they themselves have indicated the need for a clearer framework in which to operate.

A new framework

14. The Law Society's Working Party has recommended that multi-party actions should be managed from the outset. Multi-party actions, of whatever description, will almost invariably merit the full hands-on judicial control which I am recommending for the most complex cases. The system of case management which I propose generally will provide judicial scrutiny at the stage when a defence is filed and appropriate handling thereafter. But in multi-party actions there is a need for the court to exercise control at a much earlier stage. Special arrangements will be required.

15. My proposals are designed to ensure that the court is notified of the existence of potential multi-party actions as early as possible. At this early stage no immediate decision is required but from then on the judge will be required to take a succession of decisions, all of which will impact on the successful handling of the actions. In this chapter I set out the factors which should be taken into account in relation to three main aspects:

(a) *the initial stages,* involving the application for and certification of a multi-party situation (MPS), appointment of a designated judge and the arrangements for lead representation;

(b) *the strategic priorities for court management,* including the definition of the group, the establishment of a register, the need to provide an effective filter, costs; and

(c) *protecting the interests of litigants* through the court's oversight of lawyers, the appointment of a trustee, the court's approval of settlements.

The initial stages

16. The earlier the court exercises control in a potential multi-party action the better chance of managing the case to a satisfactory resolution. Other jurisdictions have achieved this by requiring certification of a group or class action where there is an identifiable class or a specified number of persons, and the claims give rise to common issues of fact and law and where handling them together appears to the court to provide the best and the most practicable approach. The disadvantage of the solution usually adopted in other jurisdictions is that there may be many claimants with similar complaints but their claims may be more satisfactorily dealt with, at least in part, in separate proceedings. In this situation, it is likely that a group action will not be certified even though the case would benefit from collective management by the court.

17. Another approach is to stipulate that for the application of multi-party treatment the claims should give rise to common but not necessarily identical issues. The Law Society's rule extends this concept of flexibility. It recognises that there are clear advantages in drawing together claims which may be in some way related. I would wish to go further and to make it clear that cases that have been drawn together could be dealt with in different ways.

A multi-party situation

18. To achieve this I recommend that where proceedings will or may require collective treatment to a greater or lesser degree, provision should be made for a multi-party situation (MPS) to be established. This should be achieved with minimum expense by providing that the parties or the Legal Aid Board should make an application to the court which contains a formal declaration that the action meets the criteria for a multi-party situation and the grounds to demonstrate this. There should also be a power for the court itself to initiate or encourage an application. The application will be an executive act. The simplicity and lack of expense will encourage the proposed parties not to delay such a request, thus ensuring that the matter is brought to the attention of the court at the earliest opportunity.

19. The criteria to be met suggested by the Law Society's working party (draft rule 1.1) are:

"(a)   ten or more persons have claims against one or more parties;

(b)   the claims are in respect of, or arise out of, the same or similar circumstances;

(c)   a substantial number of the claims give rise to common questions of fact or law; and

(d)   the interests of justice will be served by proceedings under this rule."

20. I would broadly follow this suggestion, subject to two points. First, the minimum number of ten parties should not be written into the rules but be regarded simply as a guide. Especially in local cases, five may be a sufficient number. Secondly, the common issues need not necessarily predominate over issues affecting only individuals. All that is required is that the court is satisfied that the group will be sufficiently numerous and homogenous for the cases within the MPS to be more viable if there is a collective approach than if they are handled individually.

21. The MPS will provide maximum flexibility in that it may be proposed that parts of the proceedings are common to some or all of the claimants, and other parts are limited to individual claimants. In addition, individual and common proceedings should take place in parallel or the individual proceedings should take place in advance of or following the common proceedings. One MPS could accommodate the common tools used for disposal of multi-party proceedings, namely test or lead cases, and preliminary or common issues. It could also accommodate a representative action. All actions relating to the MPS could be stayed with their claimants fully protected as to limitation, at minimum cost and without the action being swamped by an influx of new claimants. An MPS will be a suitable framework for handling all the different types of multi-party actions common in this jurisdiction from local housing and environmental actions, consumer cases, financial actions such as the Lloyds litigation, single 'one-off' disasters and large scale complex environmental actions and product liability actions, including pharmaceutical and medical cases. The possible options for dealing with cases within the MPS are explored later in this chapter.

22. The subsequent procedure for the initial stages of the MPS following the application will be similar to that outlined in the Law Society's rule: a judge will need to decide whether an MPS which has been established should be certified. If it is, then a managing judge should be appointed and should have control of all proceedings arising out of the cases within the MPS. He will need to make decisions about notification of the action, lead lawyers, arrangements for representing the interests of the group, and on how costs will be treated. I deal with these detailed arrangements below.

Joining the MPS

23. Individual claimants would be able to participate in the application for the MPS by entering their names on a register, as suggested by the Law Society (paragraph 6.10.1-6.10.6) rather than by issue of a separate application for each possible action. Joining the register in this way would, after notification to the proposed defendants of the application for the MPS, suspend the operation of the Limitation Act. While this helps those who are on the register, it does not provide equivalent protection for those in the broader class who have not yet joined the register and the managing judge will therefore need to consider at an early stage the best means of achieving this. I consider this also in paragraph 45 below.

Certification

24. Certification is confirmation by the court that the criteria for the MPS have been met, so that cases can be treated within it and appropriate orders made and procedures applied. The court will arrange to consider certification after the initial application. If necessary it will ask for further information to enable it to reach a decision. The period for fixing a hearing may vary depending on the scale and complexity of the subject matter of the cases within the MPS but should be no more than three months. Parties may request an earlier hearing.

25. There is no need for the court to take a view of the merits at the certification stage. The discussion paper on multi-party actions of the Scottish Law Commission (*Multi-Party Actions*, Discussion Paper No.98, p. 184) describes the problems that consideration of the merits would involve for both the court and the parties:

> "... the applicant would no doubt be obliged, as in Quebec and Ontario, to lodge documents vouching the facts alleged in the application, such as affidavits and experts' reports; and in fairness the proposed defenders would have to be given an opportunity to inspect these documents and lodge documents of their own. The procedure would be elaborate and expensive, and the judge's task might be insuperably difficult, even with the assistance of counsel: he would

have to try to digest the materials lodged and the submissions made …There are the further objections that the applicant would be required to satisfy the court on the merits twice over, once at certification and again at the trial."

26. If the certificate were refused then a date for the determination of the MPS would be fixed. If a party wanted to continue proceedings the party would have to file a claim prior to that date to avoid the action coming to an end. A power to decertify is also needed because the situation can change so it is subsequently found that a multi-party situation is no longer appropriate.

Appointment of a managing judge

27. I have proposed generally that complex cases requiring full hands-on judicial control should be assigned to a single judge. This is to ensure continuity of decision making and will be of particular importance in cases involving complex technical subject matter. The Law Society's Working Party similarly recommended the appointment of a designated High Court judge with power to transfer the proceedings to a designated Circuit judge if "damages were likely to be modest and/or the litigation has a particular connection with a given locality." The appointment of an alternate judge was also recommended. All of this should be done either at or immediately after the certification stage.

28. Those responding to the issues paper have emphasised that it would be helpful to have arrangements for handling multi-party actions not only in the High Court in London but at courts elsewhere in the country although there is concern that it may not be possible to provide a single managing judge outside London. However, experience over the last year has demonstrated that it is possible to achieve this, particularly at major trial centres on Circuit or by coming to other arrangements such as the transfer of the multi-party estate litigation in Hackney, London to an Official Referee for management throughout the life of the action. I consider that it is important for lower value or local cases to be tried locally at appropriate courts and by either a High Court or Circuit judge. In making these arrangements it is important that the managing judge is appointed as soon as possible following certification and that the judge will be available throughout the life of the action.

29. The Law Society's working party recommended that the managing judge should appoint a designated Master or district judge. Experience of previous multi-party actions indicates that the judicial workload may be heavy and involve considerable time which it may be difficult for full-time Masters and district judges to provide alongside their other responsibilities. In these circumstances I see benefit in the temporary appointment of a deputy Master or deputy district judge, drawn from those practitioners who already have considerable experience of such litigation. There may also be a role in heavy, complex cases for a law clerk, as I recommend in relation to other complex cases in chapter 8 on the supporting structure.

30. At this stage, so early in the proceedings, it will be very difficult for any appointed judge to have reached the same stage of familiarity with the subject matter as the claimants and defendants. This problem was specifically discussed at the multi-party action seminar in February 1996 and it was generally agreed that it would be helpful for the judge to have background material made available before he makes any key decisions so that those decisions are based on a reasonable familiarity with the background. Ideally the information made available to the judge should be in the form of a joint submission prepared by the parties and including the background facts, stated jointly, in so far as they are agreed, or the different versions so far as they are not agreed, and a reading list, agreed as far as possible, together with instructions on technical matters.

Arrangements for lead representation

31. The Law Society's working party suggested that the court should have power to approve the lead lawyer for the group. In privately funded actions, private litigants will normally organise themselves efficiently. In legal aid cases the Legal Aid Board has special arrangements for this purpose. The court's responsibility is not to ensure that the legal services are adequate but to ensure the efficient conduct of the litigation. As this might be hindered by disagreements about lead lawyers in a mixed legal aid and private case such as tenants on a housing estate, or in a private case alone, where parties did not agree, the court should have a residual power to approve the lead lawyer if a difficulty arises. I deal later (paragraphs 70 - 74) with the court's general oversight of lawyers.

Court management: strategic priorities

32. The Law Society's working party recommended that the designated judge in a multi-party action should be given wide ranging powers to control the litigation and to ensure that it is expeditiously and economically progressed. The need for imagination and creativity in dealing with such litigation is attested to by every judge who has tried such a case. The kernel of the problem is the claimant's desire to pursue generic or common issues and the defendant's equally strong wish to investigate every individual case. There are three basic matters which a judge is almost invariably going to have to start to tackle at the certification stage and immediately after in an MPS.

(a)   Deciding whether there are generic issues present and whether they can be effectively decided within the MPS (this bears particularly on the composition and identity of the proposed beneficiaries of the proceedings).

(b)   Deciding whether there are issues applicable to certain individuals which need to be determined separately as to those individual claims; and if so to establish machinery for that purpose.

(c)   Deciding the order in which the issues identified at (a) and (b) are to be determined.

33. It is likely to be the case that the judge will usually need to treat (a) as the priority. On the whole, this is likely to be the most rational and economic way of working through the case. But this cannot be a rigid rule. There may be cases where, for example, it will be possible to establish, at relatively limited cost, that there are so few cases in the group in which damage can be proved that it is simply not worthwhile going into the generic issues in any detail.

34. In many cases, testing the likely viability of a sufficient number of individual cases cannot fairly be postponed until resolution of the generic issues is completed. This is because of the interdependence of the generic and individual issues. The latter shape the former. The cost-benefit justification of the proceedings depends on an adequate number of sufficiently promising cases. And, bearing in mind the adverse effects of a group action on defendants, it is necessary as a matter of basic justice to which they too are entitled.

35. This does not of course mean that examination of each case is required initially. More selective methods can be used. Although defendants traditionally oppose any selection of lead cases, there is a growing recognition that statistically valid samples of the wider group may be helpful in establishing criteria which individuals must meet to join the action. But above all, consideration of individual cases must not be allowed to paralyse overall progress of the group action.

36. At this early point the managing judge needs to be pro-active in addressing various key matters with the parties. Some of these will be decisions common to all complex litigation: identifying main and preliminary issues; drawing up a strategy for disclosure, for further investigative work and for the use of expert evidence; establishing a timetable. Others are specific to multi-party actions:

(a) definition of the group;

(b) considering the utility of sub-groups, lead cases or sampling;

(c) considering whether the MPS should be managed on an 'opt-out' basis;

(d) arrangements for giving notice of the action;

(e) establishing a filter by agreeing with the parties the diagnostic or other criteria to facilitate the identification of valid claims and the early elimination of weak or hopeless claims;

(f) determining the approach to costs.

37. There may be value in the court adopting a less formal approach to proceedings at this stage in order to encourage a more co-operative atmosphere of mutual endeavour to find the best ways of resolving the problems ahead. I understand that at the outset of the Lloyds litigation the court held an informal meeting with interested parties to identify the categories of case involved and to receive information so as to enable the court to apply management techniques.

Definition of the group

38. In some actions, the claimant group will be already well defined. In a transport disaster there will be a finite group. In a housing case, the group will be the tenants of the estate or lessees of a block of flats and although sub-groups may be helpful there will be a finite number of claimants. In other cases there will be a potential group defined by its circumstances; for instance all those within a specific geographical area in an environment case, or in medical cases, all those treated over a specific period. In some cases the potential group may be very numerous. In each case the judge will need to decide on the most efficient way of bringing potential claimants into the action, on the stage at which this should be done and whether it is appropriate to do this before or after examination of issues of principle or some of the generic issues common to all potential claimants. Clearly, it is pointless establishing a register for a large number of potential claimants if a decision on a key issue of liability or causation might determine the action at an early stage.

Sub-groups, lead cases and sampling

39. If there is already a substantial number of claims the court can proceed at once to identifying groups and sub-groups, agreeing on lead cases or samples. Most cases will fall into this category. But in large, generally pharmaceutical or other consumer cases, the problems are more complex. The court must be pro-active in considering how best to progress the action so that valid claims are included and weak or hopeless claims excluded. This involves considering whether claimants should be required to join a register: to 'opt-in', or whether unidentified potential claimants should be deemed to be included unless they 'opt-out' and the notice that should be given to potential claimants. It also involves consideration of the best way of providing an effective filter. I consider each of these below.

40. There are, however, difficulties in relation to test cases. Firstly, both claimants and defendants need to accept that the case will be a test case in relation, say, to liability for all those claimants in the same position. It is therefore necessary to make express orders in advance of determination that parties will be bound by the results. Secondly, there are also problems if the test case turns out to be atypical – if it is disposed of on particular grounds or if the judgment is couched in such a way that it leaves undetermined the similar issues in other cases. It is therefore necessary for the difficulties of identifying cases as test or lead cases to be specifically addressed by the court at an early stage. Thirdly, the current rules on legal aid make it difficult to pursue the test case approach, even though it may offer the most economical way of resolving actions affecting numbers of people in cases as diverse as pharmaceutical products and housing disrepair. It would clearly be sensible for the legal aid provisions to support, rather than to impede cost effective resolution by this means. I recommend that this should be looked at especially in relation to the sharing of costs between privately paying and legally aided clients.

41. The Lloyds litigation gives an example of what can be achieved. At an early stage the court identified and decided a number of preliminary issues of principle common to one or more categories of cases. With the active co-operation of the Court of Appeal and the House of Lords, appeals were expedited. The court selected from cases in a particular category lead or pilot cases for trial as to liability and principles relating to quantum in the hope that decisions in these cases would provide firm guidance in relation to other cases in the same category.

'Opt-out' or 'opt-in'

42. Typically multi-party rules in other jurisdictions adopt an 'opt-out' approach, in that a person's rights may be determined in a multi-party action without his or her express consent to or participation in the litigation (the approach is under rule 23 in the US, and similar rules in Ontario, British Columbia and Australia). Members of the group may, however, opt out – in other words, indicate that they wish to be excluded. If they opt out, a person is not able to benefit from any award of damages, although they may always bring a separate action. It has generally been considered that there would be difficulties in this jurisdiction in taking forward cases on an 'opt-out' basis because of the cost sharing rules, but the experience of 'opt-in' registers with cut-off dates has not been altogether positive or, indeed, helpful in resolving the allocation of costs, particularly since most multi-party actions are legally aided.

43. For personal injury claims, it has been argued that an 'opt-out' scheme is unfair to defendants because it does not enable them to know the size of the group and the number of claims and their nature. The Law Society's working party therefore recommended an 'opt-in' approach with the establishment of a register at the initial stage of certification; provisions for varying the criteria for joining the register, as the case developed; and provisions for establishing cut-off dates and for costs sharing. This is the preferred approach where there is a well defined or identifiable group of claimants.

44. There are, however, problems in establishing an 'opt-in' register too early in the life of a potential multi-party action where there is a large pool of unidentified claimants. Although the register may appear to give defendants an idea of the size of the group, experience has shown that early cut-off dates tend to result in a rush to register which encourages many weak or hopeless claims to be registered and inflates the pool of potential claimants. The bandwagon effect may raise unrealistic hopes of compensation from claimants. Adverse publicity may have a severe negative impact on the business of defendants at a stage when there has been insufficient investigative work to establish clear criteria for the claims or, in some cases, to establish any clear indication of causation.

45. In some circumstances defendants and the Legal Aid Board may be well aware that there are large numbers of people who might be affected by the product in question. In those circumstances the claim may be more manageable if the initial certification puts any further individual applications for legal aid on hold and provides for deemed inclusion of unidentified potential claimants on an 'opt-out' basis until definitive criteria can be established to provide for the effective filtering of potential claims before they are entered on the register. There is, however, a need for action to be taken in relation to the limitation period and this can only be effective if there are provisions to suspend or freeze the running of the limitation period on certification of the MPS, as in many other jurisdictions, so that further claimants whose claims were not being considered in detail at this stage were not disadvantaged. This will require primary legislation. In the absence of such legislation I have no doubt that courts will continue to exercise their discretion to admit latecomers since the existence of the MPS ensures that defendants are already aware of the potential claims against them.

46. The court should have powers to progress the MPS on either an 'opt-out' or an 'opt-in' basis, whichever is most appropriate to the particular circumstances and whichever contributes best to the overall disposition of the case. In some circumstances it will be appropriate to commence an MPS on an 'opt-out' basis and to establish an 'opt-in' register at a later stage.

Notice

47. If members of a group are to opt out, or to join the register, they must know about the multi-party action. Notice may also be necessary at various other times throughout the course of the proceedings, eg, determination of generic issues; on settlement. In reaching the decision on notice the court must have in mind the cost of such notice and its usefulness: in some cases notice may be so expensive as to be disproportionate to the costs and benefits of the litigation, or it may not serve a useful purpose.

48. In a multi-party action where there are many claims, each of which is small, there is little to recommend in a rule making notice to each potential claimant mandatory. The costs of identifying potential claimants, and preparing and sending the notice, will make the litigation as a whole uneconomic. In any event, where such claimants receive the notice and choose to opt out, they will receive nothing. Because with small claims it is uneconomic for them to litigate individually, they will almost invariably remain members of the group. In the United States, in small claims group actions, very few of the tens of thousands – in some cases millions – of potential claimants actually notified choose to opt out. Accordingly, courts must have the discretion to dispense with notice enabling parties to opt out having regard to factors such as the cost, the nature of the relief, the size of individual claims, the number of members of a group, the chances that members will wish to opt out and so on.

49. Once the claims become more substantial, however, individual notice is economically possible. It is difficult to set a figure and the matter must be left to judicial discretion, taking into account the factors I have already mentioned. Yet even if the court decides that notice must be given to members of a group, it should have a discretion as to how this is to be done – individual notification, advertising, media broadcast, notification to a sample group, or a combination of means, or different means for different members of the group. In each case the court must take into account the likely cost and benefit before deciding on the course of action.

50. The court should have a discretion to order by whom the advertising should be undertaken. The Law Society's working party recommended that the Law Society should provide further guidance to solicitors on advertisements placed in the early stages prior to the establishment of a group action. I welcome that. The Law Society also recommended that the timing and placement of subsequent advertisements should be approved by the court. There is also a need to approve the content of the advertisements and for the court to decide on the appropriate body who should place the advertisement – either the lead solicitor, the Law Society itself with its substantial media expertise, the Legal Aid Board or the court itself.

Establishing a filter

51. It is important for the court to address one of the major problems identified in every response: the need to find better ways of weeding out weak and/or hopeless claims or, if possible, to prevent them entering the action in the first place. In legally aided cases, it also requires consideration of the best way in which the legal aid decisions on merits and cost-benefit can be meshed in with court procedures.

52. Once sufficient investigative work has been completed, it should be possible to establish criteria for entry to or removal from the register. Such an agreement, reached at an early stage, even if that in itself takes several months to arrive at, should lead to a considerable saving of time and legal costs both to the Legal Aid Board and for the defendants. The court, in effect will have drawn up the criteria for the merits test that will be applied to each individual claim. It would also mean that parties who have no realistic chance of bringing a claim are weeded out at an earlier stage or not brought in. This will be beneficial not only for defendants but also for the individuals themselves and for those claimants with stronger claims who do proceed. It has been emphasised that the bandwagon effect, in cases such as benzodiazepine, has the effect of swamping stronger claims with a host of weaker claims, many of them with very questionable foundation, and making the action as a whole unviable. While criteria for entry will be of most concern in 'creeping disaster' cases including pharmaceutical and environmental claims, I see a clear need to establish equivalent criteria in all multi-party situations.

53. Agreement on criteria should assist in drawing up standard questionnaires, agreed between the parties, the court and the Legal Aid Board. These would ensure that the initial information obtained from potential claimants enables all concerned to make a clearer assessment of the number of claimants who might actually have a case. They would enable the Board to make a more accurate cost-benefit assessment, than it can at present. They would provide the criteria for the merits test for the initial wave of entrants to a register if the Board decides to grant legal aid.

54. In legally aided cases, the present arrangements for assessing the merits of potential multi-party actions rest largely with the Legal Aid Board. Many commentators consider that it has proved difficult to establish appropriate and satisfactory arrangements despite repeated endeavours. Suggested refinements include the obtaining of an independent opinion from counsel on the merits and allowing representations from defendants as in Scotland.

55. Through the registration of an MPS the court will be involved from an early stage and will determine the shape and progress of the action. It will provide an independent focus on the preliminary investigative effort and will provide a more natural context in which to consider the defendant's representations. The Legal Aid Board has difficulty, at least procedurally, in dealing with these and getting the claimants' response to the defendants' allegations. It is difficult for the Board to 'adjudicate' between them. This essentially adversarial process is more naturally controlled by the court. The alternative is parallel assessment of the merits by the court and the Board. The preferred approach is for the court to delineate the shape of the action and determine the criteria which must be met by those wishing to join the action. The Board would make its decisions on funding in the light of the court's decision.

Costs of multi-party actions

56. The Chief Taxing Master drew attention, at the Inquiry's seminar, to the need for the court to address the question of costs at an early stage, and for the judge to make costs sharing orders in respect of both claimants and defendants. These orders have to apply both to the costs of clients in respect of their own solicitors and of the opposing party should it obtain an order for costs. Orders on costs may need the assistance of the Taxing Masters if appropriate.

57. If the treatment of costs is not examined from the outset, the result is either subsidiary litigation or protracted problems when the matter comes to taxation. My general proposals for information on costs to be made available at every stage when the managing judge is involved are all the more important in relation to multi-party actions, where many claimants will be legally aided and have no direct control over costs and where costs can escalate dramatically. At every stage in the management of the MPS the judge should consider, with the help of the parties, the potential impact on costs of the directions that are contemplated, and whether these are justified in relation to what is at issue. Parties and their legal representatives, as in other cases on the multi-track, should provide information on costs already incurred and be prepared to estimate the cost of proposed further work. It has been suggested that such examination should occur at intervals of three months. That must be for the managing judge to determine in each individual case.

58. Other common law jurisdictions with a cost-shifting rule have not changed it when introducing special rules for multi-party actions. Multi-party actions are not so significantly different from ordinary litigation as to justify such a change. However, there are several respects in which the ordinary approach to costs needs to be modified.

59. The court needs a wide discretion in deciding what are costs for the purposes of the ordinary rule. Multi-party actions involve costs which do not normally arise in individual litigation, such as co-ordinating and communicating within the group and liaising with the media in what are often high profile cases. At present the costs of action groups or claimants' co-ordinating committees are not generally met on taxation, although they have been in some cases. Yet without such groups it may be difficult to co-ordinate an action. It is also probably the case that effective co-ordination of the action saves defendants costs overall. It is necessary that the costs of action groups should be met on taxation and that a reasonable basis for acknowledging these, and any others considered necessary or appropriate, should be established and applied by the court from the start. The Law Society's working party recommended that work done to co-ordinate between claimants and their solicitors should be recoverable *inter partes* and I support this.

60. Thirdly, in some cases it will be fair that the group as a whole bears a proportionate share of any costs. This was the approach in the well known decision involving the drug Opren, *Davies (Joseph Owen) v Eli Lilly & Co.*

[1987] 1 WLR 1136, CA. However, this approach cannot be adopted as an invariable rule for multi-party litigation. The Scottish Law Commission has cogently set out the reasons (op.cit., p.278):

> "Similarly, we think it is only reasonable that the members of a class should contribute to the expenses of a class action brought on their behalf. It would be difficult, however, to give effect to this policy in a class action procedure with an opt out scheme. It is significant that in those jurisdictions with opt out schemes the other class members are not obliged by the rules to contribute to the representative party's expenses. It would obviously be impossible to enforce an order for contribution against class members who could not be identified, and inequitable to enforce it only against those who could be identified."

61. The result of always adopting the Davies approach would be that in non-legally aided cases there would be a denial of access to justice. Indeed, this was evident in the Opren litigation itself. The claimants' legal advisers hoped that the lead cases could be chosen entirely from those legally aided claimants with nil contributions. When the Court of Appeal in Davies held that costs should be borne equally amongst all claimants, the privately funded clients were advised to discontinue because of the threat which costs posed to them. Ultimately a private benefactor agreed to underwrite their costs and the case was soon after settled without trial.

62. It is therefore essential that the court approves any cost sharing arrangement at the outset, and that this includes any arrangements between the privately paying and legally aided claimants. Information on costs already incurred and to be incurred in the future will allow claimants to assess their eventual liability as the case develops.

Legal aid funding

63. At present in most group actions the Legal Aid Board is underwriting the majority of claimants' costs. The Lloyds litigation, although it is largely privately funded, includes a number of legally aided claimants. In other smaller cases, notably housing cases, there is often a mix of legally aided and private claimants. Until now the cost of large product liability actions has been a significant deterrent to unassisted claimants. It therefore seems sensible to consider whether it would be possible for future actions affecting substantial numbers of people to be handled in a way which either combines funding from legal aid and private sources or extends financial eligibility to those who might normally be ineligible.

64. Tight control by the court over the management of the case should reduce cost and make it more predictable. The arrangements I outline for establishing an effective filter prior to entry on the register should reduce the overall numbers of claimants and particularly those with weak claims. This of itself should enable privately paying litigants to enter into cases with more confidence than they can at present where costs are totally uncontrolled.

65. Legally aided clients already contribute to the costs of their cases through contributions and the operation of the statutory charge. At present this is an open-ended commitment. I consider it appropriate that legally aided clients should continue to contribute to the costs, but there should be scope within a more managed system for this to be estimated as the case develops. There may also be scope to extend the upper limits of financial eligibility on the basis of increased contributions. In appropriate cases, with tight judicial management and control on costs it may be possible to make an estimate of overall liability in advance. Such an approach could be structured in a way which included a requirement to make a personal financial commitment to the action at the stage of initial entry to the register, and perhaps at later stages, when, for example, the judge imposes a cut-off date. At each stage the commitment should be for a fixed and finite amount rather than the present general open-ended liability.

66. The requirement of a personal financial commitment would reduce the element of speculative litigation which is one of defendants' main concerns. If it could be balanced by a limit on individual claimants' liability for costs at each stage, that would meet the main concern of claimants.

67. A number of those who represent the interests of claimants and consumers have suggested that such a scheme could be combined with the often-floated idea of a contingency legal aid fund (CLAF) funded by percentage success fees from successful claimants or an institutionalised conditional fee scheme for multi-party actions. They believe that their clients would be more than happy to forgo such a percentage if it meant that they could be on the register for a specified entry fee and that their maximum liability for costs could be known in advance. There may be interest in developing this approach from those currently providing legal expenses insurance. While personal injury cases could be funded on the basis of conditional fees without the establishment of a CLAF, such funding is a possibility at present for other multi-party actions. I hope that the Lord Chancellor's Department and Legal Aid Board can reconsider the possibility of a CLAF in the context of the greater financial control over litigation which my proposals represent.

68. A precedent for such a multi-party action fund, started initially by government, but subsequently funded by a percentage levy on successful litigants, is Ontario's 'class proceedings fund', funded by the Law Foundation of Canada. With its counterparts elsewhere, the Law Foundation derives its income mainly from interest on trust accounts. The fund is to provide financial support for claimants to class proceedings in respect of disbursements – not legal costs generally – related to the proceedings, and for payments to defendants in respect of costs awards made in their favour against claimants who have received financial support from the fund. The principal advantages of such a fund are that it would be entitled to assist all multi-party litigants, not just those with incomes low enough to qualify for legal aid.

Protecting the overall interests of litigants

69. The rationale behind multi-party actions is that the diminution of the individual rights of claimants and defendants makes the overall action more practicable and less costly to progress. But there is a need to ensure that those rights are protected: for defendants by the perceived fairness of the balance between generic issues and by establishing effective criteria for entry to the action. For claimants, the court has a more explicit role in ensuring that their interests are protected:

(a)   in supervising the activity of lawyers;

(b)   in ensuring the effective representation of their interests through the appointment of a trustee in appropriate cases;

(c)   in approving settlement.

Lawyers and multi-party actions

70. There is nothing wrong with lawyers taking the initiative in multi-party actions. A typical claimant in such cases is often poorly informed, or ignorant of the particular facts, and it will only be the lawyer who recognises the potential for claiming. Moreover, even if a claimant does suspect a violation of the law and seeks redress, the cost of doing so may act as a disincentive to action. Enhancing access to justice demands that those ignorant of their legal rights, or unable because of the cost to pursue them, be given the opportunity of vindicating them. If this requires lawyer initiative, then so be it.

71. But because the lawyers will often be taking the initiative in multi-party actions, there are potential conflicts between their interests and those of group members. This can derive from the very reasons which make multi-party litigation attractive in the first place – the possible ignorance of potential claimants, and that they are disorganised and possibly also dispersed. Thus the opportunities for self-interested behaviour are generally greater in group litigation than in ordinary litigation. Particular forms which this has taken include bringing claims known to be unfounded for harassing purposes and genuine but limited value claims, knowing in both cases that defendants will feel impelled to settle on terms advantageous to the lawyer though possibly of little benefit to the group members. It would be remiss of the Inquiry not to make some recommendations to anticipate problems which experience here and elsewhere demonstrates can arise.

72. In general terms the problems arise because of the relative absence of client control. When a group is large, members may not even be aware of the litigation until it is well under way. Even if they are aware of the litigation, how are claimants to have an influence? The view of individual claimants is greatly diluted, if not excluded, in a large group. As for a majority view, the costs of communicating between claimants, and organising meetings, may be so great as to make it impractical in many cases. If claimants are not involved in the conduct of litigation, however, they cannot really act as a monitor on the way the lawyers handle it.

73. Among the strongest disincentives to meritless or frivolous multi-party litigation will be prompt dismissal by the courts. Court control from the very early days will ensure this. So too will an early determination of the merits. Courts must also be prepared to visit sanctions on lawyers who do not live up to the standards of professional behaviour expected. The Bar and the Law Society must give special attention to the ethical problems involved in multi-party litigation.

74. Lawyers conducting multi-party litigation are entitled, of course, to reasonable remuneration but there are reports that working excessive hours and inflation of the time spent on a case are common abuses in multi-party action litigation in the United States. Where multi-party litigation in this country is legally aided, the Legal Aid Board has a duty to oversee the lawyers and to call a halt to this type of behaviour. Courts, too, have a role in this regard. I am recommending generally that costs should be actively considered by the judge throughout the case and that, if appropriate, a Taxing Master should also be involved throughout. Because of this continuing involvement, they will have a store of knowledge about the case. That involvement at the taxing stage will be invaluable. Moreover, if the lawyers know that the judge and his team managing the case may have an influence on their remuneration, this is likely to act as a strong incentive to proper and reasonable behaviour on their part.

Multi-party litigants and their support

75. Multi-party actions are in any event an area of litigation which is even more lawyer-driven than any other. This may be exacerbated when the lead firm is funded on contract by the Legal Aid Board and the case will become driven by the legal team in conjunction with the Board. In those circumstances the court has a duty to ensure that the interests of the client group are protected. In the past it has been assumed that this was achieved by individuals being represented by their own solicitor and the action co-ordinated by a steering committee or lead firm. While this may provide a degree of local hand-holding and support, it does not enable the client group, either individually or as a whole, to assume the role of an informed client.

76. But there is a wider issue here which may be particularly relevant in legally aided cases. That is the need to represent the interests of all the group, including those not specifically identified, and to ensure effective conduct of the litigation from the claimants' point of view.

77. The Inquiry has heard how action groups can take on the role of an informed client, with formal constitutions established at the outset to provide for later problems, particularly in relation to settlement. Such groups can take account of their members' interests and ensure that these are reflected in the instructions to their legal representatives. Where there is no formal group representing the interests of the claimants, or where it is considered that the litigants' interests require separate representation, a trustee should be appointed by the court. There may also be a need for a trustee in cases where there are both privately paying and legally aided litigants, to ensure that the interests of both are taken into account. The trustee would be publicly funded, in some cases by the Legal Aid Board, on the basis that he or she would be fulfilling a role that would otherwise be met by an assisted person's own solicitors, or by arrangements under an 'all work' contract, which would require the lead firm to make arrangements for looking after individual clients as well as fulfilling a wider role.

78. The role of trustee would be flexible but the main elements might be:

(a) to identify the objectives and priorities of the parties (by meeting them at an early stage to determine their needs), and to assist with devising a plan to meet those objectives;

(b)   to maintain a watching brief on the public interest elements of the action to ensure that opportunities to instigate change are not missed;

(c)   where necessary, to look after the interests of unidentified or unborn claimants and to act as protection against defendants picking out lead cases for settlement;

(d)   if appropriate, to assist in the formation of an informal support group, if one does not come into being spontaneously (this could be done by advertising and holding regional meetings to inform people of the impending action and put them in touch with one another).

Approving settlement

79. There is a strong case for court approval of all multi-party settlements, especially where the defendant offers a lump sum settlement, because:

(a)   it is necessary to ensure that the lawyers do not benefit themselves while obtaining minimal benefit for their clients, or, alternatively, profiting from the vulnerability of commercially sensitive defendants;

(b)   all members of the group are bound although they may be only indirectly represented;

(c)   a lump sum settlement must be fair although it explicitly does not try to match individual loss exactly.

80. There are two possible approaches to enabling the court to provide additional safeguards in this context. First, and particularly in cases where there may be unidentified or unborn potential claimants, the judge should satisfy himself that proper arrangements have been made, or request the trustee to do so.

81. Secondly, the court could require an identified and finite group of claimants to have in place from the outset a constitution including provisions relating to acceptance of settlement, such as majority voting. The Inquiry heard how important this was considered to be by the action groups in the Lloyds litigation, which represented numbers of largely privately paying claimants. In such a case where a minority objected to the settlement, it would be open to the judge to hear their objections. The court may also have a role in administering settlements or resolving points of difficulty in borderline cases where criteria for settlement have been agreed.

82. Experience elsewhere suggests that the court also has a role in cases which are before the court solely for settlement purposes. Experience, particularly in the USA, suggests that judicial oversight of settlements is not effective unless there are understood criteria for approval, which provide for cases which may be before the court solely for settlement purposes. Although the MPS is primarily a vehicle for managing actions, it could, if necessary, be requested to provide court oversight and approval of settlement. In such a case the criteria might cover such matters as whether:

(a)   the pre-requisites for a multi-party situation have been met;

(b)   the multi-party definition is appropriate and fair, taking into account, among other things, whether it is consistent with the purpose for which it is certified, whether it may be over-inclusive or under-inclusive, and whether division into sub-groups may be necessary or advisable;

(c)   persons with similar claims will receive similar treatment, taking into account any differences in treatment between present and future claimants;

(d)   notice to members of the group is adequate, taking into account the ability of persons to understand the notice and its significance to them;

(e)   the representation of members of the group is adequate, taking into account the possibility of conflicts of interest in the representation of persons whose claims differ in material respects from those of other claimants;

(f)   'opt-out' rights are adequate to fairly protect interests of group members;

(g)   provisions for lawyers' fees are reasonable, taking into account the value and amount of services rendered and the risks assumed;

(h)   the settlement will have significant effects on parties in other actions pending;

(i)   the settlement will have significant effects on potential claims of group members for injury or loss arising out of the same or related occurrences but excluded from the settlement;

(j)   the compensation for loss and damage provided by the settlement is reasonable, taking into account the balance of costs to defendant and benefits to class members; and

(k)   any claims process under the settlement is likely to be fair and
        equitable in its operation.

A special tribunal?

83. In the issues paper published in January 1996, views were sought on
the merits of establishing a special tribunal to act as a substitute for
proceedings in court as to liability. The response has been overwhelmingly
negative. There is a general consensus that the courts are rapidly developing
case management techniques that will be further assisted by my general
proposals and that the substitution of an inquiry would necessitate greatly
increased funding to allow for the representation of the interests of the
parties. It is considered that there would be no benefits to the process or to
the funding of multi-party actions.

84. There was also concern about my proposal that, in appropriate
circumstances, a judge in charge of a multi-party action should move into
'inquiry' mode. The powers which the new rules will give to judges to
control and limit evidence will result in far greater judicial control over the
pace, scope and ordering of litigation. At a time of significant change this in
itself represents a major shift of responsibility towards a more pro-active
judicial involvement. I see no need for any further rules in this respect.

Inquiries

85. The Law Society's working party recommended that legal aid be
extended to boards or inquiries and that the costs of such representation
should in principle be recoverable in any subsequent group action. It also
recommended that there should be a presumption that any findings of fact
be binding on the parties to any subsequent proceedings and inquests if the
presumption was agreed by the parties before the inquiry. My own
preference would be for a *prima facie* assumption that the findings are
correct.

86. The Scottish Law Commission has pointed out the difficulty of devising
a single set of proceedings to serve with fairness all the purposes envisaged:
the fatal accident inquiry is concerned with establishing, in the public
interest, the circumstances surrounding particular fatalities; the criminal
trial is obviously concerned with commission of a criminal offence, and
there are strong rules excluding certain evidence in relation to this; and
civil proceedings are concerned with person's claims, mainly to damages
(Scottish Law Commission, *Multi-Party Actions*, Discussion Paper No.98,
pp.50-1). It is clear from responses to the Inquiry that there appears to be a
considerable element of duplication in the current approach to the
establishment of disaster inquiries, inquests and subsequent criminal and

civil litigation. There are also useful lessons to be learned from the study of previous inquiries and subsequent litigation. It was not part of the remit of my Inquiry to investigate this area but, despite the difficulties identified by the Scottish Law Commission, I consider that this is an area which requires further work, in particular in relation to its potential to inform or in part replace litigation in appropriate cases.

Conclusion

87. Although in the Inquiry's issues paper I encouraged consideration of more radical alternatives to the new rule proposed by the Law Society's working party, I have been persuaded by the strength of the response that such approaches are not yet necessary, given the continuing development of more effective ways of handling multi-party actions. I hope that my proposals of a multi-party situation, of pro-active judicial control and prospective arrangements as to how costs should be dealt with (although not the actual amounts involved) as well as the other recommendations in this chapter, will contribute to that process. It will be for the Lord Chancellor, if these proposals meet approval, to develop them in conjunction with the relevant interests.

Recommendations

My recommendations are as follows.

(1) Where proceedings will or may require collective treatment, parties or the Legal Aid Board should apply for a multi-party situation (MPS) to be established. This would suspend the operation of the Limitation Act. The court may also initiate an application. Within the MPS, part of the proceedings could be common to some or all of the claimants, and other parts could be limited to individual claimants.

(2) Individual claimants would be able to join the MPS at the application stage and subsequently by entering their names on an initial register.

(3) The court should certify an MPS if it is satisfied that the group or groups will be sufficiently large and homogeneous, and that the cases within the MPS will be more viable if there is a collective approach than if they are handled individually.

(4) Lower value or local cases should be dealt with locally at appropriate courts by either a High Court or Circuit judge.

(5) A managing judge should be appointed at or as soon as possible following certification and should handle the action throughout.

(6) In appropriate cases additional support may be provided by the appointment of a deputy Master or deputy district judge from those

practitioners who already have considerable experience of multi-party litigation.

(7)   The court should have a residual power to approve the lead lawyer if a difficulty arises in appointing one.

(8)   The court should usually aim to treat as a priority the determination of the generic issues while establishing economic methods of handling the individual cases.

(9)   The court should have power to progress the MPS on an 'opt-out' or 'opt-in' basis, whichever contributes best to the effective and efficient disposition of the case.

(10)   In reaching a decision on notice of the action to potential claimants, the court must take into account the cost of such notice and its usefulness.

(11)   The court should be responsible for determining whether the action has merit and should proceed and the criteria which must be met by those wishing to join the action.

(12)   The court should determine the arrangements for costs and cost sharing at the outset. The costs of action groups should be recoverable on taxation.

(13)   The Lord Chancellor's Department and Legal Aid Board should consider the possibility of extending the upper limits of financial eligibility on the basis of increased contributions. In appropriate cases, with tight judicial management and control on costs it may be possible for assisted persons' liability to be assessed and fixed in advance.

(14)   The possibility of a contingency legal aid fund should be reconsidered in the context of these proposals.

(15)   The court has a duty to protect the interests of claimants, especially those unidentified or unborn.

(16)   In appropriate cases the court should appoint a trustee.

(17)   Multi-party settlements should be approved by the court especially where the defendant offers a lump sum settlement.

(18)   The court should require an identified and finite group of claimants to have in place from the outset a constitution including provisions relating to acceptance of settlement.

Chapter 18   Crown Office List

Introduction

1. Many of the public law proceedings which are administered by the Crown Office are of considerable constitutional significance, since they are the means whereby the lawfulness of decisions of public bodies can be examined by the courts and individuals who have been improperly detained can secure their liberty. As has so often been stated, the growth of public law and, in particular, of judicial review has been one of the most significant developments in the English legal system in the last 25 years. It is therefore important to consider how the procedure and management of these proceedings are to be absorbed into the reformed civil justice system which I am advocating.

2. My objective is to secure greater uniformity of procedure among those cases which are dealt with by the Crown Office, which can at present be bedevilled by disputes as to procedure, notably where there may be an option as to what remedy to seek. For the same reason, there also needs to be greater uniformity between the procedures in public law cases and those in private law cases. The procedural exclusivity rule, whereby it is normally an abuse of process not to use judicial review when it is the appropriate procedure, has led to wholly undesirable procedural wrangles and has been much criticised by distinguished commentators. It continues to cause problems, notwithstanding some clarification by the House of Lords in the *Roy* case (*Roy v Kensington and Chelsea and Westminster FPC* [1992] 1 AC 624).

3. The Law Commission, in its 1994 report, *Administrative Law: Judicial Review and Statutory Appeals,* has made a series of recommendations for procedural reform which for the most part I warmly endorse. That report was published before the date of my interim report, on which my present proposals are also based. I have benefited considerably from the advice of the Crown Office Working Group under the chairmanship of Lord Justice Brooke, the former chairman of the Commission. I am also grateful to the members of the Justice/Public Law Project and to those who have organised and attended a series of conferences on public law proceedings, and made written submissions to me arising out of them.

4. Cases administered by the Crown Office List rarely involve determining factual evidence or hearing witnesses. Any necessary evidence is nearly always given by affidavit. Discovery, too, is rare. Crown Office proceedings are therefore on the whole free of the excesses that plague other proceedings. They can proceed rapidly to a hearing which will usually be quite short. They should involve relatively modest expenditure by the parties.

Nominated judges

5. The use of judges specially nominated to hear Crown Office cases is one of the strengths of the Crown Office List. I hope, however, that in the future more judges from other Divisions can be nominated to hear Crown Office cases where their experience in a specialist area would be valuable.

Local disposal

6. There is also a real need for the resolution of some Crown Office List cases on Circuit. Some cases, for example those which involve central government or an issue of general importance, would not be appropriate for this, but many Crown Office List cases are no less local than disputes between two individuals. An example is judicial review of those housing cases which are not disposed of by the new procedure I am recommending. There has been a number of experiments designed to ascertain whether it is practicable for selected cases to be heard on Circuit, but they have not been successful. Nevertheless I am convinced that certain cases ought to be heard locally. The problem is that until the facility for cases to be heard at a local centre is firmly established, the cases do not surface. How best to achieve this depends on the resources available. However, I recommend that a start should be made. One way would be to select a single provincial centre for the hearing of Crown Office List cases. Unless a High Court judge could be made available, which I accept is unlikely, one or preferably two Circuit judges, sitting as deputy High Court judges, should be nominated for the purpose. The experience with Chancery and Mercantile lists suggests that it is essential to have a judge with the required expertise available with sufficient regularity to persuade local practitioners to take what will be on offer seriously.

Judicial review

7. Some of the general recommendations which I am making apply as much to Crown Office cases as to private law cases. Some apply even more strongly. Among these is the recommendation that applicants should be encouraged to resolve their complaints without resorting to litigation. There is an increasing number of grievance procedures and ombudsmen available for this purpose. Applicants should normally use these procedures first. Judicial review ought to be conserved as a remedy of last resort. Before an application is made to initiate proceedings for judicial review, the proposed applicant should have taken advantage of any system of dispute resolution available, unless it would be unreasonable to do so, for example because the complaints procedure is too slow. If there is no satisfactory system of ADR the applicant should notify the proposed defendant of the claim, giving sufficient information to enable a response to be made rapidly so that the applicant could still comply with the three month time limit within which the claim must usually be brought. The defendant would not be obliged to respond, but should notify the applicant that there was to be no response. The fact that the court can extend time should avoid an applicant who waits for a reasonable period for a response from being prejudiced. This will put on a slightly more formal basis the growing practice of writing a letter before commencing proceedings, which was strongly urged by Brooke J in *R v Horsham DC ex p Wenman* [1994] 4 AER 681.

The form of application

8. Rather than being a completely separate form, as at present, an application for judicial review should follow the standard claim form. In other words, it must include a summary of the facts relied on and its contents must be verified. It will therefore replace the application and principal affidavit in support. I hope that it will also overcome the current problem of excessively lengthy applications and affidavits. There will, of course, be particular requirements for claims for judicial review, for example that a copy of the decision which is the subject matter of the claim and any response by the defendant to the pre-application process must be attached.

The remedies which should be available

9. I see no reason why any remedies which could be obtained in a private law action, or a writ of *habeas corpus,* should not also be included in a claim for judicial review, so long as it is not inconvenient to do so. The court should be able to direct that additional claims should be disposed of separately or made the subject of a separate claim if their inclusion would interfere with the disposal of the claim for judicial review. When considering whether to grant relief the court should be able to take into account any offer by the defendant to pay compensation.

10. I recommend that the court should have an express power to grant advisory declarations when it is in the public interest to do so. However, this should be limited to cases where the issue was of public importance and was defined in sufficiently precise terms, and where the appropriate parties were before the court.

11. Litigants will be encouraged to issue their claims for judicial review at the Crown Office, since it will continue to administer them. However, the originating process will not be invalidated if the claimant issues a claim in another court and it will be for that court to transmit the claim to the Crown Office.

Preliminary consideration

12. I agree with the Law Commission that the leave stage should be renamed the preliminary consideration stage. This will also demonstrate that the initial filtering process is very much the same as that which will take place in private law proceedings. It should, however, take place on the application being made, before any defence is filed, rather than after the defence has been filed, as usually happens in private law proceedings. The same criteria should also be applied in determining whether the case should proceed, namely whether there is a realistic prospect of success or some other reason why the case ought to be disposed of at a substantive hearing. The judge should give brief reasons where he refuses permission to proceed.

13. After a written refusal there should be a right of renewal to a single judge at an oral hearing and a further right of appeal to the Court of Appeal, but only with the leave of the judge or a Lord Justice, from a refusal at the oral hearing. In my view it would be sensible if this procedure applied in criminal causes and matters as well as civil causes. I recognise, however, that it raises questions of judicial deployment in criminal cases and further consultation will be needed to ensure that any difficulties can be overcome.

14. The preliminary consideration should be in writing, as the Law Commission proposes, unless the court directs an oral hearing. The judge conducting the preliminary consideration should be able to call upon the defendant to provide information, in a standard questionnaire, or to make representations, although I hope that greater use of the pre-application process will mean that this is not normally necessary. It would not be obligatory for the defendant to respond but failure to do could be taken into account in the decision whether the application should proceed.

15. The court should be able to grant interim relief before the preliminary consideration of the claim, although interim relief on an *ex parte* basis would only be granted in a very clear and urgent case. The rules should also make it clear that any appropriate remedy, including a stay, an interim declaration and bail, can be granted. The provisions on bail will be clarified, as recommended by the working group.

16. Case management is applicable to judicial review claims as well as to private law claims. At the preliminary consideration the judge should consider giving directions for the future conduct of the proceedings and the claimant should be able to indicate on a *pro forma* or standard form what directions should be given. The judge should also be able to ask the defendant for his views, although in most cases it will be preferable to make the directions subject to any written representations by him. Directions could be given as to:

(a)   the persons on whom the claim should be served (the court should consider whether any public body other than the proposed defendant will be affected by the decision);

(b)   whether there should be a defence;

(c)   what, if any, further evidence is required and the form it should take (usually witness statements but exceptionally affidavits);

(d)   the form which the hearing should take.

The judge should lay down a timetable, with as precise a date for the hearing as can be given. By giving directions the court should be able to limit the number of interlocutory hearings.

Defence

17. If the issues are sufficiently clear from the claim the judge may decide to inform the defendant that he need only provide a skeleton argument. Otherwise, he will indicate that there should be a defence, although the defendant will have the option of saying on the notice of intention to defend that he will not file a defence. The defence should be in the standard form of a defence to the claim. Like the claim, it will not be a lengthy and complex document but should be restricted to a succinct statement of the facts (so far as they differ from those set out in the claim) relied on by the defendant and his contentions. It should have annexed to it any documents relied on. It would replace the present principal affidavit, since there will be a requirement that the defendant verify the truth of its contents.

18. The defendant should be able to counterclaim for a declaration or other appropriate remedy which arises out of the matters to which the claim relates, unless the counterclaim could not be dealt with conveniently with the claim, as might happen where it would add extra parties. In certain cases it may be appropriate to impose a condition that a public authority should not seek the costs of the counterclaim.

Further evidence

19. The parties will be allowed to put in additional evidence, but they will have to justify the costs of doing so, since judicial review is not the normal way of resolving issues of fact.

Standing

20. I support the Law Commission's recommendation that the present generous practice of the courts in interpreting the requirement that the applicant must have a 'sufficient interest' in the matter to which the application relates should be incorporated in the new rules. This should be in general terms, although a practice guide could indicate relevant factors. I agree with the Commission that the applicant will have standing if he has been or will be adversely affected or if it is in the public interest that the proceedings should be brought. This is the test which I consider should be of general application: in appropriate private law cases, such as claims for a declaration, the courts should on occasion be able to allow proceedings to continue if it is in the interests of justice or in the public interest that they should do so. As the Justice/Public Law Project paper points out, the question of the applicant's standing can ultimately be treated as secondary to the merits of the case.

21. Consideration should be given to conferring on the court a discretion to allow third party intervention, both in the applicant's interest and in the public interest. If this is thought desirable, it should be a principle of general application, although the courts' approach should be more cautious when considering whether to allow intervention in proceedings concerning private rather than public law rights.

Costs

22. I agree with the Law Commission that legislation should confer a discretion on the court to order costs to be paid out of public funds where it is in the public interest that proceedings should be brought. If this recommendation is not implemented I recommend that the court should have a discretion not to order an unsuccessful party to pay the other party's costs, on the grounds that the proceedings have been brought in the public interest. Initially the discretion should only be exercised where there would otherwise be substantial hardship.

Written determination

23. As judicial review and some statutory applications in the Crown Office List do not usually involve oral evidence, they are susceptible to disposal in writing. This would not be appropriate for cases involving a point of principle, but it could sometimes be a valuable option for a straightforward case where the parties agreed on its use. Arrangements would need to be made for the documents and the judgement to be inspected by the public. Subject to these points I recommend that the judge should have a discretion to direct that there should be no hearing.

Divisional Court and appeals

24. At present judicial review in criminal causes and in the heaviest civil cases are heard by a Divisional Court of at least two judges. The justification in criminal causes is the restricted right of appeal to the House of Lords. In my view all cases of judicial review should be heard by a single judge unless there are exceptional circumstances. The proposals in paragraph 13 as to renewal at the preliminary consideration stage should be applied to appeals from substantive decisions. In criminal causes the appeal should be to the Criminal Division of the Court of Appeal and in non-criminal causes to the Civil Division. In both cases leave from the judge or the appeal court would be required. The requirement of leave is justified because of the need for certainty in criminal matters; it already exists in most civil appeals. As with the proposals on renewal of applications, there should be further consultation about this.

The prerogative orders

25. Although I am an enthusiast for adopting modern English, I am not in favour of the Law Commission's proposal to replace the names *certiorari*, prohibition and *mandamus* with a quashing, prohibiting and mandatory order. The Latin names are used throughout the common law world and have become synonymous with the duty of superior courts to protect the public against the abuse of power. I am not sure that the proposed alternatives are that much easier to comprehend. On the other hand I agree with the Treasury Solicitor that the title of judicial review proceedings, R v A, *ex parte* B, is outmoded and should be changed to A v B.

Bridging the divide

26. The recommendations which I have made are intended to bridge the divide between public law and private law claims by bringing the two procedures together. The same statements of case will be used in both, so that there will be no need for a claim in one area to be treated as though it had been begun by another procedure. It is nevertheless important that the safeguards of the three month time limit and of standing, which are necessary in judicial review claim, should not be bypassed, but these can be retained without making it an abuse of process to adopt the wrong procedure.

27. If a question arises as to whether the proceedings should have been brought by judicial review it will be possible to transfer the claim to the Crown Office for a case management conference, at which the same filtering process, without the court having to consider whether the issues are ones of public or private law, will apply, unless the answer is obvious or unless the issue needs to be resolved for substantive as opposed to procedural reasons. If the case is without merit, it can be dismissed irrespective of whether it raises public or private law issues; if it has merit the judge can direct it to proceed without determining whether it is a public or private law case. Furthermore, if the court thinks this is the best course to adopt in all the circumstances, it will be possible to leave consideration of standing and time limits until the final hearing. This is often necessary at present because the merits can affect both questions of standing and delay.

Habeas Corpus

28. So venerated is the writ of *habeas corpus* that law reformers have been cautious about interfering even with the procedure by which it is obtained. I share the Law Commission's view that it should not be absorbed into judicial review. However, I believe that its procedure should be as similar as possible to that for judicial review and it should be possible to seek a writ of *habeas corpus* on a claim for judicial review.

29. The application will be made by using a claim and will be verified by the applicant or some other appropriate person. The applicant will be able to apply *ex parte* to a single judge orally or in writing and the judge will be able to order the claimant's release, dismiss the claim, adjourn a written application for a hearing or adjourn for a full *inter partes* hearing, giving directions for the hearing. The person served with a claim should answer it in a defence, setting out the facts relied on to justify the detention.

30. At present, in a criminal case where the judge does not order release, he has to refer the application to a Divisional Court. I recommend that he should have the same powers as the Divisional Court. Otherwise the judge on the *inter partes* hearing should have the same powers as at present. There should be the same routes of appeal as in judicial review. The Law Commission favoured assimilating the procedure in criminal and civil cases but were concerned about adding to the burdens of the Criminal Division of the Court of Appeal. If judicial resources are an impediment then I recommend that the appeal should be heard by a Divisional Court.

31. I also recommend that English names (writ of release, writ to give evidence, writ to answer a charge and writ of transfer) should replace the Latin names of the four forms of the writ. These names do not have the same significance as the names of the prerogative orders.

Committal

32. The working group has made suggestions to clarify and improve RSC Order 52, which deals with committal for contempt of court. I agree that the rules should distinguish more clearly between civil contempt, ie breach of an order or undertaking, and criminal contempt, which usually relates to conduct interfering with the administration of justice. The former should be dealt with by general provisions, since applications are made to the court which made the order, whereas the latter is dealt with in the Crown Office List. The new rules will give effect to the working group's proposals and will aim to treat all litigants in the same way.

33. The same form of order should be used in the High Court and the county courts and there should be a requirement that copies of all orders for committal should be sent to the Official Solicitor. I also agree that the county courts should have the same power as the High Court to issue bench warrants for the arrest of contemnors, so that orders for committal are not made in their absence. It would be desirable if the Official Solicitor were to review all orders which, for whatever reason, had not been served within six months.

Recommendations

My main recommendations are as follows.

(1)   The procedures in public law cases should be brought into line with one another and with those in private law cases wherever possible. Use of the wrong procedure should not lead to the case being dismissed. Instead it should be dealt with so far as possible under the proper procedure.

(2)   More judges from other Divisions should be nominated to hear Crown Office List cases.

(3)   Certain Crown Office List cases should be heard outside London.

(4)   Claimants for judicial review should use available methods of ADR.

(5)   Claimants should notify the defendant of their proposed claim before starting proceedings.

(6)   A claim for judicial review and any defence should follow the standard claim form and defence. Unless it would inconvenience the hearing of the claim for judicial review, it should be possible for the claimant to include any remedies which could be obtained in a private law action and for the defendant to make a counterclaim.

(7)   The court should be able to grant advisory declarations in limited circumstances.

(8)   At the preliminary consideration stage (formerly 'leave'), which should be in writing, the judge should allow the claim to proceed if there is a realistic prospect of success or some other reason why the claim should be disposed of at a substantive hearing. He should consider giving directions for the conduct of the claim and set a timetable.

(9)   There should be a right to renew the application in non-criminal cases at an oral hearing before a single judge and a further renewal to the Court of Appeal, with leave. Consideration should be given to the same procedure applying in criminal causes.

(10)   The court should be able to grant interim relief before the preliminary consideration but should only do so *ex parte* in a clear and urgent case.

(11)   The claimant will have standing if he has been or will be adversely affected or if it is in the public interest that the claim should be brought.

(12)   All cases of judicial review should normally be heard by a single judge. There should be an appeal, with leave, to the Court of Appeal, Civil Division in non-criminal causes and consideration should be given to enabling appeals in criminal causes to lie, with leave, to the Court of Appeal, Criminal Division.

(13)   The court should have a discretion to order costs to be paid out of public funds or to order that the unsuccessful party is not to pay the other party's costs where the proceedings have been brought in the public interest.

(14)   It should be possible to determine some claims in the Crown Office List in writing where the parties agree.

(15)   The rules on *habeas corpus* and committal for contempt will be clarified and simplified.

Introduction

1. In chapter 26 of my interim report I stressed that the same general principles, rules and procedures need to apply as far as possible throughout the system. High Court and county court procedures should be brought together in a single code of rules, and different procedures within the Chancery Division and the Queen's Bench Division of the High Court and within the High Court and county courts should be assimilated wherever possible. Divergences of approach which make the civil justice system more complex, expensive and slower should be avoided. Some special types of case do require different procedural provisions, but I believe that their number and extent should be kept to a minimum.

2. Accordingly I invited a number of judges in specialist areas of High Court work to appoint small working groups to advise on those matters in their areas for which it would be essential to have provisions which departed from the standard procedure. I also wished to know of specialist practices or procedures which might usefully be adopted more generally. The areas covered are Chancery, Intellectual Property, Commercial Court, Official Referees, Admiralty and Crown Office. All six groups produced substantial reports, which will be available on request. They have made a significant contribution to this report and their advice has been invaluable. Having considered their reports I have come to the conclusion that the matters for which there will need to be special provision for particular areas of litigation are limited.

3. Most cases in the Commercial Court and the Official Referees' Court follow the present procedure for writ actions. The focus here has therefore been on elements of the new claim procedure, in particular, case management, disclosure of documents, witness statements and expert evidence. They have few rules of their own. (RSC Order 36 applies to Official Referees' and RSC Order 72 to commercial actions.) The same is true, although to a lesser extent, of the Intellectual Property and Admiralty groups. The Chancery and Crown Office groups, on the other hand, have had to cover a wide range of existing rules dealing in detail with questions with which they are concerned. The Crown Office List is covered in chapter 18.

4. The rules for the different specialist areas are in part as diverse as they are because hitherto there has been no particular desire to harmonise the different procedures. Many of the differences of detail are either unintentional or for reasons no longer relevant or remembered.

Chancery
The business
of the Division

5. The principal business of the Chancery Division, leaving aside insolvency and patents, concerns proceedings involving charities, civil fraud, companies, contracts for the sale and purchase of land, intellectual property, landlord and tenant, mortgages, partnership, professional negligence and trusts, wills and probate.

6. The Chancery Division, therefore, contains a number of specialist areas. It was partly for that reason that in chapter 12 of my interim report I accepted that the Chancery Division should not be merged with the Queen's Bench Division. However, because much of its work is now similar to that heard in the Queen's Bench Division, in particular the Commercial Court, I recommended that the administration of the two Divisions be brought closer together. This would enable judges of the Queen's Bench Division with appropriate experience to hear cases in the Chancery Division and vice versa when this would result in the more efficient disposal of cases. It would also mean that it would be of less significance in future which Division the case was commenced in.

7. The report of the working group makes it clear that many of the present Chancery procedures can be readily accommodated by the general provisions of the new rules.

8. At present jurisdiction to hear family provision claims under the Inheritance (Provision for Family and Dependants) Act 1975 is shared by the Chancery Division and the Family Division. The group considers that this is inefficient and can lead to inconsistency and recommends that all such claims should be heard by the Family Division. The judges of the Family Division agree. I accept that this should be the normal practice but, as the Vice-Chancellor has pointed out to me, claims under the 1975 Act may be linked to other claims which are more appropriate for disposal in the Chancery Division, and there should therefore be no rigid rule confining proceedings to the Family Division.

9. My Inquiry does not extend to proceedings under the Insolvency Act. This is a largely quasi-administrative jurisdiction, and concerns issues of enforcement, rather than ordinary civil litigation between two parties. There are a number of applications under the Companies Act which are dealt with by the Companies Court and governed by the Rules of the Supreme Court. I recommend that such proceedings should be entitled "In the Companies Court", which reflects what happens in practice, even though technically only Insolvency Act matters ought properly to be so described. Indeed, I recommend generally that where proceedings are usually disposed of in a particular list the heading of the case should identify that list.

10. In the new rules the definition of 'the Court' will continue to include the Companies Court Registrar. They will also make it clear that the Registrars in Bankruptcy have all the powers of Masters in addition to those specifically conferred upon them by the Insolvency and Companies Acts and the Insolvency Rules.

11. The group's suggestion that the Vice-Chancellor institutes an annual review for the Chancery Division, similar to those published by the Court of Appeal and Commercial Court, is welcome. This could summarise the procedural developments of the previous year, draw attention to any common procedural shortcomings, give current targets for hearing dates and look ahead to forthcoming changes. Again I would go further and recommend that the Head of Civil Justice publish an annual review covering the civil justice system as a whole.

Procedure

12. Many Chancery actions proceed at present by way of writ and will be suitable to the new claim procedure. Issues arising from the Chancery Group's comments on such general matters as case management, experts, witness statements etc will be found in chapter 12. The Chancery Guide, which was produced in April 1995, already provides very useful advice on the conduct of cases. As I have indicated in chapter 12, cases which are at present begun by originating summons will proceed by way of a verified claim form which will replace the originating summons and affidavit in support, and, where necessary, a defence in the standard form, which will replace the affidavit. The claimant will still be able to ask for a date to be fixed for the hearing when he issues the claim. Where the defendant does not return the notice of intention to defend or indicates on it that he will not be filing a defence, the procedural judge will then fix a date for the hearing. Where a defence is filed the judge will consider the statements of case and fix a date or give directions as to the conduct of the claim.

13. The Chancery Working Group has provided me with invaluable advice for the new rules, in particular in relation to rules and procedures for the more specialised areas of their work. The new rules will reflect the great majority of their advice and so it is not necessary for me to include in this report all the technical details to which they refer. I should, however, give some indication of ways in which the working group has met the aims of my detailed study of specialist jurisdictions.

Simplifying complex matters

(a)   The working group points to RSC Order 102 (The Companies Act 1985) as a prime example of unnecessary complexity in the types of originating process and a prime candidate for simplification. Although it will be more appropriate for some applications to be heard by a judge and some by the Companies Registrar, that is not something which needs to be reflected in the form of originating document. Nor is there any logical reason for certain applications to be begun by petition (although there is a statutory requirement that applications under section 459 of the Companies Act 1985 should be begun by petition). A petition, unlike an originating summons or motion, must itself contain all the facts necessary to found the relief required. In future, the claim form will do this and the new rules will merely record that a claim which does so will be a petition for the purposes of that section.

Removing separate rules where these are no longer necessary

(b)   An example is the present RSC Order 86. I agree with the group that there is no longer a need for a special order on summary judgment in actions for specific performance. Order 86 is therefore to be combined with Order 14.

Taking matters out of the rules which are more suitable for practice directions and guides

(c)   The group refers to RSC Order 31. This Order gives the court wide powers to refer matters to Conveyancing Counsel. It also goes into details as to the reference, which are matters more appropriate to a practice direction or guide. Order 43, rules 4 to 7 contain various matters of detail which could be incorporated into a practice direction. Order 44, rules 4 to 8 (accounts of debts) relate to the old administration action, which is now almost obsolete and need only be put in a practice direction or guide. A third example is that the procedure for inquiries as to creditors in the context of a reduction of capital under section 136 (3) to (5) of the Companies Act (now in Order 102, rules 7 to 15) can be left to a practice direction or guide, as again such inquiries are very rare.

Achieving uniformity with equivalent county court rules

(d)   The particulars required from both parties in a number of Landlord and Tenant Act applications are more extensive in the county court. I agree with the working group that these are more useful and informative for the court and that these should be the model for the new rules.

Pointing to existing rules which already fit well with my proposals

(e) The wide powers contained in Order 43, rule 3 and Order 44, rule 3 (directions in accounts and proceedings under judgments) are very much line with the approach which I am proposing generally and should continue.

Indicating which matters will continue to need separate treatment

(f) Probate actions, in which the court is asked to pronounce for or against the validity of wills in order that proof of a will in solemn form may be obtained, have characteristics which require special rules. Because the court has to consider the evidence, it is not possible either to obtain judgment by default or, usually, judgment by consent and the rules which indicate this and make alternative provision (Order 76, rules 6 and 10 to 12) need to be included in the new rules. The importance of the documents, ie the disputed wills, is also such that the special rules for tracking them down and bringing them into the custody of the court should remain (rule 5).

Making useful suggestions which are of general application

(g) The group notes that at present it is possible to transfer only the whole case and they suggest that there should be power to transfer particular issues to another court. I adopt this suggestion. It accords well with my proposal for more emphasis to be placed on the identification and disposal of specific issues in a case.

Intellectual property

14. In the case of *Chaplin Patents Holdings v Group Lotus* (The Times, 12 January 1994), Sir Thomas Bingham MR summarised very clearly the developments that have taken place in patent litigation in the last 10 or 15 years. He noted that the high reputation of the Patents Court within the High Court had never been in question but that in the 1980s problems of cost, delay and complexity were felt to be making access to justice difficult for smaller enterprises. As a result, the Patents County Court had been created by the Copyright, Designs and Patents Act 1988 with the purpose of improving access to justice by providing cheaper, speedier and more informal procedures than those in the Patents Court. Its object was to handle smaller, shorter, less complex, less important, lower value actions, but in considering whether to transfer cases to the Patents Court it was also to have regard to the financial position of the parties.

15. The creation of the Patents County Court was supported by industry but there are now differing views as to its success. It has been pointed out by some commentators that the number of cases which are brought in the court has been falling, although this is also true of the Patents Court. The court has also been the subject of some adverse comments by the Court of Appeal, most recently in *Sony Corporation v Pavel* (The Times, 22 March 1996), a case which had involved over 250 pages of pleadings, nearly eight days of hearings about interlocutory disputes and a trial lasting nearly four weeks. Aldous LJ said that "some alteration is necessary if the purposes of the PCC are to be achieved". Again, I am aware that supporters of the Court have said that this was not a typical case.

16. Clearly improvements could be made to the ways in which intellectual property litigation is handled. It continues to suffer from the vices of cost, delay and complexity. As the new draft rules make clear, dealing with a case justly includes handling it so as to ensure that, so far as is practicable, the parties are on an equal footing, and handling it in ways which are proportionate to the amount of money involved, the importance of the issues and the parties' financial position. I recognise that these matters may point in different directions, when it comes to considering which court should hear a case in intellectual property litigation. For example, the likely commercial effect on each party if relief is, or is not, granted, may not be apparent from a figure representing the value of the right being litigated.

17. In my view there is a pressing need for both the Patents Court and, more especially, the Patents County Court to develop procedures which go further than existing ones in providing rapid resolution of disputes, with a strict timetable and a trial limited in time, and a fixed budget for costs, as I am recommending for the fast track. This will enable smaller firms to compete on a more level footing with larger companies. I outline my proposals for such a procedure in chapter 5.

18. Like the Chancery Working Group, the Intellectual Property Group has made a number of valuable recommendations to me about specific procedural issues and these will influence the new rules.

19. I accept that there are a number of rules in RSC Order 104 which cannot be assimilated into the general rules and need to be retained. The Patents Acts require an amendment to the specification of a patent to be advertised and the group has proposed a simpler rule for the procedure to be followed on an application for leave to amend, since the present procedure can be cumbersome and expensive. The rules requiring certain matters to be pleaded, such as obviousness and commercial success, also need to be retained, although it might be possible to put them in a practice direction rather than in the rules themselves. Other rules which need to be retained are those on scientific advisers, the inspection of equipment etc pleaded in relation to an allegation of prior use, the requirements on the Patent Office to inquire and report and employee compensation claims. The recently made rules on service at the address for service given at the Patent Office in respect of certain registered rights held by foreign proprietors should also be preserved.

20. A recently introduced practice in the Patents Court, and in the Official Referees' court, is the use of telephone summonses. I looked forward to the possibilities of using telephone and video conferencing in chapter 13, paragraphs 15-18 of my interim report and if the experience of the Patents Court and Official Referees is favourable I would hope that greater use can be made of telephone summonses in other courts. I appreciate that initially the profession is showing little enthusiasm for this initiative but with experience I would expect its popularity to grow.

21. The Intellectual Property Group also helpfully draws attention to the Patents Court's practice, contained in a practice direction, of requiring the parties, about a week before the trial, to produce an agreed reading guide indicating to the judge the material he should pre-read and the order in which it should be read, as well as identifying what the parties conceive to be the issues. In the future more active case management could mean that the guide would be useful at an earlier stage. I welcome the use of pre-reading guides and agree with the group that they should be extended to other areas of multi-track litigation.

22. At present, under the Copyright, Designs and Patents Act 1988, the High Court does not have the power, which it has in relation to other county court cases, to entertain an application to transfer a case from the Patents County Court to itself. The majority of the Intellectual Property Group has said that where either party wishes to have a case transferred from one court to the other, such an application should be heard by the High Court judge in charge of the Intellectual Property List, in order for there to be predictability and uniformity of approach. They add that uncertainty as to which court will hear a case is a factor affecting foreign parties' choice of the jurisdiction in which to bring their litigation. The contrary view is that an application to transfer should be made to the judge of the court in which the case has begun and that it would go against the policy accepted by Parliament in the 1988 Act to permit the High Court to transfer Patents County Court cases to itself. I do not recommend at present that intellectual property litigation should differ from other litigation, in which the general principle will be that decisions on allocation should be taken by the procedural judge at the court where the claimant issues his claim. Nevertheless, I recognise that there are strongly held views on the issue, and it may be that the Head of Civil Justice, in consultation with all those with an interest in intellectual property litigation, will wish to look again at the question of allocation. To my mind improving the procedures of both courts is the first task.

Commercial Court

23. The Commercial Court is a good example of a specialist court which has a valuable and detailed practice guide to its proceedings but relatively few rules which are specific to it. Such rules as there are are contained in RSC Order 72 and in CCR Order 48C for the Central London Business List. Most of the working group's very valuable report deals with general issues such as pleadings, discovery, witness statements and case management, which I discuss in chapters 12 and there is little to which I need draw attention here.

24. I recommend the continuance of the Commercial List in the High Court in London. The definition of 'commercial action', which refers to 'merchants and traders', should be replaced by a more modern definition. I also welcome the growing use of the Central London County Court's Business List and of the Mercantile Lists in the High Court outside London.

25. I propose that there should be uniformity in the description of claims and defences. I do not see any necessity for the Commercial Court to retain the description of points of claim and points of defence, since the requirements as to statements of case reflect what their use was intended to achieve. Nor do I consider that special rules are needed for the transfer of commercial actions, since the new rules will contain wide provisions on the transfer of cases.

Official Referees

26. In my interim report I noted that many contributors to the Inquiry had commented on the advantage of having specialist judges in certain areas, among them Official Referees' business. I said that specialisation was likely to increase but added that most judges should hear more than one type of case. I recommended that Official Referees' business should form one of the lists to which all High Court proceedings should be attached.

Accordingly, I do not propose to alter the existing arrangements whereby the Official Referees' court is a 'court' for the purposes of the Rules, or the entitlement of a party to begin proceedings in the Official Referees' court. Nor do I believe that the nature of their business should be changed (subject to possible drafting modifications, since it is not readily apparent from the present provisions that their work essentially concerns construction cases).

27. As with the Commercial Court I believe that the wide, general provisions as to transfer should apply to transfers to and from the Official Referees' court.

28. I welcome the proposal in the working group's report that the rules should provide that trials or other hearings may take place anywhere and I agree that this power should be generally available.

29. Again like the Commercial Court Group's report, the Official Referees' Group's report deals chiefly with issues which are common to all ordinary claims on the multi-track: discovery, witness statements and experts, which are covered in chapters 12 and 13 of this report. Their proposals for case management in the Official Referees' courts are also covered in chapter 12. I agree with the group that there may be occasions when it would be useful to hold a case management conference even before the defence has been filed. The management needs of each case must be considered. However, there must also be consistency in the approach to case management and I do not favour the practice whereby each judge works from his own standard directions.

Admiralty

30. Admiralty proceedings are another specialised area which clearly needs to retain a number of special rules. Examples are the provisions relating to arresting a vessel, the sale of a ship and limitation actions. Again I should like to pay tribute to the detailed work which the Admiralty Working Group has carried out, which is of great use to those who are assisting in drafting the new rules. Consideration should also be given to reducing the number of county courts which have Admiralty jurisdiction. About one third of them have heard no Admiralty cases in the last five years and many others have heard very few.

The Crown

32. Government departments and the Treasury Solicitor have at my request reviewed the existing rules which give the Crown advantages which are not available to other litigants. They have concluded that a number of provisions are no longer justifiable and these will be omitted from the new rules. This is a small but not totally insignificant step.

Recommendations

My main recommendations are as follows.

(1) Many of the present Chancery procedures should be accommodated by the general provisions of the new rules.

(2) Where proceedings are usually disposed of in a particular list or court, the heading of the case should identify that list or court. For example, all Companies Act proceedings should be entitled 'In the Companies Court'.

(3) The Vice-Chancellor should institute an annual review of the Chancery Division, similar to those published by the Court of Appeal and the Commercial Court.

(4) The Head of Civil Justice should publish an annual review covering the civil justice system as a whole.

(5) There should be a power to transfer particular issues, as well as whole cases, to another court.

(6) The Patents Court and the Patents County Court should develop procedures which go further than existing ones in providing rapid resolution of disputes, with a strict timetable and a trial limited in time, and a fixed budget for costs.

(7) A number of the special rules for intellectual property, Chancery and Admiralty proceedings should be retained.

(8) Pre-reading guides for trial judges, as currently used in the Patents Court, should be extended to other areas of multi-track litigation. Where it would assist with case management, they should be made available at an earlier stage in the litigation.

(9) Both the Official Referees' Court and the Commercial List in the High Court in London should continue. The definition of 'commercial action' should be replaced with a more modern one.

(10) There should be uniformity in the description of claims and defences, and there is no need for the Commercial Court to retain the description of points of claim and points of defence.

(11) There should no longer be special rules for the transfer of commercial actions, since the new rules will contain wide provisions on the transfer of cases.

(12) As proposed by the Official Referees' Working Group, there should be a general provision in the rules that trials or other hearings may take place anywhere.

(13) Consideration should be given to reducing the number of county courts with Admiralty jurisdiction.

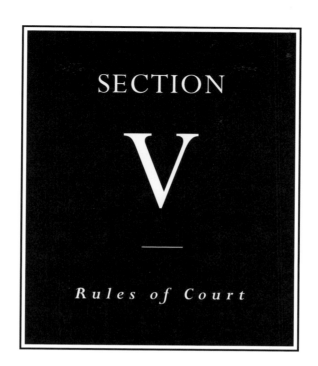

SECTION

V

Rules of Court

Chapter 20   The New Rules

1. It is part of my remit to produce a single body of rules of court to replace the existing Rules of the Supreme Court and County Court Rules. A draft set of rules is published at the same time as this report. It constitutes the main core of general rules which in my opinion will be needed to support the new arrangements for civil justice. It is intended to form the basis of consultation with all relevant interests.

Overall objectives for the rules

2. I set myself five specific objectives for the rule-making exercise:

(a)   to identify the core propositions in the rules and to cut down the number of interconnecting provisions which are used;

(b)   to provide procedures which apply to the broadest possible range of cases and to reduce the number of instances in which a separate regime is provided for a special type of case;

(c)   to reduce the size of the rules and the number of propositions contained in them;

(d)   to remove verbiage and to adopt a simpler and plainer style of drafting;

(e)   to give effect to the substantive reforms which I am proposing.

3. Genuine access to justice requires people to be able to understand how the legal procedure works. The procedure, working properly, is a vital guarantee that justice will be done; that it can be seen to work properly helps to ensure that justice will be seen to be done.

4. Given the size of the existing rules, reducing the amount of material in them is obviously desirable in itself. However, reduction of the amount of specialised material in favour of greater reliance on general rules also serves the broader purpose of emphasising the similarities between different types of jurisdiction rather than their differences. In the past the fragmentation of civil justice has undermined its claims to equal treatment with criminal and family justice in such matters as resources. It has also made civil justice substantively less efficient. My proposals overall are directed towards reversing these features. New rules of broader application will support the new policy. Greater reliance on broader propositions makes it easier for users of civil procedure to keep in mind the objects of the procedure. It reduces complexity and so makes the system more amenable to actual users and more acceptable to ordinary citizens, whether litigants or not. It should reduce the learning and processing costs of courts and lawyers.

**Method of working
on the rules**

5.   To help carry forward the work on the new rules, I set up a small working group. It incorporated judicial, consumer and lay advisory viewpoints. The role of the group has been to advise on the preparation of instructions to the draftsman and to comment on the drafts as they were prepared. It has made an enormous contribution to the work, for which I am immensely grateful. To my knowledge, this is the first time on which representatives of consumer and advice organisations have been directly involved in the preparation of rules of court. I recommend that they should have a permanent role as a counterbalance to the professional legal viewpoint in the new rule-making committee which will be needed to enact the combined rules.

6.   I have also been assisted in preparing the rules by the specialist working groups whose work is described in chapter 19. Their contribution has been particularly helpful in enabling me to decide how much of the existing rules relating to specialised areas of jurisdiction can be removed altogether or put into practice directions.

7.   The draft rules published at the same time as this report do not yet contain those specialised rules which I consider are needed. Before reaching a final conclusion about what should be kept, I consider it is important that the working groups should have an opportunity of seeing the new general rules. In addition, certain other topics still need to be inserted. These include appeals, costs and enforcement. Work will of course continue until the body of material is complete.

Unified rules

8.   The interim report discussed the problems of the existing rules of court. There are two separate sets of rules, which partly overlap but which often diverge for no obvious reason. This is merely the most obvious symptom of the general problem of complexity in the existing rules, which I broke down under the following main heads:

(a)   too many ways of doing the same or similar thing;

(b)   the use of specialist terms without explanation;

(c)   over-elaborate language;

(d)   the desire to give every single word a definite meaning and to cover every eventuality;

(e)   piecemeal amendment over the years.

9. Some of the steps towards a more integrated system involve substantive procedural changes, such as the introduction of a single method of starting all types of case (the 'claim'). These are discussed in separate chapters. Others effectively involve the integration of existing, separate procedures: for example, the new summary judgment procedure in Part 14 of the draft rules, which is available both to claimants (as now) and defendants. Within the new rules, the emphasis wherever possible is on providing general rules to apply to the widest range of cases. I have carefully examined existing variations both of method and terminology to see whether they really justify separate treatment. The effect will eventually be seen in the treatment of some of the specialist areas which at present have their own, separate provisions, for example, RSC Order 36 (Official Referees' business) and RSC Order 72 and its county court equivalent CCR Order 48C, which deal with commercial actions. I am confident that it will prove possible substantially to reduce the size of provisions such as these.

Interpretation of the rules: overall objective

10. Every word in the rules should have a purpose, but every word cannot sensibly be given a minutely exact meaning. Civil procedure involves more judgment and knowledge than the rules can directly express. In this respect, rules of court are not like an instruction manual for operating a piece of machinery. Ultimately their purpose is to guide the court and the litigants towards the just resolution of the case. Although the rules can offer detailed directions for the technical steps to be taken, the effectiveness of those steps depends upon the spirit in which they are carried out. That in turn depends on an understanding of the fundamental purpose of the rules and of the underlying system of procedure.

11. In order to identify that purpose at the outset, I have placed at the very beginning of the rules a statement of their overriding objective. This is intended to govern the operation of all the rules and in particular the choices which the court makes in managing each case and in interpreting the rules. In the interim report I set out the likely text of this rule. Because of its importance, I make no apology for setting it out again here, in its updated form.

"(1)   The overriding objective of these Rules is to enable the court to deal with cases justly.

(2)   The court must apply the Rules so as to further the overriding objective.

(3)   Dealing with a case justly includes –

(a)   ensuring, so far as is practicable, that the parties are on an equal footing;

(b)   saving expense;

(c)   dealing with the case in ways which are proportionate –

(i)   to the amount of money involved;

(ii)   to the importance of the case;

(iii) to the complexity of the issues; and

(iv)   to the parties' financial position;

(d)   ensuring that it is dealt with expeditiously; and

(e)   allotting to it an appropriate share of the court's resources, while taking into account the need to allot resources to other cases."

12. The new rules are deliberately not designed expressly to answer every question which could arise. Rule 1, the statement of the objective, provides a compass to guide courts and litigants and legal advisers as to their general course. Where detailed instructions are needed, matters of general application will be dealt with in the rules; other matters will, I hope, be capable of being dealt with in practice directions and practice guides.

Simpler and clearer language

13. I said in the interim report that one of my aims was to modernise terminology. I have not approached this dogmatically but on the basis that terminology should be changed where it is useful to do so. I have sought to remove expressions which are meaningless or confusing to non-lawyers (such as 'relief' when used to mean a remedy) or where a different expression would more adequately convey what is involved (such as 'disclosure' of documents instead of the archaic 'discovery'). The various terms for methods of starting a case, such as writ, summons, originating application, will all be replaced by a 'claim'. The word 'plaintiff' will be replaced by 'claimant'.

14. I have suggested that the word 'pleading' should be replaced by 'statement of case'. Although it is a very familiar expression to lawyers and in some respects a convenient one, the word has become too much identified with a process which the legal profession itself readily acknowledges has to change. This is an instance where a change of language will, I believe, help to underpin a change of attitude and a real change of practice to a more open and straightforward method of stating a claim or defence.

15. I recognise that changes of terminology are discomforting and temporarily inconvenient for those who are very familiar with the existing expressions. But, as I made clear in the interim report, the system of civil justice and the rules which govern it must be broadly comprehensible not only to an inner circle of initiates but to non-professional advisers and, so far as possible, to ordinary people of average ability who are unlikely to have more than a single encounter with the system.

16. A system of procedure cannot completely avoid technical terms. Some of them are, I believe, reasonably well understood and are difficult to replace conveniently. Where these are kept, the rules will define them where it is possible to do so. Provisions defining the exact meaning of expressions are a standard tool of legislative drafting: in the new rules, for example, 'child' is defined as a person under 18 and 'filing', in relation to a document, means delivering it to the court. However, some expressions are useful to keep but not so easy to define precisely. An example is 'service' of documents. The existing rules provide a limited number of permissible methods of serving a document. I am proposing (see chapter 12) that in future any method which is reasonably likely to bring the relevant document to the intended recipient's attention may suffice, so it will no longer be possible to 'define' service by reference to specific ways of doing it. Even under the existing rules, it is not easy to define service in terms of bringing the document to a person's attention, because the process may be effective in certain circumstances even though the document has not come to his attention. I am attempting, in the new rules, to make the basic legal test of good service somewhat clearer. In addition, however, I am also proposing the inclusion in the rules of a glossary of terms. This gives a brief, general explanation of certain terms used by the rules. For example, the rules refer to legal concepts such as special damages, contribution and indemnity. These expressions take their meaning, not from the rules themselves, but from the general law. Often they have a broad meaning but one which is well understood by the legal profession. Their meaning may have been refined by case-law. They do not have an exact definition and, for the purposes of the rules, they do not need one. It is, nevertheless, helpful to the non-specialist reader to give a broad indication of their meaning. Unlike the definition of terms within the main rules, the explanation of terms in the glossary would not directly affect the way in which the relevant rules operate. It is simply an aid to understanding.

Incorporating case-law

17. The right balance between general statements and detail has to be considered afresh in each case. In some cases, where the present rules are very brief, I have chosen to be more detailed. An important example is the power to set aside judgment for failure to defend (Part 12 in the new rules). The existing rule in the Rules of the Supreme Court is extremely short and deceptively simple; it provides that the court may, on such terms as it thinks just, set aside or vary a default judgment. In fact the courts have had to evolve different tests for setting aside judgment depending on specific factors, such as whether the judgment was correctly or incorrectly obtained in the first place. Since this is a common situation and the various considerations are well-established, I have thought it helpful to set out these matters in the rules themselves.

Cross-references

18. When dealing with a particular subject in the rules, it would often be simpler to set out all the relevant provisions in one place, even if that meant repeating provisions set out elsewhere in the rules. But this would go against the general aim of reducing their size wherever possible. A balance has to be found, though it is not necessarily the same balance in all cases.

19. For example, throughout the rules there are references to parties making applications to the court. I have tried to gather in one part (Part 10) all the provisions about applications: parties, time limits, notice, court's powers ,etc, rather than setting these matters out individually in relation to each type of application. Generally speaking, I have chosen to accept a system of cross-referring between related provisions in preference to duplication. Several methods of drawing attention to such provisions were considered. They included footnotes, side notes, modifying the appearance of the relevant text or direct references to the relevant rule in the text itself. Footnotes and side-notes were thought likely to distract the reader's eye from the main text and purely visual modifications (such as shading, use of capital letters or bold print) need some further key to explain their meaning, and are likely to cause difficulties in reproducing the text of the rules.

20. In general, therefore, I have chosen the conventional approach of referring in the text of the rule to another rule but in such a way as to make it clear what the rule referred to does. For example, in Part 9, which is about defending and counterclaiming, rule 9.1(2) provides that, if a defendant does not file a defence within the relevant period, "judgment for failure to defend may be entered if Part 11 allows it". In one or two instances, I have thought it desirable to repeat provisions for the sake of clarity. For example, rule 9.3 provides that a defendant may apply to the court for an extension of the time for filing a defence. Strictly speaking, this is unnecessary because Part 5 of the rules includes a general power to extend time limits; I considered the point sufficiently important to be worth repeating here.

21. The current rules sometimes use the device of applying another provision of the rules but with modifications. I believe it is confusing for readers, whether practitioners or not, to keep in their minds a notional textual modification introduced by the words 'as if'. As an example, CCR Order 7 rule10A deals with service of a summons by post by solicitors. It provides that Order 7 rule 10(3) and (4) and rule 13 and Order 37 rule 3 shall apply, with the necessary modifications, as if the summons had been served by a court officer. It is laborious to have to look up those provisions to find out what it is that is being applied and then it is not immediately obvious what the necessary modifications would be. I have sought to avoid this kind of cross-reference in the new rules on service and generally.

22. I have chosen, where it is necessary, to set out the full version afresh. It will be obvious, however, that this approach must in some cases make a provision longer than its current equivalent. In one case, I have applied rules in a different context without setting them out again: that is the application of the rules about claims to counterclaims. Given that these are fairly lengthy and detailed, and that they are applied almost in their entirety to counterclaims, I believe that this approach is justified here.

Simpler drafting structure

23. In the interim report, I commented on the density of drafting which is often to be found in the existing rules. When analysed, this is because the existing rules will habitually bring together in a single paragraph three, four or more ideas. While this approach can provide a degree of compression, it has not overall prevented the existing rules from becoming very lengthy, and it assumes a high level of understanding or familiarity on the part of the reader. I have chosen instead to adopt a simpler structure in which each paragraph generally contains not more than one or two ideas. Where it contains more, I have tried to ensure that the links between them are clearly set out.

24. Comparison between an existing rule and its equivalent in the new rules will help to illustrate the new approach. RSC Order 29 rule 17, the present rule dealing with the adjustment of an interim payment, provides as follows:

"Adjustment on final judgment or order or on discontinuance

17. Where a defendant has been ordered to make an interim payment or has in fact made an interim payment, whether voluntarily or pursuant to an order, the Court may, in giving or making a final judgment or order, or granting the plaintiff leave to discontinue his action or to withdraw the claim in respect of which the interim payment has been made, or at any other stage of the proceedings on the application of any party, make such order with respect to the interim payment as may be just, and in particular

(a) an order for the repayment by the plaintiff of all or part of the interim payment, or

(b) an order for the payment to be varied or discharged, or

(c) an order for the payment by any other defendant of any part of the interim payment which the defendant who made it is entitled to recover from him by way of contribution or indemnity or in respect of any remedy or relief relating to or connected with the plaintiff's claim."

25. Draft rule 16.7 provides as follows:

"Powers of court where it has made an order for interim payment

16.7 (1) The court may make an order to adjust an interim payment at any time.

(2) The court may in particular –

(a) order all or part of the interim payment to be repaid;

(b) vary or discharge the order for the interim payment.

(3) If a party who has made an interim payment claims, in respect of the payment he has made, a contribution, indemnity or other remedy against some other party, the court may order the other party to reimburse the party who has made the interim payment, either wholly or partially.

(4) If the claim or the part to which the interim payment relates

has not been discontinued or finally determined, the court may make an order for reimbursement under paragraph (3) only in the same circumstances that an order for interim payment could be made under rule 16.5 or 16.6.

(5) Where

(a) the court has made an order for an interim payment; and

(b) the person against whom the court made the order paid more by way of an interim payment than he was liable to pay under the final judgment or order,

he shall be entitled to interest on the overpaid amount from the date when he made the interim payment.

(6) This rule applies whether the interim payment was made voluntarily or pursuant to an order."

Internal structure of rules

26. Each Part of the rules deals with a distinct topic. Each Part begins with a contents list of the individual rules which it contains; this would conventionally appear at the very beginning of a statutory instrument, but I think it is helpful if the detailed list of provisions appears close to the relevant material. So, for example, Part 11 begins with the following:

Scope of this Part	Rule 11.1
Claims in which judgment under this Part may be obtained	Rule 11.2
Conditions to be satisfied – judgment for failure to file notice of intention to defend	Rule 11.3
Conditions to be satisfied – judgment for failure to defend	Rule 11.4
Procedural requirements	Rule 11.5
Claimant's right to chose rate of payment	Rule 11.6
Nature of judgment for failure to defend	Rule 11.7
Interest	Rule 11.8
Costs	Rule 11.9
Directions to be given where further decision of the court is needed	Rule 11.10
Defendant's rights following judgment under this Part	Rule 11.11
Claim against more than one defendant	Rule 11.12

27. Reference to the contents of each Part helps to illustrate another technique which I have applied. It helps the reader if the material in each Part appears, so far as possible, in a standard order. I have aimed to achieve this where possible, not only in the ordering of individual rules within each Part but also, where appropriate, within individual rules. The broad order of topics which I have sought to follow is:

(a)   purpose of the process;

(b)   types of case in which it may be used;

(c)   grounds to be established;

(d)   procedure to be followed;

(e)   court's powers.

28. The contents list set out in paragraph 26 provides an example of this approach. It is not always appropriate to follow this structure or possible to follow it exactly in the order indicated in the previous paragraph.

Concluding observations

29. In the interim report I commented that the rules had become a tactical weapon used to obstruct progress and inflate costs. They have also become, in significant respects, a dead letter. Experience shows that changes to rules of procedure by themselves cannot achieve significant improvements. As part of a comprehensive package of reforms, however, modernised and improved rules have a major part to play. The changes which I have discussed in this chapter are aimed at enabling the rules to perform their proper function once more.

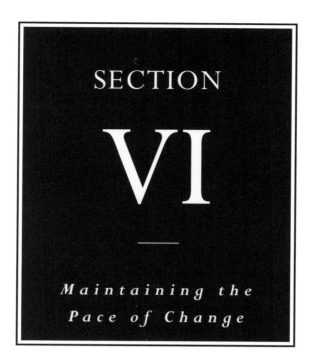

SECTION

VI

Maintaining the
Pace of Change

Chapter 21   Information Technology

Introduction

1.   In chapter 13 of the interim report, I stressed the importance of the role of information technology (IT) in supporting the implementation of my more general recommendations. I looked, in broad terms, at some potential applications of IT and also addressed central questions of costs, infrastructure and strategy. The additional information I have received since the publication of that report, both here and abroad, has strengthened my conviction that sensible investment in appropriate technology is fundamental to the future of our civil justice system. IT will not only assist in streamlining and improving our existing systems and processes; it is also likely, in due course, itself to be a catalyst for radical change as well. It is necessary now to distinguish between those systems which can be implemented quite quickly, bringing immediate benefits, and those which are far longer term ventures. Our planning must reflect this distinction.

2.   This chapter builds on the interim report in two ways. First, as I undertook to do, I summarise the progress that has been made during the intervening year in respect of each of the nine recommendations on IT that I put forward. Most of these anticipated some short term actions. Second, I consider three related topics in further detail – judicial case management technology, the Private Finance Initiative (PFI) procurement scheme and IT strategy for the civil justice system – and I make further recommendations in respect of each. These are fundamental, as they concern the tools needed to support my main proposals, the infrastructure and financing of the required technology and the way in which progress can be planned and controlled.

3.   This chapter must be read against the background of the procurement exercise in which the Court Service is currently engaged under the PFI. The main focus of this is the system known as LOCCS (the Local County Court System). It is generally anticipated that the scheme will lead to the establishment of a long term partnership between the Court Service and the selected private sector PFI provider. In due course, this relationship will extend well beyond LOCCS and this provider will deliver most, if not all, IT services to the civil courts. This PFI project is a major (and not uncontroversial) initiative of considerable significance to the civil justice system. It bears on most IT-related issues arising for the court system.

Progress since the interim report

4.   My first recommendation was directly related to this initiative. It was that consideration should be given to the extent to which my proposed IT requirements for case management could be integrated into the LOCCS framework. I have since been assured by specialists in the Court Service that, from a technical point of view, they are confident that the modular approach they have taken to the development of LOCCS and the use of PFI could indeed provide an appropriate platform for the implementation of the new case management procedures which I am recommending in this report.

5. My second recommendation focused on judges. They should be fully equipped with appropriate IT. I encouraged wider consultation on the needs of all judges and not just those who are already enthusiastic about technology. I also expressed the view that there should be more comprehensive in-house training and technical support to encourage substantial uptake amongst judicial users. I understand the current position to be that, under the JUDITH project, around 330 judges have now been supplied with personal computers, a number of which are regularly connected to the judicial communications network known as FELIX. Further, the JUDITH project board has agreed with representatives of JSCIT (the Judicial Standing Committee on Information Technology) that a Post Implementation Review (PIR) of the JUDITH project should be carried out in the final quarter of 1996. This will assess the benefits of the project to date, identify lessons to be learned and make recommendations for the future. Procedures for judicial training on IT are also said to have been improved, with peer group training programmes and arrangements for judicial cover in place. More remains to be done and later paragraphs of this chapter deal with various applications of judicial and courtroom IT in an attempt to suggest a way ahead (see paragraphs 13-23). IT training is not likely to be cheap, but the Judicial Studies Board should be resourced appropriately to make sure it happens.

6. My third recommendation was for the more widespread use of litigation support technologies (document indexing, full text retrieval and document image processing) within the legal profession to assist with the management of document loads in preparation for trials; and, more specifically, to help cope with discovery. My general impression has been that litigation support systems do continue to be used in earnest by many solicitors and barristers but no more so during the past year than before. Advocates of these systems still speak forcefully of their benefits and I continue to believe that they will bring cost savings and improvements in quality and productivity which can benefit clients and lawyers alike. To encourage greater usage within the professions, I would like to call on the energies and experience of the Society for Computers and Law, assisted, where appropriate, by ITAC (the Information Technology and Courts

Committee) to build on the solid work of the Official Referees' Solicitors' Association which produced the ORSA Protocol. This is ORSA's set of standard formats which encourage opposing parties to agree compatible systems and, where possible, to share the costs of setting up these systems. I have in mind that an extended protocol might be developed for use across the entire civil justice system. The developing use of IT will also require separate consideration on the question of the recoverability of expense incurred on IT in the course of dispute resolution, a matter of ongoing uncertainty for litigants and so still of concern to me. A decision is required on whether the cost of IT should be included in general overheads and/or whether, in specific cases, the costs of specially tailored systems can be recovered.

7. Telephone and video conferencing facilities were the subject of my fourth recommendation. I suggested these technologies be piloted with a view to helping procedural judges (in particular) with case management. I understand from the Court Service that the successful LOCCS/PFI supplier will, in due course, be asked to assess the feasibility and costs of video conferencing facilities, although this will not be a mandatory service under the contract and work will not commence before the successful provider starts the service delivery for LOCCS. Although I would have preferred earlier piloting of the technology and I am to that extent disappointed, I appreciate that this may have been difficult in the light of the PFI project. I do reiterate, however, that I anticipate, in the medium and long term, that video conferencing will be one vital tool for case management. Further consideration should be given as to whether this should be reflected in the contractual arrangements with the PFI supplier. As for telephone conferencing, I understand that the Court Service is to consider its potential later this year and identify the technical changes and costs involved in its widespread introduction. This is a matter of more immediate concern to me because I regard telephone conferencing a very important tool for judicial case management. I address this in more detail in paragraph 21 of this chapter.

8. My fifth recommendation was that video recording and viewing facilities should be introduced in appropriate centres to assist with the presentation of expert evidence, the replay of pre-recorded statements and the examination of expert witnesses. I am told that adequate television and video recording facilities are now readily available at most trial centres. The challenge is to integrate this technology with everyday court practice.

9.   My sixth recommendation suggested that technology could provide the basis for information systems, available in court buildings and other public places, to guide the public on court and legal matters. I saw potential in the use of dedicated kiosk technology. Other developments during the past year have refined my views. The global information system, known as the World Wide Web, has gained enormously in popularity. The Court Service has its own Web site and is working on the electronic publication of guidance for court users. Given the projected level of usage of the World Wide Web, this should be one of the preferred means of delivery of information for the public. Additionally, I am impressed by the idea of using more general community information systems for the delivery of legal guidance. For example, the Chief Clerk on the Midland and Oxford Circuit of the Court Service has agreed with Lincolnshire County Council that he may place guidance onto their system (called LINNET) which provides a wide variety of general, local information. This is an eminently sensible precedent which should be extended when opportunities arise.

10.   My seventh recommendation was for clarification of government policy in relation to the allegedly excessive costs being levied by HMSO for permission to reproduce primary legal source materials – especially statutes – in electronic form. Around the date of publication of my interim report, there was considerable and passionate debate about the extent to which access to legal materials in electronic form should incur any cost whatsoever. Since then, however, there have been very considerable developments. On 12 February 1996 it was announced by the government that the liberal licensing position which has applied in the past to printed statutes would now extend to their reproduction in electronic form. And both Houses of Parliament have also expressed interest and reported on the subject. Overall, so long as the government's concessions extend also to those additional materials which are important for the interpretation of the primary sources, I believe that the current public policy and application of Crown copyright now support rather than inhibit the widespread use of legal information systems for lawyers and the public at large.

11.   My eighth recommendation was that there should be an evaluation of the implications of the proposed PFI procurement scheme. The procurement exercise may well lead to the development and introduction of advanced systems which might otherwise not be possible, and I continue to support this. I also raised the question of whether the IT infrastructure of the civil justice system should be run by the private sector. I drew particular attention to the challenge of retaining control over policy and strategy where there are powerful and capable service providers running the IT infrastructure. I am assured by the Court Service that it is fully aware of the risks of dealing with a large multi-national service provider and that the appropriate safeguards will be put in place to ensure that control is retained by the Court Service and the Lord Chancellor's Department. I am also told that similar controls will be in place to enable other sponsors and stakeholders to be fully involved with the design and development of systems. Nevertheless, this is so central an issue that I have chosen to express my views more fully later in this chapter in the hope that these will provide a useful benchmark for the Court Service and will clarify others' understanding of the scope and nature of the project.

12. My ninth and final recommendation was that the provision of IT in the civil justice system should be co-ordinated, involving all the key bodies, such as the Judicial Studies Board, who are affected and involved. This is currently subject to the attention of the Court Service, with a view to establishing a strategic body for the development and review of IT strategy for the courts. This is again a vital issue for the future of the civil justice system generally, so I return to it later.

Judicial case management technology

13. Turning now to the future, judges will need support in facing the challenges and fulfilling the demands of case management. Here IT should play a major role. There are two broad categories of what can be called 'case management systems'. These overlap. There are case load management systems, which assist in the management of a group of cases, with particular attention to the allocation of all the resources involved (courtrooms, judges and witnesses for example). On the other hand, there are case flow management systems, which in a variety of ways support the management and progress of individual cases, from inception through to final disposal. I believe both categories of systems are crucial if judicial case management is to succeed. In turn, they are closely associated with the more general applications of technology for judges and the courts.

14. Turning, first, to case load management, I have one major recommendation to make – that a distinct project be launched to address the many ways in which existing and projected court administration systems can and should be extended for use as soon as possible by judges (and later by others, including lawyers and their clients). The principal challenge, therefore, is to extend and to make more widely available any case load management facilities of systems such as LOCCS and, indeed, those of all systems which deal with the allocation of resources, the scheduling of judges' workloads and the listing of cases, including the electronic diarising of cases. Concern has been expressed by judges that this extension of systems to them is not being made. Yet, if judges are to be responsible for the management of individual cases, they must also have ready access to information about groups of cases as well. It is here we see the overlap between the two categories of case management systems, because case load management systems should hold all manner of useful and up-to-date information about the status and progress of individual cases; and judges and parties would find it invaluable to have access to this information. The PFI suppliers must be alive to this project, because it will be a natural extension of the systems they are to take over and run.

15. With regard to case flow management, I can see here some immediate benefits as well as some very promising longer term possibilities. My assessors have explored this field in depth over the past year – and have developed a small prototype personal computer-based system to demonstrate some of the initial ideas, including techniques for allocating cases to the correct tracks – and so it is appropriate to deal with this matter in some detail.

16. A sensible starting point is the need to develop some standard techniques for judicial case management. Some judges are already adept at managing their cases while others will need training and encouragement. One possibility is to regard each case as a separate project; each, from the outset, with its own phases, activities, tasks and events and each to be driven through to final disposal against allocated time scales. The judge could be said to have two responsibilities in this context. The first is to formulate a case plan, which will specify, and stipulate time frames for, all relevant phases, activities, tasks and events; and the second is to progress each case by reference to its own case plan.

17. In developing case plans, however, judges and the parties themselves should have access to standards and guidelines. These should provide basic models and illustrations of case plans for various categories of cases, with standard life cycles assigned by the court for each. This will assist the parties to give judges concrete help in pinpointing all central tasks, identifying the critical paths, and recognising those milestones which may and may not be subject to variation, as well as the preferred elapsed timescales for entire cases or phases within cases. Thus, when judges come to draw up individual case plans, they will not do so in a vacuum but will have basic common structures within which to operate. These could be refined and developed as experience of using them becomes more general. These basic structures would also help lawyers and their clients to know what is expected of them and will provide greater insight into the likely progress of the types of cases with which they are involved. We already have positive experience, here and abroad, of case management by solicitors. It has been popular with lawyers and clients alike, with everyone seeming to feel comfortable with the greater certainty that it brings.

18. New tools are needed for judges, especially as so much of this kind of work (plans and schedules, for instance) is best expressed graphically rather than in words. IT should be of help here because there are a wide variety of project management systems available which are designed precisely to create easily understood graphics of the sort I envisage. I suggest, at this early stage in the evolution of judicial case management, that very simple, PC-based project management software is gradually made available to all judges to enable them to generate their own case plans. This software should be tailored so that, for example, the use of a fairly basic *project schedule* is possible, one which clearly depicts time spans (of phases, activities and tasks), particular events (say, milestones), and any dependencies that there might be (for example, that one phase cannot begin until the achievement of some milestone). When a case is being reviewed or further aspects are being planned, such a schedule should also be able to show what progress has been made against individual project steps (project managers would call such a schedule a combined *Gantt Chart* and *Milestone Schedule*).

19. Such systems can be extremely easy for any computer user to master (about an hour's training for an already competent computer user). The schedules themselves can be generated either by directly entering symbols and lines onto the charts; or, far easier, by completing a simple form, responses to which would then automatically create the appropriate lengths of bars and so forth. Inexpensive, off-the-shelf packages can be used for this purpose, although it would be necessary to tailor such a system for judges so that there would be standardisation of notation (for instance, the same symbols should be used across the court system for the same types of milestone). Ideally, the tailoring should also extend to the loading of the standard models for particular categories of case, so that all the basic phases and milestones – a basic structure – would be dropped into place on the screen of the judge who would then be free to focus on the specifics of timing and resources of any case at hand. The schedules themselves can also be 'cut and pasted' from the project management package into a standard word processing system, so that the charts and commentary can all be incorporated in the one document.

20. I am optimistic that this kind of tool could be introduced very rapidly to the judiciary and would become central to judges' use of IT. Experience gained by the first group of judicial users would be invaluable as the basis for the gradual introduction of this system across the entire judiciary. The development of such a tool must clearly be a collaborative venture, involving, at least, the Court Service, the PFI supplier, the Judicial Studies Board, judges (beginners as well as advanced users) and the profession. I recommend that a working group (with representatives of each) is set up immediately to analyse and specify the requirements of case flow management of the kind I have described. That work should investigate and allow for a variety of enhancements, such as systems which will produce daily reminders, progress reports and lists of outstanding tasks (indicating who is responsible for further actions). I suggest that the relevant technologies, usually described as 'workflow' and 'groupware', be explored in this context. I would hope the work of my proposed working group can progress hand-in-hand with the plans for the practical implementation of my general case management proposals. Subject to the timing of that more general work, I would like to see the working group's project finished within six months and training and implementation to follow immediately thereafter for all judges currently equipped with appropriate IT, and extended to others as they are provided with systems.

Telephone conferencing

21. Another basic tool for judicial case management is telephone conferencing. There are mixed views on the potential scope of this technology. Those who are sceptical claim that information is lost where there is no eye contact or body language. Proponents, on the other hand, suggest that the purpose of telephone conferencing is not to replace existing hearings or meetings but to encourage greater, proactive communication where in the past there may have been silence. For judicial case management, regular telephone conferencing should become an important tool for judges in maintaining the progress of cases where formal meetings would be impractical. At the very least, I recommend, as I did in my interim report, that this technology is piloted extensively so that decisions about its applicability can be based on practical and extensive experience.

The future

22. In the longer term in relation to case flow management, although not technically feasible today, advances in telecommunications technology will eventually enable judges to be able to gain access to the entire set of documents relating to the individual cases on which they are working – including full case histories, pleadings, affidavits, orders and document bundles, for example – and to retrieve these, either as images or as searchable text, from some central location. These documents would be accessible from anywhere, so long as the judge had appropriate computer and telecommunications equipment. And far more powerful video conferencing facilities are also in sight. These possibilities should be monitored as part of the long term strategic planning process to which I refer in paragraph 36.

23. Other basic applications of technology for judges will also be invaluable in supporting both the conventional judicial role, as well as the extended case management responsibilities of judges. Electronic communications technology will allow judges to send and receive messages and documents, communicating internally with other judges, externally across the profession generally, to and from any location. In the courtroom itself, judges will increasingly use laptops to take notes and to produce standard text, while document storage, retrieval and display technologies will facilitate speedier and more efficient management of documents. The pilot project in the Exeter group of courts also suggests that IT can support team working by judges.

The Private Finance Initiative procurement scheme

24. There have been a variety of forceful objections to the PFI procurement scheme. The objections raise political issues on which I do not consider it appropriate to comment. However, I am advised that the PFI/IT project offers an unparalleled opportunity to put in place an adequately funded, first rate IT infrastructure for the court system, with powerful applications in court administration, case management and in the courtroom, and backed up by thoroughly professional support, maintenance and training. Experts agree that this comprehensive introduction of IT to the courts would give rise to major cost savings and, in turn, enable and fuel further investment in the PFI project itself. Furthermore, the improved and streamlined court system which should result will help this country to continue to provide a world class civil justice system for many years to come.

25. I accept also, however, that there are threats and pitfalls which arise from the proposed PFI project and these must be understood widely and addressed squarely. There is widespread concern that policy, strategy and control of future developments in these areas may, unless appropriate precautions are in place, be lost to the third party private sector supplier which is eventually selected. There is also the worry that increasing reliance on an external third party for so vital a social function may create a monopoly situation in which transfer of the service to another party in the future may be impractical.

26. In order to realise the opportunities and, at the same time, to tackle the threats just noted in the previous paragraph, I suggest four initial steps are taken (notwithstanding the reassurances I have been given – see paragraph 11). First, ministers and senior judges, agency and departmental policy makers should be seen personally to be involved, proactively, with the progress of this project and not simply in responding to criticisms. Although the project relates to IT, its implications go well beyond technology – to the heart of the legal system and to the core of society itself. This is not simply an outsourcing exercise. IT will be the foundation of the court system in the near future and now is the time that it should be seen to be receiving attention at the highest levels. Second, the Court Service must be seen to recognise that the management of the third party providers, under the proposed project, should be undertaken largely by its senior management and not by technical specialists. Third, other branches of the professions, the judges and relevant bodies should have a reasonable opportunity to specify their own requirements, for these might have a direct bearing on the shape of the project. Fourth, the legal profession and the public at large should be formally assured that the ongoing effects of the PFI project will be monitored and evaluated regularly and independently.

27. To put the PFI work in context and to move forward generally, we also need a widely agreed vision of what our IT-based court system should look like in, say, seven to 10 years. I recommend the development of an exhibit – a 'Courtroom of the Future' – a step that has been taken both in the USA and Australia to capture a model of, and to stimulate interest in, the future. Additionally, we must also have a full IT strategy for the courts extending in detail for the medium term; and reaching in aspiration well beyond this period.

IT strategy for the civil justice system

28. In my interim report, I expressed concern on a number of occasions about the lack of co-ordination of IT across the civil justice system. Greater co-ordination, I argued, should lead to an overarching strategy for the civil justice system. Little progress has been made in this direction, however, and so significant problems remain.

29. A stumbling block is that various agencies within the civil justice system and the justice system as a whole are pursuing their own individual initiatives concurrently but with little mutual regard, which has resulted both in unnecessary duplication of effort as well as in incompatible systems (or at least systems which do not operate alongside one another). Electronic communication is a prime illustration. The FELIX system has been developed for the exclusive use of around 300 judges, although its actual user base is much smaller. A more general purpose system – LINK – is said to be in use by over 7,000 practising lawyers, and countless other lawyers and judges are reported to be using the Internet. If judicial case management is to become a reality – and I pick this as but one example of the need for co-ordination – it is surely sensible that all participants in the legal process can communicate easily with one another across the same system (while still preserving the facility for individuals to communicate in complete security with each other). Yet this is unlikely to happen unless there is some overarching attempt to co-ordinate, guide and lay down sensible standards for all interested parties.

30. In summary, the civil justice system is treated today as though it were a collection of separate information systems; and there has been no effective mechanism in the past for bringing these together as one coherent system. What is needed is a more strategic, co-ordinated and longer term approach for the entire system. I am convinced, both from consultation here and abroad, that it is possible (technically and logistically) to have such an overarching IT strategy for the civil justice system; and I have no doubt also that this approach is both desirable and necessary if the applications I am recommending are to be put in place cost effectively and in a way that is most likely to lead to substantial uptake across the court system and within the profession.

31. I have in mind that the strategic IT planning should be in two dimensions: one should relate to the medium term (two to four years) and the other should have a far longer term focus (five to 10 years). Both strategic plans should state clearly (but with differing and appropriate degrees of confidence and detail) what the civil justice system intends to achieve through technology and why (in social and economic terms). The plans should be widely available and also indicate how the objectives and the vision are to be realised, within what timescales and with what interim achievements. This is standard practice for any major organisation investing in IT.

32. The development of the medium term plans should remain the province of the Court Service. But there should be a new, formal mechanism for other relevant bodies and agencies (for example, the Bar, solicitors and judges) to contribute to the strategic thinking and to have a realistic opportunity to comment upon draft proposals (see paragraph 34).

33. As to the responsibility for the development of the long term plans, I can see, of course, because this topic goes to heart of the Court Service, that again this Agency must play a prime role in the exercise. However, there are many other interested parties – not the least of whom are the judges, the Judicial Studies Board, the Bar, solicitors, consumer bodies and advice centres – and they too must have a genuine opportunity to shape the future. There is a need for a body, in which they can be involved, charged with the responsibility of articulating the long term IT strategy for the civil justice system.

34. Accordingly, I recommend the establishment of a new independent body, which in due course should become attached, as a sub-committee, to the proposed Civil Justice Council. The body will have four main responsibilities. First, it will be responsible for promoting the development of the long term IT strategy to be implemented by the Court Service for the entire civil justice system. Secondly, it will be a review body through which the medium term IT plans of the Court Service should be passed and, thirdly, the body will monitor and report on the progress of the PFI. Fourthly it will have to co-ordinate initiatives in other parts of the justice system. This body will have to show leadership and general direction for the use of IT in the civil justice system.

35. In the first instance, the group should develop a high level statement, which would provide a broad vision of IT in the civil justice system, offering overall direction and purpose and providing, I would suggest, some basic standards, parameters and guidelines.

36. This broad, high level, long term strategic statement would indeed represent the long term view. I have in mind a period of anything up to 10 years. I am fully aware that there may be all manner of changes within the world of IT within this period. Nonetheless, we can look ahead with some confidence, on the strength of current laboratory activities and developments in other industries, and recognise, for example, that video conferencing, document image processing, video and audio recording of evidence and voice recognition could exert enormous influence on the manner in which we practise law and administer justice in this country. The general thrust, therefore, in the long term planning would be to present a vision of where we would like to be in seven to 10 years' time.

37. A further issue is the way in which the PFI project bears on the development of the strategy. It has been suggested to me that it may be too late to develop the overarching long term strategy which I have in mind because the PFI scheme has already progressed so far. I do not think that this is the case. As I have explained in paragraph 3, the main focus of the PFI project today is LOCCS. The details of the longer term relationship which is anticipated have not yet been settled.

38. It must also be recognised that the development of an IT strategy for the civil justice system in isolation would of itself be a short sighted exercise. Given that the civil and criminal systems share so many resources (buildings, judges, listing facilities and administrators, for example), there can be no question that the optimum approach to IT strategy would be one that produced a long term framework for the justice system as a whole, thereby bringing together the civil and criminal dimensions. The new body which I am proposing must therefore work hand in hand with those responsible for IT in the criminal justice system, including CCCJS (Co-ordination of the Computerisation of the Criminal Justice System).

Recommendations

My main recommendations are as follows.

(1)   A new independent and representative IT strategy body should be set up, which in due course should become attached, as a sub-committee, to the proposed Civil Justice Council. This body should have four main responsibilities. First, it should be responsible for promoting the development of long term IT strategy to be implemented by the Court Service for the entire civil justice system. Secondly, it should be a review body through which the medium

term IT plans of the Court Service should be passed. Thirdly, the body should monitor and report on the progress of the PFI exercise. Fourthly, it should co-ordinate initiatives in other parts of the justice system.

(2) There should be close liaison between the new body and those responsible for IT in the criminal justice system, so that there is a coherent approach to IT across the entire justice system.

(3) A project should be launched to address the ways in which existing court administration systems can and should be extended for use by judges (and by others, including lawyers and their clients), especially the caseload management facilities which deal with the allocation of resources, the scheduling of judges' workloads, the listing of cases and the electronic diarising of cases.

(4) A working group (involving, at least, the Court Service, the PFI supplier and judges) should be set up to analyse and specify the requirements of simple, PC-based case flow management systems for judges.

(5) A 'Courtroom of the Future' exhibition should be created, similar to those in the USA and Australia, to capture a vision of, and to stimulate interest in, the future.

(6) Telephone conferencing should be piloted more extensively so that decisions about its applicability for case management can be based on practical and extensive experience.

(7) An extended civil litigation protocol should be developed for use across the entire civil justice system, building on the protocol developed by the Official Referees' Solicitors' Association.

ACCESS
TO
JUSTICE

Recommendations

I set out here a combined list of the recommendations from the interim report and from this report. Recommendations from the interim report are in italics and the number is shown in brackets.

Case management

1. *There should be a fundamental transfer in the responsibility for management of civil litigation from litigants and their legal advisers to courts. (IRR 1)*

2. *The management should be provided by a three-tier system: an increased small claims jurisdiction, a new fast track for cases in the lower end of the scale and a new multi-track for the remaining cases. (IRR 2)*

3. *All cases where a defence is received will be examined by a procedural judge who will allocate the case to the appropriate track. (IRR 4)*

Fast track: detailed procedure

4. *The fast track, which is primarily for cases where the value does not exceed £10,000, will have a set timetable of 20–30 weeks, limited discovery, a trial confined to not more than three hours and no oral evidence from experts; it would also have fixed costs. (IRR 6)*

5. *All personal injury cases up to £10,000 should be dealt with in the fast track. If the small claims limit is increased before the introduction of the fast track, the increase should not apply to personal injury cases. (IRR 40)*

6. When appropriate, cases shall be allocated to the fast track by a district judge after service of the defence. A case should not be included in the fast track if:

(a)   it raises issues of public importance; or

(b)   it is a test case; or

(c)   oral evidence from experts is necessary; or

(d)   it will require lengthy legal argument or significant oral evidence which cannot be accommodated within the fast track hearing time; or

(e)   it will involve substantial documentary evidence.

7. Additional information to assist allocation to the appropriate track may be provided by questionnaires filed by the parties.

8. When allocating a case to the fast track the judge should decide on venue, allocate a 'trial week' and set a timetable for the steps to be taken which will ensure that the case can be tried by the date given; and give directions for preparing the case.

9.   Judges should have the power to direct a preliminary hearing where a litigant is in person so as to assist the litigant in the preparation of the case.

10.   There should be a discretion to allocate to the fast track other defended actions which fall outside the recommended monetary band but which are otherwise appropriate for disposal on the fast track.

11.   Directions orders will be framed as a series of requirements which must be completed by specified dates.

12.   Applications to vary the timetable must be made within the relevant time limit. If that time has passed, a sanction will apply automatically, unless relief is applied for.

13.   There should be no oral evidence from expert witnesses but parties will be able to put written questions to experts.

14.   Where possible a single expert should be instructed. Any relevant protocols should be observed. (supersedes IRR 112)

15.   The court will have a residual power to appoint a single expert.

16.   Where a party legitimately requires experts from more than one discipline then they may be instructed, although no more than two experts can be instructed without leave of the court.

17.   Leave of the court will be required to instruct any expert, other than a medical expert, in road traffic accident cases.

18.   The court will give a fixed date for trial at a set time and for a limited hearing time.

19.   Normally cases should be completed in three hours but if otherwise suitable may go up to a day.

20.   Cases are to be heard on the date fixed. If the Court Service fails to honour a fixed date, through no fault but its own, it should be liable for the wasted costs except where the failure is the result of a specific judicial direction.

Fast track costs

21.   There should be a regime of fixed recoverable costs for fast track cases.

22.   The guideline maximum legal costs on the fast track should be £2,500, excluding VAT and disbursements.

23. The costs payable by a client to his own solicitor should be limited to the level of the fixed costs plus disbursements unless there is a written agreement between the client and his solicitor which sets out clearly the different terms.

24. The costs regime should reflect case value in two bands; up to £5,000 and up to £10,000. There should be two levels of costs within each value band, one for straightforward cases and the other for cases requiring additional work.

25. The fixed costs should be divided into tranches relating to the stage the case reaches.

26. There should be a fixed advocacy fee for each band payable in cases which go to trial whether the advocate is a solicitor or a barrister. A cancellation fee should be payable to the advocate to cover work undertaken on cases which settle shortly before trial.

27. The Law Society's rule of conduct requiring a solicitor to attend trial with counsel except in specified circumstances should be revoked.

28. The costs of interlocutory hearings, applications for interim injunctions and hearings for the court to approve a settlement should be additional to the fixed costs.

29. The indemnity principle should be modified so that the costs recoverable are the fixed costs.

30. There should be further detailed work to establish the levels of the fixed costs, standard fees for experts' reports and an appropriate fee for defended debt cases.

31. The levels of the fixed costs should be reviewed each year, and the general operation of the fixed costs regime should be reviewed every three years by a committee reporting to the Lord Chancellor through the Civil Justice Council.

Multi-track

32. On the multi-track the nature of management required will be decided by the procedural judge as part of the initial scrutiny once the defence is received. The court can:

    (a)   fix a case management conference;

    (b)   issue directions in writing for the preparation of the case;

    (c)   fix a date for the trial;

(d)   specify a period within which it is intended that the trial shall take place;

(e)   fix a pre-trial review.

33.   Information to assist the judge may be provided by the parties in a questionnaire and called for by the court.

34.   *On the multi-track, case management will usually be provided through at least two interlocutory management hearings: the first will be a case management conference shortly after the defence is received (usually conducted by the procedural judge) and the second will be a pre-trial review (normally conducted by the trial judge). (IRR 7)*

35.   The objective of the case management conference is to set the agenda for the case before significant costs have been incurred and too much time has elapsed. At a case management conference the procedural judge will narrow the issues, decide on the appropriate future work and case management required, set a trial date and a timetable for the case and consider ADR and the question of costs.

36.   Parties should file statements of issues, if possible agreed beforehand, for the conference.

37.   *Among the information to be made available at the case management conference and the pre-trial review will be estimates of the amount of costs already incurred by each party and of the costs which will be incurred if the case proceeds to trial. (IRR 8)*

38.   *The case management conference should be attended by a solicitor with responsibility for the conduct of the case and at the pre-trial review the counsel or solicitor instructed to attend the trial must appear; the lay client, or someone fully authorised to act on his behalf, will be required to attend both hearings. (IRR 9)*

39.   *At the case management conference and pre-trial review the parties should be required to state whether the question of ADR has been discussed and, if not, why not. (IRR 70)*

40.   *In deciding on the future conduct of a case, the judge should be able to take into account the litigant's unreasonable refusal to attempt ADR. (IRR 71)*

41.   Where a party has refused unreasonably a proposal by the court that ADR should be attempted, or has acted unco-operatively in the course of ADR, the court should be able to take that into account in deciding what order to make as to costs.

42. *On the multi-track, cases will always be proceeding to a fixed timetable and initially to approximate and subsequently to a fixed date of trial.* (IRR 10)

43. The dates of the case management conference, the pre-trial review and the trial date cannot be changed except with the permission of the court. Parties would be able to agree other changes to the timetable subject to the overriding power of the court to intervene if appropriate, and any such agreement should be notified to the court, with the proposed new timetable.

44. Applications to vary the timetable must be made within the relevant time limit. If that time has passed, a sanction will apply automatically, unless relief is applied for.

45. A listing questionnaire should be sent out by the court at a time specified in the initial directions to establish whether directions have been complied with and to inform the decision on hearing time.

46. At a pre-trial review about eight to 10 weeks before the hearing the judge will settle the statement of issues to be tried and set a programme for the trial.

47. A general streamlined procedure should be developed with the assistance of judges and practitioners for more straightforward cases on the multi-track. This should involve limited disclosure and expert evidence, a short timetable and limited trial time and a system of controlled costs, which, while less restrictive than the fast track, would provide many of the same benefits to parties.

48. Particular streamlined procedures should be developed for small medical negligence claims, Crown Office cases and intellectual property cases where there is substantial disparity between the financial status of the parties.

49. It should be possible for suitable cases to be determined on the statements of case, without the need for an oral hearing, where this would save time and costs.

50. *To provide time for case management, civil trials on the multi-track would not normally be heard on Fridays.* (IRR 11)

51. The new rules will provide that only the Lord Chancellor and the Head of Civil Justice will be able to issue practice directions to ensure that case management systems are uniform and consistent.

Sanctions

52. As part of a case-managed system, sanctions should be designed to prevent, rather than punish, non-compliance with rules and timetables.

53. The rules themselves should specify what will happen where there has been a breach. All directions orders should include an automatic sanction for non-compliance.

54. The court should intervene and impose sanctions on parties who conduct litigation in an unreasonable or oppressive manner even if they have not breached specific rules, orders or directions.

55. The courts should make more use of their power to tax or assess the costs of an application and order them to be paid immediately.

56. The onus should be on the party in default to seek relief from a sanction, not on the other party to apply to enforce the sanction.

57. The power to make wasted costs orders should continue, but they should be reserved for clear cases and not allowed to develop into satellite litigation.

58. The client should personally be sent any costs order made against him and be made aware of his right to apply for a wasted costs order against his solicitor. He should also be sent a copy of any order, breach of which will lead to striking out, so that he knows the directions of the court and the effect of non-compliance.

Costs

59. *It should be a professional obligation for lawyers, before they are retained in connection with litigation, to explain to the prospective client how their charges for litigation are to be calculated and what the overall cost might be; and for the solicitor to give reasonable notice where that estimate is likely to be exceeded and the reason for this.* (IRR 120)

60. *Legal professional bodies should encourage their members, where this is practical, to undertake litigation on fixed fees either for stages of the proceedings or the proceedings as a whole.* (IRR 121)

61. *Courts, in making orders for costs, should pay greater regard than they do at present to the manner in which the successful party has conducted the proceedings and the outcome of individual issues.* (IRR 122)

62. Orders for costs need to reflect more precisely the obligations the new rules place on parties.

63. The court should have power to deal with the question of costs even where all other issues have been resolved without litigation.

64. Where one of the parties is unable to afford a particular procedure, the court, if it decides that that procedure is to be followed, should be entitled to make its order conditional upon the other side meeting the difference in the costs of the weaker party, whatever the outcome.

65. The court should be able to order payment of interim costs in cases where the opponent has substantially greater resources and where there is a reasonable likelihood that the weaker party will be entitled to costs at the end of the case.

66. Benchmark costs should be established by the court with the assistance of user groups, for multi-track proceedings with a limited and fairly constant procedure.

67. The new standard basis of taxation should be based on the wording of the Solicitors' (Non-Contentious Business) Remuneration Order 1994, ie, that the amount allowed should be what is "reasonable to both parties to the taxation". The indemnity basis should remain as it is.

68. There should be a review of the rules on the costs recoverable by a litigant in person with a view to simplifying them.

69. *As part of the wider discussion of legal aid, consideration should be given to the position of the unassisted litigant who succeeds against a legally aided opponent.* (IRR 123)

70. *As part of the review of court fees, the position of a litigant of modest means should be protected from the undue impact of increased court fees.* (IRR 124)

The supporting structure

71. A Civil Justice Council should be established to contribute to the development of the proposed reforms.

72. The new rule-making authority which will be needed to enact the new combined rules should contain in its membership people who can advance consumer, advisory and other lay viewpoints, as a counterbalance to the professional legal interests.

73. *There should be a Head of Civil Justice who will have overall responsibility for the civil justice system in England and Wales.* (IRR 12)

74. *A Presiding Judge on each Circuit should be nominated as having primary responsibility for civil work.* (IRR 13)

75. *The two Chancery judges responsible for overseeing Chancery work on Circuit should also oversee the business and mercantile lists.* (IRR 14)

76.   A Circuit judge responsible for each civil trial centre and its satellite courts should be designated by the Head of Civil Justice as soon as the centres are identified. (supersedes IRR 15)

77.   *The Court Service should appoint officials who correspond to the judges responsible for judicial administration to act in partnership. (IRR 16)*

78.   *The High Court and the county courts should be retained as separate courts and the separate status of the High Court judge should not be undermined. (IRR 24)*

79.   *The High Court and the county courts should generally have the same jurisdiction and outside London should be administered together. Cases should be remitted to the lowest appropriate level for trial. (IRR 25)*

80.   *The specialist judges on Circuit should provide support to each other's lists. (IRR 26)*

81.   *The Chancery and the Queen's Bench Divisions should retain their separate identities. (IRR 27)*

82.   *Outside London there should be three or four designated civil trial centres on each Circuit. (IRR 28)*

83.   *Small claims and fast track cases should be dealt with at local county courts. (IRR 29)*

84.   *Cases on the multi-track should be managed by teams of judges. (IRR 17)*

85.   *Each team should have a Master or district judge as the manager of the team and, except in unusually complex cases, as the procedural judge. (IRR 18)*

86.   *An appropriate share of judicial resources should be allocated to civil business. The trial judges for heavier civil cases should be identified earlier than at present to enable them to conduct the pre-trial reviews in those cases. (IRR 20)*

87.   *High Court and Circuit judges should concentrate on fewer areas of work without becoming single subject specialists. (IRR 19)*

88.   Judges should be nominated for appropriate areas of specialisation. A record of judges' preferences should be established and taken into account in determining the allocation of judges to specialised areas.

89.   Judges who specialise in areas such as medical negligence and housing should be given appropriate training. The possibility of providing joint training with the legal profession, under the general aegis of the Judicial Studies Board, should be explored.

90. Procedural judges should be given proper clerical and secretarial support to enable them to carry out their new duties in relation to case management effectively.

91. The Court Service should encourage members of staff, including clerks to High Court judges, to become members of the Institute of Legal Executives.

92. High Court and Court of Appeal judges should have law clerks, initially on a selective basis.

93. *Consideration should be given to the way in which members of the professions who are experienced in litigation and who retire at an early age can be involved as 'civil magistrates' or otherwise, in support of the civil justice system.* (IRR 73)

94. *Masters and district judges should be eligible for appointment as Circuit judges, without having to sit as Recorders in crime.* (IRR 21)

95. *High Court judges should continue to visit Circuits and not be resident on Circuit.* (IRR 22)

96. *There should be training and monitoring of judges in relation to case management. This should be under judicial supervision.* (IRR 23)

Pre-action protocols

97. *There should be a new ethos of co-operation on the part of litigants and their legal representatives before proceedings are begun.* (IRR 74)

98. *The appropriate professional bodies should draw up guidelines for pre-proceedings conduct of legal representatives.* (IRR 75)

99. Pre-action protocols should set out codes of sensible practice which parties are expected to follow when faced with the prospect of litigation. They should not cover all areas of litigation, but should deal with specific problems in specific areas, including personal injury, medical negligence and housing.

100. When a protocol is established for a particular area of litigation, it should be incorporated into the relevant practice guide.

101. Unreasonable failure by either party to comply with the relevant protocol should be taken into account by the court, for example in the allocation of costs or in considering any application for an extension of the timetable.

102. The operation of the protocols should be monitored and their detailed provisions modified so far as is necessary in the light of practical experience.

Offers

103. *Offers to settle can be made by a plaintiff as well as a defendant.* (IRR 115)

104. *Offers to settle can relate to individual issues.* (IRR 116)

105. *Offers to settle can be made before the commencement of proceedings.* (IRR 117)

106. *The extent of entitlement to costs and interest in respect of an offer should be in the court's discretion and should depend on the extent of disclosure by the parties.* (IRR 119)

107. A defendant's ability to make a payment into court should be retained, but the making of an offer, in accordance with rules of court, should be the primary requirement, with payments in being a secondary and optional means of backing an offer. The absence of a payment in should not normally influence the court's view of whether an offer was reasonable. (supersedes IRR 114)

108. A party may withdraw an offer, but an offer which is open for less than 21 days should be disregarded by the court for costs purposes.

109. *Offers to settle can result in substantially enhanced costs and interest being payable.* (IRR 118)

110. The rates of additional interest which I now recommend should be payable to a claimant who makes an offer which is not accepted and which the claimant matches or exceeds at trial are:

awards up to £10,000	25%
more than £10,000 and up to £50,000	15%
above £50,000	5%.

111. Extra interest will normally run from the date of the offer, but the court may order a different start date where appropriate.

112. A party who recovers at trial the amount which he claimed should be treated as if he had made an offer for that amount, and be entitled to extra interest.

Practice and procedure
Starting a claim

113. It will usually be possible to start proceedings in any High Court district registry or county court. Claims for possession of land will be an exception, being brought in the court where the relevant land is situated. It will normally not be possible to bring claims worth £50,000 or less in the Royal Courts of Justice in London. The commencement of proceedings in the wrong court will not nullify them.

114. All claims should be started on a single claim form with appropriate variations.

115. *A claim should contain the following:*

(a)   *a succinct statement of the facts entitling the claimant to a remedy;*

(b)   *the remedy or remedies claimed;*

(c)   *any matters of law arising out of the stated facts which entitle the plaintiff to a remedy; and*

(d)   *the legal nature of the claim where it would otherwise not be clear.* (IRR 81)

116. The defendant will be required to complete a notice of intention to defend, within 14 days of service of the claim, and the period for filing a defence will be 28 days, unless the parties agree to extend it.

117. *A defence should contain:*

(a)   *the parts of the claim admitted and not admitted;*

(b)   *the defendant's version of the facts so far as different from those stated in the claim;*

(c)   *specific defences (voluntary assumption of risk, failure to mitigate loss, etc,) and any grounds for denying the claim arising out of the facts stated by the defendant, or for disputing its value or denying entitlement to a particular remedy; and*

(d)   *where no specific facts or legal grounds are relied upon, that the defendant does not know whether the facts stated in the claim are true and requires the plaintiff to prove them and, if appropriate, why this is required.* (IRR 82)

118. In debt cases the claimant must file a reply if the defendant's defence is that he has paid the whole of the money claimed. In other cases it will be possible for the claimant to file a reply without the leave of the court, before any initial case management conference. (supersedes IRR 83)

Statements of case

119. *The term 'pleading' should be replaced by 'statement of case'.* (IRR 86)

120. *Statements of case will refer to the principal documents relied upon. A party would be permitted, but not obliged, to attach to his statement of case the principal documents to which he refers and the names of his anticipated witnesses or summaries of their evidence.* (IRR 84)

121. *Statements of case will contain a declaration on behalf of the party of belief in the accuracy and truth of the matters put forward.* (IRR 85)

122. One amendment of the claim, after service, and one amendment of the defence will be allowed without leave.

123. *As part of its responsibility for managing cases, the court will ensure that the parties plainly state the factual ingredients of their case so that true nature and scope of the dispute can be identified.* (IRR 76)

124. *The basic function of pleadings is to state the facts relied upon.* (IRR 77)

125. *The claim and defence will be considered by the procedural judge after the defence is filed and, if the issues cannot be readily identified from the pleadings, directions will be given with a view to rectifying this.* (IRR 78)

126. *Where there has been a case management conference, a major aim will be to produce a statement of the issues in dispute, which will effectively take over from the pleadings.* (IRR 79)

127. *If, unavoidably, new facts and new issues emerge during the proceedings, the statement of issues can be altered to reflect this.* (IRR 80)

Service

128. In principle there should be no restriction on the methods by which court process can be served. Instead the court will have to be satisfied that the method used had either put the recipient in a position to ascertain the document's contents or was reasonably likely to enable him to do so.

129. Service by first class post and service on a solicitor will be the 'standard' method of service, with a simpler burden of proving service than other methods. A party who uses another method will have to describe the method, the date of service and why the method was expected to be effective.

130. A party should be free in all cases to serve process himself.

Summary judgment

131. *The court should have an enlarged jurisdiction to give summary judgment on the application of either a claimant or defendant or on the court's own initiative, on the grounds that a case or part of a case has no realistic prospect of success.* (IRR 3)

132. The test for summary judgment would be that there was no realistic prospect of success at trial. Exceptionally, notwithstanding that the test was satisfied, the court could allow a case or issue to continue if it considered there was a public interest in the matter being tried.

133. Summary judgment would be available at all stages of a case up to judgment.

Disclosure of documents

134. *A requirement to disclose documents should be retained, but subject to controls.* (IRR 87)

135. *In fast track cases, discovery should normally be confined to documents on which a party relies or which to a material extent undermine his case or support another party's case ('standard discovery').* (IRR 88)

136. *In the multi-track, standard discovery should be the first stage, the extent and timing of 'extra discovery' being determined by the procedural judge.* (IRR 89)

137. *Standard discovery should be limited to documents of whose existence a party is aware at the time when the obligation to disclose arises. If the documents involved are likely to be voluminous, a party can state that he was initially limiting disclosure to those which were capable of being located without undue difficulty and expense.* (IRR 90)

138. *It will normally be necessary to disclose only one version of a document.* (IRR 91)

139. *In determining whether to order extra discovery, the procedural judge should have regard to the issues in the case and the order in which they are likely to be resolved, the resources and circumstances of the parties, the likely cost of extra discovery and the likely benefit.* (IRR 92)

140. *The restriction of the court's powers in respect of pre-action discovery to personal injury cases should be removed.* (IRR 93)

141. The test for documents to be initially disclosed is whether a party is aware of those documents at the time when the obligation to disclose arises. In the case of a company, 'awareness' will be that of individual employees with relevant knowledge. A company will be required to appoint a supervising officer to identify such individuals.

142. A potential claimant in proceedings for injury or death should be able to make a pre-action application for disclosure against a person who is not expected to be a defendant.

143. Pre-action applications for disclosure will have to be in respect of specified documents which will be relevant to a potential claim; the court must be satisfied that the benefit of allowing such disclosure will outweigh any cost and inconvenience to the disclosing party.

Witness statements

144. *On the multi-track, before the case management conference, only the identity of witnesses and the issues with which they deal need be disclosed. After the case management conference, when the issues have been identified, witness statements should be exchanged.* (IRR 96)

145. *A party should be entitled to require his witnesses to amplify summaries or statements but not to raise new matters except with leave of the judge.* (IRR 97)

146. *Cross-examination on the contents of witness summaries and statements should only be allowed with the leave of the judge.* (IRR 98)

147. *A practice guide dealing with the preparation and use of witness summaries and statements should be issued.* (IRR 99)

148. *The costs allowed for witness statements and summaries should reflect the fact that they are not intended to be elaborate documents.* (IRR 100)

149. Witness statements should:

    (a)   so far as possible, be in the witness's own words;

    (b)   not discuss legal propositions;

    (c)   not comment on documents;

    (d)   conclude with a signed statement by the witness that the evidence is a true statement and that it is in his own words.

150. When the Civil Evidence Act 1995 is in force, allowing a witness statement to refer to matters beyond the direct knowledge or observation of the witness, the statement should indicate where appropriate the sources of knowledge, belief or information on which the witness relies.

151. Especially on the fast track witness statements should be concise. (supersedes IRR 95)

Representation of companies

152. Rules of court should no longer require a company to act by a solicitor.

153. The court should normally exercise its discretion in favour of allowing an employee of a company to take any steps on behalf of the company which a litigant in person could take in High Court or county court proceedings.

Expert evidence

154. The employee would have to show, if required, that he was duly authorised to act by the company.

155. A practice direction should indicate the considerations relevant to the exercise of the court's discretion.

156. *The calling of expert evidence should be subject to the complete control of the court.* (IRR 101)

157. *The court should have discretion, with or without the agreement of the parties, to appoint an expert to report or give evidence to the court.* (IRR 102)

158. *The court should have wide power to appoint assessors.* (IRR 103)

159. *Experts should be given clear guidance that, when preparing evidence or actually giving evidence to a court, their first responsibility is to the court and not their client.* (IRR 104)

160. *Any report prepared for the purposes of giving evidence to a court should be addressed to the court.* (IRR 105)

161. *Such a report should end with a declaration that it includes everything which the expert regards as being relevant to the opinion which he has expressed in his report and that he has drawn to the attention of the court any matter which would affect the validity of that opinion.* (IRR 106)

162. *If experts instructed by the parties meet at the direction of the court, it should be unprofessional conduct for an expert to be given or to accept instructions not to reach agreement. If the experts cannot reach agreement on an issue they should specify their reasons for being unable to do so.* (IRR 107)

163. *Codes of practice providing guidance as to the practice in relation to experts should be drawn up jointly by the appropriate professional bodies representing the experts and the legal profession.* (IRR 109)

164. *Unless the plaintiff is relying on the doctor by whom he is being treated, the defendant should be told whom the plaintiff intends to instruct and invited to make any comments as to the proposed instructions.* (IRR 110)

165. *Before a doctor reports on behalf of a plaintiff or a defendant, the opposing party should have the opportunity to give instructions to that doctor.* (IRR 111)

166. *Every effort should be made by the court to avoid doctors having to attend court, or if they have to attend court, to reduce the inconvenience this involves. Video technology should be used for this purpose.* (IRR 113)

167. As a general principle, single experts should be used wherever the case (or the issue) is concerned with a substantially established area of knowledge and where it is not necessary for the court directly to sample a range of opinions.

168. Parties and procedural judges should always consider whether a single expert could be appointed in a particular case (or to deal with a particular issue); and, if this is not considered appropriate, indicate why not.

169. Where opposing experts are appointed they should adopt a co-operative approach. Wherever possible this should include a joint investigation and a single report, indicating areas of disagreement which cannot be resolved.

170. Expert evidence should not be admissible unless all written instructions (including letters subsequent upon the original instructions) and a note of any oral instructions are included as an annex to the expert's report. (supersedes IRR 108)

171. The court should have a wide power, which could be exercised before the start of proceedings, to order that an examination or tests should be carried out in relation to any matter in issue, and a report submitted to the court.

172. Experts' meetings should normally be held in private. When the court directs a meeting, the parties should be able to apply for any special arrangements such as attendance by the parties' legal advisers.

173. Training courses and published material should provide expert witnesses with a basic understanding of the legal system and their role within it, focusing on the expert's duty to the court, and enable them to present written and oral evidence effectively. Training should not be compulsory.

Appeals

174. Leave to appeal should be required for all interlocutory appeals.

175. Appeals from interlocutory decisions should lie, in fast track cases:

(a)   from a district judge to a nominated Circuit judge;

(b)   from a Circuit judge to the Court of Appeal;

and, in multi-track cases:

(c)   from a Master or a district judge to a High Court judge;

(d)   from a Circuit judge or a High Court judge to the Court of Appeal.

176. In case (a) the Circuit judge should be able to refer the appeal to a Presiding Judge or, with his agreement, to the Court of Appeal. In cases (a) and (c) there should be a further appeal to the Court of Appeal with leave if there was certified to be an important point of principle or practice or one which for some other special reason should be considered by the Court of Appeal.

177. It should be possible to make an application for leave to appeal from an interlocutory order to the judge taking the decision, there and then, or *ex parte* in writing to the appellate court within three days. The appellate judge should decide on the papers whether to refuse leave, or to direct that there be an oral hearing of the appeal or a determination on the basis of written submissions. Where the judge appealed from gives leave to appeal the appeal should be listed for hearing within 10 days. There should be no further renewal of the application for leave.

178. Appeals from final decisions should be to the Court of Appeal. Leave to appeal would be required from final decisions in fast track cases.

179. The Court of Appeal should be able to delegate its jurisdiction to hear interlocutory and final fast track appeals to any judge of the Supreme Court or to request a Circuit judge to sit as a member of the Court. It should also be able to determine such appeals without a hearing.

180. There should be a procedure involving the preliminary consideration of all appeals to the Court of Appeal, usually by a single judge, with the power to dispose of appeals with no merit summarily.

181. All appeals should be of the limited Court of Appeal rehearing type and not complete rehearings.

182. All appeals should be heard in open court.

183. There should be greater uniformity in the procedure for statutory appeals to the courts.

184. Further consideration should be given to enabling decisions to be referred to the House of Lords or Court of Appeal where no appeal has been brought or is possible, so as to ensure proper development of the law.

185. It should be possible for third parties, with the leave or at the request of the court, to make submissions to the Court of Appeal or House of Lords.

186. The rules on appeals should be rationalised. Eventually there should be a single procedure for all appeals to the courts, using a claim and defence and with a preliminary consideration by the court at which it will be possible to dispose of the proceedings summarily. If there have been two stages already the appeal should normally be to the Court of Appeal, and if not more than one stage, then to the High Court.

Medical negligence

187. The training of health professionals should include an introduction to the legal context of medical work, including an indication of what is involved in a claim for negligence.

188. The General Medical Council and other regulatory bodies should consider whether a rule of professional conduct is needed to clarify the responsibility of healthcare professionals to their patients when they discover an act or omission in which they may have been negligent in their care and treatment.

189. The NHS should consider tackling the problem of tracing former hospital staff, by improving hospital record systems or making more use of existing information.

190. A pre-litigation protocol for medical negligence cases should be developed. As part of the protocol, claimants should be required to notify defendants of a firm intention to sue in a letter before action. The letter should include the fullest available information about the basis of the intended claim, and should wherever possible give at least three months' notice that a statement of case is to be served. If liability is disputed, defendants should be required to provide a reasoned answer.

191. The use of alternative dispute resolution mechanisms should be encouraged in medical negligence, especially for smaller claims. Solicitors acting for patients should not automatically advise litigation but should inform their clients of all the available options, including the Health Service Ombudsman, and consider the possibility of alternative dispute resolution at all stages of the case.

192. The specialist lists in the Queen's Bench Division of the High Court should include a separate medical negligence list.

193. Outside London, medical negligence cases at both High Court and county court level should be handled at specially designated court centres.

194. There should be regional lists, or a single national list, to facilitate the flexible allocation of cases for trial and reduce delay.

195. The Judicial Studies Board should investigate, with appropriate medical experts, the scope and content of training in medical issues for procedural and trial judges, and organise the necessary training.

196. Standard tables should be used wherever possible to reduce the cost of quantifying complex medical negligence (and other personal injury) claims.

197. There should be a practice guide to indicate how the new rules on case management and procedure will apply in detail to medical negligence litigation. The guide should be developed by the new 'umbrella' organisation for medical negligence or under the aegis of the Civil Justice Council.

198. The Court Service should facilitate a pilot study of the various options for dealing with medical negligence claims below £10,000, to establish which is the most effective procedure for enabling these cases to be litigated on a modest budget.

Housing

199. Judges should be encouraged to specialise in housing cases, and more training should be provided to ensure that they are aware of the special problems in this area.

200. The Law Commission should be invited to carry out a review of housing law with a view to consolidating the various statutory and other provisions in a clear and straightforward form.

201. All claims for repossession of domestic property, including actions for the eviction of squatters, should start in the local county court. It should be possible for cases to be listed before a High Court judge only if there are exceptional circumstances which make this necessary.

202. There should be a new, two-stage possession procedure for arrears of rent cases. The first stage would be a paper procedure leading to a court order for the repayment of arrears. Failure to comply with its terms would lead to a second stage involving a hearing, which could then result in an order for possession.

203. The need to reform the accelerated possession procedure for assured shorthold tenancies should be considered in the light of the responses to the Inquiry, and of the results of research by the Department of the Environment.

204. All hearings involving discussion of a party's financial affairs should be held in private. The best approach is for all possession proceedings to take place in the informal surroundings of chambers. There should be no overall ban on public attendance, but either party should be able to apply for members of the public to be excluded.

205. There should be an expedited possession procedure, including an element of case management and a target date for trial within 10-13 weeks, for claims by local authorities and registered social landlords within the meaning of the current Housing Bill, where it is alleged that there has been violence or harassment.

206. County courts, solicitors, law centres and any other agencies dealing with enquiries about housing matters should provide information to potential claimants about the 1994 Right to Repair Regulations, the Local Government Ombudsman, and any other options such as local mediation schemes.

207. There should be a pre-action protocol for housing disrepair cases including:

(a) a clear procedure for tenants to report disrepair;

(b) an obligation on landlords to issue receipts for reports of disrepair; and

(c) provision for inspection of the property by a single expert chosen from an agreed list.

If the agreed protocol, or the protocol set out in the practice guide, is not complied with by the parties, this should be reflected in the court's approach to costs and discretionary relief.

208. There should be a new route of appeal to the county courts, on judicial review principles, against local authorities' decisions on homelessness.

209. The existing rules on the standing of organisations to bring representative actions in the housing field should be clarified and made less restrictive.

210. The discretion of the public Ombudsmen to investigate issues involving maladministration which could be raised before the courts should be put on a formal basis. The Ombudsman should be able to refer points of law (including questions of statutory interpretation) to the courts, and compensation recommended by the Ombudsman should be enforceable through the courts.

211. *The law in relation to housing should be simplified.* (IRR 58)

Multi-party actions

212. Where proceedings will or may require collective treatment, parties or the Legal Aid Board should apply for a multi-party situation (MPS) to be established. This would suspend the operation of the Limitation Act. The court may also initiate an application. Within the MPS, part of the proceedings could be common to some or all of the claimants, and other parts could be limited to individual claimants.

213. Individual claimants would be able to join the MPS at the application stage and subsequently by entering their names on an initial register.

214. The court should certify an MPS if it is satisfied that the group or groups will be sufficiently large and homogeneous, and that the cases within the MPS will be more viable if there is a collective approach than if they are handled individually.

215. Lower value or local cases should be dealt with locally at appropriate courts by either a High Court or Circuit judge.

216. A managing judge should be appointed at or as soon as possible following certification and should handle the action throughout.

217. In appropriate cases additional support may be provided by the appointment of a deputy Master or deputy district judge from those practitioners who already have considerable experience of multi-party litigation.

218. The court should have a residual power to approve the lead lawyer if a difficulty arises in appointing one.

219. The court should usually aim to treat as a priority the determination of the generic issues while establishing economic methods of handling the individual cases.

220. The court should have power to progress the MPS on an 'opt-out' or 'opt-in' basis, whichever contributes best to the effective and efficient disposition of the case.

221. In reaching a decision on notice of the action to potential claimants, the court must take into account the cost of such notice and its usefulness.

222. The court should be responsible for determining whether the action has merit and should proceed and the criteria which must be met by those wishing to join the action.

223. The court should determine the arrangements for costs and cost sharing at the outset. The costs of action groups should be recoverable on taxation.

224. The Lord Chancellor's Department and Legal Aid Board should consider the possibility of extending the upper limits of financial eligibility on the basis of increased contributions. In appropriate cases, with tight judicial management and control on costs it may be possible for assisted persons' liability to be assessed and fixed in advance.

225. The possibility of a contingency legal aid fund should be reconsidered in the context of these proposals.

226. The court has a duty to protect the interests of claimants, especially those unidentified or unborn.

227. In appropriate cases the court should appoint a trustee.

228. Multi-party settlements should be approved by the court especially where the defendant offers a lump sum settlement.

229. The court should require an identified and finite group of claimants to have in place from the outset a constitution including provisions relating to acceptance of settlement.

The Crown Office List

230. The procedures in public law cases should be brought into line with one another and with those in private law cases wherever possible. Use of the wrong procedure should not lead to the case being dismissed. Instead it should be dealt with so far as possible under the proper procedure.

231. More judges from other Divisions should be nominated to hear Crown Office List cases.

232. Certain Crown Office List cases should be heard outside London.

233. Claimants for judicial review should use available methods of ADR.

234. Claimants should notify the defendant of their proposed claim before starting proceedings.

235. A claim for judicial review and any defence should follow the standard claim form and defence. Unless it would inconvenience the hearing of the claim for judicial review, it should be possible for the claimant to include any remedies which could be obtained in a private law action and for the defendant to make a counterclaim.

236. The court should be able to grant advisory declarations in limited circumstances.

237. At the preliminary consideration stage (formerly 'leave'), which should be in writing, the judge should allow the claim to proceed if there is a realistic prospect of success or some other reason why the claim should be disposed of at a substantive hearing. He should consider giving directions for the conduct of the claim and set a timetable.

238. There should be a right to renew the application in non-criminal cases at an oral hearing before a single judge and a further renewal to the Court of Appeal, with leave. Consideration should be given to the same procedure applying in criminal causes.

239. The court should be able to grant interim relief before the preliminary consideration but should only do so *ex parte* in a clear and urgent case.

240. The claimant will have standing if he has been or will be adversely affected or if it is in the public interest that the claim should be brought.

241. All cases of judicial review should normally be heard by a single judge. There should be an appeal, with leave, to the Court of Appeal, Civil Division in non-criminal causes and consideration should be given to enabling appeals in criminal causes to lie, with leave, to the Court of Appeal, Criminal Division.

242. The court should have a discretion to order costs to be paid out of public funds or to order that the unsuccessful party is not to pay the other party's costs where the proceedings have been brought in the public interest.

243. It should be possible to determine some claims in the Crown Office List in writing where the parties agree.

244. The rules on *habeas corpus* and committal for contempt will be clarified and simplified.

Other specialist jurisdictions

245. Many of the present Chancery procedures should be accommodated by the general provisions of the new rules.

246. Where proceedings are usually disposed of in a particular list or court, the heading of the case should identify that list or court. For example, all Companies Act proceedings should be entitled 'In the Companies Court'.

247. The Vice-Chancellor should institute an annual review of the Chancery Division, similar to those published by the Court of Appeal and the Commercial Court.

248. The Head of Civil Justice should publish an annual review covering the civil justice system as a whole.

249. There should be a power to transfer particular issues, as well as whole cases, to another court.

250. The Patents Court and the Patents County Court should develop procedures which go further than existing ones in providing rapid resolution of disputes, with a strict timetable and a trial limited in time, and a fixed budget for costs.

251. A number of the special rules for intellectual property, Chancery and Admiralty proceedings should be retained.

252. Pre-reading guides for trial judges, as currently used in the Patents Court, should be extended to other areas of multi-track litigation. Where it would assist with case management, they should be made available at an earlier stage in the litigation.

253. Both the Official Referees' Court and the Commercial List in the High Court in London should continue. The definition of 'commercial action' should be replaced with a more modern one.

254. There should be uniformity in the description of claims and defences, and there is no need for the Commercial Court to retain the description of points of claim and points of defence.

255. There should no longer be special rules for the transfer of commercial actions, since the new rules will contain wide provisions on the transfer of cases.

256. As proposed by the Official Referees' Working Group, there should be a general provision in the rules that trials or other hearings may take place anywhere.

257. Consideration should be given to reducing the number of county courts with Admiralty jurisdiction.

Information technology **258.** *Consideration should be given to the extent to which the IT requirements of case management, as proposed in this report, can be integrated into the LOCCS framework.* (IRR 30)

259. *Judges should be equipped with personal computers powerful enough to support all the proposals outlined in this report. There should be consultation with a wider range of judges to establish the full range of applications. The specification of minimum requirements for judicial systems should be reconsidered in this light. There should be enhanced training and technical support to encourage a wider range of judicial users.* (IRR 31)

260. *Litigation support systems should be used more widely by the professions. The position of recoverability under legal aid and taxation should be clarified.* (IRR 32)

261. *Video and telephone conferencing facilities should be piloted and introduced as a priority to assist judges, particularly procedural judges, in case management and the legal aspects of the use of new technology should be considered.* (IRR 33)

262. *Video recording and viewing facilities should be introduced in appropriate cases.* (IRR 34)

263. *There should be exploration of the provision of IT to inform and assist the public and the scope for its provision in public places and advice centres.* (IRR 35)

264. *The policy in relation to providing primary source materials, especially statutory materials, in electronic form should be clarified.* (IRR 36)

265. *There should be an evaluation of the implications of the proposed PFI procurement scheme for the civil courts, including the necessary safeguards and infrastructures.* (IRR 37)

266. *There should be co-ordination of the provision of IT in the civil justice system, involving all the key bodies. The proposed Civil Justice Council and ITAC should consider how best to advise on and assist in this.* (IRR 38)

267. A new independent and representative IT strategy body should be set up, which in due course should become attached, as a sub-committee, to the proposed Civil Justice Council. This body should have four main responsibilities. First, it should be responsible for promoting the development of long term IT strategy to be implemented by the Court Service for the entire civil justice system. Secondly, it should be a review body through which the medium term IT plans of the Court Service should be passed. Thirdly, the body should monitor and report on the progress of the PFI exercise. Fourthly, it should co-ordinate initiatives in other parts of the justice system.

268. There should be close liaison between the new body and those responsible for IT in the criminal justice system, so that there is a coherent approach to IT across the entire justice system.

269. A project should be launched to address the ways in which existing court administration systems can and should be extended for use by judges (and by others, including lawyers and their clients), especially the caseload management facilities which deal with the allocation of resources, the scheduling of judges' workloads, the listing of cases and the electronic diarising of cases.

270. A working group (involving, at least, the Court Service, the PFI supplier and judges) should be set up to analyse and specify the requirements of simple, PC-based case flow management systems for judges.

271. A 'Courtroom of the Future' exhibition should be created, similar to those in the USA and Australia, to capture a vision of, and to stimulate interest in, the future.

272. Telephone conferencing should be piloted more extensively so that decisions about its applicability for case management can be based on practical and extensive experience.

273. An extended civil litigation protocol should be developed for use across the entire civil justice system, building on the protocol developed by the Official Referees' Solicitors' Association.

Small claims in the county courts

274. *Except for personal injury cases, the financial limit of the small claims jurisdiction should be increased to £3,000. The effect of the increase, and of the measures recommended below, should be monitored with a view to a possible further increase to £5,000. (IRR 39)*

275. *The district judge's discretion to transfer complex cases out of the small claims jurisdiction should be widened by removing the requirement that complexity must be "exceptional". (Implemented) (IRR 41)*

276. *Unless there are genuinely exceptional circumstances, small claims should be disposed of at a single hearing. If clarification is required from the parties this should, wherever possible, be done by correspondence or telephone. (IRR 42)*

277. *Businesses should be allowed to continue to use the scheme. (IRR 43)*

278. *All district judges and deputy district judges should be trained in handling small claims, to ensure a more consistent approach. (IRR 44)*

279. *The option of paper adjudication in small claims should be more effectively publicised. (IRR 45)*

280. *The court should have power to appoint an expert assessor from a list provided by the appropriate professional body. Subject to the judge's discretion the cost of the assessor should be recoverable from the unsuccessful party or shared between the parties. (IRR 46)*

Litigants in person

281. *The provision of assistance to litigants should be an invariable obligation of the courts.* (IRR 47)

282. *In the context of the consultation paper on legal aid and the aims of the Court Service, the Lord Chancellor should determine and implement the best way of providing advice through court-based or duty advice and assistance schemes funded by the Legal Aid Board.* (IRR 48)

283. *Information technology kiosks should be introduced on a trial basis at selected courts.* (IRR 49)

284. *Research should be conducted into litigants' information needs and the most helpful way of presenting information. The feasibility of providing an explanatory video on the court process should be investigated.* (IRR 50)

285. *The courts should provide reasonable facilities, preferably in private, for filling in forms.* (IRR 51)

286. *Both professional litigators and unrepresented litigants should have access to court libraries.* (IRR 52)

287. *All the Civil Justice Review's recommendations on the provision of information and advice to litigants should be fully implemented.* (IRR 53)

288. *There should be a permanent advice centre in larger courts. In courts with smaller workloads, there should be an investigation as to whether court-based advice agencies are more effective than those located elsewhere.* (IRR 54)

289. *Permanent facilities should be provided for all court-based advice schemes, where possible.* (IRR 55)

290. *There should be a duty advice scheme funded by legal aid at each of the courts identified as handling substantial levels of debt and housing work. Ways of providing more general assistance, by the provision of a Citizens Advice Bureau or similar facility at court centres where the workload would justify it, should be explored and the possibility of legal aid funding for such a service should be considered.* (IRR 56)

291. *Judges should be prepared to adopt an interventionist approach in all cases involving an unrepresented party and the handling of such cases should be fully covered in judicial training.* (IRR 57)

292. *Alternative ways of providing court services in rural areas should be explored, including mobile courts providing small claims hearings, as well as advice and information.* (IRR 59)

293. *The possibility of holding evening or weekend courts should be re-examined.* (IRR 60)

Alternative approaches to dispensing justice

294. *Court buildings should be clearly signposted, in appropriate minority languages as well as English.* (IRR 61)

295. *Developments abroad, particularly those in the United States, Australia and Canada, in relation to ADR should be monitored, the Judicial Studies Board giving as much assistance as is practicable in relation to this exercise.* (IRR 62)

296. *The retail sector should be encouraged to develop private ombudsman schemes to cover consumer complaints similar to those which now exist in relation to service industries; the government should facilitate this.* (IRR 63)

297. *The relationship between ombudsmen and the courts should be broadened, enabling issues to be referred by the ombudsman to the courts and the courts to the ombudsman with the consent of those involved.* (IRR 64)

298. *The discretion of the public ombudsmen to investigate issues involving maladministration which could be raised before the courts should be extended.* (IRR 65)

299. *In the review of legal aid, the funding of voluntary organisations providing mediation services should be considered.* (IRR 66)

300. *The courts should encourage and facilitate mini-trials in appropriate cases and use of mini-trials should be tested on an experimental basis in a selected number of courts.* (IRR 67)

301. *The courts should, where appropriate, consider taking advantage of bodies such as the City Disputes Panel, to give authoritative guidance on particular practices from those who have experience at the highest level.* (IRR 68)

302. *Where there is a satisfactory alternative to the resolution of disputes in court, use of which would be an advantage to the litigants, then the courts should encourage the use of this alternative: for this purpose the staff and the judiciary must be aware of the forms of ADR which exist and what can be achieved.* (IRR 69)

303. *The Lord Chancellor and the Court Service should treat it as one of their responsibilities to make the public aware of the possibilities which ADR offers.* (Implemented) (IRR 72)

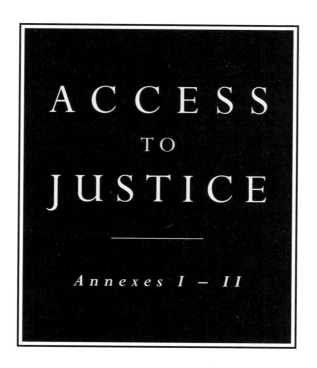

ACCESS TO JUSTICE

Annexes I – II

Inquiry Team and Working Groups

The Inquiry Team	Amanda Finlay
	Michael Kron
	Nicholas Hodgson
	Chris Pulford
	Catherine Davidson
	Brenda Griffith-Williams
	Melanie Field
	Clare Funnell
	Margaret MacDonald
	Ian Johnson
	Elizabeth Marshall
	Sarah Brown
	Betty Blatt
	Suzy Johnson
	Rose Lenihan

I am also especially grateful to my secretary at the House of Lords, Lesley Minster.

Rules Working Group

Michael Kron, Secretary to the Inquiry (Chairman)
Helen Brown, Information Officer, National Association of Citizens Advice Bureaux
Catherine Davidson, Woolf Inquiry Team ✓
District Judge Greenslade, Assessor
Senior Master Turner, Assessor
Marlene Winfield, Senior Policy and Development Officer, National Consumer Council

Admiralty Working Group

Master Miller, Admiralty Master (Chairman)
Geoffrey Brice QC
Tony Ferrigno, Admiralty Marshal
H R Heward, solicitor, Norton Rose
J M M Johnson, solicitor, Davies Grant and Horton
Jervis Kay QC
Nigel Meeson, barrister
Senior Master Turner, Assessor

Chancery Working Group

Mrs Justice Arden DBE (Chairman)
District Judge Beattie
Richard Clark, solicitor, Slaughter and May
David Chivers, barrister

Amanda Finlay, Secretary to the Inquiry
Nicholas Hodgson, Woolf Inquiry Team
Master Moncaster, Chancery Division
Senior Master Turner, Assessor

Commercial Court Working Group

Mr Justice Waller (Chairman)
Richard Aikens QC
David Bird MBE, Commercial Court, Royal Courts of Justice
Amanda Finlay, Secretary to the Inquiry
Nicholas Hodgson, Woolf Inquiry Team
Mark Humphreys, solicitor, Linklaters & Paines
Senior Master Turner, Assessor

Crown Office Working Group

Mr Justice Brooke (now Lord Justice Brooke) (Chairman)
Diana Babar, solicitor, Treasury Solicitor's Department
Professor Jack Beatson, St. John's College, Cambridge
Amanda Finlay, Secretary to the Inquiry
Stephen Grosz, solicitor, Bindman & Partners
Nicholas Hodgson, Woolf Inquiry Team
Lynne Knapman, Crown Office, Royal Courts of Justice
Mr Justice Laws
Master McKenzie QC, Master of the Crown Office
David Pannick QC
Senior Master Turner, Assessor

Fast Track Working Group

Amanda Finlay, Secretary to the Inquiry (Chairman)
David Bean, barrister
Dave Beaumont, Courts Administrator, Liverpool
Carlos Dabezies, solicitor, Kensington Citizens Advice Bureau
Melanie Field, Woolf Inquiry Team
District Judge Frenkel
District Judge Greenslade, Assessor
Janet Howe, Lord Chancellor's Department
Paulette James, Court Service (Chris Tye until January 1996)
Paul Johnson, solicitor, Oldham Law Centre
Margaret MacDonald, Woolf Inquiry Team
David Marsh, London County Courts & Tribunals Administrator
Simon Parrington, solicitor, Wayman-Hales
Chris Pulford, Woolf Inquiry Team
Henry Witcomb, barrister

Housing Working Group	Brenda Griffith-Williams, Woolf Inquiry Team (Chairman)
	Wendy Backhouse, solicitor, Hodge Jones & Allen
	John Bryant, National Federation of Housing Associations
	Russell Campbell, solicitor, Shelter
	Bernard Crofton, Director of Housing, London Borough of Hackney
	District Judge Greenslade, Assessor
	Roger Griffiths, City Housing Officer, Coventry City Council
	Alastair Jackson, National Federation of Housing Associations
	Jan Luba, barrister
	Margaret MacDonald, Woolf Inquiry Team
	District Judge Madge
	Jo Miller, solicitor, City of Liverpool Personnel & Administration Directorate
	Chris Moores, Wrekin Council
	Melissa Morse, Lord Chancellor's Department
	Steve Mycio, Director of Housing, Manchester City Council
	Pauline Prosser, Department of the Environment
	Jeanette York, Association of District Councils
Intellectual Property Working Group	Mr Justice Jacob (Chairman)
	Terry Crowther, European Patent Operations, Lilly Industries Ltd
	Amanda Finlay, Secretary to the Inquiry
	Judge Ford, Patents County Court
	Nicholas Hodgson, Woolf Inquiry Team
	Christopher Tootal, solicitor, Herbert Smith
	Senior Master Turner, Assessor
	Andrew Waugh, barrister
Medical Negligence Planning/Steering Group	Sarah Leigh, solicitor, Leigh Day & Co (Chairman)
	Charles Blake, Assistant Solicitor, Department of Health
	Suzanne Burn, Secretary, Civil Litigation Committee, The Law Society
	Jane Chapman, Association of Litigation and Risk Managers
	Roger Clements, FRCS, FRCOG
	Brenda Griffith-Williams, Woolf Inquiry Team
	Paul MacNeil, solicitor, Field Fisher Waterhouse
	David Mason, solicitor, Capsticks
	Keith Miles, Director, Action for Victims of Medical Accidents
	Jean Ritchie QC (now Judge Ritchie QC)
	Arnold Simanowitz, Chief Executive, Action for Victims of Medical Accidents
	Adrian Whitfield QC

Multi-Party Action Working Group	Amanda Finlay, Secretary to the Inquiry (Chairman)
	Paul Bowden, solicitor, Freshfields
	Daniel Brennan QC
	Professor Ross Cranston, London School of Economics, Academic Consultant to the Inquiry
	Martyn Day, solicitor, Leigh Day & Co
	Clare Funnell, Woolf Inquiry Team
	Jonathan Isted, solicitor, Freshfields
	Rodger Pannone, solicitor, Pannone & Partners
	Lord Justice Phillips
	Michael Spencer QC
	Colin Stutt, barrister, Legal Adviser to Legal Aid Board
	Senior Master Turner, Assessor
	Marlene Winfield, Senior Policy and Development Officer, National Consumer Council
Official Referees' Working Group	Judge Esyr Lewis QC, Official Referees' Courts (Chairman)
	Judge Bowsher QC, Official Referees' Courts
	Richard Fernyhough QC
	Amanda Finlay, Secretary to the Inquiry
	Nicholas Hodgson, Woolf Inquiry Team
	James Hudson, solicitor, Bristows Cooke & Carpmael
	Rupert Jackson QC, Assessor
	Judge LLoyd QC, Official Referees' Courts
Pre-action Protocols Working Group	Amanda Finlay, Secretary to the Inquiry (Chairman)
	Peter Brennan, Guardian Insurance
	Suzanne Burn, Secretary, Civil Litigation Committee, The Law Society
	District Judge Greenslade, Assessor
	Omar Hameed, Association of British Insurers
	Denise Kitchener, Association of Personal Injury Lawyers
	Margaret MacDonald, Woolf Inquiry Team
	Frances McCarthy, solicitor, Pattinson Brewer
	Paul Parke, solicitor, Wansbroughs Willey Hargrave
	Chris Pulford, Woolf Inquiry Team
	Terry Renouf, solicitor, Berrymans
	Phil Skarrett, General Accident
	Nigel Tomkins, solicitor, Thompsons

The Consultation Process

Visits to Australia and Canada

During the course of the year since the publication of my interim report I have been fortunate to have been able to visit both Australia and Canada in order to attend conferences and to learn from the experiences of judges, court administrators, lawyers and academics. I am enormously grateful to all those who gave up their valuable time in order to meet and to talk to me and to those who helped to organise my visits. They are named below.

Australia

Federal Court Judges
Court of Appeal Judges, Supreme Court of NSW
Supreme Court of Victoria Judges
County Court Judges, Victoria
Justice Badgery-Parker
John Basten QC
Margaret-Mary Batch, Director of Research, Litigation Reform Commission, Brisbane
Chief Justice M E J Black, Federal Court of Australia
Justice Buckley, Family Court of Australia
Peter Butler, Freehill Hollingdale and Page, Melbourne
Malcolm Charlton, medical negligence practitioner, Sydney
Leah Cranston, Litigation Reform Commission, Brisbane
Justice Richard Cooper, Federal Court
Justice G L Davies, Supreme Court of Queensland
Chief Justice Gleeson, Supreme Court of NSW
Dr Gavan Griffith, Solicitor General
Chief Justice Hunt, Chief Judge at Common Law, Supreme Court of NSW
Bronwyn Jolly, Acting Director of Research, Litigation Reform Commission, Brisbane
Leonard Levy, medical negligence practitioner, Sydney
Norman Lyall, President, Law Society of NSW
Justice Kiefel
Justice Mahoney, Supreme Court of NSW
Sir Anthony Mason AC, KBE
Gillian McAllister, Executive Director, Civil Justice Research Centre
Peter McEwen, President, Environment and Planning Law Association, NSW
Richard Elgin McGarvie, Governor of Victoria
Justice McLelland, Chief Judge in Equity, Supreme Court of NSW
Justice William Ormiston, Supreme Court of Victoria
Chief Justice Phillips, Supreme Court of Victoria
Andrew Rogers QC
Commissioner Michael Ryland, Australian Law Reform Commission
Peter Sallmann, Australian Institute of Judicial Administration
Justice G F K Santow, Supreme Court of NSW

Warwick Soden, Registrar, Office of The Registrar, Federal Court of Australia

Maurie Stack, immediate past President, Law Society of NSW

Justice Paul Stein

Justice Teague, Australian Institute of Judicial Administration

Chief Judge Glen Waldron, County Court of Victoria

Margaret Wallace, Australian Institute of Judicial Administration

Justice Winneke, President of the Court of Appeal, Supreme Court of Victoria

Justice James Wood

Canada

Larry Taman, Attorney General

Robert Beaudoin, Civil Justice Review, Toronto

Mary-Lou Benotto, Canadian Bar

Justice Robert Blair

Justice Archie Campbell, Regional Senior Justice, Toronto Region

Justice Douglas Coo

Justice Charles Dubin, Chief Justice of Ontario

Justice James Farley

Justice Lee Ferrier

Justice Jack Ground

Christine Hart, Director, Alternative Dispute Resolution Centre, Toronto

Justice Dennis Lane

Justice Susan Lang

Justice Sidney Linden, Chief Judge of Ontario Court of Justice (Provincial Division)

Hugette Malyon, Courts Administration, Toronto

Mary McConville

John McMahon, Executive Legal Officer

Chief Justice Roy McMurtry

Justice Larry Morin

Terry O'Sullivan

Justice Gladys Pardu

Marc Rosenberg

Ruby Tulloch, Civil Justice Review, Toronto

Justice George Walsh

David Wires, Canadian Bar

Visit to Hong Kong

During a visit to Hong Kong I had meetings with the Chief Justice, the Hon Sir T L Yang, the Justices of Appeal, Judges of the High Court and Principal and Acting Principal Magistrates. I also met Mr Justice Leonard and Neil Kaplan QC.

Visit to the USA

During the course of the American-British Exchange there were meetings with the Chief Judge, other judges and members of staff of the District of Columbia Court of Appeal; also seminars arranged by Linklaters & Paines (in conjunction with Lord Justice Saville) in New York and Washington; and I had further discussions with Dr Roger Hanson of the National Center for State Courts and with James G Apple of the Federal Court Center.

I also had meetings with the following:

Justice Sandra O'Connor, Supreme Court of the United States
Justice Tony Kennedy, Supreme Court of the United States
Justice Stephen Breyer, Supreme Court of the United States
Judge Barbara Crabb, US Seventh Circuit
Charles Renfrew
William Schwarzer, former Director, Federal Judicial Center
Bob Clare, former President, American College of Trial Lawyers
Frank Jones, former President, American College of Trial Lawyers
Lively Wilson, former President, American College of Trial Lawyers

Conferences and seminars

The following conferences and seminars were organised to enable me to discuss my proposals and to hear the views of those invited:

Defendants in Medical Litigation Conference
Housing Seminar, Manchester
'Lord Woolf and the revolution in medical negligence' Conference
Medical Experts Conference
Multi-party Actions Conference
Royal Society of Medicine Medical Negligence Conference

I am very grateful to all those who gave up their time to attend and participate in these events.

In addition to these conferences and seminars, further seminars were organised in Birmingham, Bristol, Cardiff, Leeds, London and Manchester to enable judges and district judges to meet members of the Inquiry Team and to discuss various aspects of my proposals which were of concern to them. I am very grateful to all those who participated in this programme of seminars.

I also spoke at or participated in the following conferences and seminars

and I am grateful to the organisers of these events for inviting me; they
provided useful opportunities for me to gauge the views of those who will
be affected by my proposals:

Access to Justice Forum
Action for Victims of Medical Accidents Client Conference
'The Age of Reform' Seminar
Association of District Judges annual conference
Association of Personal Injury Lawyers Multi-Party Special Interest Group
Association of Women Solicitors
Bar Council Conference
British and Irish Ombudsman Association
Chairmen of Industrial Tribunal Conference
City Disputes Panel Conference
Consumer Congress Annual Conference
'Controlling Legal Costs' Seminar
Hare Court Judicial Review Seminar
Independent Tribunals Service
Institute of Legal Executives Conference
Law Society Civil Litigation Committee
Legal Action Group Conference
Legal Aid Practitioners Group Annual Conference
London Common Law and Commercial Bar Association
Professional Negligence Bar Association
The Law Society Conference
Sweet and Maxwell Judicial Review Conference

**Written contributions,
meetings and discussions**

I am most grateful to all the following individuals and organisations who
have contributed to my Inquiry, either through their written responses to
the interim report or the issues papers, or through meetings and
discussions.

Judiciary

The Lord Chief Justice
The President of the Family
Division
The Vice-Chancellor
Lord Donaldson
Lord Taylor
Lord Justice Auld
Lord Justice Simon Brown
Lady Justice Butler-Sloss DBE
Lord Justice Henry
Lord Justice Kennedy
Lord Justice Leggatt
Lord Justice McCowan
Lord Justice Morritt
Lord Justice Neill
Lord Justice Otton
Lord Justice Phillips
Lord Justice Saville
Lord Justice Staughton
Lord Justice Stuart-Smith
Lord Justice Thorpe

Mr Justice Aldous (now Lord
Justice Aldous)
Mrs Justice Arden DBE
Mr Justice Bell
Mr Justice Blofeld
Mr Justice Brooke (now Lord
Justice Brooke)
Mr Justice Carnwath
Mr Justice Colman
Mr Justice Chadwick
Mr Justice Cresswell
Mr Justice Drake
Mr Justice Garland
Mr Justice Harman
Mr Justice Harrison
Mr Justice Hidden
Mr Justice Holland

Mr Justice Jacob
Mr Justice Johnson
Mr Justice Kay
Mr Justice Ian Kennedy
Mr Justice Knox
Mr Justice Laws
Mr Justice Lewis
Mr Justice Lightman
Mr Justice May
Mr Justice Mance
Mr Justice Morland
Mr Justice Mummery
Mr Justice Ognall
Mr Justice Jonathan Parker
Mr Justice Potter (now Lord
Justice Potter)
Mr Justice Rattee
Mr Justice Rimer
Mr Justice Rose
Mr Justice Scott-Baker
Mr Justice Sedley
Mr Justice Stuart-White
Mr Justice Tuckey
Mr Justice Turner
Mr Justice Vinelott
Mr Justice Walker
Mr Justice Wall
Mr Justice Waller
Mr Justice Waterhouse
Mr Justice Wright
Sir Barry Sheen
Sir Peter Webster
Sir John Wood

Registrar Adams
Deputy Master Burns
Deputy Master Campbell
Deputy Master Desmond
Master Dyson, Chief
Chancery Master

Master Ellis
Master Eyre
Master Foster
Master Hodgson
Deputy Master Hoffman
Master Hurst, Chief Taxing Master
Master Miller
Master Moncaster
Master O'Hare
Master Prebble
Master Rogers
Master Seager Berry
Deputy Master Thum
Master Trench
Master Winegarten
Master Wright
Edmund Heward
Sir Jack Jacob QC
Keith Topley (formerly Senior
Queen's Bench Master)

The Council of HM Circuit Judges
Judge Altman
Judge Bassingthwaighte
Judge Bowsher QC
Judge Bradbury
Judge Butter QC
Judge Campbell
Judge Carter QC
Judge Collins
Judge Coningsby QC
Judge Cook
Judge Roger Cooke
Judge Coombe
Judge Dyer
Judge Duncan
Judge Gareth Edwards QC
Judge Marshall Evans QC
Judge Fawcus
Judge Ford

Judge Fox-Andrews QC
Judge Fricker QC
Judge Gee
Judge Barry Green QC
Judge Grenfell
Judge Hallgarten QC
Judge Hamilton
Judge Head
Judge Hicks QC
Judge Jack QC
Judge Graham Jones
Judge Hugh Jones
Judge Kershaw QC
Judge Lachs
Judge Lawrence
Judge Michael Lee QC
Judge Levy QC
Judge Esyr Lewis QC
Judge LLoyd QC
Judge Machin QC
Judge Mander
Judge Marder QC
Judge Mellor
Judge Mitchell
Judge Morrell
Judge O'Malley
Judge Stephen Oliver QC
Judge Paling
Judge Platt
Judge Pullinger
Judge Reid
Judge Steel
Judge Sumner
Judge Tetlow
Judge Tibber
Judge Anthony Thorpe
Judge Thornton QC
Judge Tyrer
Judge Urquhart
Judge White

Judge David Wilcox
Judge Wroath

The Association of District Judges
District Judge Ainsworth
District Judge Angel, Senior District
Judge of the Family Division
District Judge Armon-Jones
District Judge Bazeley White
District Judge Beattie
District Judge Berkson
District Judge Butler
District Judge Chapman
District Judge Cochrane
District Judge Donnelly
District Judge Evans
District Judge Frenkel
District Judge Glover
District Judge Green
District Judge Greenwood
District Judge Gypps
District Judge Harrison
District Judge Haythornthwaite
District Judge Hendicott
District Judge Hollis
District Judge Holloway
District Judge Howe
District Judge Jackson
District Judge Jolly
District Judge Lawood
District Judge Lay
District Judge Lee
District Judge Lingard
District Judge Llewellyn
District Judge Madge
District Judge Martin
District Judge Merrick
District Judge Mitchell
District Judge Nash-Williams
District Judge Read
District Judge Rees
District Judge Sankey

District Judge Silverman
District Judge Segal
District Judge Sparrow
District Judge Toeman
District Judge Vincent
District Judge Walker
District Judge Wilby
District Judge Wilkinson (now
Judge Wilkinson)

Judge Jean-Marc Baissons, Tribunal
de Grande Instance d'Orleans,
France
Justice Stephen Breyer, Supreme
Court of the United States
Justice John Byrne, Supreme Court
of Queensland, Australia
William H Rehnquist, Chief Justice,
Supreme Court of the United States
Lord Cullen, Court of Session,
Scotland
Justice Davies, Supreme Court
of Queensland, Australia
Chief Justice Michael de la Bastide,
Trinidad and Tobago
Justice Doogue, High Court of New
Zealand
Judge Richard Enslen, United States
District Court
Chief Justice Feldman, Chief Justice,
Supreme Court of Arizona, USA
Russell Fox QC, Australia
Chief Justice Catherine Fraser,
Alberta, Canada
Justice Friedman, Supreme Court,
Republic of South Africa
Chief Justice Constance Glube,
Supreme Court of Nova Scotia,
Canada
Chief Justice Noel Goodridge,
Supreme Court of Newfoundland,
Canada

7 12 int

Justice Sarah Grant, Supreme Court
of Arizona, USA
Justice Henry, High Court of New
Zealand
Justice Ipp, Supreme Court
of Western Australia
Justice Kaplan, Supreme Court
of Hong Kong
Justice Michael Kirby, High Court
of Australia
Judge Antonio Lamer, Supreme
Court of Canada
Mr Justice Leonard, Hong Kong
Associate Chief Justice Le Sage,
Supreme Court of Ontario, Canada
Chief Justice MacPherson,
Saskatchewan Court of Queen's
Bench, Canada
Judge John McClellan Marshall,
14th Judicial District, Texas, USA
Justice Mason, High Court
of Australia
Sheriff John McInnes QC, Perth
Sheriff Court
Chief Justice Roy McMurtry,
Ontario Court of Justice, Canada
Chief Justice Moore, Supreme
Court of Alberta, Canada
Judge Robert Myers, Superior
Court of Arizona, USA
Lord Hope, Lord President,
Court of Session, Scotland
Sheriff Principal Gordon Nicholson
QC, Scotland
Justice Sandra Day O'Connor,
Supreme Court of the United
States, USA
Justice Antonin Scalia, Supreme
Court of the United States, USA
Sheriff Marcus Stone, Edinburgh
Chief Judge Clifford Wallace, US
Nineth Circuit, USA

Barristers

Richard Aikens QC
Robin Allen QC
Kenneth Bagnall QC
Sir Louis Blom-Cooper KB, QC
Daniel Brennan QC
Andrew Buchan
Jeffrey Burke QC
Michael Burton QC
Christopher Clarke QC
Neil Cawley
Nicola Davies QC
Conrad Dehn QC
Iain Goldrein
Peter Goldsmith QC
Elizabeth Goodchild
Allan Gore
Gary Garland
Jonathan Gaunt QC
Hilary Heilbron QC
James Holman QC (now
Mr Justice Holman)
Ian Hunter QC
Michael Kalisher QC
Brian Langstaff QC
Allan Levy QC
Alun Lewis QC
Charles Lewis
Christopher Limb
Philip Naughton QC
Colin Nixon
David Pannick QC
Leolin Price QC
George Pulman QC
Chris Purnell
Santha Rasaiah
Graham Sinclair
Michael Thomas CMG, QC
Phillip Walter
Hazel Williamson QC

Solicitors

Mark Adler, Adler & Adler
Neil Aitken, McKenna & Co
Patrick Allen, Hodge Jones & Allen
Alsop Wilkinson
Hamish Anderson, Bond Pearce
Rowley Ashworth
Ashurst Morris Crisp
Richard Barlow, Browne Jacobson
Wendy Backhouse, Hodge Jones & Allen
Barlow Lyde and Gilbert
Brian Barr, Antony Hodari & Co
Richard Barr, Dawbarns
James Barrett-Hitchcock, Cameron Markby Hewitt
Keith Barritt, Haynes Duffell
Kentish & Co
Anthony Barton
Beale & Co
C R Berry, Edwin Coe
Catherine Bond, Bond Solon
P Bourne, Irwin Mitchell
Carmen Cahill, Platt Halpern
Anthony Burton, Simons Muirhead & Burton
Peter Carter-Ruck, Peter Carter-Ruck & Partners
Paul Balen, Freeth Cartwright Hunt Dickens
A J Cherry, Beachcroft Stanleys
Challinors
Chethams
Doug Christie, Thompsons
John Franks, Clarke Willmott and Clarke
Courts and Co
Timothy Daniels, D J Freeman
A E Davies, Bailey McIlquham
M L Davies, Crown Estate Office
Martyn Day, Leigh Day & Co
Charles Dewhurst

Christine Dodgson, Rowley Ashworth
Douglas Redfern and Co
Maria Eagle, Stephen Irving & Co
Greg Dwyer, The College of Law
B J Ecclestone, Health and Safety Executive
E Edwards, Son & Noice
T V Edwards
C Elgey, The College of Law
Charles Elly
Chris Esdaile, McGrath & Co
Patricia Fearnley, Thomson Snell & Passmore
G M Ferguson, Withy King & Lee
Richard Follis, Challinor Roberts Cooksey
Duncan Forbes
R M Freeman
C M Lake, Frere Cholmeley Bischoff
E C Gee, Lace Mawr
K C R Gibson, Wansbroughs Willey Hargrave
Margaret Gibson, Shoosmiths & Harrison
Deborah Girling, Mills & Reeve
Cyril Glasser, Sheridans
Richard Greenwood, J Bright Clegg Coupe & Co
Tony Guise, Silverman Sherliker
Christopher Hales, Holman Fenwick & Willan
T J Handler, Baker & MacKenzie
Alan Harrison
Colin Harvey
Paul Hurst, Anthony Hodari & Co
Michael Munden, Herbert Smith
Rhonda Hesling, Buss Murton
Hextall Erskine and Co
Gary Hickinbottom, McKenna & Co

Diana Holtham, Berrymans
Jonathan Hosie, Baker & MacKenzie
Mark Humphries, Linklaters & Paines
Colin Jacque, Jacque Simmons & Co
Andrew Jeffries, Allen & Overy
Chris Johnson, McGrath & Co
Robert Johnson, Osborne Clarke
John Kear, Kelly Cramer
John Kellcher, Theodore Goddard
G J Kendall, Allen & Overy
Crispin Kenyon, Jarvis & Bannister
Diana Kettle, Thomson Snell & Passmore
Rosaline Kilbane, McGrath & Co
Knapp Richardson
Blake Lapthorn
David Lawton, Budd Martin Burrett
Lees and Partners
Bertie Leigh, Hempsons
Jonathan Leslie, Travers Smith Braithwaite
Peter Lewis
Sonya Leydecker, Herbert Smith
Alistair Logan, The Logan Partnership
M C Longmore, Furley Page Fielding & Barton
Audrey MacDonald
Phil MacKenzie
Peter Martin, Frere Cholmeley Bischoff
David Mason, Capsticks
Frances McCarthy, Pattinson Brewer
David McIntosh, Davies Arnold Cooper
McKenna & Co
Hilary Meredith, Donn & Co
Tony Michaelson-Yates
Simon Middleton, Stephens & Scown

Mark Mildred
Razi Mireskandari, Simons Muirhead & Burton
Robert Morfee, Clarke Wilmott & Clarke
Michael Napier, Irwin Mitchell
John A Neil
J O'Hare, The College of Law
Rodger Pannone, Pannone & Partners
Paul Parke, Wansbroughs Willey Hargrave
Parry's
Paul Paxton, Shoosmiths & Harrison
Patricia Pearl, Vernor Miles & Noble
Simon Pearl, Davies Arnold Cooper
K J Perry, Pinsent & Co
Nigel Puddicombe, Cartwrights
Terry Renouf, Berrymans
Graham Ross, Ross Park Partnership
Nigel Rourke, Antony Hodari & Co
Rowe & Maw
N Ryan, Furley Page Fielding & Barton
Su Savill
Shane Sayers, Kennedys
Elizabeth Scott, Lees & Partners
Shook Hardy and Bacon
Simkins
Simmons and Simmons
G J H Smith
I R Tenquist, Cole & Cole
Peter Thomas OBE
Richard Thomas, Clifford Chance
Brian Thompson and Partners
Robin Thompson & Partners
Jade Thornley & Partners
Nigel Tomkins, Thompsons
Max Thum, Davies Arnold Cooper
D P Towler, Whittles

Desmond Trenner, Trenners
Andrew Tucker, Irwin Mitchell
W A Twemlow, Cuff Roberts
William Ware, Warner Goodman &
Steat
Garry Watson, Lovell White
Durrant
F R Maher, Weightman Rutherfords
Vizards
T W Worden, Ryan Heatons

Legal Professional Associations

Association of Law Costs Draftsmen
Association of Personal Injury
Lawyers
Birmingham Law Society
Bristol Law Society
Chancery Bar Association
The City of Westminster Law
Society
City of London Law Society
Commercial Bar Association
Devon and Exeter Incorporated Law
Society
Forum of Insurance Lawyers
The General Council of the Bar
Professor J Ross Harper,
International Bar Association
Harrogate and District Law Society
Holborn Law Society
Housing Law Practitioners
Association
The Institute of Legal Executives
The Law Society
Law Society of Northern Ireland
Law Society of Scotland
Legal Aid Practitioners Group
Liverpool Law Society
London Common Law and
Commercial Bar Association

London Solicitors' Litigation
Association
Manchester Law Society
Motor Accident Solicitors' Society
Newcastle upon Tyne Incorporated
Law Society
Norfolk and Norwich Incorporated
Law Society
Northwest Housing Law Group
Official Referees' Bar Association
Official Referees' Solicitors
Association
Patent Bar Association
Personal Injuries Bar Association
Society of Conservative Lawyers
South Yorkshire Housing Law Group

Others

Academy of Experts
Andrew Acland
Advisory Committee on Legal
Education and Conduct
David Adams
ADR Net
ADR Group
Advice Services Alliance
James Alfini
K W Alford Ltd
Dr Laurie Allen
Alliance of Independent Retailers
and Businesses
Professor Anthony Allot
Neil Andrews
R Anns, Public Trust Office
Susan Anthony
Nick Armstrong, Irwin Mitchell
Research Fellow, Nottingham Law
School
Association of British Insurers
Association of British Chambers

of Commerce
Association of Consulting Engineers
Association of District Councils
Association of Insurance and Risk
Managers
Association of London Government
Association of Metropolitan
Authorities
N B Atkinson
Dr R C Atkinson
Dr R E Atkinson
S J A Atkinson
The Automobile Association
Michael Bacon, Michael Bacon
Associates
Professor John Baldwin, University
of Birmingham
Professor Barbara Banks, University
College London
Barclays plc
S J A Barklem, Costain Group
Dr R D Barnes
Rupert Barnes
Miss M L Barron
S P Chalfu, BAT Industries
P M Beaton, Scottish Courts
Administration
Sir F D Berman
Robert Beaudoin, Civil Justice
Review, Canada
Victor Benjamin
Terrence Birmingham
Birmingham Settlement
Richard Blair
R Bland, Scottish Law Commission
R M Blanks, The Institute of
Chartered Secretaries and
Administrators
Dr Richard Bloore
Mrs M Blyth
Guy Brabiant, Commission

Superieure de Codification, France
Peter Brennan
Brighton Housing Trust
British Medical Association
Peter Brook, Building Employers
Confederation
Graham Calvert, Administrator,
Royal Courts of Justice
Carlisle Community Law Centre
Simon Carne
Keith Carter
Professor D B Casson
Alex Carlisle QC, MP
Dr S Castell
Centre of Medical Law and Ethics
Peter Champness
Chartered Institute of Patent Agents
The Chartered Institute of
Arbitrators
Patrick Cheadle
The Cheltenham Group
Dr David Cheshire
Chesterton
The Citizenship Foundation
Brian Clancy, Brian Clancy &
Partners
Dr M A Clarke
Roger Clements FRCS, FRCOG
Professor Christopher Colton,
British Orthopaedic Association
The Commission for Local
Administration in England
A M Cone-Farran
Confederation of British Industry
Construction Industry Council
Consumers' Association
Coopers and Lybrand
Council of Industrial Tribunal
Chairmen
Council of Mortgage Lenders
County Court Users Association

Dr J D M C Craig

Michael Curry, Lands Tribunal
of Northern Ireland

I F Davies

Peter Davies, Taylor Woodrow
Group

Dr Sally Davies

Dr Peter Dear

Philip Dear, Trade Union Side, Lord
Chancellor's Department

Martin Dearden, Robert Jordan
Associates

Michael Deeney, Gooda Walker
Action Group

The Disability Law Service

James Dixon

Dr John Dove

Professor Brian Doyle

Kevin Duffy

J S Elkington FRCS

Dr Carl Emery, University
of Durham

Keith Fay, Chief Clerk,
Peterborough Combined Court
Centre

Federation of Private Residents
Association

Federation of Small Businesses

Dr C E Fernando

Elizabeth Filkin, Revenue
Adjudicator

Forum of Private Business

Larry M Fox, Ministry of the
Attorney General, Canada

A M Fraser, Director of Public
Prosecutions for Northern Ireland

Richard Freeman, City Disputes
Panel

Ian Freer, Crown Office, Royal
Courts of Justice

Professor Charles Galasko

G A Gilbert

Brian Cahill, Alice Pasco, Glaxo
Wellcome

Dr R B Godwin Austen

R C L Gregory CBE, QC

Roger Grace FRCS

R D M Grant, The Dispute
Resolution Co

Roger Griffiths, Coventry City
Council

Mrs J G Tunstall, Griffiths and
Armour

Professor Andrew Grubb

Michael Grundy

The Guild of Editors

Kenneth Gulleford

John Hale, Listing Officer, Chancery
Division

Professor D M B Hall, University
of Sheffield

Angela Hammond

Kathy Hanson, Chartered Institute
of Housing

Dr Roger Hanson, National Center
for State Courts, USA

Professor Frank Harris

Nigel Harris FRCS

Dr J Harrison

Dr Peter Harvey

Donald Hayes

Robert Hazell, The Nuffield
Foundation

Health and Housing Group

Thomas Heintzman QC, past
President of the Canadian Bar

H M Customs & Excise

Dr Anthony Hopkins

Lord Howe of Aberavon PC, QC

Professor Christopher Hull

Caroline Hunter, University
of Nottingham

Ian Hyams, Deputy Administrator,
Royal Courts of Justice

Inland Revenue

Sir Donald Innes Williams, The
Royal Society of Medicine

Institute of Advanced Legal Studies

Institute of Credit Management

Institute of Directors

Institute of Traffic Accident
Investigators

Peter Jackson, Sarah Ricketts,
Nottingham City Council

Roger Jefferies, Housing
Associations Tenants' Ombudsman

The Intellectual Property Institute

Professor Jolowicz QC

A J Jones, Assistant Treasury
Solicitor

Justice for Victims

Dr Leon Kaufman

John Kershaw

Paul Knapman

KPMG Peat Marwick

Alison Lamb, Federation of
Independent Advice Centres

Alan Lambert

Ian Lang MP

Law Centres Federation

Legal Action Group

The Legal Aid Board

Eliot Levin

The Litigants Society

Litigation Protection Ltd

Lovewell Blake

Peter Lyons, Nottingham
Law School

Dr Julie Macfarlane, University
of Sussex

A D W Maclean

Donald Macrae, Treasury Solicitor's
Department

Dr Christopher Mallinson

Manchester Housing

Manchester Housing Advice Service

Professors Richard Marcus

William Marsh, Centre for Dispute
Resolution

William J Marshall and Partners

Sir Bruce Martin QC, NHS
Litigation Authority

Professor Stephen Mason

David de Massey

E T Matthews

Patrick McCartan

Suzanne McClure

J C McCluskie QC, Legal Secretary
and First Scottish Parliamentary
Counsel

M McGarry

Mediation UK

Medical Defence Union

D N Menzies

Barbara Mills QC, Director
of Public Prosecutions

M C T Morrison

Wilma Morrison, Central London
Law Centre

Peter Morton, Elmbridge Council

Rob Ferguson, Mosscare Housing
Ltd

A S Murrie

G Murray

Dr Iain Murray-Lyon

Tom Murtha, Merseyside Improved
Homes

National Association for the Care
and Resettlement of Offenders

National Association of Citizens
Advice Bureaux

National Consumer Council

National Federation of Consumer
Groups

National Federation of Housing
Associations
NatWest Group
Jonathan Noble, British
Orthopaedic Association
E A Norden
H W S Norvill
Edward Northcote
Professor A Ogus, University
of Manchester
Huw Owen
Dr Chris Pamplin, UK Register
of Experts
Professor Martin Partington,
University of Bristol
Naran Patel, President, Royal
College of Obstetricians and
Gynaecologists
Professor Sir Alan Peacock
Mrs Nancy Pearce
Sarah J Pearce
Personal Injury Medical Services
Ltd
Sir Keith Peters FRCS
John Peysner, Nottingham Law
School
David Pipkin, Institute of Legal
Executives
Hilary Platten, Finance and Leasing
Association
David Pollock, The Newspaper
Publishers Association
Gordon Proudfoot, President of the
Canadian Bar
Professor J A Raeburn
Terry Rayson, Listing Officer,
Queen's Bench Division
William Reid, Health Service
Commissioner
Professor Judith Resnick, University
of Southern California, USA

T J Rhodes, Citizens Advice Bureau,
Liverpool
Ian Richardson, Home Housing
Association
Professor Peter Richards,
Northwick Park Hospital
William Ricketts
Dr R K Rondel
Dr Lewis Rosenbloom
The Royal Institute for Deaf People
Royal Institute of Chartered
Surveyors
Dr Adrian Rozkovec
B J Russell, Trade Marks, Patents
and Designs Federation
John Sacher CBE
Peter Sainsbury
City of Salford Housing Services
Roger Samuel, Canterbury City
Council
Professor Frank Sander, University
of Harvard Law School
Dr Michael Saunders
Mrs Jennifer Savage, Clifton Ingram
Dr A M Seywood
Professor Ian Scott, University
of Birmingham
Robert Sell
David Shapiro, JAMS Endispute
Europe
Bernard Shaw, Chief Clerk,
Birmingham County Court
David Shaw
Shelter
C J Shepley, The Planning
Inspectorate
Caroline Sheppard, Parking Appeals
Service
Laurence Shurman, The Banking
Ombudsman
Ms A Simon

G Simons
E A Simpson, Northern Ireland
Court Service
Nicola Simpson
Graham Sinclair, Adroit Dispute
Resolution Ltd
Rodney Stares, Foundation for
Community Leadership
Development
Janet Stephens
Frances Stobbs
Roy Swanston, Royal Institution
of Chartered Surveyors
Brian Swift, DTI Business Law Unit
Professor Malcolm Symonds,
University of Nottingham
Robert Taylor, Dispute Mediation
Ltd
Professor Ron Taylor
Dr John Temperley
Patricia Thomas, Commission for
Local Government in England
P K J Thompson, Department
of Health
Dr Christine Tomkins
UNEX Group
Owen Tudor, Trades Union
Congress
Union of Independent Companies
Kevan Verdun, The Lighting
Association
Professor Vickers
Dr John Wall, The Medical Defence
Union
S C Walters
C H Walton
G W Waterson
V D L Williams
Clive Wilson, Office of the Health
Service Commissioner
Ruth Wilson, North Cheshire

Housing Association
Sheona York, Hammersmith Law
Centre
Professor Michael Zander, London
School of Economics
Rya Zobel

SURVEY
OF
LITIGATION
COSTS

Summary of Main

Findings

Survey of Litigation Costs: Summary of Main Findings

Background

1.   In order to provide information about costs and to inform the work of the Inquiry into civil litigation, in 1995 Lord Woolf asked the Supreme Court Taxing Office (SCTO) to collect comprehensive information about costs from bills submitted for taxation. The results of a preliminary analysis of litigation costs in 673 cases were published as part of the Inquiry's interim report *Access to Justice* in June 1995. Following further data collection, a fuller analysis of costs and case length in High Court litigation has been carried out on 2,184 cases sampled from those submitted to the SCTO during the period 1990–1995[1]

2.   The analysis describes total average costs (on the winning party's side only[2]) in cases of different type, weight and value, and provides a breakdown of average costs for particular elements in bills, such as counsel fees, expert fees, discovery and documents. Variations in case length have been analysed in relation to factors such as case type, weight, claim value, and the presence of legal aid. In addition, three separate statistical modelling exercises were undertaken, in order more fully to understand the factors that affect the length and cost of litigated cases. Some of the significant findings of the study are summarised here.

Characteristics of sample

3.   *Case type:* The sample comprises 2,184 cases divided roughly equally between 10 case types: medical negligence, personal injury, professional negligence, Official Referees', breach of contract, judicial review, Chancery, Queen's Bench 'other', Commercial, and bankruptcy/ Companies Court cases.

4.   *Claim value:* Claim value was based on the amount of money recovered in the action. The highest claim value in the sample was £660 million in a Commercial case, and the lowest was £5 in a breach of contract case. There was a wide range of claim values in the sample both within and between case types. Commercial cases had the highest median[3] claim value at £118,454. Other case types with high median claim values were bankruptcy/Companies Court (£50,269), personal injury (£50,000) and breach of contract (£37,875). The lowest median claim value was among Queen's Bench 'other' cases (£29,000). About one-third of cases in the

---

1 The full results of the Costs Survey are reported in a separate volume, entitled *Survey of Litigation Costs*.
2 It should be recalled at all times that the analysis is based only on the costs of the winning party (ie, those submitted for taxation). The total costs of actions, ie, the combined costs of the winning and the losing party, would be substantially higher.
3 The median represents the point at which half the measurements fall above and half fall below. Median figures are given in addition to the arithmetic average for costs and duration, because the arithmetic average is strongly affected by extreme values. Thus average cost figures will be higher than median cost figures where there are cases with very high costs within the sample or case type.

sample had claim values of £25,000 or less, and one-quarter had claim values of £100,000 or more.

5. *Case weight:* The weight of cases in the sample was assessed by the taxing office using five categories: category A (heaviest weight) to category E (least heavy). Factors taken into account in the categorisation were: complexity of issues, importance of case to the parties and to other litigants and potential litigants, unusual expedition, number and importance of documents, and quantum. The vast majority of cases (90 per cent) were assessed as being at the light end of the range (C–E). There was, however, much variation between case types in this respect.

6. *Legal aid:* Some 35 per cent of all winning parties had legal aid, but the proportions varied among different case types. Legal aid was most prevalent among medical negligence (92 per cent), personal injury (59 per cent), judicial review (58 per cent), and professional negligence cases (38 per cent). Among other case types, only a minority of winning parties had legal aid (29 per cent Chancery; 18 per cent Official Referees'; 17 per cent breach of contract; 18 per cent Queen's Bench 'other' and 9 per cent bankruptcy and Companies Court).

7. *Stage of proceedings reached:* There was considerable variation among cases in the stage that had been reached before proceedings ended. About a quarter of cases got only as far as the issue of proceedings before the case was settled. In just over a quarter of cases the matter was concluded after it had been set down, but before trial. In 17 per cent of cases the parties reached the doors of the court before settling, and about one-third of cases had proceeded all the way to trial.

8. *How proceedings were concluded:* Nearly half the cases had been concluded on the basis of a consent order, and one-quarter on the basis of a judgment. In a further 9 per cent of cases, a payment into court had been accepted; 4 per cent of cases were concluded on the basis of a consent judgment; 2 per cent of cases had been struck out; 1 per cent of cases had been dismissed; 7 per cent had been concluded following summary judgment; and a further 1 per cent had been withdrawn or discontinued.

9. *Successful party:* 86 per cent of cases in the sample had been won by plaintiffs, reflecting the kinds of cases that are submitted for taxation. Among medical negligence cases none had been won by the defendant.

Average costs

10. *Costs and case type:* A little under one-half of bills in the sample were allowed at £10,000 or less (42 per cent); just over one-quarter of bills (28 per cent) were allowed at between £10,000 and £20,000; 10 per cent of all bills were allowed at between £20,000 and £30,000; and just over one-fifth (21%) of all bills in the sample, on the winning side only, were allowed at more than £30,000. Average costs varied between different case types. Official Referees' and Commercial cases had the highest average costs (median £19,320 and £18,897 respectively) and judicial review cases had the lowest average costs (median £7,642). The highest minimum costs were found among medical negligence cases (minimum £3,759). Only a quarter of medical negligence and Official Referees' bills were for less than £10,000 (Table 1). The case types with the highest percentage of costs over £50,000 were Commercial cases, Official Referees' cases, professional negligence cases and medical negligence cases.

Table 1: Categories of costs by case type

Case type	Costs allowed £						
	<=10,000	>10,000 & <=20,000	>20,000 & <=30,000	>30,000 & <=40,000	>40,000 & <=50,000	>50,000	Total
Medical Negligence (N=206)	25%	35%	11%	9%	4%	16%	100%
Personal Injury (N=323)	38%	36%	10%	5%	3%	7%	100%
Professional Negligence (N=205)	32%	28%	10%	9%	5%	16%	100%
Official Referees' (N=206)	24%	28%	11%	13%	6%	17%	100%
Breach of Contract (n=214)	43%	27%	12%	6%	3%	9%	100%
Judicial Review (N=206)	68%	20%	5%	4%	1%	1%	100%
Chancery (N=204)	46%	29%	11%	6%	3%	5%	100%
Queen's Bench 'other' (N=205)	58%	23%	8%	2%	6%	3%	100%
Commercial (N=106)	29%	21%	15%	9%	3%	23%	100%
Commercial (no value) (N=102)	36%	22%	15%	9%	8%	11%	100%
Bankruptcy/Companies Court (N=77)	65%	17%	6%	5%	3%	4%	100%
Bankruptcy/Companies Court (no value) (N=130)	59%	29%	4%	5%	1%	2%	100%
All cases (N=2184)	42%	28%	10%	7%	4%	10%	100%

<= Less than or equal to   >= Greater than or equal to

11. *Costs and case weight:* Average costs tended to be higher among heavier cases. The difference in the weight profile of case types to some extent accounts for observed variation in average costs between case types. For example, medical negligence and Commercial cases had a relatively high proportion of heavy cases, while the vast majority of breach of contract, judicial review and Queen's Bench 'other' cases were assessed as being light (Table 2). Differences in median costs between case types appear somewhat smaller when comparing cases of similar weight (Table 2). However, it is also clear that average costs among the most straightforward cases are relatively stable at around £6,000, irrespective of case type. It should be borne in mind that these represent the costs of only the winning side in the actions.

12. The average level of costs in cases of different weight is quite striking. Among most case types, simply moving up from weight E to weight D doubles average costs, and there were substantial differences in average costs between the heaviest and lightest cases (Table 2).

13. There is an association between claim value and claim weight which is to be expected since quantum was one of the factors taken into account in assessing case weight. Thus the average claim value among cases in category A is much higher than the average claim value among cases in category E. The pattern is not, however, consistent since there were high value cases that were not assessed as very heavy and vice versa.

Table 2: Median costs among case types in relation to case weight

Median costs* Number and % of cases in category	Assessment of weight of case																
	A (Heaviest)			B			C			D			E (Lightest)			Total	
	£	N	%	£	N	%	£	N	%	£	N	%	£	N	%	N	%
Medical Negligence	92,472	(21)	10	56,746	(29)	14	24,982	(49)	24	12,418	(75)	36	6,139	(32)	16	206	100
Personal Injury	91,720	(3)	1	54,962	(29)	9	21,429	(68)	21	12,879	(104)	32	7,264	(119)	37	323	100
Professional Negligence	150,556	(9)	4	70,408	(24)	12	31,974	(46)	22	12,845	(76)	37	6,096	(50)	24	205	100
Official Referees'	133,805	(7)	3	88,220	(20)	10	35,384	(57)	28	15,382	(69)	33	7,462	(53)	26	206	100
Breach of Contract	245,208	(2)	1	89,484	(15)	7	33,418	(34)	16	14,626	(72)	34	6,471	(91)	43	214	100
Judicial Review	29,207	(3)	1	27,782	(11)	5	15,234	(42)	20	7,807	(55)	27	6,132	(95)	46	206	100
Chancery	199,222	(3)	1	122,061	(2)	1	31,779	(33)	16	12,374	(84)	41	6,329	(82)	41	204	100
Queen's Bench 'other'	231,395	(5)	2	42,546	(4)	2	27,761	(27)	13	11,382	(68)	32	6,208	(101)	50	205	100
Commercial	135,521	(12)	11	45,321	(17)	16	21,697	(32)	30	13,606	(23)	22	6,494	(22)	21	106	100
Commercial (no value)	95,911	(5)	5	39,997	(10)	10	27,690	(33)	32	10,153	(35)	34	5,774	(19)	19	102	100
Bankruptcy/Comp Ct	170,129	(1)	1	44,795	(3)	4	22,168	(15)	19	9,306	(28)	36	5,559	(30)	39	77	100
Bankruptcy/Comp (no val)	42,280	(4)	3	54,700	(1)	1	18,110	(18)	14	10,446	(50)	38	6,076	(57)	44	130	100
Whole Sample	107,089	(75)	3	54,962	(165)	7	27,277	(454)	21	12,094	(739)	34	6,469	(751)	35	2,184	100

*Median = 50 per cent of cases have costs higher and 50 per cent lower than the median figure.

14. *Costs and claim value:* There was a huge amount of variation in the level of costs charged for cases of similar value. Among the lowest value claims (up to £12,500) median costs in the sample as a whole were £8,318, but costs for claims with value not exceeding £12,500 ranged from £1,798 to £200,515. The highest value claims (more than £250,000) had median costs of £36,951, with costs ranging from £3,001 to £2,135,412.

15. Analysis of the broad relationship between costs and claim value reveals that, as claim value rises, the proportion of costs allowed at less than £10,000 steadily falls. Among the lowest value claims, 60 per cent of cases had costs of less than £10,000; among the highest value claims (over £250,000), only 18 per cent had costs of less than £10,000, and 41 per cent had costs of over £50,000.

16. There is a lack of proportionality between costs and claim value at the lower end of the claim value scale. Among cases with a value of less than £12,500, about one-third (31 per cent) had costs between £10,000 and £20,000, with a further 9 per cent of cases having costs in excess of £20,000. Thus, in 40 per cent of the lowest value claims, the costs on one side alone were close to, or exceeded, the total value of the claim. By way of contrast, in 60 per cent of claims over £250,000, costs represented less than 20 per cent of the value of the claim.

17. There were substantial differences between case types in the average levels of costs for similar value claims (Table 3). For example, among cases with a claim value below £12,500, the median costs figure in medical negligence cases was £10,482, and in Official Referees' cases the figure was £12,245; median costs in Commercial cases in this claim value category were about half, at £6,187, and the median figure for personal injury cases was £7,099.

18. Table 3 also shows the differences between case types in the proportion of cases falling within different claim value brands. Personal injury and Commercial cases had the lowest proportions of cases with values of £12,500 or less (14 per cent and 9 per cent respectively), while all of the other case types had between a fifth and a quarter of cases in the lowest claim value band.

Table 3: Median costs allowed by claim value

Median costs* £ Number and % of cases in category	Claim value £																
	<= 12,500 N=361			>12,500 – <= 25,000 N=287			>25,000 – <= 50,000 N=355			>50,000 – <= 100,000 N=303			>100,000 – <= 250,000 N=248			<250,000 N=192			Total	
	£	N	%	£	N	%	£	N	%	£	N	%	£	N	%	£	N	%	N	%
Med Negligence	10,482	56	27	12,464	30	15	15,655	44	21	24,982	27	13	35,936	19	9	76,011	30	15	206	100
Personal Injury	7,099	45	14	8,006	47	14	10,474	71	22	14,881	76	23	18,688	66	20	64,435	18	6	323	100
Professional Neg	9,440	42	20	9,688	42	20	13,250	41	20	27,524	37	18	34,208	23	11	78,904	20	10	205	100
Official Ref	12,245	51	25	19,696	38	18	17,272	41	20	34,355	25	12	43,865	36	17	133,805	15	7	206	100
Breach of Cont	8,882	43	20	7,774	30	14	13,405	57	27	14,993	47	22	14,632	19	9	31,610	18	8	214	100
Chancery	7,316	49	24	11,150	33	16	13,434	35	17	10,757	35	17	9,421	27	13	11,906	25	12	204	100
Queen's Bench	6,693	51	25	7,751	43	21	10,677	43	21	9,912	21	10	8,876	24	12	16,199	23	11	205	100
Commercial	6,187	10	9	10,907	10	9	13,522	13	12	20,262	15	14	27,537	26	24	26,503	32	30	106	100
Bankruptcy/Comp	6,785	14	18	7,050	14	18	5,748	10	13	9,015	20	26	16,592	8	10	13,042	11	14	77	100

<= Less than or equal to   >= Greater than or equal to

*Median = 50 per cent of cases have costs higher and 50 per cent lower than the median figure.

19. When costs are expressed as a percentage of the value of the claim[4], median costs among the lowest value claims (under £12,500) consistently represent more than 100 per cent of claim value, and this holds true among all case types (Table 4). The lower the claim value, the higher the percentage of the claim value that costs represent. At the lowest end of the claim value spectrum, the costs of the winning party only substantially exceed the value of the claim. Among claims with a value of between £12,500 and £25,000, costs as a percentage of claim value range from 41 per cent among personal injury cases to 96 per cent among Official Referees' cases. At the highest end of the claim value scale, costs range from around 1 per cent of claim value among Chancery, and bankruptcy/ Companies Court cases, to 19 per cent of claim value among Official Referees' cases.

4 This was calculated as follows: for each case, costs allowed were divided by claim value x 100; then the median value was taken across all cases in each case type.

Table 4: Costs as a percentage of claim value (costs/value x 100)

Costs as a % of claim value (median)	Claim value £					
	<=12,500 N=361	>12,500 – <=25,000 N=287	>25,000 – <=50,000 N=355	>50,000 – <=100,000 N=303	>100,000 – <=250,000 N=248	>250,000 N=192
Medical Negligence	137%	57%	46%	33%	21%	12%
Personal Injury	135%	41%	28%	22%	13%	11%
Professional Negligence	135%	54%	43%	41%	27%	15%
Official Referees'	158%	96%	48%	53%	31%	19%
Breach of Contract	138%	46%	32%	21%	12%	5%
Chancery	119%	62%	40%	17%	8%	2%
Queen's Bench 'other'	154%	44%	33%	14%	5%	3%
Commercial	174%	54%	27%	38%	16%	2%
Bankruptcy/Companies Court	115%	39%	18%	15%	10%	1%

<= Less than or equal to   >= Greater than or equal to

20. *Costs and case duration:* A simple analysis of costs in relation to case length reveals higher average costs among longer cases. For example, cases lasting less than one year had average costs of £14,745 (median £8,008); cases lasting two to four years had average costs of £28,921 (median £14,758); and cases lasting for more than six years had average total costs of £30,373 (median £15,685).

Case duration data

21. *Case type:* Duration was measured from the date of first instruction to the date of conclusion. Medical negligence cases lasted longest on average (mean 65 months), followed by personal injury cases (56 months) and professional negligence cases (41 months). The most rapidly concluded cases were judicial review (12 months), Companies Court cases (about 13 months) and Commercial cases without a claim value (16 months) (Table 5).

Table 5: Average duration (in months) from date of instruction to conclusion by case type

Case type	Mean	Median	Max	Min	Number of case in category
Whole sample	34	29	214	0	2184
Medical Negligence	65	61	214	26	206
Personal Injury	56	54	117	1	323
Professional Negligence	41	35	118	7	205
Official Referees'	34	30	116	1	206
Chancery	32	27	152	0	204
Breach of Contract	29	25	114	1	214
Queens Bench 'other'	28	21	128	2	205
Commercial	25	20	100	0	106
Commercial (no value)	16	7	93	0	102
Bank/Company (no value)	15	9	118	0	130
Bankruptcy and Company	13	7	118	0	77
Judicial Review	12	11	36	0	206

22. *Claim value:* Analysis of case length and claim value revealed no consistent pattern in the sample as a whole.

23. *Legal aid:* In the sample as a whole, cases where the winning party had legal aid lasted longer, on average, than cases where the winning party did not have legal aid. With the exception of judicial review cases, this difference held true within case type. The mean duration of case from first instruction to conclusion for the whole sample was 26 months among cases without legal aid (median 22 months) as compared with 49 months among cases with legal aid (median 48 months).

24. *Means of concluding proceedings:* Cases with the longest average duration in the sample as a whole were those that were concluded on the basis of a consent judgment (48 months), acceptance of money in court (44 months) or a consent order (42 months). The average length of cases ending after judgment was 25 months from instruction to conclusion, while cases concluded on the basis of a summary judgment had an average duration of 19 months. The association between duration and means of concluding proceedings varied between cases of different type.

25. *Weight of case:* In the sample as a whole, heavier cases appeared to take longer to conclude. The heaviest cases (weight A) took, on average, 48 months, as compared with 29 months among the lightest cases (weight E). The pattern was not consistent within case types.

26. *Interlocutory activity:* In the sample as a whole, there was an association between the average length of case and the number of interlocutory applications made. In cases where there were no interlocutory applications, the average length of case was 28 months. This figure rose to 50 months in cases where there were seven or more interlocutory applications, and the pattern held true within every case type.

Delay between first instruction and issue of proceedings

27. *Case type:* Medical negligence and personal injury cases had the longest average delays between instruction and issue of proceedings. The average delay in medical negligence cases was 21 months and in personal injury cases it was 17 months. The shortest average delays were in Commercial cases with no claim value (two months), Companies Court cases with no value (two months), and judicial review cases (three months).

28. *Legal aid:* Within the sample as a whole, cases with legal aid generally appeared to have a longer period of delay between instruction and issue of proceedings than those without legal aid. The average period of delay among cases with legal aid was 15 months (median 12 months), as compared with an average of seven months (median three months) among cases without legal aid.

Statistical modelling

29. In order to attempt to understand, rather than merely describe data relating to costs in litigation, a series of statistical modelling exercises was undertaken. Such procedures help to isolate, from the wealth of data collected, systematic relationships between costs and other variables, and to disentangle some of the relationships. For example, an apparent association between costs and claim value might be explained by the fact that cases with higher claim values tend to be more complicated, and therefore when cases of similar levels of complexity are compared, differences in claim value actually make little or no difference to costs levels. It is therefore helpful to analyse the independent effect of such factors as value and weight on costs levels, in order to assess which factors are the most important in explaining costs. Using modelling procedures, it is possible, simultaneously, to compare cases of similar type (in terms, for example, of weight, value and case length) and to assess the effect of different factors on costs levels.

30. Three separate modelling exercises were undertaken to explore the effects of a number of factors on costs, on case length and on delay between date of instruction and issue of proceedings. The objective of the modelling exercises was to indicate general trends in case duration and costs. There is considerable scope for further work to be done on analysing both case duration and costs levels in civil litigation.

Modelling of delay between instruction and issue

Effect of case weight / complexity on delay

31. The results of the modelling exercises suggest that the weight / complexity of cases significantly affects delay between instruction and issue of proceedings in five case types, but the impact of case weight is inconsistent. In professional negligence cases, Official Referees' cases and breach of contract cases, increasing weight of cases significantly increases the period of delay between instruction and issue of proceedings. Thus, the heavier the case, the longer the delay.

32. In personal injury cases and Queen's Bench 'other' cases, increasing weight appears to lessen the period of delay between instruction and issue; thus, the more straightforward the case, the longer the period of delay.

33. In medical negligence, judicial review and Chancery cases, weight appeared to have no significant effect on the period of delay between instruction and issue of proceedings. There was no evidence that the period of delay in lighter cases was systematically shorter than in heavier cases, holding other factors constant.

Effect of legal aid on delay

34. When the winning party had legal aid, the period of delay between instruction and issue was affected in most case types, with the exception of medical negligence, Official Referees' and judicial review cases. Whenever legal aid had an impact on delay, the effect was always that the period of delay between instruction and issue was independently lengthened (by about 50 per cent among personal injury and professional negligence cases; by about 60 per cent among Chancery cases; by about 70 per cent among breach of contract cases; and by about 75 per cent among Queen's Bench 'other' cases).

35 Among professional negligence, breach of contract and Queen's Bench 'other' cases, the increase may amount to little more than the time taken to apply for legal aid since those case types have relatively low median periods of delay (nine months, three months and four months respectively). Among personal injury cases, on the other hand, an estimated 50 per cent increase in delay in legal aid cases is likely to be in excess of the time taken to apply for legal aid, since the median period of delay in personal injury cases was found to be 15 months.

Effect of date of first instruction on delay: is delay increasing or decreasing?

36. Among all case types, with the exception of judicial review, there was clear evidence that the period of delay between date of first instruction and issue of proceedings has been declining in recent years. The extent of the decline was as much as 20 per cent or 25 per cent per year among some case types. This effect may be a reflection of change in litigation strategy, or the result of falling workloads among litigation lawyers.

Modelling of case duration between instruction and conclusion of claim

Effect of case weight / complexity on case duration

37. The various models suggest that the weight of cases significantly affects the total length of cases among only four of the case types (Official Referees', breach of contract, Chancery and Queen's Bench 'other' cases). Whenever case weight did affect duration, the effect was always to increase the total length of the case.

38. Among medical negligence, personal injury, professional negligence and judicial review cases there was no evidence that heavier cases systematically took longer than lighter cases, holding other factors constant, and the explanation for variations in case length among those case types must lie elsewhere.

Effect of legal aid on case duration

39. Among all case types, with the exception of judicial review, the fact that the winning party had legal aid significantly affected case length, holding other factors constant, and the effect was always that cases were longer when the successful party had legal aid. For example, the independent effect of legal aid on case length was a 20 per cent increase in the length of personal injury cases, a 25 per cent increase in the length of medical negligence cases and an increase of 45 per cent among breach of contract cases. Given the median case lengths found among these case types (Table 5), the period of increase appears to be well beyond the time taken to apply for legal aid.

40. There are a number of possible explanations for the apparent effect of legal aid on case length. First, the administrative time taken in applying and dealing with the Legal Aid Board; second, the possibility that legal aid work is given a low priority, resulting in cases not being rapidly progressed and hearing dates adjourned; third, the possibility that more work is being done on legal aid cases, or that legal aid cases are being run harder and further than might otherwise be the case, because there is no risk of costs for the party with legal aid.

Effect of date of conclusion on case duration: is case length increasing or decreasing?

41. The date of case conclusion appeared to affect case length among Official Referees', breach of contract, Chancery and Queen's Bench 'other' cases. Among each of these four case types, there was clear evidence that the length of case has been decreasing in recent years. The rate of decrease in overall case duration is about 8 per cent among Official Referees' cases, about 10 per cent among breach of contract and Queen's Bench 'other' cases, and about 13 per cent among Chancery cases. Thus, whenever a change in case duration over time was identified in the models, the change was always in a downward direction. In none of the case types modelled was there any evidence that the overall length of case has been increasing in recent years.

Modelling of costs

Effect of case weight / complexity on costs

42. The weight/complexity of cases significantly affected costs in every case type analysed. The effect of weight on costs was always to increase the level of costs, although the impact of increasing weight on costs varied in different case types.

Effect of case duration on costs

43. The total duration of cases, from date of first instruction to conclusion of case, was found significantly to affect costs in all case types, except medical negligence and judicial review. When duration has an independent impact on costs, the effect of increased case length is always increased costs, although the impact of long case duration varies between case types.

44. Among medical negligence cases and judicial review cases, there was no evidence that case duration had a significant, independent effect on costs, when other factors were held constant.

Effect of claim value on costs

45. The results of the analysis of costs indicates that the value of claims (in terms of the amount recovered) affects costs in personal injury, professional negligence, Official Referees', Chancery and Queen's Bench 'other' cases. In general, the effect is that, holding factors such as weight and duration constant, increasing claim value increases costs, although the pattern is not always consistent. For example, among personal injury and professional negligence cases, doubling claim value independently increases costs by about 15 per cent.

Effect of legal aid on costs

46. The costs models suggest that legal aid has a significant and independent effect on costs in personal injury cases and in judicial review cases. When the winning party has legal aid in personal injury cases, the costs of cases of the same weight, value and length will be about 10 per cent higher than if the winning party does not have legal aid, and this is in addition to the contribution of legal aid to costs in personal injury cases through increased case duration.

Effect of date of conclusion on costs: have costs been increasing or decreasing?

47. In only one of the case types analysed did the date of case conclusion affect costs. In medical negligence cases, there is clear evidence that costs are increasing at the rate of about 7 per cent per year, independent of case weight, case length or claim value.

48. In all other case types analysed, the date of conclusion has no significant impact on costs. This means that costs in all case types, other than medical negligence, have remained relatively stable in recent years, neither increasing nor decreasing. Since costs have not been adjusted to take account of inflation this means that there has probably been a decline in costs in real terms in recent years, in all case types other than medical negligence.

Summary profiles of case types

Medical Negligence

(a) Case type characteristics

	Mean	Median
Costs allowed	£29,380	£15,531
Claim value	£134,748	£33,381
Delay between instruction and issue	21 months	20 months
Duration	65 months	61 months
Average total counsel fees	£7,028	
Average total expert fees	£4,413	
Average costs discovery + documents	£7,590	
% of successful parties with legal aid	92%	

(b) Results of statistical modelling

Delay between instruction and issue of proceedings: Case weight and legal aid were not found to have a significant effect on the period of delay between instruction and issue of proceedings in medical negligence cases. The period of delay has declined in recent years. The median period of delay has fallen from about 28 months among cases commenced in 1975, to 22 months among cases commenced in 1980, to 13 months among cases commenced in 1990.

Case duration: The only explanatory variable found to have a significant effect on total case duration among medical negligence claims was whether or not the winning party had legal aid. The effect is that cases in which the winning party had legal aid were about 25 per cent longer than those in which the winning party did not have legal aid. Lighter cases were not found to be systematically shorter than heavier cases, holding other factors constant. The length of medical negligence cases has remained stable in recent years, neither increasing nor decreasing.

Costs: Case weight and year of conclusion were the only variables included in the costs model found to have a significant effect on costs in medical negligence cases. The heaviest medical negligence cases are estimated to cost about 12 times more than the lightest cases, holding other factors constant. The level of costs in medical negligence cases has been increasing by about 7 per cent per year in recent years, holding other factors constant.

Personal Injury

(a) Case type characteristics

	Mean	Median
Costs allowed	£19,382	£12,134
Claim value	£98,434	£50,000
Delay between instruction and issue	17 months	15 months
Duration	56 months	54 months
Average total counsel fees	£3,744	
Average total expert fees	£2,413	
Average costs discovery + documents	£5,016	
% of successful parties with legal aid	58%	

(b) Results of statistical modelling

Delay between instruction and issue of proceedings: Case weight, legal aid and the year of instruction were found to have a significant effect on the period of delay between instruction and issue of proceedings in personal injury cases. The period of delay has been decreasing in recent years, by about 15 per cent per year. The period of delay is longer among lighter cases than among heavier cases. Delay among weight A cases (heaviest) is about 50 per cent shorter than among weight E cases (lightest). If the winning party has legal aid, the period of delay between instruction and issue of proceedings among personal injury cases will be about 50 per cent longer than when the winning party does not have legal aid.

Case duration: The only explanatory variable found to have a significant effect on total case duration among personal injury cases was whether or not the winning party had legal aid. The effect is that cases in which the winning party had legal aid were about 20 per cent longer than those in which the winning party did not have legal aid. Lighter cases were not found to be systematically shorter than heavier cases, holding other factors constant. The length of personal injury cases has neither increased nor decreased in recent years.

Costs: Several of the explanatory variables were found to have a significant effect on costs in personal injury cases. Case weight affects costs, with costs increasing as case weight increases. Weight A cases (heaviest) cost about eight times as much as weight E cases (lightest). The value of claims also independently affects costs in personal injury cases. Doubling the value of a personal injury case will increase costs by about 15 per cent, holding other factors constant. The duration of personal injury cases also independently affects costs. Doubling the length of a personal injury case will increase costs by about 25 per cent, holding other factors constant. Legal aid also has an impact on costs in personal injury cases. In addition to the effect on costs through increased duration, when the winning party has legal aid, costs will be about 10 per cent higher, holding other factors constant. Finally, costs in personal injury cases have been neither increasing nor decreasing in recent years. If inflation is taken into account, this implies that there has been a decrease in costs in real terms.

Professional Negligence

(a) Case type characteristics

	Mean	Median
Costs allowed	£32,866	£14,834
Claim value	£107,849	£34,000
Delay between instruction and issue	12 months	9 months
Duration	41 months	35 months
Average total counsel fees	£5,757	
Average total expert fees	£6,445	
Average costs discovery + documents	£11,320	
% of successful parties with legal aid	38%	

(b) Results of statistical modelling

Delay between instruction and issue of proceedings: The year of instruction, the weight of the case and the presence of legal aid all have a significant effect on the length of delay in professional negligence cases. There is unequivocal evidence that the length of the delay between instruction and issue, in professional negligence cases, has been declining in recent years, by about 10 per cent per year. However, when the winning party has legal aid, the period of delay between instruction and issue will be about 50 per cent longer than when the winning party does not have legal aid. The heaviest cases (weight A) have a period of delay between instruction and issue of proceedings which is about two-and-a-half times that of other cases (B/C/D/E).

Case duration: The only explanatory variable having a significant effect on case length was the presence of legal aid. When the successful party had legal aid, total duration was almost 60 per cent longer than when the successful party did not have legal aid, holding case weight constant. None of the other explanatory variables appeared to have any significant effect on case duration. There was no convincing evidence that weight or year of conclusion affects duration in professional negligence cases, suggesting that there has been no systematic increase or decrease in case duration in recent years, and that, holding other factors constant, lighter cases are not systematically shorter than heavier cases.

Costs: The main effects on costs are the weight of the case, the duration of the case and the value of the claim. There is a systematic increase in costs with increasing weight: weight A cases cost nearly 14 times as much as weight E cases, holding other factors constant. Duration also affects costs. If the total length of a professional negligence case doubles, costs will increase by about 20 per cent. The value of claims also affects costs; doubling claim value increases costs by about 15 per cent, irrespective of other factors. Although legal aid does not have an independent effect on costs, it has some impact through its effect on duration, which clearly affects costs in professional negligence cases. The year in which the case was concluded had no significant effect on costs. Thus there is no evidence that costs have been increasing in recent years, and given that costs have not been adjusted for inflation, it is possible that the apparent stability of costs levels represents a decline in real terms.

Official Referees' cases

(a) Case type characteristics

	Mean	Median
Costs allowed	£35,844	£19,320
Claim value	£112,633	£34,764
Delay between instruction and issue	8 months	5 months
Duration	34 months	30 months
Average total counsel fees	£5,396	
Average total expert fees	£9,653	
Average costs discovery + documents	£9,956	
% of successful parties with legal aid	18%	

(b) Results of statistical modelling

Delay between instruction and issue of proceedings: The only explanatory variables that have a significant effect on the period of delay are the year of first instruction and the weight of the case. Delay does not appear to be affected by whether or not the winning party had legal aid (18 per cent of winning parties had legal aid). The period of delay in Official Referees' cases has been declining by almost 20 per cent per year. Heavier cases (categories A/B/C) have a period of delay between instruction and issue of proceedings which is about 50 per cent longer than that of lighter cases (categories D/E).

Case duration: The total duration of cases is affected by the weight of cases, the presence of legal aid and the date on which the case was concluded. Increasing weight has quite a substantial effect; the heaviest cases with weight A/B take twice as long as weight E cases; weight C cases take about one-and-a-half times as long as weight E cases; and weight D cases take about 20 per cent longer than weight E cases. Legal aid also affects duration. Cases in which the successful party had legal aid lasted about 90 per cent longer than non legal aid cases. The length of cases has been decreasing by about 8 per cent per year.

Costs: Costs are affected by the weight of the case, the value of the case and the duration of the case. There is also an interaction effect, in that the effect of weight on costs varies according to the value of the claim. Among cases of weight D and E the value of the claim has no impact on costs. Among more weighty cases, however, costs do appear to increase as claim value rises. Doubling the value of a weight B case will increase costs by about 30 per cent, irrespective of the length of the case. Increasing duration also leads to increased costs. Doubling the length of cases increases costs by about 20 per cent. There was no evidence that legal aid had any independent impact on costs, although it has an influence through its effect on case duration, which affects costs. There is no evidence to suggest that costs in Official Referees' cases have been increasing in recent years. Given that costs have not been adjusted for inflation, it is possible that the apparent stability of costs levels represents a decline in real terms.

Judicial Case Management
Standard timetable for fast track cases

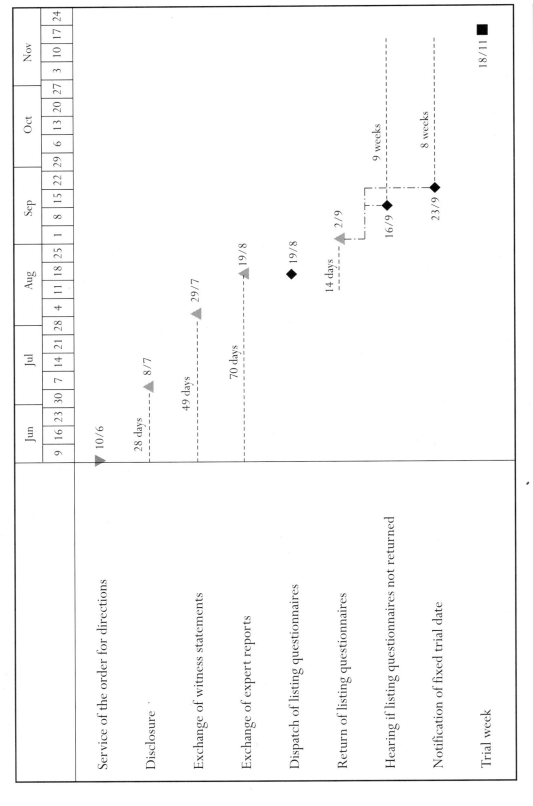